Handbook of Advances in Culture and Psychology

Advances in Culture and Psychology

SERIES EDITORS

Michele J. Gelfand, *Stanford University*
Chi-yue Chiu, *The Chinese University of Hong Kong*
Ying-yi Hong, *The Chinese University of Hong Kong*

ADVISORY BOARD

Patricia Greenfield, *University of California, Los Angeles*

Yoshihisa Kashima, *University of Melbourne*

Shinobu Kitayama, *University of Michigan*

Mark Schaller, *University of British Columbia*

Richard Shweder, *University of Chicago*

Colleen Ward, *Victoria University of Wellington*

Li Liu, *Beijing Normal University*

Handbook of Advances in Culture and Psychology

VOLUME 9

Edited by

Michele J. Gelfand
Chi-yue Chiu
Ying-yi Hong

OXFORD
UNIVERSITY PRESS

Oxford University Press is a department of the University of Oxford. It furthers
the University's objective of excellence in research, scholarship, and education
by publishing worldwide. Oxford is a registered trade mark of Oxford University
Press in the UK and certain other countries.

Published in the United States of America by Oxford University Press
198 Madison Avenue, New York, NY 10016, United States of America.

© Oxford University Press 2022

All rights reserved. No part of this publication may be reproduced, stored in
a retrieval system, or transmitted, in any form or by any means, without the
prior permission in writing of Oxford University Press, or as expressly permitted
by law, by license, or under terms agreed with the appropriate reproduction
rights organization. Inquiries concerning reproduction outside the scope of the
above should be sent to the Rights Department, Oxford University Press, at the
address above.

You must not circulate this work in any other form
and you must impose this same condition on any acquirer.

Handbook of Advances in Culture and Psychology
ISSN 2155-2622
ISBN 978–0–19–763167–6 (pbk.)
ISBN 978–0–19–763166–9 (hbk.)

DOI: 10.1093/oso/9780197631669.001.0001

9 8 7 6 5 4 3 2 1

Paperback printed by Marquis, Canada
Hardback printed by Bridgeport National Bindery, Inc., United States of America

CONTENTS

Contributors • ix

Chapter 1

Cultural Influences on Memory: Integrating Top-Down and Bottom-Up Perspectives • 1

Angela Gutchess and Ashley N. Gilliam

   I. Introduction • 1

  II. Origins of Ideas About Culture and Cognition • 2

 III. Framework for Cultural Differences in Cognition • 6

 IV. Cultural Differences in Specific Aspects of Memory • 9

  V. Framework for Cultural Differences in Memory • 21

 VI. Influence of Aging on Cultural Differences in Cognition • 31

 VII. Future Directions • 36

VIII. Summary • 38

Chapter 2

Worldwide Changes in the Lives of Children and Youth: A Socioecological Approach • 51

Uwe P. Gielen and Sunghun Kim

   I. Introduction • 51

  II. A Socioecological Approach to the Long-Term Study of Children and Youth • 54

 III. Societal Evolution: From Foraging Bands to Digital Information Societies • 57

 IV. Issues in the Development of Children and Adolescents in China and South Korea • 74

  V. Childhood and Youth: Worldwide Changes and the Broad Sweep of History • 84

 VI. A Look Into the Future: The CRC, the Promotion Of Child Welfare, and the Internationalization Of Psychology • 106

 VII. Conclusion • 111

v

vi Contents

Chapter 3
On the Causes and Consequences of Cross-Cultural Differences: An Economic Perspective • 125
Nathan Nunn
I. Introduction • 125
II. Conceptual Framework • 126
III. Global Variation in Cultural Traits • 128
IV. Longer-Run Determinants • 134
V. Shorter-Run Determinants • 150
VI. Cultural Persistence and Change • 157
VII. Economic Consequences of Cultural Differences • 162
VIII. The Interplay of Culture and Policy • 170
IX. Conclusions • 176

Chapter 4
The Pursuit of Honor: Novel Contexts, Varied Approaches, and New Developments • 189
Susan E. Cross and Ayşe K. Üskül
I. Introduction • 189
II. Major Themes in Our Research • 197
III. Bottom-Up Approaches • 199
IV. Top-Down Approaches • 206
V. Expanding the Theory of Honor Cultures • 218
VI. Themes, Implications, and Future Directions • 230

Chapter 5
Culture and Negotiation Strategy • 245
Jeanne M. Brett
I. Introduction • 245
II. Key Concepts • 247
III. Origins of Negotiation Strategy Theory • 248
IV. Motivational Theory • 248
V. Behavioral Theory • 253
VI. Motivational and Behavioral Theories: A Comparison • 259
VII. Culture and Negotiation Strategy and Joint Gains • 261
VIII. Intercultural Negotiation Strategic Adjustment and Outcomes • 271

Contents **vii**

IX. Discussion and Future Directions • 274

X. Conclusion • 279

Chapter 6

Foresight, Punishment, and Cooperation • 291

Sergey Gavrilets

I. Introduction • 291

II. Theoretical Framework and Major Concepts • 299

III. Major Predictions and Evidence • 305

IV. Implications • 317

V. Extensions • 320

VI. Conclusion • 322

Index • 333

CONTRIBUTORS

Jeanne M. Brett
Kellogg School of Management
Northwestern University
Evanston, IL, USA

Susan E. Cross
Department of Psychology
Iowa State University
Ames, IA, USA

Sergey Gavrilets
Department of Ecology and
Evolutionary Biology, Department of
Mathematics
National Institute for Mathematical
and Biological Synthesis, Center for
the Dynamics of Social Complexity
University of Tennessee
Knoxville, TN, USA

Uwe P. Gielen
Department of Psychology
St. Francis College
Brooklyn, NY, USA

Ashley N. Gilliam
Department of Psychology
Brandeis University
Waltham, MA, USA

Angela Gutchess
Department of Psychology
Brandeis University
Waltham, MA, USA

Sunghun Kim
Department of Psychology
St. Francis College
Brooklyn, NY, USA

Nathan Nunn
Department of Economics
Harvard University and Canadian
Institute for Advanced Research
Cambridge, MA, USA

Ayşe K. Üskül
School of Psychology
University of Kent
Canterbury, Kent, UK

CHAPTER 1

Cultural Influences on Memory

Integrating Top-Down and Bottom-Up Perspectives

ANGELA GUTCHESS AND ASHLEY N. GILLIAM

Abstract

This chapter will review behavioral and neuroimaging findings on cross-cultural differences in memory, including cultural differences in the prioritization of object versus context information, the use of categories in memory, memory specificity, and self-referencing in memory. A model drawing on the contribution of top-down versus bottom-up processes will be used to account for some of the findings of cross-cultural differences and highlight the need for more consideration of the lower-level processes that contribute to cultural differences in memory. This framework will also consider effects of cognitive aging and predict what types of processes should evoke magnification, maintenance, or minimization of cultural differences across the life span.

Key Words: culture, memory, cognition, aging, cognitive neuroscience, memory specificity, context, self-reference effect, categorization

---

I. INTRODUCTION

Why study memory across cultures? Memory not only serves as a record of past events in one's life and of knowledge and facts that have been acquired. But there are arguments that memory inherently shapes one's sense of self— knowing what one has experienced, how one has behaved in the past, the people with whom these events were shared, and using all of this knowledge

Angela Gutchess and Ashley N. Gilliam, *Cultural Influences on Memory* In: *Handbook of Advances in Culture and Psychology*. Edited by: Michele J. Gelfand, Chi-yue Chiu, and Ying-yi Hong, Oxford University Press. © Oxford University Press 2022. DOI: 10.1093/oso/9780197631669.003.0001 to make predictions about what to expect in the future. As memory is malleable, changeable, and subject to distortion, culture can act as a lens that filters one's representation of the world and shapes one's representation of the past. If culture can shape memory, that means that peoples' representation of knowledge, past events, predictions for the future, and even understanding of themselves could systematically differ across cultures.

In this chapter, we will discuss our exploration of the effects of culture on memory. The chapter will begin by describing our theoretical roots in the field of culture and cognition, as well as considering how the fields of cognitive neuroscience and memory shaped the development of our thinking. Next, we will consider routes through which culture can influence cognition. Specifically considering the effects of culture on memory, we will review our findings that pertain to cultural differences in object versus context processing, the use of categories to support accurate as well as erroneous memory, and memory specificity. In the next section, we will describe a model to account for the ways in which culture can shape memory, including top-down processes (e.g., motivational and experiential factors), intermediate processes (e.g., attentional factors), and bottom-up processes (e.g., lower-level visual factors). Findings illustrating each of these levels will be reviewed. Ways in which cognitive aging can influence the effects of culture on memory will be considered and integrated into the model. The chapter will conclude with a consideration of opportunities and challenges that lie ahead for the study of memory, and cognition more broadly, across cultures.

II. ORIGINS OF IDEAS ABOUT CULTURE AND COGNITION

Richard Nisbett's framework initially shaped how we thought about the ways in which culture could influence cognition. His perspective has its roots in social psychology as agricultural practices shaped the social culture (e.g., social interaction, social pressures and obligations, norms), resulting in divergent approaches for ancient China and ancient Greece (Nisbett, 2003; Nisbett & Masuda, 2003; Nisbett & Miyamoto, 2005; Nisbett et al., 2001). Whereas Chinese agriculture was based in farming, and specifically rice farming, requiring people to work together collectively, Greek agriculture was based in herding, a more individualistic enterprise. Nisbett argued that these different agricultural systems profoundly shaped rules, norms, and philosophies for each society, leading Greek culture to embrace the individual and one's unique attributes, whereas Chinese culture emphasized fitting in with the social group and discouraged distinguishing one's self as unique. The cultural differences in practices eventually pervaded the very way of thinking, broadly shaping cognition (see support for how agriculture impacts cognition in Uskul et al., 2008). His analysis was based on a breadth of materials; in addition to considering different agricultural traditions, his theory of cultural differences incorporated analysis of ancient scripts, such as the teachings of Confucius and Greek laws, and consideration of norms and social orientation (e.g., group or individual). Although ancient China and Greece were the focus of the framework, these cultural traditions were thought to more broadly shape Eastern and Western civilizations such that the influence of Chinese thought extended to Japanese and Korean cultures, whereas the influence of Greek thought shaped western Europe, the United Kingdom, Canada, and the United States.

A variety of studies provided empirical support for the theory (for reviews, see Nisbett, 2003; Nisbett et al., 2001). These illustrated cultural differences in attention and memory such that Easterners attended broadly to field and context, whereas Westerners attended to focal objects and parts of the field (Masuda & Nisbett, 2001, 2006). These findings were consistent with those based on a classic rod-and-frame test (Witkin, 1954), in which Westerners were less field-dependent than Easterners (Ji et al., 2000). Cultures also differed in categorization, with Westerners exhibiting a bias toward using taxonomic categories, in terms of how they sorted information and the explanations provided for the groupings, and Easterners focusing on functional relationships (Ji et al., 2004). Cultural differences in reasoning emerged, with Easterners being more holistic, integrating object and background information together, and Westerners being more analytic, breaking information into parts; Easterners exhibited more sensitivity to covariation in the environment and greater expectations for change, whereas Westerners predicted trends would continue (Ji et al., 2000, 2001).

This framework is not without critics, including research highlighting the agricultural diversity within China such that some areas grow rice whereas others grow wheat, which is a more solitary enterprise. Comparing regions of China that grow rice versus wheat provides support for the idea that rice-growing regions are more collectivistic, whereas wheat-growing regions are more individualistic (Talhelm et al., 2014), suggesting that the impact of agricultural practices on culture is relatively local and does not account for country- (or region-) wide effects. Not only does the framework fail to capture some of the richness of different aspects of culture within a country (e.g., rice vs. wheat regions, ethnic majority vs. minority, rural vs. urban populations), it also can be interpreted as equating "East" to China and "West" to Greece, ignoring the many other cultural traditions beyond this bisection of the globe.

Another consideration about predominant frameworks is that initial theories accounting for cultural differences were largely based on social factors. Nisbett's theory (Nisbett, 2003; Nisbett et al., 2001) emphasizes the social practices—more group-based or individualistic—that led to different cognitive styles across cultures. Another predominant theory emphasizes how different construals of the self, conceptualizing of the self as interdependent and defined by its relationships with others or as an independent entity separate and unique from others, shape cognition, emotion, and motivation (Markus & Kitayama, 1991). Cultural differences in the tightness or looseness of social norms, which vary in the degree of tolerance for deviations from norms (low for tight societies, high for loose societies), relate to a number of behaviors and attitudes, including government structures, judicial systems, and the role of the media (Gelfand, 2012; Gelfand et al., 2011). Although we initially anticipated that social factors would account for differences in memory across cultures, reflecting motivational influences on what information should be remembered, our results have led us to question the role of social influences on memory. Given the limited number of theoretical frameworks, reflecting the relative "newness" of the study of culture and cognition, the development of unifying frameworks and distinguishing mechanisms from those considered in past studies is an important, yet challenging, endeavor. We will discuss these challenges in later sections.

In addition to questioning which cultural forces contribute to differences in cognition, difficulties have arisen with how to define *culture*. Our work has stayed within the East/West dichotomy, based on our roots in the Nisbett theoretical model. To define participant samples, we compare participants from the United States with participants originating from East Asia. These samples reflect our location and allow for the comparison of Americans to those samples that are most accessible through collaborations or relocation to the United States for study. Our "Eastern" samples are largely Chinese; in various studies these include participants tested in mainland China or Taiwan and those who are ethnically Chinese residing in Singapore. When tested in the United States, the sample is defined as a heterogeneous mix of East Asians that includes Japanese and Koreans, in some cases extending to Southeast Asians. Our Eastern samples also have focused on Turkey, again based on the potential through collaboration as well as the potential for the original East/West framework to extend to this part of the world. Turkey has historically been a prime route for traders and invaders coming from both the East and the West, and social values emphasize family and collectivism, in line with Eastern philosophies (Kagitçibaşi, 1994, 2000). As our understanding of mechanisms advances and our findings do not always fit the anticipated pattern of results based on social factors, we acknowledge the need for a more fine-grained consideration of the complex concept of *culture*, considering the specific experiences or environments through which culture can shape cognition. We will discuss these issues further in Section VII, in which we consider the importance of studying acculturation and defining samples in a more nuanced manner.

Integrating a cognitive neuroscience perspective to the work highlighted the importance of considering the varying life experiences that are afforded by culture. With Denise Park, we initially framed cognitive neuroscience work on culture around well-known examples of plasticity that shaped the structural and functional development of regions of the cortex (Park & Gutchess, 2002, 2006). These included training in juggling (Draganski et al., 2004), navigating London as a taxicab driver (Maguire et al., 2000), and, in the case of Canadian postal workers, sorting zip codes and consequently integrating letters and numbers into a single category (Polk & Farah, 1995). At the time we began this work, there was some resistance to the idea that culture could shape the "hardware" or "software" of the brain, necessitating links to this early work that demonstrated plasticity in the adult brain. Remarkably, nearly 20 years later it now seems intuitive to many cognitive psychologists and neuroscientists that the immersive experiences of culture can shape neural development and activation. This change in the zeitgeist partially reflects the efforts of Joan Chiao (Chiao, 2009; Chiao et al., 2013), Shinobu Kitayama (Kitayama & Uskul, 2011), Shihui Han (Han & Ma, 2015), and others to establish a field of cultural neuroscience. However, numerous and widespread demonstrations of how life experiences, such as adversity (McLaughlin et al., 2017; Sheridan & McLaughlin, 2016) or socioeconomic status (Hackman & Farah, 2009; Hackman et al., 2010), affect the brain have also shaped the thinking of many in the field.

The final influence that we must acknowledge in shaping our thinking about how culture influences cognition is the research on the malleability of memory. From the early studies of Elizabeth Loftus, illustrating how misleading information can distort or be implanted into memory (Loftus, 1979, 2005), to the explosion of research on false memory in the 1990s (e.g., Koutstaal & Schacter, 1997; Norman & Schacter, 1997; Roediger & McDermott, 1995), including research in the lab in which the first author began working in research as an undergraduate (Reinitz & Hannigan, 2001; Reinitz et al., 1992), the understanding of memory underwent a rapid change. Instead of being conceptualized as a fixed, highly accurate recording of past events, memory was understood to be reconstructive, pulling together different aspects of information (e.g., visual, auditory, emotional, contextual, and temporal elements) to re-create the memory each time it was retrieved. As such, these reconstructed memories were subject to distortion and error, reflecting multiple "sins" of memory (Schacter, 1999, 2001). Neural data added another interesting overlay to the understanding of memory, in that true and false memory exhibited a high degree of overlap in the underlying brain regions (Cabeza et al., 2001; Gonsalves & Paller, 2000, 2002; Schacter & Slotnick, 2004; Slotnick & Schacter, 2004). These regions included the hippocampus, long recognized as playing a critical role in forming memories (Scoville & Milner, 1957). These findings indicated that brain activity often went along with the subjective experience of detecting whether an event was experienced before, whether or not it actually had been. Our thinking about memory was profoundly shaped by this revolution in the conceptualization of memory; the malleability provides a fertile ground for considering how cultural milieu could differently shape reconstructive processes in memory. In the next section, we will outline some general routes for how culture can shape cognition, before turning to the specific consideration of memory and reviewing relevant findings in the subsequent section.

III. FRAMEWORK FOR CULTURAL DIFFERENCES IN COGNITION

An initial framework we used to think about the ways in which culture influences cognition is in terms of the recruitment of distinct cognitive *processes*, possessing different cognitive *content*, and experiencing different levels of *difficulty* with tasks (Gutchess et al., 2011). Effects of culture on processes include many of the ideas highlighted in the work of Nisbett, as reviewed in the preceding section (Nisbett, 2003; Nisbett & Masuda, 2003; Nisbett & Miyamoto, 2005; Nisbett et al., 2001). For example, cultural differences in preference for analytic versus holistic processing could impact memory such that East Asians' emphasis on holistic processing could support better memory for contextual information, whereas Americans' emphasis on analytic processing could support better memory for objects and parts of information.

Cross-cultural differences in the type of content could reflect accumulated life experiences that shape knowledge. For example, lychees and durians are common fruits in China, whereas many Americans may never encounter these fruits. Even if someone unfamiliar with it determined a durian to be a type of fruit, its distinctive spiky appearance and pungent smell might make it seem unlike any other exemplar of fruit, challenging the ways in which *fruit* might be conceptualized as a category. Categorization and organization are important for forming and retrieving memories (Bousfield, 1953). The relative value placed on items and their hierarchical organization can differ cross-culturally and influence what information is recalled. In the case of the durian, it may be more likely to be forgotten by Westerners when presented alongside more recognized exemplars like apples and oranges.

The third route that we suggested could influence how culture shapes cognition is through differences in task difficulty. For this route, both cultural groups would apply the same cognitive processes to a task, but they would differ in the relative difficulty it would take to successfully enact those processes. Increased difficulty could be expected to recruit additional neural networks such as frontoparietal attentional networks or frontal control regions in line with the greater cognitive demands of the task for the culture that was less facile or familiar with the process. See Figure 1.1 for an illustration of the frontoparietal control network. Such effects could be similar to those seen when cognitive load increases for participants; trying to use working memory

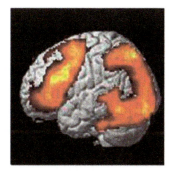 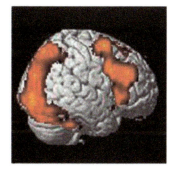

FIGURE 1.1: Frontoparietal Control Network
This image illustrates activation of regions of the frontal lobes and parietal lobes that are discussed as part of the executive control network that is implicated in demanding tasks. Reproduced from Gutchess A. H., Hedden, T., Ketay, S., Aron, A., & Gabrieli, J. D. E. (2010). Neural differences in the processing of semantic relationships across cultures. *Social Cognitive and Affective Neuroscience*, 5(2–3), 254–263, Figure 2. Copyright © 2010 by Oxford University Press. Reproduced with permission.

to remember the item that appeared three trials ago engages the dorsolateral prefrontal cortex more than trying to remember the item that appeared two trials ago (Braver et al., 1997).

Challenges with using this framework reflect the ways in which these three mechanisms are often intertwined. Cultural differences in the content of cognition can be difficult to entirely separate from cultural differences in processes. Take, for example, the study of cross-cultural differences in categorization. Sorting objects into categories would presumably operate quite differently across cultures when people differ in their familiarity with items. But it might be unclear whether cultures differ in the process of categorization versus knowledge of the items themselves (e.g., rather than categorizing durian into *fruits*, Americans might create additional categories or subcategories based on their lack of familiarity with the item). In studies of cognition across cultures, the goal is typically to remove effects of item familiarity and avoid potential disadvantages for one culture by using culture-fair tests.

Distinguishing cultural differences in strategies from those reflecting difficulty also can be challenging. Neuroimaging methods can be helpful in distinguishing the two routes for cultural differences, as illustrated in a study by Hedden and colleagues (2008). In this study, the frontoparietal attentional network is engaged more for the less preferred task for each culture. That is, when making judgments about the length of a line relative to the surrounding frame, Westerners tend to excel at absolute judgments, in which the length of the line is reproduced exactly without considering the size of the frame, whereas Easterners excel at relative judgments, in which the length of the line is reproduced relative to the size of the frame (Kitayama et al., 2003). When functional magnetic resonance imaging (fMRI) methods were used to investigate the neural regions associated with this task, the frontoparietal network responded more when people from each culture performed their less preferred task, that is, when Easterners performed the absolute task (ignoring context) and Westerners performed the relative (context-dependent) task (Hedden et al., 2008). This pattern of findings indicates that the culturally nonpreferred tasks were more demanding, requiring more cognitive control and attentional resources to support performance. In this case, attributing the pattern of cultural differences to effects of difficulty rather than strategy is fairly straightforward because cultural differences in neural activity occurred in a network known to reflect effects of difficulty and attentional demand. In addition, the pattern of double dissociation, with the same region responding to the more difficult task in each culture, is reassuring in terms of attributing effects to difficulty. In many cases, however, the interpretation is not so straightforward, with different regions responding to the task in each group, which could reflect contributions from task differences as well as differing levels of demand.

IV. CULTURAL DIFFERENCES IN SPECIFIC ASPECTS OF MEMORY

In this section, we will describe our study of memory. Most of the findings are in line with cultural differences in terms of strategies rather than in the content or difficulty of tasks. These reflect cultural differences in the prioritization of processing information about objects compared to backgrounds, in the use of categories in memory, and in the emphasis on specificity, or amount of detail that is represented in memory.

A. Memory for Objects Versus Background Information

Building on the studies illustrating cultural differences in attention to contextual information versus objects in complex scenes and environments (Chua et al., 2005; Ji et al., 2000; Masuda & Nisbett, 2001), we further probed cultural differences in processing these different types of information, including measures of memory. We initially approached this work with the expectation that Westerners would be focused on individual objects, in line with their individualistic perspective, whereas Easterners would prioritize context and relationships, in line with their more interdependent, collectivistic perspective. We used fMRI to assess cultural differences during the viewing of objects, backgrounds, and combined (object + background) images (Gutchess, Welsh, et al., 2006). The study was positioned to be able to separately evaluate cultural differences in the processing of both objects and backgrounds, distinguishing the two types of information in a way that is not always possible to accomplish in behavioral studies. That is, reporting more background information could take away from the reporting of object information, though using fMRI, regions that respond selectively to objects or backgrounds can be probed simultaneously.

In this study, American and East Asian participants, all tested on the same magnetic resonance (MR) scanner in the United States, viewed images, and rated them in terms of pleasantness—either pleasant, neutral, or unpleasant—to ensure that participants attended to the stimuli. Critically, a third of the pictures consisted of a background and lacked a central target object (e.g., a savannah), another third consisted of a target object on a white background (e.g., an elephant), and the final third consisted of "combined" images, with target objects placed in an environmentally meaningful background (e.g., an elephant in the savannah). To separately probe cultural differences in object and background processing, we created masks of regions that responded more to objects or to backgrounds and then tested for cultural differences during the viewing of the combined images. The major finding from this study was that American participants activated more regions associated with object processing than East Asian participants. These differences were particularly evident in the posterior cortical regions, such as the left middle temporal gyrus, a region potentially reflecting processing of semantic information. There were few cultural differences in the activation of background-processing regions, including greater activation of a region of the left superior occipital cortex in Americans. The results suggest that Americans attend more to focal objects than East Asians; together with the eye-tracking findings in which Americans fixated on objects earlier than East Asians (Chua et al., 2005), the work established the importance of considering cultural differences in object processing, enriching the story that, up until that point, had largely emphasized greater processing of contextual information in East Asians.

Another set of fMRI studies (Chee et al., 2006; Goh et al., 2007, 2004) built on this initial finding of cross-cultural differences in object processing while simultaneously testing for potential differences in the processing of backgrounds and in the binding, or association, of objects to background. Michael Chee and Joshua Goh had the innovative idea to apply an adaptation approach to further probe cultural differences in object and background processing. Adaptation capitalizes on the tendency for neural regions to reduce their response upon repeated presentations (Grill-Spector et al., 2006). Thus, regions critically involved in processing aspects of information (e.g., objects, backgrounds) would be expected to reduce their response over time when that information is repeated.

Participants were recruited in both the United States and Singapore; the cross-site collaboration necessitated establishing that the scanners were comparable across sites, ruling out the possibility that cultural differences actually reflected differences in the scanner hardware (Sutton et al., 2008). The research also incorporated the study of aging, sampling younger and healthy older adults from both countries; we will discuss the broader framework and implications of studying cross-cultural differences with age in Section VI. In this study (Goh et al., 2007), participants viewed picture stimuli in which objects were placed against congruent backgrounds, much like the stimuli in Gutchess, Welsh, et al. (2006). In order to capitalize on adaptation, pictures were presented in quartets, in which (1) both the object and background were repeated across all four pictures (adaptation of both object and background), (2) the object was repeated but against a novel background (adaptation of object only), (3) the background was repeated behind a novel object (adaptation of background only), or (4) a novel object and background appeared for each image in the quartet (no adaptation). Using the combination of different conditions allowed for the examination of cultural differences in binding, in addition to assessing adaptation to objects and backgrounds.

Converging with the prior findings (Gutchess, Welsh, et al., 2006), cultures differed in object processing such that there was less adaptation to objects in the lateral occipital complex, a visual region implicated in object recognition, for Easterners than for Westerners, although this difference only emerged in older adults (see Figure 1.2). Adaptation to objects in older Easterners could be restored when objects were presented in isolation against a blank background or when instructions emphasized attention to objects, as opposed to passive viewing (Chee et al., 2006). These boundary conditions indicate that cultural differences in adaptation to objects might only emerge when object information is less salient; when older East Asians attend to object information, they exhibit an intact adaptation response. Young adults did not differ across cultures, and neither did background processing or object–background binding.

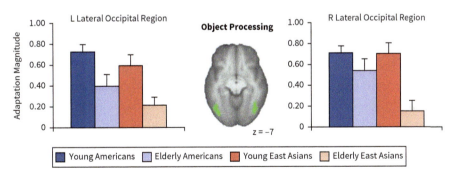

FIGURE 1.2: Cultural Differences in Object Adaptation
In the lateral occipital complex, there is a larger effect of aging on adaptation for older East Asians (right two bars in each graph) than for Americans (left two bars in each graph). Adapted from Goh, J. O., Chee, M. W., Tan, J. C., Venkatraman, V., Hebrank, A., Leshikar, E. D., Jenkins, L., Sutton, B. P., Gutchess, A. H., & Park, D. C. (2007). Age and culture modulate object processing and object–scene binding in the ventral visual area. *Cognitive, Affective, and Behavioral Neuroscience, 7*, 44–52, Figure 2. Copyright © 2007 by Springer Nature. Reproduced with permission.

There were, however, age differences in object–background binding such that older adults, across both cultures, exhibited reduced response to object–background binding in the right hippocampus and right parahippocampal gyrus, regions related to memory and memory for associations, compared to younger adults. Taken together, these results indicate both cultural differences in object processing, exhibited via the reduced adaptation response in older East Asians, and universal effects of aging on binding across cultures, with an impaired medial temporal response to associative information for Eastern and Western older adults.

Although Goh et al. (2007) did not identify cultural differences in young adults, a later study by Jenkins et al. (2010) suggested that congruency could influence the presence of cultural differences even in young adults. Chinese participants exhibited greater adaptation in the lateral occipital complex to incongruent than congruent scenes, whereas adaptation did not differ for these types of images for Americans. These results were interpreted as evidence of East Asians' sensitivity to context.

These studies take advantage of the sensitivity of cognitive neuroscience methods to detect cultural differences in object processing, even when behavioral measures do not detect cultural differences or participants are passively viewing stimuli. These studies did not directly assess neural responses in service of memory but tested for cultural differences when people simply viewed or made judgments about different types of visual information. Even so, the findings have implications for memory as the reduced object responsivity for East Asians suggests that the information may have reduced salience, perhaps particularly in complex environments in which many streams of information compete for attention and processing. If object information is not attended to or has an impoverished representation, these deficiencies would be expected to feed forward and impact memory for information. Despite these cultural differences in neural responsivity to objects, the cultural groups did not differ in behavioral measures of memory in the Gutchess, Welsh, et al. (2006) fMRI study. This could reflect, in part, the relatively high memory performance in the study; a follow-up behavioral study with a shorter window for encoding provided some suggestive data that East Asians may remember pictures containing objects worse than Americans (Gutchess, Welsh, et al., 2006).

Our subsequent work on cross-cultural differences more directly probed memory and moved beyond the type of accuracy measures employed in our work on cultural differences in memory for object and background information.

As described in the following sections, we employed more sensitive assays of memory, focusing on strategy usage, memory errors, and qualities of memory.

B. Use of Categories in Memory

1. Categorical Strategies for Accurate Memory

One common mnemonic strategy is the use of categories to organize information in memory. When people recall information, they spontaneously sort information into categories. For example, if people learn a list of items that includes items intermixed from different categories—some exemplars of fruits (e.g., *apple*, *banana*, *pear*), some animals (e.g., *pig*, *cow*, *sheep*), and some modes of transportation (e.g., *car*, *airplane*, *train*)—they will tend to output their recall by category. This categorization strategy has long been recognized (Bousfield, 1953) and likely reflects the use of a retrieval strategy whereby recalling some items can cue recall of other items, perhaps reflecting a strategic search for related items (e.g., "I remember *apple*, and I know there were other fruits on the list. What were they?").

We examined the use of a categorization strategy in memory across cultures. Although prior work revealed that cultures differed in their tendency to use taxonomic categories (Chiu, 1972; Ji et al., 2004; Unsworth et al., 2005), this work had not assessed the impact of these cultural differences in memory. Two experiments compared free recall for word lists across groups of younger and older adults from the United States and China (Gutchess, Yoon, et al., 2006). Participants were presented with words (in their native language as testing was conducted in the two different countries); the words were selected from category norms from both age groups and cultures (Yoon et al., 2004) to equate the strength of the categorical association across cultures and languages. The first experiment used word lists with strong category associates, which are those exemplars generated by most participants in response to a categorical cue (e.g., *apple* or *orange* in response to *fruit*, for an American). The second experiment used words with weaker category associations (e.g., *peach*, which was generated by a subset of Americans in response to the categorical cue of *fruit*). In both experiments, participants encoded two word lists, one categorically related and one unrelated. After the word lists were presented, participants free-recalled all of the words that they could remember. The use of categories could be measured with clustering scores, measuring the extent to which people recalled words in order by category. The highest score would occur when participants outputted all of the words that they could remember from one category before moving to the next category; switching between categories and returning to a category multiple times would result in lower clustering scores.

The results generally indicated that cultural differences in categorization extended to impact memory. For the experiment with strong category associates, the strategy measure of clustering indicated that older adult Chinese used categories less than older adult Americans. For the experiment with weak category associates, Chinese younger and older adults also used categories less than Americans. Although cultural differences emerged in the use of categories as a strategy, interestingly, these cultural differences did not extend to the amount of information remembered. This suggests that Chinese participants' memory performance was not necessarily harmed by their reduced use of a categorization strategy and that perhaps they were able to recruit other strategies, not identified in this study, to support their memory performance. The results illustrate the ways in which cultural practices and styles of thought can influence memory representations through the types of strategies that are used to retrieve information from memory.

2. Categorical False Memories

Although our initial work assessed the role of categories as strategies supporting accurate memory, we wanted to illustrate alternate outcomes from using strategies in memory. Part of this stemmed from a desire to present a balanced view, illustrating both advantages and disadvantages, of how cultures fared from employing different strategies. One approach could involve comparing the effects of multiple strategies, differing in how much they are preferred across cultures (e.g., comparing the taxonomic strategy preferred by Americans to the functional relational strategy preferred by East Asians [Ji et al., 2004]). Such an approach is challenging, given the need to norm words for multiple types of relationships in multiple groups and match word lists across cultures for the types of semantic and orthographic properties that are typically considered in word lists (e.g., word frequency, length, and commonness). We adopted an alternate approach in which we continued to focus on the strategy of categorization but examined it as a liability in memory. Thus, we predicted that Americans' greater use of a categorical strategy would make them more prone to committing memory errors for categorically related information. In addition, our experience with the previous study—in which categorical strategy usage did not directly account for memory performance—led us to reflect about sensitive assays of memory. Whereas there are a number of routes to achieve accurate memory—perhaps people accurately recollected the original experience, relied on a vague sense of familiarity, or guessed the information based on related cues—memory errors seem to reflect a cleaner assay of memory processes. When people misremember a categorically related piece of information as having been encountered earlier (when in fact it had not), this error reflects the role of categories in directing and reconstructing memory.

A cultural comparison of categorical memory errors was conducted through a collaboration in Turkey, as a result of a Fulbright semester spent in Ayşecan Boduroğlu's lab (Schwartz et al., 2014). Drawing on our experience creating word lists for the categorical memory studies, we used existing category norms from the United States and Turkey to develop sets of categorical word pairs for each culture and language. Young adults from the United States and Turkey studied lists of word pairs, with half of the pairs categorically related (e.g., *apple–banana*) and the other half categorically unrelated (e.g., *apple–magazine*). Participants were "set up" to commit memory errors by having categorical pairs within the list but also by having a categorically related lure present in another unrelated pair (e.g., for a participant who studied *apple–magazine*, the word *banana* could appear in another unrelated word pair, such as *chair–banana*). After studying the word pairs, participants completed a cued recall test in which they were given the first word as a cue (e.g., *apple*) and asked to recall the second word from each pair. Participants committed many memory errors, including generating words that had not been on the list (e.g., generating *grape*). Responses were coded based on whether it was an accurate response or, in the case of an error, labeling the type of error (e.g., *categorical, other semantic relationship, phonological, other word pair,* or *random*).

The results indicated that Americans committed more categorical errors than Turks (see Figure 1.3). This suggests that not only is the use of strategies to support accurate recall shaped by culture but false memory also can serve as a rich assay of cultural differences. These types of errors have profound impacts in terms of illustrating the ways in which people from different cultures can reconstruct their worlds in systematically different ways. Memory errors have the potential to contribute to cross-cultural misunderstandings if people from different cultures not only have the tendency to prioritize different information in memory but also can distort their memories in line with different cultural biases (e.g., preference for taxonomy) and priorities in information processing.

We also extended our study of categorical memory errors across cultures to older adults. This provided an opportunity for us not only to attempt to replicate our results in different samples but also to test a domain in which

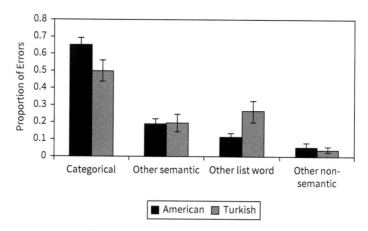

FIGURE 1.3: Cultural Differences in Categorical Memory Errors
American young adults have a larger portion of memory errors based on categories than do Turkish young adults.
Figure from Schwartz, A. J., Boduroglu, A., & Gutchess, A. H. (2014). Cross-cultural differences in categorical memory errors. *Cognitive Science*, *38*(5), 997–1007, Figure 2. https://doi.org/10.1111/cogs.12109. Copyright © 2014 by John Wiley & Sons, Inc. Reproduced with permission.

aging dramatically affects memory. Older adults tend to commit more memory errors than younger adults (Balota et al., 1999; Gallo, 2006, 2010; Tun et al., 1998), though the extent to which this tendency is universal, occurring across cultures, has not been assessed. Older adults in the United States and Turkey were tested on the paradigm from A. J. Schwartz et al. (2014), and to ensure consistency, the young adult data were rescored by the same research assistants who scored the older adult data. The results indicated that the pattern of cultural differences in memory errors seen in younger adults extended to older adults, with American older adults committing more categorical memory errors than Turkish older adults (Gutchess & Boduroglu, 2019). In addition, the data provided evidence for the consistent effects of aging on false memory across cultures as older adults, in the United States and Turkey, made more categorical and other semantic memory errors than younger adults (see Figure 1.4). The results provide additional support for our finding that memory errors can reflect cultural influences and, in this case, illustrate that those influences can persist across different generations of cultures. In addition, the work tested the extent to which our understanding of cognitive aging, thus far based largely on the study of Westerners, extends across cultures, to different populations. We will discuss the study of aging further in Section VI.

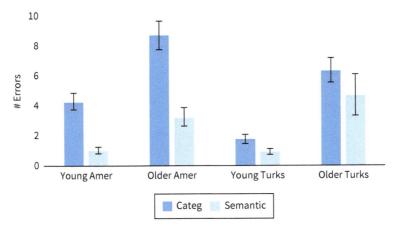

FIGURE 1.4: Cultural Differences in Categorical Memory Errors With Age
The finding that Americans commit more memory errors than Turks based on categorical relationships holds for both younger and older adults. In addition, the tendency for older adults, compared to younger adults, to commit more memory errors for meaningfully related information (here, both categorical and other types of semantic relationships) is true across both cultures.
Figure from Gutchess & Boduroglu (2019, Figure 1). Copyright © 2019 by Taylor & Francis. Reproduced with permission.

C. Memory Specificity

Another aspect of memory that differs across cultures is the amount of perceptual detail that is contained in memories. We initially hypothesized that Americans' bias toward categorization could push them to represent information more globally, in line with the superordinate category and potentially reducing the amount of detail specific to an individual exemplar that is contained in memory. In fact, we found the opposite: that Americans remember more perceptual details than do East Asians.

Our initial paper on cultural differences in memory specificity contained two experiments (Millar et al., 2013). Participants encoded images of focal objects (e.g., an ice cream cone, a bicycle) on a white background in the first experiment and images of focal objects on a meaningful background in the second experiment. For the recognition tests, participants encountered some of the same images seen earlier, some entirely new ones, and some that were similar, sharing the same verbal label as those originally studied (e.g., a new exemplar of a bicycle that is perceptually distinct—perhaps in terms of color, shape, or orientation—from the image of a bicycle that was studied originally). Participants made a decision of *same*, *similar*, or *new*, allowing for assessment of whether they recognized the exemplars with a high amount of detail (i.e., correctly assigning *same* to original images) or recognized the exemplars at a general level, corresponding to recognizing the items but not necessarily with perceptual detail (i.e., responding *same* or *similar* to an exemplar of a bicycle, reflecting that participants know that they studied a bicycle previously).

The results showed that Americans and East Asians did not differ in general memory but that Americans exhibited greater accuracy in specific memory for objects. There was evidence that these cultural differences extended to memory for the background details in Experiment 2 (see Figure 1.5). These results indicated that Americans encode information with more perceptual detail than East Asians. This finding may reflect Americans' preferential attention to features and emphasis on feature analysis strategies (Nisbett, 2003; Nisbett et al., 2001). Although we initially thought that memory for detail could be in line with greater attention to processing objects by Americans compared to East Asians (Gutchess, Welsh, et al., 2006), as discussed in Section IV.A, the tendency for these cultural differences to emerge for backgrounds as well as objects suggests that the mechanism may be distinct from that of object-centric biases.

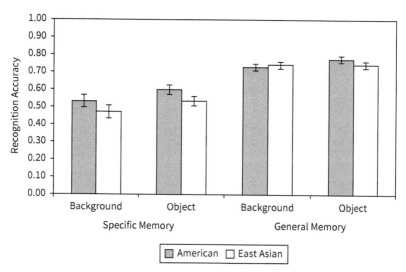

FIGURE 1.5: Cultural Differences in Memory Specificity
Americans tended to remember more specific perceptual details for both objects and backgrounds than East Asians, whereas the groups did not differ in general memory. Figure from Millar, P. R., Serbun, S. J., Vadalia, A., & Gutchess, A. H. (2013). Cross-cultural differences in memory specificity. *Culture & Brain*, 1(2–4), 138–157, Figure 4. Copyright © 2013 by Springer Nature. Reproduced with permission.

An important factor to consider is to what extent cultural differences are robust across different encoding tasks. Our cultural differences in memory specificity findings were stronger in the original behavioral studies (Millar et al., 2013) than in a subsequent fMRI study (Paige, Ksander, et al., 2017). Not only did the encoding environment vary across these studies (testing in a more controlled lab environment than in a constrained MR scanner with potentially lower-quality visual input) but the encoding instructions also varied. For these reasons, we directly compared the effect of the instructions in a follow-up experiment in the laboratory (Paige, Amado, & Gutchess, 2017). The stimuli were the same as in previous studies, with an object placed against a white background. During the encoding stage, participants made a decision of whether someone they know would purchase the depicted object (*purchase* decision) or if they would approach, avoid, or stay at the same distance from the object when encountering it in real life (*approach* decision). Two days later participants took a recognition test in which they responded as to whether items were the same, similar, or new compared to those from encoding.

The results indicated that although there was an overall effect wherein the approach decision enhanced performance for specific memory compared to the purchase decision (and particularly when the approach task was completed first), this effect did not vary cross-culturally. In terms of the cultural differences, Americans had higher hit rates (e.g., correctly recognizing old items) than East Asians for specific memory of objects despite instruction type, a finding that converged with prior work (Millar et al., 2013). However, the cultural differences in memory did not translate to differences in sensitivity of discriminating old same items from new items, based on a signal detection measure of d'. Cultural differences instead emerged in a measure of response bias, suggesting that East Asians had a more stringent response bias than Americans in their use of the "same" response to items, be they the same, similar, or new items.

Based on the results thus far, there is some inconsistency in our findings of whether sensitivity—what we typically think of as memory accuracy (ability to discriminate old from new)—or biases in how people respond account for cultural differences. Another set of studies further probed this issue, using a new set of stimuli and some further work to ensure selection of culture-fair stimuli, finding evidence that both memory sensitivity and response bias can differ across cultures (Leger & Gutchess, 2021). Interestingly, cultural differences in correct recognition of items was most pronounced for the easiest trials, failing to support suggestions that East Asians were disadvantaged due to the stimuli that were unfamiliar. Another candidate explanation that the study failed to support was the possibility that sociocultural values (e.g., individualism, collectivism) account for cultural differences in memory performance. The measures of cultural values neither differed across the groups nor related to memory performance. Thus, this set of studies substantiated the potential for cultural differences in memory sensitivity as well as response biases but failed to support other explanations (e.g., difficulty of the task, cultural values). More work is needed in order to disentangle the influences of culture on memory sensitivity from the influences on response bias, by both manipulating factors that would be expected to influence one and not the other as well as collecting measures that separately assess memory accuracy and response bias.

Other work has probed candidate mechanisms to account for cultural differences in memory specificity. Using hierarchical modeling, we tested for cultural differences in the specificity of memory while using participants' individual ratings of each image to control for scene congruency and the emotional intensity of the stimuli (Mickley Steinmetz et al., 2018). Compared to East Asians, Americans' tendency to better recognize items persisted, even when controlling for the factors of scene congruency and emotional intensity. In addition, Americans exhibited higher levels of background memory than East Asians, again suggesting that cultural differences in memory specificity might be distinct from biases to process objects. The lack of an effect of item–background congruency is somewhat surprising, considering previous research that shows cross-cultural differences for semantic congruency (Goto et al., 2010; Ishii et al., 2010), but could reflect the emotional nature of the images or other details of task demands.

Another way to investigate cross-cultural differences in memory specificity is to probe the effects of culture on neural activation using fMRI (Paige, Ksander, et al., 2017). Using the same paradigm as the original behavioral study (Millar et al., 2013), participants viewed pictures of common objects on a blank background while in the scanner and returned 48 hours later to complete a surprise recognition test using *same*, *similar*, or *new* judgments. Analyses sorted trials based on whether participants later correctly recognized the image as *same* versus *similar*. These analyses allowed brain activity to be compared across cultures at the time of encoding, based on whether pictures were accurately encoded with a high level of detail (specific memory) or at the item level (general memory). Based on prior work in which Americans engaged the right fusiform more for specific recognition but the left fusiform for specific or general recognition (Garoff et al., 2005), we predicted that Americans would engage the right fusiform more than East Asians during the successful encoding of pictures that are later recognized with a high level of detail (e.g., correct *same* responses). Instead, the results indicated that East Asians exhibited greater activation in the left fusiform and left hippocampus than Americans for specific memory. To further understand this unexpected result, we conducted follow-up analyses to test whether these results reflected greater difficulty in the task or less familiarity with the items for East Asians, but neither of these measures seemed to account for the results.

The surprising pattern of fMRI findings led us to question the types of mechanisms that might underlie cultural differences in memory specificity. We will discuss how our thinking has evolved over time in the next section and the subsequent work that has led us to our current model of cultural influences on memory.

V. FRAMEWORK FOR CULTURAL DIFFERENCES IN MEMORY

Initially, we broadly conceptualized culture as a lens through which the world is perceived (Gutchess & Indeck, 2009). In a complex environment, some information is attended to while other aspects are not; bottlenecks (e.g., Ferreira & Pashler, 2002) in cognitive processing further limit how much information can be managed at any one time. Culture can determine what information is selected at the expense of other information (Gutchess et al., 2011). For example, if a culture prioritizes contextual information, that type of information might be attended to and selected for further processing, which can enhance the encoding of the information into memory. Culture can also shape memory through retrieval processes, such as what information is accessible through many different cues or reconstructed in line with cultural values and expectations. Some work supports a role for culture in attentional processes that can contribute to memory. For example, after viewing animated vignettes, Japanese individuals describe more background and contextual information, whereas Americans' descriptions focus on the focal objects (Masuda & Nisbett, 2001). Examining eye movements can be a valuable technique through which to measure attention. When viewing complex scenes, Americans fixate on objects sooner than Chinese; Americans also fixate more on central objects than Chinese, whereas Chinese saccade to the background more than Americans (Chua et al., 2005). These cultural differences in what is reported from eye movements may reflect attentional processes that contribute to differences in what is later remembered.

Our initial approach to conceptualizing the role of culture in memory emphasized top-down processes, the motivational processes by which individuals could attend to certain parts of a scene or fit information in memory to conform to cultural values and expectations. However, over time this framework developed to encompass both top-down and bottom-up processes, classic frameworks from cognitive and perceptual psychology. Bottom-up processes are based on the physical energy that comes from the stimulus and is received by a sensory organ. For example, the wavelength of light that is reflected off an object interacts with the perceiver's retina and is transmitted to the visual cortex, beginning the process of visual perception. Top-down processes are those that rely on the observer's interpretation of the signal that is detected in sensory organs, such as interpreting a wavelength of light between 620 and 750 nanometers as *red* and the shape of the object as a *ball*. Both top-down and bottom-up levels of analysis necessarily interact when encountering information in the world as there must be some stimulus energy to be detected and the observer must detect and interpret it in order to impose meaning on the signals. An observer brings their past experiences to interpret basic stimuli (e.g., *red ball*) as well as more complex ones (e.g., reading words when a letter is smudged, interpreting a social interaction as sarcasm), which allows for a rich array of top-down processes than can be brought to bear on interpreting stimuli in the complex perceptual, cognitive, and social environments that we navigate.

These processes are often considered in terms of how observers are fooled by visual illusions, such as the debate over "the dress."[1] Debate over whether a dress was yellow and gold or blue and black "broke the internet" in 2015, and people were incredulous about the possibility that others could perceive in a way that differed from their own perception. Different individuals perceived the dress differently due to top-down influences. Depending on how one accounted for the levels of lighting, one might mentally subtract out the influence of shadows and adjust one's interpretation of the colors accordingly (Wallisch, 2017). Importantly, these adjustments happen instantaneously and without conscious effort, illustrating the pervasive nature of top-down processes in perception.

Top-down and bottom-up processes not only account for visual illusions but arguably shape all aspects of perception. And the influences are not circumscribed only to the domain of perception but extend to other domains of cognitive processing, including memory. An influential model for the study of memory, signal detection theory, conceives of memory strength as a signal to be detected (e.g., how familiar does this information seem?) (Green & Swets, 1966; Stanislaw & Todorov, 1999). Decisions about whether a particular stimulus was encountered before reflect not only the strength of the signal (e.g., this person seems very familiar because I live with him and see him every day) but also motivational aspects that lead someone to have biases to respond in a certain way (e.g., I may be more likely to smile at someone I deem "familiar" when I am on campus, surrounded by students I may have taught in past large lecture courses than when I am at a coffee shop far from home and do not expect to encounter people I know).

The distinction between top-down and bottom-up influences is a useful framework for the study of culture. It provides a framework to consider the types of processes that can be shaped by culture and the level at which cultural differences might emerge in terms of processes and brain systems. Figure 1.6 depicts the ways in which we conceptualize culture as influencing different levels of processing, and we will review each of these in this section, covering examples of how this has been tested in our work and the research that has influenced it. Critically, there are not sharp distinctions between these levels of processing; our levels are meant to represent tasks that evoke more of one type of process than another. We fully acknowledge that all perceptual and cognitive processes represent a combination of top-down and bottom-up

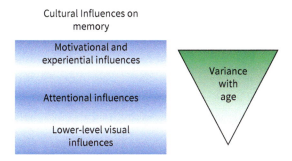

FIGURE 1.6: Hypothesized Cultural Influences on Memory
Culture is hypothesized to influence memory at three different levels, ranging from motivational and experiential influences, which are the most top-down, to attentional influences to lower-level visual influences. The text describes various examples of findings at each of these levels. Furthermore, cultures are hypothesized to differ the most for the top-down processes, whereby strategies can be selected based on cultural values and motivations. Because the influences of culture are driven by lower-level processes, there will be less variation across cultures as effects will be largely driven by neurobiological universals of aging.

A. Motivational and Experiential Influences

The highest level of top-down differences reflects the role of motivation and experiences in information processing, potentially including what knowledge has been taught or gained through one's life experiences. Our work has examined these types of influences in two different studies.

The line of work that most clearly addresses this approach examines cultural differences on self-referencing in memory. The self-reference effect is a mnemonic strategy whereby information that is related to the self (e.g., Does this word describe me? Imagine owning this object) improves the encoding of information (Rogers et al., 1977). The benefits of self-referencing emerge, at least in Western cultures, when compared to relating information to another person, even someone personally close to the self (e.g., one's mother or friend). Past research suggests that self-referencing effects hold for younger and older adults and that the strategy similarly engages neural regions for both groups, even during the encoding of the information into memory (Gutchess, Kensinger, & Schacter, 2007; Gutchess, Kensinger, Yoon, & Schacter, 2007; Gutchess et al., 2015). Most self-referencing studies have been conducted with Western samples. Given the ways in which the concept of the self differs across cultures (e.g., more independent versus more interdependent self-construal), one might expect that East Asians would have less of a unique benefit from referencing the self, compared to referencing another person, than Americans. Indeed, that had been found in some studies, including findings of less of a self-reference effect or less differentiation between the neural signal for self and mother for Chinese younger adults (Sui et al., 2007; Zhu et al., 2007). Work has suggested that for bicultural individuals, both the interdependent self and the independent self may become available (Sui et al., 2007). However, in the case of a Chinese sample, the interdependent self is more accessible (Sui et al., 2007).

We extended these tests of self-referential memory across cultures in a few ways, including incorporating older adults as well as a control condition that allowed for the exploration of other-referencing effects, apart from self-referencing. In this study, Zhang and colleagues (2020) compared samples of younger and older adults from Taiwan to those from the United States, based on the idea that the Taiwanese should be a sample with a more interdependent self-construal than Americans. In this study, participants made judgments about adjectives, deciding on different trials how well the word described themselves, the close other they selected to reference throughout the task, or the category *dogs*, as a control condition.

The critical effect of culture interacted with age and condition; young Taiwanese benefit more from self-referencing than older Taiwanese, but Americans did not mirror this pattern of age differences. Put another way, young adults from Taiwan and the United States responded similarly and benefited from self-referencing, but older Taiwanese did not benefit as much as older Americans (see Figure 1.7). Although we had not predicted that the effects of self-referencing would vary across younger and older Taiwanese, the finding could reflect either generational differences (e.g., global influences, such as shared media, have made younger generations more similar across cultures) or that older adults are more constrained in their ability to adopt less familiar strategies due to cognitive resource limitations (an idea discussed further in Section VI). But overall, the results illustrate the ways in which cultural differences in thinking about the self, shaped by learning and experiences within a culture, can exert top-down influences on memory, such that people

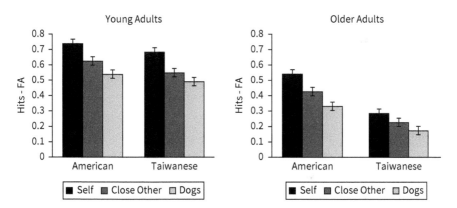

FIGURE 1.7: Cultural Differences With Age in Self-Reference Effects in Memory
Although the self condition enhances memory over the close other person condition for both young Americans and Taiwanese (left panel), the benefits of self-referencing are constrained for older Taiwanese compared to older Americans (right panel). "Hits – FA" on the y-axis corresponds to a corrected recognition measure of hit rates minus false alarms (FA).
Figure from Zhang W., Hung, I. T., Jackson, J. D., Tai, T.-L., Goh, J. O. S., & Gutchess, A. (2020). Influence of culture and age on the self-reference effect. *Aging, Neuropsychology, and Cognition, 27*(3), 370–384, Figure 2. https://doi.org/10.1080/13825 585.2019.1620913. Copyright © 2020 by Taylor & Francis. Reproduced with permission. (Taylor & Francis Ltd., http://www.tandfonline.com).

may be motivated to benefit the most from strategies that are congruent with their cultural perspective on the self.

Another way in which top-down influences can shape memory is through the use of categories, as reviewed in Section IV.B. As taxonomic categories likely differ in the ways in which they are emphasized and instructed across cultures through educational practices, cultural differences in the use of this strategy likely emphasize the influence of cultural differences in knowledge.

B. Attentional Influences

The next level of influences, less top-down than motivational ones (as depicted in Figure 1.6), are those by which cognitive resources are directed differently across cultures. These could reflect motivational or learned influences, such as prioritization of the self for Westerners or context for Easterners, but are marked by their more direct intersection with limited cognitive abilities than those at the highest level of top-down influences (as noted in Figure 1.6, there is a soft distinction rather than a firm one between levels).

One example of how culture influences attention investigates differences in the emotion-induced memory trade-off effect. This effect emerges when people view complex images, with a central object that is either emotional (positively or negatively valenced, e.g., a cake or a snake) or neutral (e.g., a book) against a neutral background (e.g., a table or a forest). The trade-off effect consists of two components: (1) people remember emotional items better than neutral items and (2) neutral backgrounds, or the peripheral information, are remembered worse when they occur with emotional items than with neutral items (Kensinger, 2007; Waring et al., 2010). That is, emotional items are thought to attract attention, potentially drawing it from backgrounds, resulting in the poorer memory for backgrounds than when there was only a neutral item with a background. Previous studies on the phenomenon had primarily been conducted with Western populations. Given the work suggesting cultural differences in the processing of visual environments, with East Asians prioritizing contextual information more than Americans (Masuda & Nisbett, 2001; Nisbett & Masuda, 2003), we wanted to test whether Easterners exhibited a reduced memory trade-off effect (Gutchess et al., 2018). American and Turkish participants viewed visual scenes, each containing a positive, negative, or neutral item placed on a neutral background. Memory for items and backgrounds was tested separately in the surprise recognition test.

The results revealed that while Americans exhibit the typical emotion-induced trade-off effect, Turks have a reduced trade-off effect in emotional memory. Although the Turks exhibited the typical emotional enhancement in item memory (positive and negative items remembered better than neutral items), unlike the Americans, they had no decrease in memory for the backgrounds that had been paired with emotional items compared to memory for the backgrounds that had been paired with the neutral items (see Figure 1.8). This suggests that Eastern cultures, which have an attentional bias for backgrounds rather than focal objects, are less likely to exhibit the emotion-induced memory trade-off effect.

C. Lower-Level Visual Influences

We initially approached the study of memory anticipating that top-down influences would account for cultural differences, perhaps intersecting with cognitive resource constraints in the middle level. Many of our results,

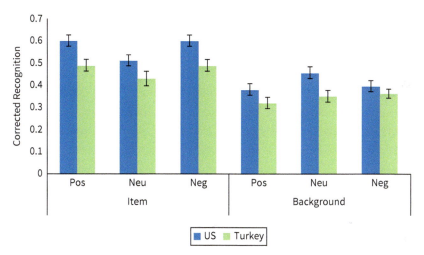

FIGURE 1.8: Cultural Differences in Emotion-Induced Memory Trade-Off Effects
Both groups show the expected benefit of emotion on item memory (left side, positive and negative > neutral). In contrast, cultural differences emerge in the memory for backgrounds. Americans, but not Turks, show the expected trade-off such that memory is better for backgrounds that had been paired with neutral items, compared to memory for those backgrounds that had been paired with positive or negative items.
Figure from Gutchess, A. H., Garner, L., Ligouri, L., Konuk, A. I., & Boduroglu, A. (2018). Culture impacts the magnitude of the emotion-induced memory trade-off effect. *Cognition & Emotion, 32*(6), 1339–1346, Figure 1. https://doi.org10.1080/02699 931.2017.1386620. Copyright © 2018 by Taylor & Francis. Reproduced with permission. (Taylor & Francis Ltd., http://www.tandfonline.com).

however, have led us to suspect that even lower-level visual processes can account for differences in memory across cultures. One line of work that led us to this conclusion was based on a reanalysis of the fMRI data from the Paige, Ksander, et al. (2017) study investigating memory specificity. Using a multivoxel pattern analysis approach (Norman et al., 2006), we compared East Asians and Americans when viewing objects (without regard to later memory performance). A left occipital region in Brodmann area 18/19 (but not in the primary visual cortex) emerged as the sole region in which object representations differed between East Asians and Americans (Ksander et al., 2018). The location of this region in the visual cortex could reflect cultural sensitivities to different image features. Some work (Freeman et al., 2013; Ziemba et al., 2016) indicates this region is particularly sensitive to textures, rather than the lower-level visual properties of stimuli (e.g., line orientations) to which V1 responds. Early-life visual experiences, such as with written languages (Dehaene & Cohen, 2007; Horie et al., 2012), built environments (Miyamoto et al., 2006), density of environments (Chee et al., 2011), or other experiences (Kuwabara & Smith, 2012, 2016), could reflect culture and could tune the visual system's preference for particular ranges of spatial frequencies (Piazza & Silver, 2014, 2017). This tuning would be manifest in perceptual behaviors.

This finding has led us to consider cross-cultural differences in memory from a new perspective focused on bottom-up visual processes, rather than one focused on top-down motivational and attentional processes that influence memory. In addition to the Ksander et al. (2018) results, re-examining the literature guided our thinking in that the observed cultural differences in neural activation patterns might reflect cultural differences in prioritized processing of different spatial frequencies. This idea is based on some behavioral findings that suggest that East Asians tend to use low spatial frequencies, associated with coarser, more global information, whereas Westerners tend to use high spatial frequencies, associated with fine details and more local information during face processing (Blais et al., 2008; Caldara et al., 2010; Estephan et al., 2018; Im et al., 2017; Kelly et al., 2010; Miellet et al., 2013; Rodger et al., 2010; Tardif et al., 2017). This implies that across cultures people could differ in their attention to, or have cortex differentially tuned to, particular spatial frequencies. Cross-cultural distinctions in sensitivity to particular ranges of spatial frequencies could impact the visual processing of objects, though this has yet to be tested. Should this be the case, the left hemisphere cultural differences that emerged in Paige, Ksander, et al. (2017) could reflect East Asians' disproportionate neural response to high spatial frequencies, compared to Americans. This inference is based on evidence that hemispheres differ in their response to high versus low spatial frequency information. High spatial frequencies tend to be preferentially processed in left hemisphere temporoparietal regions, including the fusiform gyrus, compared to low-spatial frequency information, which is processed more in the right hemisphere (Iidaka et al., 2004).

These findings push us to think of memory in terms of its intersections with visual processing. We are currently testing for cultural differences in the prioritization of low versus high spatial frequencies using basic visual stimuli, such as Gabors. This is an important step because many of the prior studies finding cultural differences in spatial frequencies relied on face stimuli, which contain a range of spatial frequencies. Our eventual goal is to test whether cultural differences in these visual processes account for cultural differences in memory specificity.

D. Other Candidate Mechanisms

When we began our investigation of cross-cultural differences in memory, we expected frontal control processes to be implicated in cultural differences, reflecting difficulty in implementing different strategies. When memory tasks require elaboration or organization of information (e.g., thinking about the meaning and importance of information or sorting related information together), as well as executive functions, such as selecting relevant information, inhibiting irrelevant information, and maintaining goals, regions of the prefrontal cortex are engaged (e.g., Blumenfeld & Ranganath, 2007; Miller & Cohen, 2001; Simons & Spiers, 2003). Perhaps, for example, attending to objects would invoke more frontal control processes, either to select this isolated component of the scene for Americans or to inhibit attention to background contextual information for East Asians. Yet in our hands, differences in the engagement of frontal regions across cultures have not emerged for memory, though have been implicated in some of our work outside of the domain of memory. In a categorization task East Asians and Americans were instructed to use either a categorical (e.g., *head–neck*) or a relational (e.g., *head–hat*) strategy while inhibiting the other strategy that may be culturally preferred. The results indicate that East Asians engaged the frontoparietal attentional network more than Americans to make these judgments, whereas Americans engage regions of the temporal lobes to a greater extent, perhaps reflecting the semantic content (Gutchess et al., 2010). These findings are in line with those of Hedden and colleagues (2008) in implicating a domain-general executive function in cultural differences when individuals are working with competing strategies or information. The results are also in line with much of our work on memory that reveals strategy differences across cultures in that different neural regions, reflecting different sets of cognitive processes, are engaged by each culture.

Another way in which we anticipated that control processes would be evoked across cultures is when bicultural individuals are primed to use one of their two cultural frames. A rich body of behavioral research has demonstrated that multicultural individuals can switch between cultural frames (Hong et al., 2000), as a result of viewing pictures and icons associated with their distinct cultural knowledge (e.g., for a Chinese American individual, pictures of the Great Wall of China or dragons to evoke the Chinese knowledge or pictures of the Washington Monument or Mickey Mouse to evoke the American knowledge). Thus, the same bicultural individual can respond in a manner congruent with either culture based on what cultural knowledge is at the forefront at any given time, responding in a way that reflects collectivist values, such as following as part of a group, or that reflects individualistic values, such as leading a group or acting as a unique individual. We anticipated that switching between cultural frames might require cognitive control processes to support bringing one set of knowledge to the foreground and inhibiting the other set of knowledge. Although few studies have investigated this question using cognitive neuroscience methods that could aid in pinpointing the involvement of cognitive control processes, none of the studies thus far have implicated cognitive control networks. Our work indicated some changes in the midline prefrontal cortex (dorsal and ventral medial prefrontal cortex) in response to frame-switching (Huff et al., 2013). These regions respond to thinking about the self and social cognition and are distinct from the prefrontal regions implicated in cognitive control. Our finding that priming different cultural sets of knowledge impacts these medial prefrontal regions is consistent with other studies (Harada et al., 2010; Ng et al., 2010), all of which investigated frame-switching when making judgments about self and others.

Although our research on memory has not implicated cognitive control processes, studies beyond Hedden et al. (2008) have found cultural differences in prefrontal regions associated with this process. In examining cognitive persistence over time, Chinese participants evinced more cognitive persistence, indicated by continued improvement on a demanding task over blocks, whereas American participants made more errors over time; self-reported desire for self-improvement mediated the cultural differences in cognitive performance (Telzer et al., 2017). In addition, fMRI data implicate the inferior frontal gyrus, a region that is part of the frontoparietal control network, in cognitive persistence, with Chinese participants engaging the region more over blocks than Americans. Thus, it is certainly possible that control processes, and the frontoparietal network associated with them, can differ across cultures. It may be the case that the studies investigating memory thus far have not investigated tasks that place strong demands on executive control, such as inhibiting a prepotent strategy (e.g., ignoring the categorical information, for Americans) or culturally prioritized information (e.g., ignoring the information associated with the context, for East Asians) when in direct opposition to what the task demands. It is also possible that these types of task demands could implicate frontoparietal control networks in frame-switching; more research is needed to evaluate these possibilities.

VI. INFLUENCE OF AGING ON CULTURAL DIFFERENCES IN COGNITION

We have mentioned throughout the chapter some of our findings involving age differences. At one level, simply establishing the universality of the cognitive aging literature is an important endeavor. Even though the study of young adults is limited to largely Western samples (Henrich et al., 2010), this problem is even greater for the study of aging as the vast majority of the literature studies people in the West and does not systematically consider individual differences related to culture. Beyond the importance of testing the extent to which cognitive aging findings generalize across cultures, we will explicate models for thinking about how aging might impact cultural differences that will aid in understanding the ways in which cultural effects on cognition can change across the life span.

A. Combined Effects of Age and Culture: Initial Model

Our work initially was framed in terms of Denise Park's ideas. Her model (Park & Gutchess, 2002; Park et al., 1999) emphasized the distinction between *culture-invariant* (not requiring or influenced by cultural knowledge or strategies) and *culture-saturated* (requiring or influenced by cultural knowledge or strategies) tasks. Younger adults across cultures should perform similarly on culture-invariant tasks, and effects of aging on cognitively demanding tasks should emerge equivalently across cultures (e.g., Corsi blocks). For culture-saturated tasks, the effects of aging would depend on the extent to which the task is automatic or whether it requires effortful, controlled processing (e.g., digit span). For automatic tasks, cultural differences should magnify with age. This reflects the fact that older adults have spent more years absorbing cultural learning and influences; due to the automatic nature of the task, they are able to apply culturally crafted strategies and biases. For controlled tasks, cultures should converge with age, reflecting the reliance of culturally specific strategies on cognitive resources that are limited by cognitive aging. The model also emphasizes the importance of comparing samples across cultures that have been equated on cognitive resources; drawing differently abled samples would confound understanding of the effects of culture. Initial work (Hedden et al., 2002) focused on developing a battery of culture-fair neuropsychological tasks that could be used be ensure that samples of healthy younger and older adults were equated on basic cognitive resources (e.g., speed of processing, working memory).

Introducing a neuroscience perspective to the model allowed for the possibility of achieving similar behavior across cultures using different neural mechanisms, as we discussed in Section III for young adults. Whereas younger adults from different cultures might recruit different neural circuits, reflecting distinct strategies or processes, these neural pathways may become more similar with age. This could reflect limited cognitive resources but also the tendency for older adults to recruit neural resources more generally, in a less specialized fashion. For example, regions of the prefrontal cortex are specialized for either verbal or visuospatial working memory tasks in young adults, but older adults recruit the regions from both hemispheres during challenging working memory tasks of either modality (Park & Gutchess, 2002, 2006).

B. Proposed Revision to Model

Our thinking has undoubtedly been influenced by Park's notions of the tension between the processes through which life experiences sculpt neural networks and neurobiological processes of aging limit the plasticity of neural systems, restricting the ability to engage neural systems in culturally unique ways. This framework has led us to think about culture, the brain, and behavior as ever malleable and plastic. In addition, the emphasis on cognitive resource demands, particularly with aging, has aided our thinking about when to expect cultural differences (e.g., more effortful and demanding processes), as well as highlighting the complexity in understanding when and where in the brain cultural differences do and do not emerge in younger adults, depending on task demands and domains of processing (e.g., lateral occipital complex and middle temporal cortex for object processing).

Our data, however, have challenged the utility of thinking about automatic versus controlled processes. What we initially may have thought of as automatic processes (e.g., self-referencing, use of categories), in that they are well practiced over a lifetime, nevertheless seem to interact with cognitive resources. For example, even though older Americans use categories more than older Chinese in their free recall output, this does not directly map onto memory performance (Gutchess, Yoon, et al., 2006), indicating that additional cognitive processes are at play. Similarly, we find that differences in self-referencing effects in memory are larger for older than younger adults (Zhang et al., 2020), again potentially indicating the role of cognitive resources in the task. We have struggled with defining the presence of cognitive effort and resource demands in a way that avoids being circular, in defining cognitive effort through its impact on the performance of older adults. We have also seen ways in which tasks can combine automatic components with effortful components or be highly dependent on task instructions and demands, such as the older Singaporeans' lack of an adaptation response in the lateral occipital complex during passive viewing of objects but having adaptation restored when they make a response about the object or see objects in isolation without a background (Chee et al., 2006; Goh et al., 2007). These findings highlight the ways in which resource demands are flexible and may vary across different aspects of a task or performance.

We propose a variation on the Park model by including aging in the right-side portion of Figure 1.6. Rather than focusing on the degree to which a task requires controlled or automatic processing, we think about how the top-down or bottom-up processes evoked by a task may allow for a smaller or larger influence of culture with age. When task performance is profoundly shaped by top-down processes, such as motivation or goals, the performance of older adults can vary greatly across cultures. This reflects that tasks have a large degree of flexibility such that multiple strategies or different types of motivations can shape performance. This is in line with our examples in which cultural differences are larger for older than younger adults for categorization and self-referencing in memory (Gutchess, Yoon, et al., 2006; Zhang et al., 2020). When more bottom-up processes drive the ability to do the task, there is a limited role for strategies to contribute to different patterns of performance. In these cases, tasks will be very resource-dependent (e.g., on speed of processing, working memory, sensory acuity).

Due to neurobiological aging processes, these resources are limited with age; older adults should perform similarly across cultures as there is less room for culture to differentially shape performance. This would predict that cultural differences in lower-level tasks, such as prioritization of high versus low spatial frequency information, would be fixed with age. This means that cultural differences present for younger adults would be maintained with age or that limitations to visual and attentional systems with age would eliminate cultural differences in older adults. Although either of these patterns might occur, cultural differences would not be predicted to magnify with age for tasks that are more bottom-up. The intermediate attentional level would be predicted to support the entire range of patterns of cultural differences with age—magnification, maintenance, and reduction. Effects may be highly dependent on the precise attentional demands, task instructions, and task content. The importance of these aspects of task demands is illustrated in the finding that cultural difference in adaptation to visual objects is larger with age but that directing attention to the objects—based on instructions or task context—restores older Singaporeans' adaptation response (Chee et al., 2006; Goh et al., 2007) (presumably eliminating cultural differences, though a direct comparison was not possible as these manipulations were not conducted in older Americans).

C. Test of Model

In current work with Joshua Goh, we are testing the effects of aging across cultures on multiple behavioral and neural systems. In this work, we adopt the framework in which the medial temporal system that supports accurate and detailed memory is a lower-level system than the frontostriatal system that supports value-based decision-making. See Figure 1.9 for a depiction of our framework and expectations for cultural differences in neural engagement with age. In addition to roughly mapping onto the continuum of top-down processes (decision-making) and a relatively lower-level system (memory), our approach emphasizes the unique properties of different brain systems and makes predictions of the effects of culture based on the malleability and flexibility of these systems with age. The medial temporal (or temporoparietal, according to one framework) system is vulnerable to the effects of pathological aging (e.g., Alzheimer's disease), and thus may have less plasticity to be shaped by culture than systems that are predominantly affected by normal aging processes, such as the frontostriatal system (Fjell et al., 2014). Interestingly, based on these

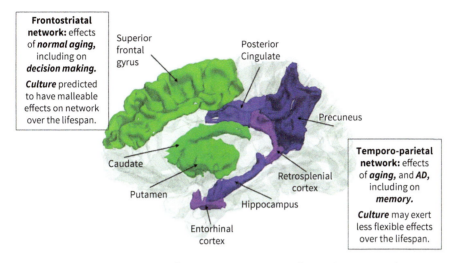

FIGURE 1.9: Proposed Cultural Differences in Engagement of Neural Systems With Age
As described in the text, we predict that effects of aging on the medial temporal lobe system may be more fixed, reflecting the vulnerability of the region to pathology (such as from Alzheimer's disease [AD]), and thus less prone to the influence of culture. In contrast, culture may be able to exert malleable effects on the frontostriatal system over the life span.
Figure adapted from Fjell, A. M., McEvoy, L., Holland, D., Dale, A. M., & Walhovd, K. B. (2014). What is normal in normal aging? Effects of aging, amyloid and Alzheimer's disease on the cerebral cortex and the hippocampus. *Progress in Neurobiology, 117,* 20–40, Figure 8. Copyright © 2014 by Elsevier. Reproduced with permission.

ideas, we would predict that the cultural differences in memory specificity and the corresponding patterns of neural activation that we have found in younger adults (Leger & Gutchess, 2021; Millar et al., 2013; Paige, Amado, & Gutchess, 2017; Paige, Ksander, et al., 2017) would be eliminated with age, due to the constrained functioning of the medial temporal lobes with age. In contrast, cultural differences in value-based decision-making (i.e., making a choice based on subjective value, such as deciding what to eat for dinner or which of two gambles to accept), which we have observed in pilot data, should be maintained or even exaggerated with age. Distinct patterns of behavior and corresponding neural activity across cultures can emerge due to the considerable flexibility of the frontostriatal system with age, including its reflection of individual differences in risk preferences in older adults (Goh et al., 2016). In these ways, we can see how understanding the effects of aging on particular neural systems can inform predictions of how much culture can be expected to contribute to performance differences across the age groups.

VII. FUTURE DIRECTIONS

As we have illustrated throughout this chapter, the study of culture and cognition, including consideration of memory, has begun to enter maturity. This reflects the number of converging findings on specific topics (e.g., object–context processing, memory specificity), as well as the breadth in approaches that have been applied to increase our understanding of processes, such as the integration of behavioral, eye-tracking, and neuroimaging methods to probe the effects of culture on object versus background processing (Chua et al., 2005; Goh et al., 2007; Gutchess, Welsh, et al., 2006; Masuda et al., 2008, 2016; Masuda & Nisbett, 2001, 2006). In addition, the field benefits as frameworks are developed to predict how culture would be expected to influence behavior and neural activity.

Even though we are at the point in the field where findings are replicating and building on each other in a way that supports the development of new theories and frameworks, we need to further embrace open science practices. Larger sample sizes will ensure that the field reports replicable effects and better support the understanding of individual differences. Pre-registrations may help null results of culture to find their way into the literature (Hakim et al., 2017); failures to find predicted cultural differences are important to consider when developing frameworks and understanding boundary conditions or limitations to effects. The study of culture and cognition is fairly unusual in its relatively young state; additional theoretical frameworks are critically needed as the extant ones do not always succeed in accounting for patterns of cultural differences. One example from our own work is that our findings of cultural differences in memory specificity do not extend to comparisons of Turkish and American populations. We cannot determine whether this null result reflects unexpected effects of the task design or true convergence across American and Turkish cultures, representing a way in which "Eastern" cultures are differentiated from each other. Yet knowing this could be important for understanding the nature of cultural differences (e.g., what mechanism differentially affects Chinese and Turks?).

Despite the advances in the field, many questions and challenges to the study of culture and cognition remain. Chief among these are questions of mechanism. Although there is some support that social processes that differ across cultures can lead to cognitive differences, some of our work reviewed here suggests that is not the most straightforward explanation. In our hands, individual differences in values, such as independence, interdependence, and each of the values comprising the Schwartz Values Scale (S. H. Schwartz, 1992), fail to explain cultural differences in memory specificity (Leger & Gutchess, 2021); and priming different cultural mindsets (e.g., Chinese or American sets of knowledge) does not impact what type of information is remembered or what biases in memory (e.g., to remember objects versus contexts) emerge (see Gutchess & Sekuler, 2019, for a discussion of this issue). We believe that our work contributes to the field by suggesting the lower-level mechanisms that must be considered when attempting to explain cross-cultural differences in cognition, representing a focus on more perceptual and cognitive processes in their own right, as opposed to social ones.

Even when specific mechanisms are suggested to account for cultural differences in cognition, such as differences in attention to context or built environments that might direct attention away from objects (e.g., Miyamoto et al., 2006; Nisbett & Miyamoto, 2005) or differences in prioritization of low versus high spatial frequencies (Blais et al., 2008; Estephan et al., 2018; Tardif et al., 2017), questions remain about the source of these differences. For example, does the built physical world simply reflect social expectations, in terms of number and salience of objects? Do visual experiences contribute to prioritization of different spatial frequencies, or are there physical differences in the visual systems across cultures (e.g., confounds such as cultural differences in the prevalence of astigmatism)? We consider these challenges elsewhere (Gutchess & Sekuler, 2019) and here only acknowledge the importance, and difficulty, of answering questions about mechanism.

Two important avenues to further our understanding of mechanism require systematically investigating the richness of culture, by studying a greater breadth of cultural groups and examining the effects of acculturation, as individuals move to and acquire a new cultural frame. Much of the work thus far, including our own, has been largely based on convenience sampling. This includes testing populations available at one site (e.g., Chinese students who have moved to the United States for study) or cross-site collaborations that are largely selected based on shared interests and common training. To some extent, these are necessary approaches as establishing the rigor and reproducibility of methods across sites requires coordination, resources, and a high degree of trust; these concerns are compounded when considering the equipment and technical demands of using cognitive neuroscience methods. But as the field matures, broadening the scope of cultures being studied will help in understanding the limits to effects (e.g., ending the treatment of "Eastern" and "Western" as monoliths) and inform theory. Likewise, systematically studying cultural change as people adapt to a new culture is an approach that has been adopted little in the study of the effects of culture on cognition. Although dramatic changes in cultural experiences, such as relocating to an urbanized environment for a seminomadic people, have been demonstrated to impact perceptual processes (Caparos et al., 2012), most studies systematically comparing samples with different levels of cultural adaptation focus on socioemotional processes, such as perceiving out-groups (Hughes et al., 2019) or emotion recognition (Elfenbein & Ambady, 2003). Studying cognition as people are exposed to a new culture offers an opportunity to examine the malleability and shift in strategies and styles of information processing.

VIII. SUMMARY

To conclude, our work provides evidence that culture can impact memory, potentially through a combination of top-down and bottom-up processes. Applying a cognitive neuroscience approach has the potential to aid in our understanding of cultural differences by offering a sensitive assay of strategic and processing differences across cultures, in some cases having the potential to identify cultural differences in difficulty or cognitive demand. Integrating the work with aging allows for important tests of the universality of the effects of aging on cognition, which thus far have largely been investigated in Western samples. When culture does influence cognition with age, the effects are expected to emerge more strongly when the culture impacts behavior and neural engagement via top-down, rather than bottom-up, processes.

The study of culture and cognition has entered an exciting period: It is embraced by the mainstream fields of psychology and neuroscience, and converging findings are accumulating. Yet many, many questions remain to be answered; these puzzles offer opportunities for creative experimentation and theory-building.

ACKNOWLEDGMENTS

We wish to acknowledge the people and resources who have made this body of work possible. This work would not have been possible without Aysecan Boduroglu and Joshua Goh as collaborators, Denise Park and Richard Nisbett as mentors, as well as the many students who collaborated on these studies. Funding from the Fulbright Scholars program, the National Science Foundation (BCS 1147707 and BCS 1921644), and the National Institute on Aging (R01 AG061886) supported this research. We also thank readers who offered comments on earlier drafts of the manuscript and Tong Lin for assistance with figures.

NOTE

1. Thanks to James Pomerantz for priming this example at the Culture & Cognition pre-conference to the 2019 meeting of the Psychonomic Society.

REFERENCES

Balota, D. A., Cortese, M. J., Duchek, J. M., Adams, D., Roediger, H. L., III, McDermott, K. B., & Yerys, B. E. (1999). Veridical and false memories in healthy older adults and in dementia of the Alzheimer's type. *Cognitive Neuropsychology*, *16*(3–5), 361–384. https://doi.org/10.1080/026432999380834

Blais, C., Jack, R. E., Scheepers, C., Fiset, D., & Caldara, R. (2008). Culture shapes how we look at faces. *PLoS One*, *3*(8), Article e3022. https://doi.org/10.1371/journal.pone.0003022

Blumenfeld, R. S., & Ranganath, C. (2007). Prefrontal cortex and long-term memory encoding: An integrative review of findings from neuropsychology and neuroimaging. *Neuroscientist*, *13*(3), 280–291. https://doi.org/10.1177/1073858407299290

Bousfield, W. A. (1953). The occurrence of clustering in the recall of randomly arranged associates. *Journal of General Psychology*, *49*, 229–240.

Braver, T. S., Cohen, J. D., Nystrom, L. E., Jonides, J., Smith, E. E., & Noll, D. C. (1997). A parametric study of prefrontal cortex involvement in human working memory. *Neuroimage*, *5*(1), 49–62. https://doi.org/10.1006/nimg.1996.0247

Cabeza, R., Rao, S. M., Wagner, A. D., Mayer, A. R., & Schacter, D. L. (2001). Can medial temporal lobe regions distinguish true from false? An event-related functional MRI study of veridical and illusory recognition memory. *Proceedings of the National Academy of Sciences of the United States of America*, *98*(8), 4805–4810.

Caldara, R., Zhou, X., & Miellet, S. (2010). Putting culture under the "spotlight" reveals universal information use for face recognition. *PLoS One*, *5*(3), Article e9708. https://doi.org/10.1371/journal.pone.0009708

Caparos, S., Ahmed, L., Bremner, A. J., de Fockert, J. W., Linnell, K. J., & Davidoff, J. (2012). Exposure to an urban environment alters the local bias of a remote culture. *Cognition*, *122*(1), 80–85. https://doi.org/10.1016/j.cognition.2011.08.013

Chee, M. W., Goh, J. O., Venkatraman, V., Tan, J. C., Gutchess, A. H., Sutton, B., Hebrank, A., Leshikar, E., & Park, D. C. (2006). Age-related changes in object processing and contextual binding revealed using fMR adaptation. *Journal of Cognitive Neuroscience*, *18*(4), 495–507. https://doi.org/10.1162/jocn.2006.18.4.495

Chee, M. W., Zheng, H., Goh, J. O., Park, D. C., & Sutton, B. P. (2011). Brain structure in young and old East Asians and Westerners: Comparisons of structural volume and cortical thickness. *Journal of Cognitive Neuroscience, 23*, 1065–1079.

Chiao, J. Y. (2009). Cultural neuroscience: A once and future discipline. In J. Y. Chiao (Ed.), *Cultural neuroscience: Cultural influences on brain function* (Progress in Brain Research, Vol. 178, pp. 287–304). Elsevier.

Chiao, J. Y., Cheon, B. K., Pornpattanangkul, N., Mrazek, A. J., & Blizinsky, K. D. (2013). Cultural neuroscience: Progress and promise. *Psychological Inquiry, 24*(1), 1–19. https://doi.org/10.1080/1047840X.2013.752715

Chiu, L. H. (1972). A cross-cultural comparison of cognitive styles in Chinese and American children. *International Journal of Psychology, 7*, 235–242.

Chua, H. F., Boland, J. E., & Nisbett, R. E. (2005). Cultural variation in eye movements during scene perception. *Proceedings of the National Academy of Sciences of the United States of America, 102*(35), 12629–12633.

Dehaene, S., & Cohen, L. (2007). Cultural recycling of cortical maps. *Neuron, 56*(2), 384–398. https://doi.org/10.1016/j.neuron.2007.10.004

Draganski, B., Gaser, C., Busch, V., Schuierer, G., Bogdahn, U., & May, A. (2004). Changes in grey matter induced by training. *Nature, 427*(6972), 311–312. https://doi.org/10.1038/427311a

Elfenbein, H. A., & Ambady, N. (2003). When familiarity breeds accuracy: Cultural exposure and facial emotion recognition. *Journal of Personality and Social Psychology, 85*(2), 276–290. https://doi.org/10.1037/0022-3514.85.2.276

Estephan, A., Fiset, D., Saumure, C., Plouffe-Demers, M. P., Zhang, Y., Sun, D., & Blais, C. (2018). Time course of cultural differences in spatial frequency use for face identification. *Scientific Reports, 8*(1), Article 1816. https://doi.org/10.1038/s41598-018-19971-1

Ferreira, V. S., & Pashler, H. (2002). Central bottleneck influences on the processing stages of word production. *Journal of Experimental Psychology: Learning, Memory, and Cognition, 28*(6), 1187–1199.

Fjell, A. M., McEvoy, L., Holland, D., Dale, A. M., & Walhovd, K. B. (2014). What is normal in normal aging? Effects of aging, amyloid and Alzheimer's disease on the cerebral cortex and the hippocampus. *Progress in Neurobiology, 117*, 20–40.

Freeman, J., Ziemba, C. M., Heeger, D. J., Simoncelli, E. P., & Movshon, J. A. (2013). A functional and perceptual signature of the second visual area in primates. *Nature Neuroscience, 16*(7), 974–981. https://doi.org/10.1038/nn.3402

Gallo, D. A. (2006). *Associative illusions of memory: False memory research in DRM and related tasks.* Psychology Press.

Gallo, D. A. (2010). False memories and fantastic beliefs: 15 years of the DRM illusion. *Memory & Cognition, 38*(7), 833–848. https://doi.org/10.3758/mc.38.7.833

Garoff, R. J., Slotnick, S. D., & Schacter, D. L. (2005). The neural origins of specific and general memory: The role of the fusiform cortex. *Neuropsychologia, 43*(6), 847–859.

Gelfand, M. J. (2012). Culture's constraints: International differences in the strength of social norms. *Current Directions in Psychological Science, 21*(6), 420–424. https://doi.org/10.1177/0963721412460048

Gelfand, M. J., Raver, J. L., Nishii, L., Leslie, L. A., Lun, J., Lim, B. C., Duan, L., Almaliach, A., Ang, S., Arnadottir, J., Aycan, Z., Boehnke, K., Boski, P., Cabecinhas, R., Chan, D., Chhokar, J., D'Amato, A., Ferrer, M., Fischlmayr, I. C., . . . Yamaguchi, S. (2011). Differences between tight and loose cultures: A 33-nation study. *Science, 332*(6033), 1100–1104. https://doi.org/10.1126/science.1197754

Goh, J. O., Chee, M. W., Tan, J. C., Venkatraman, V., Hebrank, A., Leshikar, E. D., Jenkins, L., Sutton, B. P., Gutchess, A. H., & Park, D. C. (2007). Age and culture modulate object processing and object–scene binding in the ventral visual area. *Cognitive, Affective, and Behavioral Neuroscience, 7,* 44–52.

Goh, J. O., Siong, S. C., Park, D. C., Gutchess, A. H., Hebrank, A., & Chee, M. W. (2004). Cortical areas involved in object, background, and object-background processing revealed with functional magnetic resonance adaptation. *Journal of Neuroscience, 24*(45), 10223–10228. https://doi.org/10.1523/jneurosci.3373-04.2004

Goh, J. O., Su, Y. S., Tang, Y. J., McCarrey, A. C., Tereshchenko, A., Elkins, W., & Resnick, S. M. (2016). Frontal, striatal, and medial temporal sensitivity to value distinguishes risk-taking from risk-aversive older adults during decision making. *Journal of Neuroscience, 36*(49), 12498–12509. https://doi.org/10.1523/jneurosci.1386-16.2016

Gonsalves, B., & Paller, K. A. (2000). Neural events that underlie remembering something that never happened. *Nature Neuroscience, 3*(12), 1316–1321.

Gonsalves, B., & Paller, K. A. (2002). Mistaken memories: Remembering events that never happened. *Neuroscientist, 8*(5), 391–395.

Goto, S. G., Ando, Y., Huang, C., Yee, A., & Lewis, R. S. (2010). Cultural differences in the visual processing of meaning: Detecting incongruities between background and foreground objects using the N400. *Social Cognitive and Affective Neuroscience, 5*(2–3), 242–253. https://doi.org/10.1093/scan/nsp038

Green, D. M., & Swets, J. A. (1966). *Signal detection theory and psychophysics.* John Wiley & Sons.

Grill-Spector, K., Henson, R., & Martin, A. (2006). Repetition and the brain: Neural models of stimulus-specific effects. *Trends in Cognitive Sciences, 10*(1), 14–23. https://doi.org/10.1016/j.tics.2005.11.006

Gutchess, A., & Boduroglu, A. (2019). Cultural differences in categorical memory errors persist with age. *Aging & Mental Health, 23,* 851–854. https://doi.org/10.1080/13607863.2017.1421616

Gutchess, A. H., Garner, L., Ligouri, L., Konuk, A. I., & Boduroglu, A. (2018). Culture impacts the magnitude of the emotion-induced memory trade-off effect. *Cognition & Emotion, 32*(6), 1339–1346. https://doi.org/10.1080/02699931.2017.1386620

Gutchess, A. H., Hedden, T., Ketay, S., Aron, A., & Gabrieli, J. D. E. (2010). Neural differences in the processing of semantic relationships across cultures. *Social Cognitive and Affective Neuroscience*, *5*(2–3), 254–263. https://doi.org/10.1093/scan/nsp059

Gutchess, A. H., & Indeck, A. (2009). Cultural influences on memory. In J. Y. Chiao (Ed.), *Cultural neuroscience: Cultural influences on brain function* (Progress in Brain Research, Vol. 178, pp. 137–150). Elsevier.

Gutchess, A. H., Kensinger, E. A., & Schacter, D. L. (2007). Aging, self-referencing, and medial prefrontal cortex. *Social Neuroscience*, *2*(2), 117–133.

Gutchess, A. H., Kensinger, E. A., Yoon, C., & Schacter, D. L. (2007). Ageing and the self-reference effect in memory. *Memory*, *15*(8), 822–837. https://doi.org/10.1080/09658210701701394

Gutchess, A. H., Schwartz, A. J., & Boduroglu, A. (2011). The influence of culture on memory. In D. D. Schmorrow & C. M. Fidopiastis (Eds.), *Foundations of augmented cognition: Directing the future of adaptive systems* (Lectures Notes in Computer Science, Vol. 6780, pp. 67–76). Springer-Verlag.

Gutchess, A. H., & Sekuler, R. (2019). Perceptual and mnemonic differences across cultures. *Psychology of Learning and Motivation*, *71*, 131–174.

Gutchess, A. H., Sokal, R., Coleman, J. A., Gotthilf, G., Grewal, L., & Rosa, N. (2015). Age differences in self-referencing: Evidence for common and distinct encoding strategies. *Brain Research*, *1612*, 118–127. https://doi.org/10.1016/j.brainres.2014.08.033

Gutchess, A. H., Welsh, R. C., Boduroglu, A., & Park, D. C. (2006). Cultural differences in neural function associated with object processing. *Cognitive, Affective & Behavioral Neuroscience*, *6*(2), 102–109.

Gutchess, A. H., Yoon, C., Luo, T., Feinberg, F., Hedden, T., Jing, Q., Nisbett, R. E., & Park, D. C. (2006). Categorical organization in free recall across culture and age. *Gerontology*, *52*(5), 314–323. https://doi.org/10.1159/000094613

Hackman, D. A., & Farah, M. J. (2009). Socioeconomic status and the developing brain. *Trends in Cognitive Sciences*, *13*(2), 65–73. https://doi.org/10.1016/j.tics.2008.11.003

Hackman, D. A., Farah, M. J., & Meaney, M. J. (2010). Socioeconomic status and the brain: Mechanistic insights from human and animal research. *Nature Reviews Neuroscience*, *11*(9), 651–659. https://doi.org/10.1038/nrn2897

Hakim, N., Simons, D. J., Zhao, H., & Wan, X. (2017). Do Easterners and Westerners differ in visual cognition? A preregistered examination of three visual cognition tasks. *Social Psychological and Personality Science*, *8*(2), 142–152. https://doi.org/10.1177/1948550616667613

Han, S., & Ma, Y. (2015). A culture–behavior–brain loop model of human development. *Trends in Cognitive Sciences*, *19*(11), 666–676. https://doi.org/10.1016/j.tics.2015.08.010

Harada, T., Li, Z., & Chiao, J. Y. (2010). Differential dorsal and ventral medial prefrontal representations of the implicit self modulated by individualism and collectivism: An fMRI study. *Social Neuroscience*, *5*(3), 257–271. https://doi.org/10.1080/17470910903374895

Hedden, T., Ketay, S., Aron, A., Markus, H. R., & Gabrieli, J. D. E. (2008). Cultural influences on neural substrates of attentional control. *Psychological Science*, *19*(1), 12–17.

Hedden, T., Park, D. C., Nisbett, R., Ji, L. J., Jing, Q., & Jiao, S. (2002). Cultural variation in verbal versus spatial neuropsychological function across the lifespan. *Neuropsychology*, *16*, 65–73.

Henrich, J., Heine, S. J., & Norenzayan, A. (2010). The weirdest people in the world? *Behavioral and Brain Sciences*, *33*(2–3), 61–83. https://doi.org/10.1017/s0140525x0999152x

Hong, Y. Y., Morris, M. W., Chiu, C. Y., & Benet-Martinez, V. (2000). Multicultural minds. A dynamic constructivist approach to culture and cognition. *The American Psychologist*, *55*(7), 709–720.

Horie, S., Yamasaki, T., Okamoto, T., Kan, S., Ogata, K., Miyauchi, S., & Tobimatsu, S. (2012). Distinct role of spatial frequency in dissociative reading of ideograms and phonograms: An fMRI study. *Neuroimage*, *63*(2), 979–988. https://doi.org/10.1016/j.neuroimage.2012.03.046

Huff, S., Yoon, C., Lee, F., Mandadi, A., & Gutchess, A. H. (2013). Self-referential processing and encoding in bicultural individuals. *Culture and Brain*, *1*(1), 16–33. https://doi.org/10.1007/s40167-013-0005-1

Hughes, C., Babbitt, L. G., & Krendl, A. C. (2019). Culture impacts the neural response to perceiving outgroups among Black and White faces. *Frontiers in Human Neuroscience*, *13*, Article 143. https://doi.org/10.3389/fnhum.2019.00143

Iidaka, T., Yamashita, K., Kashikura, K., & Yonekura, Y. (2004). Spatial frequency of visual image modulates neural responses in the temporo-occipital lobe. An investigation with event-related fMRI. *Brain Research. Cognitive Brain Research*, *18*(2), 196–204.

Im, H. Y., Chong, S. C., Sun, J., Steiner, T. G., Albohn, D. N., Adams, R. B., & Kveraga, K. (2017). Cross-cultural and hemispheric laterality effects on the ensemble coding of emotion in facial crowds. *Culture and Brain*, *5*(2), 125–152. https://doi.org/10.1007/s40167-017-0054-y

Ishii, K., Kobayashi, Y., & Kitayama, S. (2010). Interdependence modulates the brain response to word–voice incongruity. *Social Cognitive and Affective Neuroscience*, *5*(2–3), 307–317. https://doi.org/10.1093/scan/nsp044

Jenkins, L. J., Yang, Y.-J., Goh, J., Hong, Y.-Y., & Park, D. C. (2010). Cultural differences in the lateral occipital complex while viewing incongruent scenes. *Social Cognitive and Affective Neuroscience*, *5*(2–3), 236–241. https://doi.org/10.1093/scan/nsp056

Ji, L. J., Nisbett, R. E., & Su, Y. (2001). Culture, change, and prediction. *Psychological Science*, *12*(6), 450–456.

Ji, L. J., Peng, K. P., & Nisbett, R. E. (2000). Culture, control, and perception of relationships in the environment. *Journal of Personality and Social Psychology*, *78*(5), 943–955.

Ji, L. J., Zhang, Z. Y., & Nisbett, R. E. (2004). Is it culture or is it language? Examination of language effects in cross-cultural research on categorization. *Journal of Personality and Social Psychology*, *87*(1), 57–65. https://doi.org/10.1037/0022-3514.87.1.57

Kagitçibaşi, Ç. (1994). Psychology in Turkey. *International Journal of Psychology*, *29*(6), 729–738. https://doi.org/10.1080/00207599408246562

Kagitçibaşi, Ç. (2000). Turkey. In A. E. Kazdin (Ed.), *Encyclopedia of psychology* (Vol. 8, pp. 125–127). Oxford University Press.

Kelly, D. J., Miellet, S., & Caldara, R. (2010). Culture shapes eye movements for visually homogeneous objects. *Frontiers in Psychology*, *1*, Article 6. https://doi.org/10.3389/fpsyg.2010.00006

Kensinger, E. A. (2007). Negative emotion enhances memory accuracy: Behavioral and neuroimaging evidence. *Current Directions in Psychological Science*, *16*(4), 213–218.

Kitayama, S., Duffy, S., Kawamura, T., & Larsen, J. T. (2003). Perceiving an object and its context in different cultures: A cultural look at new look. *Psychological Science*, *14*(3), 201–206.

Kitayama, S., & Uskul, A. K. (2011). Culture, mind, and brain: Current evidence and future directions. *Annual Review of Psychology*, *62*, 419–449.

Koutstaal, W., & Schacter, D. (1997). Gist-based false recognition of pictures in older and younger adults. *Journal of Memory and Language*, *37*(4), 555–583.

Ksander, J. C., Paige, L. E., Johndro, H. A., & Gutchess, A. H. (2018). Cultural specialization of visual cortex. *Social, Cognitive, and Affective Neuroscience*, *13*(7), 709–718. https://doi.org/10.1093/scan/nsy039

Kuwabara, M., & Smith, L. B. (2012). Cross-cultural differences in cognitive development: Attention to relations and objects. *Journal of Experimental Child Psychology*, *113*(1), 20–35. https://doi.org/10.1016/j.jecp.2012.04.009

Kuwabara, M., & Smith, L. B. (2016). Cultural differences in visual object recognition in 3-year-old children. *Journal of Experimental Child Psychology*, *147*, 22–38. https://doi.org/10.1016/j.jecp.2016.02.006

Leger, K. R., & Gutchess, A. (2021). Cross-cultural differences in memory specificity: Investigation of candidate mechanisms. *Journal of Applied Research in Memory and Cognition*. https://doi.org/10.1016/j.jarmac.2020.08.016

Loftus, E. F. (1979). Malleability of human memory. *American Scientist*, *67*(3), 312–320.

Loftus, E. F. (2005). Planting misinformation in the human mind: A 30-year investigation of the malleability of memory. *Learning & Memory*, *12*(4), 361–366. https://doi.org/10.1101/lm.94705

Maguire, E. A., Gadian, D. G., Johnsrude, I. S., Good, C. D., Ashburner, J., Frackowiak, R. S. J., & Frith, C. D. (2000). Navigation-related structural change in the hippocampi of taxi drivers. *Proceedings of the National Academy of Sciences of the United States of America, 97*(8), 4398–4403.

Markus, H. R., & Kitayama, S. (1991). Culture and the self: Implications for cognition, emotion, & motivation. *Psychological Review, 98*, 224–253.

Masuda, T., Ellsworth, P. C., Mesquita, B., Leu, J., Tanida, S., & De Veerdonk, E. V. (2008). Placing the face in context: Cultural differences in the perception of facial emotion. *Journal of Personality and Social Psychology, 94*(3), 365–381. https://doi.org/10.1037/0022-3514.94.3.365

Masuda, T., Ishii, K., & Kimura, J. (2016). When does the culturally dominant mode of attention appear or disappear? Comparing patterns of eye movement during the visual flicker task between European Canadians and Japanese. *Journal of Cross-Cultural Psychology, 47*(7), 997–1014. https://doi.org/10.1177/0022022116653830

Masuda, T., & Nisbett, R. E. (2001). Attending holistically versus analytically: Comparing the context sensitivity of Japanese and Americans. *Journal of Personality and Social Psychology, 81*(5), 922–934. https://doi.org/10.1037//0022-3514.81.5.922

Masuda, T., & Nisbett, R. E. (2006). Culture and change blindness. *Cognitive Science, 30*(2), 381–399.

McLaughlin, K. A., Sheridan, M. A., & Nelson, C. A. (2017). Neglect as a violation of species-expectant experience: Neurodevelopmental consequences. *Biological Psychiatry, 82*(7), 462–471. https://doi.org/10.1016/j.biopsych.2017.02.1096

Mickley Steinmetz, K., Sturki, C., Rochester, N., Liu, X., & Gutchess, A. (2018). Cross cultural differences in item and background memory: Examining the influence of emotional arousal and scene congruency. *Memory, 26*(6), 751–758.

Miellet, S., Vizioli, L., He, L., Zhou, X., & Caldara, R. (2013). Mapping face recognition information use across cultures. *Frontiers in Psychology, 4*, Article 34. https://doi.org/10.3389/fpsyg.2013.00034

Millar, P. R., Serbun, S. J., Vadalia, A., & Gutchess, A. H. (2013). Cross-cultural differences in memory specificity. *Culture & Brain, 1*(2–4), 138–157.

Miller, E. K., & Cohen, J. D. (2001). An integrative theory of prefrontal cortex function. *Annual Review of Neuroscience, 24*, 167–202.

Miyamoto, Y., Nisbett, R. E., & Masuda, T. (2006). Culture and the physical environment—Holistic versus analytic perceptual affordances. *Psychological Science, 17*(2), 113–119.

Ng, S. H., Han, S., Mao, L., & Lai, J. C. L. (2010). Dynamic bicultural brains: fMRI study of their flexible neural representation of self and significant others in response to culture primes. *Asian Journal of Social Psychology, 13*(2), 83–91. https://doi.org/10.1111/j.1467-839X.2010.01303.x

Nisbett, R. E. (2003). *The geography of thought: How Asians and Westerners think differently . . . and why*. Free Press.

Nisbett, R. E., & Masuda, T. (2003). Culture and point of view. *Proceedings of the National Academy of Sciences of the United States of America, 100*(19), 11163–11170. https://doi.org/10.1073/pnas.1934527100

Nisbett, R. E., & Miyamoto, Y. (2005). The influence of culture: Holistic versus analytic perception. *Trends in Cognitive Sciences, 9*(10), 467–473. https://doi.org/10.1016/j.tics.2005.08.004

Nisbett, R. E., Peng, K. P., Choi, I., & Norenzayan, A. (2001). Culture and systems of thought: Holistic versus analytic cognition. *Psychological Review, 108*(2), 291–310. https://doi.org/10.1037//0033-295x.108.2.291

Norman, K. A., Polyn, S. M., Detre, G. J., & Haxby, J. V. (2006). Beyond mind-reading: Multi-voxel pattern analysis of fMRI data. *Trends in Cognitive Sciences, 10*(9), 424–430. https://doi.org/10.1016/j.tics.2006.07.005

Norman, K. A., & Schacter, D. L. (1997). False recognition in younger and older adults: Exploring the characteristics of illusory memories. *Memory & Cognition, 25*(6), 838–848.

Paige, L. E., Amado, S., & Gutchess, A. H. (2017). Influence of encoding instructions and response bias on cross-cultural differences in specific recognition. *Culture & Brain, 5*, 153–168.

Paige, L. E., Ksander, J. C., Johndro, H. A., & Gutchess, A. H. (2017). Cross-cultural differences in the neural correlates of specific and general recognition. *Cortex, 91*, 250–261. https://doi.org/10.1016/j.cortex.2017.01.018

Park, D. C., & Gutchess, A. (2002). Aging, cognition, and culture: A neuroscientific perspective. *Neuroscience and Biobehavioral Reviews, 26*(7), 859–867. https://doi.org/10.1016/s0149-7634(02)00072-6

Park, D. C., & Gutchess, A. (2006). The cognitive neuroscience of aging and culture. *Current Directions in Psychological Science, 15*(3), 105–108.

Park, D. C., Nisbett, R. E., & Hedden, T. (1999). Aging, culture, and cognition. *Journals of Gerontology. Series B, Psychological Sciences and Social Sciences, 54*(2), P75–P84.

Piazza, E. A., & Silver, M. A. (2014). Persistent hemispheric differences in the perceptual selection of spatial frequencies. *Journal of Cognitive Neuroscience, 26*(9), 2021–2027. https://doi.org/10.1162/jocn_a_00606

Piazza, E. A., & Silver, M. A. (2017). Relative spatial frequency processing drives hemispheric asymmetry in conscious awareness. *Frontiers in Psychology, 8*, Article 559. https://doi.org/10.3389/fpsyg.2017.00559

Polk, T. A., & Farah, M. J. (1995). Late experience alters vision. *Nature, 376*(6542), 648–649. https://doi.org/10.1038/376648a0

Reinitz, M. T., & Hannigan, S. L. (2001). Effects of simultaneous stimulus presentation and attention switching on memory conjunction errors. *Journal of Memory and Language, 44*(2), 206–219. https://doi.org/10.1006/jmla.2000.2727

Reinitz, M. T., Lammers, W. J., & Cochran, B. P. (1992). Memory-conjunction errors: Miscombination of stored stimulus features can produce illusions of memory. *Memory & Cognition, 20*(1), 1–11. https://doi.org/10.3758/BF03208247

Rodger, H., Kelly, D. J., Blais, C., & Caldara, R. (2010). Inverting faces does not abolish cultural diversity in eye movements. *Perception, 39*(11), 1491–1503. https://doi.org/10.1068/p6750

Roediger, H. L., 3rd, & McDermott, K. B. (1995). Creating false memories: Remembering words not presented on lists. *Journal of Experimental Psychology: Learning, Memory, and Cognition, 21*, 803–814.

Rogers, T., Kuiper, N., & Kirker, W. (1977). Self-reference and the encoding of personal information. *Journal of Personality and Social Psychology, 35*(9), 677–688.

Schacter, D. L. (1999). The seven sins of memory—Insights from psychology and cognitive neuroscience. *The American Psychologist, 54*(3), 182–203.

Schacter, D. L. (2001). *The seven sins of memory*. Houghton Mifflin.

Schacter, D. L., & Slotnick, S. D. (2004). The cognitive neuroscience of memory distortion. *Neuron, 44*(1), 149–160.

Schwartz, A. J., Boduroglu, A., & Gutchess, A. H. (2014). Cross-cultural differences in categorical memory errors. *Cognitive Science, 38*(5), 997–1007. https://doi.org/10.1111/cogs.12109

Schwartz, S. H. (1992). Universals in the content and structure of values: Theory and empirical tests in 20 countries. In M. Zanna (Ed.), *Advances in experimental social psychology* (Vol. 25, pp. 1–65). Academic Press.

Scoville, W. B., & Milner, B. (1957). Loss of recent memory after bilateral hippocampal lesions. *The Journal of Neurology, Neurosurgery, & Psychiatry, 20*, 11–21.

Sheridan, M. A., & McLaughlin, K. A. (2016). Neurobiological models of the impact of adversity on education. *Current Opinion in Behavioral Sciences, 10*, 108–113. https://doi.org/10.1016/j.cobeha.2016.05.013

Simons, J. S., & Spiers, H. J. (2003). Prefrontal and medial temporal lobe interactions in long-term memory. *Nature Reviews Neuroscience, 4*(8), 637–648. https://doi.org/10.1038/nrn1178

Slotnick, S. D., & Schacter, D. L. (2004). A sensory signature that distinguishes true from false memories. *Nature Neuroscience, 7*(6), 664–672. https://doi.org/10.1038/nn1252

Stanislaw, H., & Todorov, N. (1999). Calculation of signal detection theory measures. *Behavior Research Methods, Instruments & Computers, 31*(1), 137–149. https://doi.org/10.3758/BF03207704

Sui, J., Zhu, Y., & Chiu, C. Y. (2007). Bicultural mind, self-construal, and self- and mother-reference effects: Consequences of cultural priming on recognition memory. *Journal of Experimental Social Psychology, 43*(5), 818–824. https://doi.org/10.1016/j.jesp.2006.08.005

Sutton, B. P., Goh, J. O., Hebrank, A., Welsh, R. C., Chee, M. W., & Park, D. C. (2008). Investigation and validation of intersite fMRI studies using the same imaging hardware. *Journal of Magnetic Resonance Imaging, 28*(1), 21–28.

Talhelm, T., Zhang, X., Oishi, S., Shimin, C., Duan, D., Lan, X., & Kitayama, S. (2014). Large-scale psychological differences within China explained by rice versus wheat agriculture. *Science, 344*(6184), 603–608. https://doi.org/10.1126/science.1246850

Tardif, J., Fiset, D., Zhang, Y., Estephan, A., Cai, Q., Luo, C., Sun, D., Gosselin, F., & Blais, C. (2017). Culture shapes spatial frequency tuning for face identification. *Journal of Experimental Psychology: Human Perception and Performance, 43*(2), 294–306. https://doi.org/10.1037/xhp0000288

Telzer, E. H., Qu, Y., & Lin, L. C. (2017). Neural processes underlying cultural differences in cognitive persistence. *Neuroimage, 156*, 224–231. https://doi.org/10.1016/j.neuroimage.2017.05.034

Tun, P. A., Wingfield, A., Rosen, M. J., & Blanchard, L. (1998). Response latencies for false memories: Gist-based processes in normal aging. *Psychology and Aging, 13*(2), 230–241.

Unsworth, S. J., Sears, C. R., & Pexman, P. M. (2005). Cultural influences on categorization processes. *Journal of Cross-Cultural Psychology, 36*, 662–688.

Uskul, A. K., Kitayama, S., & Nisbett, R. E. (2008). Ecocultural basis of cognition: Farmers and fishermen are more holistic than herders. *Proceedings of the National Academy of Sciences of the United States of America, 105*(25), 8552–8556. https://doi.org/10.1073/pnas.0803874105

Wallisch, P. (2017, April 12). Two years later, we finally know why people saw "the dress" differently. *Slate.* https://slate.com/technology/2017/04/heres-why-people-saw-the-dress-differently.html

Waring, J. D., Payne, J. D., Schacter, D. L., & Kensinger, E. A. (2010). Impact of individual differences upon emotion-induced memory trade-offs. *Cognition and Emotion, 24*(1), 150–167. https://doi.org/10.1080/02699930802618918

Witkin, H. A. (1954). *Personality through perception, an experimental and clinical study.* Harper.

Yoon, C., Feinberg, F., Hu, P., Gutchess, A. H., Hedden, T., Chen, H.-Y. M., Jing, Q., Cui, Y., & Park, D. C. (2004). Category norms as a function of culture and age: Comparisons of item responses to 105 categories by American and Chinese adults. *Psychol Aging, 19*(3), 379–393. https://doi.org/10.1037/0882-7974.19.3.379

Zhang, W., Hung, I. T., Jackson, J. D., Tai, T.-L., Goh, J. O. S., & Gutchess, A. (2020). Influence of culture and age on the self-reference effect. *Aging, Neuropsychology, and Cognition, 27*(3), 370–384. https://doi.org/10.1080/13825585.2019.1620913

Zhu, Y., Zhang, L., Fan, J., & Han, S. (2007). Neural basis of cultural influence on self-representation. *Neuroimage, 34*(3), 1310–1316.

Ziemba, C. M., Freeman, J., Movshon, J. A., & Simoncelli, E. P. (2016). Selectivity and tolerance for visual texture in macaque V2. *Proceedings of the National Academy of Sciences of the United States of America, 113*(22), E3140–E3149. https://doi.org/10.1073/pnas.1510847113

CHAPTER 2

Worldwide Changes in the Lives of Children and Youth

A Socioecological Approach

UWE P. GIELEN AND SUNGHUN KIM

Abstract

Adopting a socioecological perspective, this chapter focuses on selected long-term global changes in the lives of children and youth. After comparing children's lives in small, pedestrian hunter–gatherer groups with those in larger peasant societies and today's digital information societies, the emphasis shifts to a discussion of children and youth in China and South Korea. There follows a delineation of global trends and the impact of globalization on the lives and identities of children, adolescents, and emerging adults. The chapter concludes with a discussion of the 1989 Convention on the Rights of the Child and the ongoing efforts by the United Nations to assess and support worldwide improvements in the lives of children, especially in the poorer countries.

Key Words: Global childhood, global youth, socioecological perspective, hunter–gatherer band, peasant society, digital information society, China, South Korea, education fever, globalization

---

I. INTRODUCTION

During 1945–1948, the first author spent some of his earlier childhood years as a *Flüchtling* (refugee/displaced person) in a Bavarian mini-village that included 13 houses, 53 people, and assorted cows, foxes, field mice, and dung beetles. The second author spent his childhood and youth in the South Korean capital of Seoul, at a time when the country was recovering from its difficult past but was also beginning to evolve into a new kind of digital information

Uwe P. Gielen and Sunghun Kim, *Worldwide Changes in the Lives of Children and Youth* In: *Handbook of Advances in Culture and Psychology*. Edited by: Michele J. Gelfand, Chi-yue Chiu, and Ying-yi Hong, Oxford University Press. © Oxford University Press 2022. DOI: 10.1093/oso/9780197631669.003.0002

society. Today, however, both of us reside in one of the world's great international cities, New York, while speaking a language originally foreign to our ears and brains. Consequently, our diverse backgrounds have helped us to write this cross-culturally oriented chapter. It attempts to analyze how the lives of children and youth have changed over time in a variety of socioecological and cultural settings. In this context, we especially support the efforts of UNICEF and the world community to improve the lives of children in the poorer countries. The chapter was conceived prior to the worldwide spread of the coronavirus.

The lives and identities of children and youth have changed dramatically over the course of time. During the first 185,000+ years of the existence of *Homo sapiens*, all children presumably grew up in nomadic foraging bands and societies. During their early years, they learned to gather wild plants, hunt, fish, and scavenge. Over many years, evolution prepared humans and their hominid predecessors to adapt to this form of life. Then, around 9500 BCE, in some areas of the Fertile Crescent in the southwestern areas of Asia, and subsequently in other parts of the world, select human groups learned to domesticate animals and plants. This revolutionary process would over time lead to much larger societies based on pastoralism, horticulture, and increasingly sophisticated forms of agriculture. States began to form, while a rapidly increasing percentage of the world's children grew up in the midst of peasant or, less often, pastoralist families. Subsequently, industrialization emerged in Great Britain and in the following two centuries spread to other areas of the Western and non-Western world. An increasing number of children began to survive childhood, grew up in urban areas, attended a school for a number of years, came of age after a longer period of adolescence, and spent their adult years working in factories or service occupations rather than in the fields.

During the last few decades, the digital revolution and the forces of globalization have been spreading in various forms to many corners of the world, thereby changing substantially the ways in which young people are coming of age. Frequently, they attend school for numerous years in order to secure well-paying jobs, enter an extended period of adolescence that merges into early adulthood, get married at later ages or maybe not at all, and have fewer and fewer children. Increasingly, they are influenced by economic and cultural forces and by information about events that are taking place in other parts of the world. However, in the poorer rural areas, especially in sub-Saharan Africa and South Asia, such changes have been slower to emerge. In those regions, several hundred million children continue to lead rather traditional forms of life, are often undernourished, work from their early years onward, spend limited or no time in school, get married early, and are repeatedly becoming parents in their later teenage years and early 20s. Others are struggling with very difficult life circumstances while coming of age in the slums of Africa's, South Asia's, and Latin America's rapidly expanding cities.

It is our contention that technological innovations and changes are exerting a powerful and frequently underestimated long-term impact on children's survival together with their ways of growing up and coming of age (Gielen & Kim, 2019). Such innovations include new subsistence technologies and new ways of human adaptation to the physical environment. In addition, medical discoveries and associated health practices have reduced the worldwide child mortality rate below the age of 5 from an estimated 43.3% in 1800 to about 3.9% in 2019. These and other innovations and forces have been partially shaped by, and have interacted with, a broad range of economic, political, and religious institutions as well as a variety of family systems that emerged over the course of time in thousands of different societies. The joint and accelerating impact of these forces has resulted in a dramatic increase of the world's population from about 4 million humans around 10,000 BCE to 7.8 billion in the year 2019 (Roser et al., 2019).

The initial invention of agriculture and the domestication of animals, the subsequent forces unleashed by industrialization and digitalization, new forms of birth control, medical discoveries made during the last 200 years, and the emergence and spread of educational systems have expanded the length and altered the very nature of childhood. Together they have also led to new forms of adolescence and emerging adulthood, gender roles and family systems, identity, and knowledge cultures, as well as new ideas spelling out what life can and should be. In addition to discussing selected examples taken from China and South Korea, we provide an overview of selected worldwide trends that together have been changing the lives of the world's children and youths. They include the world's ongoing population increases and industrialization, which unfortunately have also been triggering an accelerating and highly dangerous climate crisis. This development threatens to destroy much of the impressive progress that humanity has achieved especially since 1960 (Wallace-Wells, 2019). However, a more positive development occurred in 1989–1990, when almost all nations adopted the United Nations (UN) Convention on the Rights of the Child (CRC) (UNICEF, 1989). It has instigated many important efforts to promote the welfare of children and youth, especially in the world's low- and low-medium-income countries. In spite of cultural differences and the diverse forms of childhood emerging across time and across the different regions of the world, the CRC reflects considerable agreement among the world's nations about how children's lives can and should be improved.

II. A SOCIOECOLOGICAL APPROACH TO THE LONG-TERM STUDY OF CHILDREN AND YOUTH

In this section, we discuss in more detail the overall process of societal evolution and its impact on the lives and identities of children, adolescents, and emerging adults. Initially, we focus on three diverse kinds of societies: pedestrian bands of nomadic hunter–gatherers, evolving peasant societies, and the recent emergence of digital information societies. Given that hunter–gatherers and agricultural societies are increasingly exposed to outside influences, we focus on these societies both in their original conditions as well as on their nature in today's age of rapid change. In this context, we pay special attention to the interlinked forces of digitalization, globalization, migration, and schooling that in recent decades have been reshaping the lives of numerous young people in many parts of the world.

In order to trace global trends reflecting the socioecological evolution of childhood and the beginning phases of adulthood, we rely on studies conducted by demographers, sociologists, economists, anthropologists, cross-cultural psychologists, and social scientists working in the non-Western world. In addition, we make use of important publications by UNICEF such as the annual overview entitled *The State of the World's Children*. Also influential have been the *Global Childhood Report* by Save the Children (2019) and the big global data reported on Max Roser's unique website Our World in Data. It is our purpose to integrate these and many other studies in a transdisciplinary manner. A major emphasis is placed on changes in parts of Asia and the Global South, where some 90% of the world's children and emerging adults live.

Scientists emphasizing societal differences in subsistence ecologies, technological knowledge, demographic factors, and economic structures tend to adopt a more functional approach to the analysis of childhood and beginning adulthood than researchers and theorists exploring the impact of contrasting values and normative belief systems. For instance, the invention of computers, the pervasive impact of digitalization, the emergence of artificial intelligence, and various related technological changes have in recent decades facilitated the emergence of globalized or semi-globalized forms of adolescence and beginning adulthood. The increasingly *glocal* (=both global and local) identities of many adolescents tend to reflect a mixture of sometimes conflicting global, national, and local influences (see Ozer et al., 2017, 2019, for an example from India). By way of contrast, the everyday worlds of adolescents in previous times tended to be more local in nature and resembled those that their elders had experienced.

Our functional and socioecological approach recognizes that conflicts and trade-offs both within and between individuals are part of the human condition. For instance, many families residing in well-to-do East and Southeast Asian societies such as South Korea, Singapore, Japan, Taiwan, and China have in recent decades invested enormous amounts of time, effort, and financial resources in order to support the education of their children in a highly competitive environment. Such costly efforts, however, have led to major reductions in family size never before seen in history. Given the rapid declines in East Asian total fertility rates (TFRs), their populations are now aging rapidly and are expected to shrink in size in the coming decades. At the same time, having few (if any) children is detrimental to the parents' inclusive fitness when seen from an evolutionary perspective. Moreover, many South Korean and Japanese natives oppose immigration, which otherwise could slow down the expected decreases in their countries' population sizes. Similar fertility declines, dilemmas, and conflicts can also be observed in many European societies, which otherwise embrace different and more individualistic value systems than those predominating in East Asia. These similarities between East and West suggest that the much studied differences between collectivistic and individualistic value systems are not the main engine driving the widespread decline of TFRs in East Asia, Europe, and North America. In addition, the highly desirable global decline in child mortality rates has nevertheless fueled the world's population explosion, which in turn has contributed greatly to the worsening climate crisis (Bongaarts & O'Neill, 2018; Jamieson, 2014). It is important to keep such basic contradictions and conflicts in mind rather than sweeping them under the rug of political expediency and correctness.

Figure 2.1 depicts postulated interrelationships between a variety of factors influencing the lives of children and youths. The overall conception underlying this figure has been influenced by the pioneering work of Schlegel and Barry (1991) and Triandis (2009). The thicker lines in the graph denote postulated main lines of influence, whereas the dotted lines refer to feedback loops. Ecological/physical conditions are expected to exert a major impact upon a given society's predominant mode of subsistence and survival. In addition, the ecological conditions both influence and are influenced by that society's

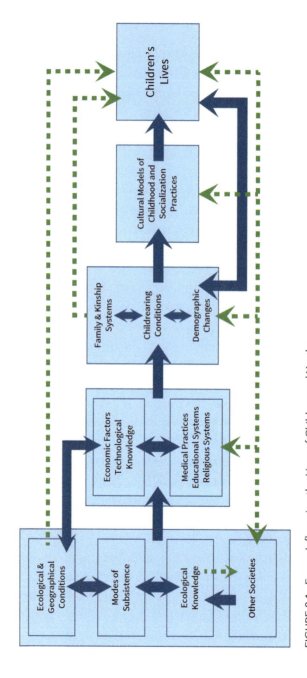

FIGURE 2.1: Forces Influencing the Lives of Children and Youths

ecology-related knowledge and technology. For instance, a society's knowledge of rice planting techniques, which originally may have been acquired from a neighboring culture, can induce that society to develop complex irrigation systems and mountain terraces for the planting of rice. Such systems, in turn, require long-term, regulated cooperation between the members of that society. This requirement, in turn, encourages the development of large-scale societies together with collectivistic and tightly regulated rather than individualistic and more loosely organized cultural belief systems, ideologies, inheritance systems, and social rules. The modes of subsistence and intertwined forms of ecological knowledge, for their part, help to structure a society's basic economic processes and social stratification systems. This influences the nature and prevalence or absence of daily labor by children and youths. They also interact with the society's technological and scientific knowledge including medical knowledge, health-related practices, means of birth control, and the educational systems that teach this knowledge to children and youths. In addition, religious ideologies and belief systems have historically been of major importance in most societies. Taken together, all these sociocultural forces influence a given society's family and kinship systems—for instance, how stable family systems are, whether the society relies on nuclear or extended family structures together with neolocal, patrilocal, or matrilocal residence, prevailing fertility rates, more or less equal and sharply defined gender roles, and more loosely or more tightly controlled sexual practices (Gelfand, 2018). Together with its religious, educational, and health-oriented institutions, a society's preferred family system(s) helps shape demographic trends, basic childrearing conditions, cultural models of childhood and socialization practices, and ultimately, the day-to-day lives and identities of its children and youths. More generally, a socioecological approach emphasizes the long-term influence of environmental conditions together with the knowledge and practices that societies develop over time to adapt to such conditions. In addition, societies and societal segments influence each other. For instance, the preoccupations and practices of today's advanced information societies are increasingly influencing those young people who are residing in the world's more traditional agricultural regions.

III. SOCIETAL EVOLUTION: FROM FORAGING BANDS TO DIGITAL INFORMATION SOCIETIES

Cultural anthropologists and macrosociologists such as Nolan and Lenski (2014) distinguish between a variety of societies based upon their technologies, subsistence economies, and societal complexity. Small-scale, pedestrian, and nomadic foraging bands engage in the hunting of small and large animals and in foraging for roots, nuts, fruits, and vegetables. Fishing societies depend on aquatic foraging including fishing, hunting of sea and other animals, the collection of eggs, and at times foraging for roots and vegetables. Nomadic pastoralists are engaged in keeping and herding animals such as goats, sheep, cattle, pigs, horses, and camels for dairy products, meat, pelts, as well as transportation services and trade. Horticultural societies rely on digging sticks and hoes to cultivate plants in gardens and small fields. Advanced agricultural societies cultivate crops on a larger scale and often depend on draft animals, plows, irrigation systems, and fertilizers to do so. Large-scale industrial societies employ technologies of mass production to produce vast amounts of goods in factories. *Digital information societies* (our term), which emerged in the postindustrial era, provide extensive information services and social media while depending on a variety of advanced electronic technologies. The initial impact of digitalization is sometimes referred to as the *Third Industrial Revolution*, while new forms of cyber physical systems, artificial intelligence, the widespread introduction of big data, and robotics are spearheading the *Fourth Industrial Revolution*.

Among these kinds of societies, we have selected three for our discussion since they are associated with three distinct forms of childrearing, adolescence, and beginning adulthood. They include bands of pedestrian hunter–gatherers, peasant societies, and today's digital information societies. Because they originally emerged and predominated during quite different periods of human history, an investigation of these three types of societies can also provide a bird's-eye view of accelerating changes in global childhood across time. By focusing on long-term trends rather than relying predominantly on research guided by experimental methods, we hope to understand different forms of childhood in their broader and changing contexts.

Notably, there also exist considerable differences within each major kind of society. For instance, bands of hunter–gatherers are strongly influenced by climatic conditions that create different environments for them. These include the desert-like conditions shaping the survival of many, though not all, Australian Aboriginal societies, the tropical jungles surrounding some groups of hunter–gatherers in central Africa, and the Arctic conditions to which Inuit people must adjust. Such varying conditions, in turn, influence which animals can be hunted and which plants can be gathered, a society's population density and size, selected physical aspects of childrearing, the prevalence of certain diseases, and physical distances between potentially competitive neighboring groups. For reasons of space, however, we are emphasizing here differences between three types of societies, while paying only limited attention to important variations occurring within each type.

Table 2.1 summarizes some key characteristics of small foraging bands, peasant societies, and modern digital information societies together with some characteristics of their respective family systems.

A. Pedestrian Foraging Bands and Their Family Systems

Although small foraging bands of hunter–gatherers have existed for many centuries in Australia, the Kalahari Desert of southern Africa, the western Congo basin, the subtropical forests of Paraguay, and elsewhere, today most of the bands are disappearing and/or are becoming more dependent upon neighbors such as pastoralists, farmers, and even civil servants and teachers representing semi-digital societies (R. B. Lee & Daly, 1999). Traditionally, however, foraging bands have relied on food resources already existing in their environments. While women collect fruits, nuts, tubers, and various small animals such as insects, worms, and lizards, men hunt both larger and smaller animals. Population densities tend to be very low, and the bands move to other areas whenever the bigger animals and other resources have become sparse where they live. Group membership changes frequently when some members leave after quarreling with each other, marry somebody from another group, or visit family members and friends in neighboring and culturally related bands. Small foraging bands frequently adopt an egalitarian and relatively "loose" (Gelfand, 2018) lifestyle, while leadership tends to be of an informal nature. Successful hunters are expected to share meat with the other group members, which helps them to gain their respect while also making them more attractive to the opposite sex. Pedestrian hunter–gatherers endorse a variety of animistic and polytheistic religious ideas that include shamanistic healing practices but do not feature writing systems, holy books, or religious specialists such as priests or monks. Foraging can be a demanding lifestyle, and learning how to hunt giraffes, antelopes, or kangaroos successfully; how to deal with dangerous predators; or where to find certain plants requires expert knowledge that needs to be perfected over the course of several decades. Our focus here is on small-scale pedestrian bands rather than on those larger and more stratified native groups in North America that, after the arrival of Europeans, began to rely on newly introduced horses or else represented more settled and stratified

60 Handbook of Advances in Culture and Psychology

TABLE 2.1: **Three Types of Society and Their Family Systems**

	Small-Scale Foraging Bands	Peasant Societies	Digital Information Societies
Examples	Australian Aborigines, !Kung San (Kalahari Desert), Aka (Congo), Hadza (Tanzania)	Traditional rural societies in Africa, Asia, Latin America, preindustrial western Europe, and United States	Present-day South Korea, urban China, Japan, Singapore, Australia, Europe, United States, Dubai
Average population size and density	Small, fluid bands of 15–45 persons; very low population densities, compact settlements; nomadic bands are embedded in larger cultural-linguistic groups	Villages and towns embedded in large to very large state societies with moderate to very high population densities	Very large, urbanized societies; very high population densities
Economic basis of society and subsistence activities	Foraging for roots, nuts, vegetables, fruits, honey, insects; hunting of small and big animals	Agriculture, subsistence farming; keeping of animals; crafts; trade; today, migration to cities is supporting basic socioeconomic changes	Information and service industries; manufacturing; limited agricultural sector; local and international trade
Division of labor and socioeconomic stratification	Limited to division by gender and age; part-time shamans; no or limited social stratification; emphasis on sharing, egalitarianism	Moderate division of labor; stratification and inequality moderate to extreme; societies becoming more heterogeneous	Extreme heterogeneity (more than 200,000 different job titles in United States); pronounced stratification
Societal complexity; rural vs. urban areas	Small bands displaying limited functional specialization mostly according to gender and age	Moderate complexity in rural areas, greater complexity in urban areas	Very high complexity especially in widespread urban areas

Worldwide Changes in the Lives of Children and Youth **61**

TABLE 2.1: **Continued**

	Small-Scale Foraging Bands	Peasant Societies	Digital Information Societies
Influence of religion(s) and supernatural conceptions	Animistic and polytheistic religions often linked to environmental features and based on oral traditions	Polytheistic and monotheistic religions; mixture of local beliefs and world religions based on sacred literature	Weakening influence of religion especially in Europe and East Asia, separation of church and state in non-Islamic societies
Impact of external and global influences	Leading to widespread decline; symbiotic relationships with pastoralists and agriculturalists; external influences increasing	Indirect and direct impact of national and global influences is increasing	Pervasive impact especially in major cities, through mass media, multinational organizations
Speed of societal change	Formerly slow but now rapidly increasing	Formerly slow and uneven but now steadily increasing	Very rapid
Balance between tradition and innovation	Traditions are/ were emphasized, but innovative influences are increasingly arriving from the outside	Traditions are emphasized but increasing exposure to innovation partially introduced from abroad	Rapid cultural change favors innovation over tradition; tensions between tradition, modernity, and religious beliefs in Islamic societies
Gender roles	Clear differentiation of gender roles; women/girls tend to collect plants and small animals, while men/older boys hunt big game and defend group; mixed gender playgroups in early childhood	Distinct gender roles considered a part of the natural and sacred order; males more aggressive, assertive; more freedom for boys, girls kept closer to home; less extreme differences in some matrilineal societies	Contested and less differentiated gender roles; gender roles perceived as human-made and changeable; extended schooling increases female expectations, possibilities, and autonomy

(continued)

TABLE 2.1: **Continued**

	Small-Scale Foraging Bands	**Peasant Societies**	**Digital Information Societies**
Gender inequality and violence against females	Low to moderate inequality and violence against women (e.g., violence among Australian Aborigines, North American larger groups)	Patriarchal and hierarchical systems predominate; inequality and female infanticide and neglect common but less so in matrilineal societies	Increasing egalitarianism; neolocal rather than patrilocal residence favors more egalitarian husband–wife bonds; marital violence fairly common
Educational institutions and literacy rates	Traditionally no educational institutions, illiteracy	Educational institutions expanding, low literacy rates are now rapidly increasing	Educational institutions of great importance, very high literacy rates
Prevalence and changes in 2020	Bands are incorporated into larger societies; they are disappearing or subject to fundamental change	Agricultural sectors remain common in the poorer countries; growing impact of modern agricultural techniques, external influences, urbanization, state institutions	Digital societies expanding globally; widespread urbanization; powerful external and global influences
Family systems			
Marriage systems and postmarital residence	Patrilineal and bilateral kinship most common; monogamy and some polygyny; patrilocal or multilocal residence	Patrilineal descent but matrilineal descent in some horticultural societies; polygyny (for the well-off) and patrilocal residence both common	Bilateral family systems becoming more important; monogamy and neolocal residence widespread; polygyny illegal or declining
Mothers' vs. fathers' impact on children	Mother–child contact strongest in early years; father–child contact often considerable in small bands	Father may be a remote authority figure; his impact is strongest in the later stages of childhood	Father's presence increasing in two-parent, middle-class families but declining in single-mother families (which are on the increase)

Worldwide Changes in the Lives of Children and Youth **63**

TABLE 2.1: **Continued**

	Small-Scale Foraging Bands	Peasant Societies	Digital Information Societies
Family size and fertility rates (total fertility rates)	Moderate family sizes; fairly high to high fertility rates	Large families; high fertility rates; pronatalist ideologies	Small nuclear families; below replacement (2.1) fertility rates
Family stability and structures	Moderate family stability; early divorces common; extensive husband–wife interaction	Often low divorce rates; few single-parent families; extended families among the well-to-do; family instability in some sub-Saharan countries	Medium to high divorce rates; many single-parent and childless families; increased variety of family types; many young adult singles
Economic activities and functions of family	Families perform main economic activities	Wide range of economic activities especially in subsistence economies and among peasants	Families are shedding many economic functions
Socialization/ teaching functions of family; alloparenting and polymatric care	Alloparenting by other adults and older children helps rear, protect, and teach children	Pervasive family influence but teaching functions now shifting toward schools	Many family functions are being transferred to schools, preschools, day-care centers
Parental reasons for having children	It is traditional; economic utility, provide support in old age; emotional companionship; a spiritual goal; children validate adult identity	Economic utility; they provide support in old age; reinforce adult status and families' influence; emotional companionship; they manifest God's blessing	Children provide emotional companionship but are expensive to raise; having children is an individual preference competing with other preferences shaped by consumerism and long years of schooling

forms of fishing societies. In general, such larger societies were more stratified than is typical for smaller foraging bands.

Because the band members live in very small groups, both adults and children are heavily dependent on other group members for daily food supplies, help in emergency situations, support for pregnant or injured mothers, and the raising of children who may need to learn survival techniques from an early age. While mothers are the primary caretakers of their children, *alloparenting* (shared parenting) by other family and non-family members is common. If needed, grandmothers and other women will at times take care and perhaps even breastfeed the youngest children. Family stability is variable under these circumstances. Moreover, because daily life is largely public, other band members are typically well aware of the nature of relationships among the various family and non-family members. Among some larger groups, such as certain interlinked bands of Australian Aborigines, older men enjoy considerable power, which they use to acquire young teenage brides through negotiations with parents and other family members.

B. Peasant Societies and Their Family Systems

The progression from hunting and gathering societies to advanced horticultural and agricultural subsistence practices and the domestication of animals led over time to much larger and more complex, stratified, and unequal societies. People began to build houses close to sources of water such as brooks, rivers, and lakes; settled down in villages and towns; planted millet, wheat, corn, and potatoes; kept animals such as chickens, lamas, cattle, sheep, goats, yaks, and dogs; developed a variety of crafts; and traded with neighbors as well as outsiders. Our term *peasant societies* refers to traditional villages, towns, and societies that rely either on instruments such as hoes and digging sticks (i.e., advanced horticulturalists who are not also relying on hunting) or on plows, irrigation systems, and fertilizers (i.e., agriculturalists). However, we do not discuss here traditional horticultural village societies in areas such as the Amazon region and New Guinea that often included hunting and fishing practices. These societies tended to attack each other because of population pressures and because no state institutions existed to control them (e.g., the Yanomamo in South America [see Chagnon, 2012]).

The nutrition of peasants relies mostly on their own activities and some local trading, whereas farmers in industrialized countries produce mostly for markets. As peasant societies grew more complex, some of their villages began to expand into towns and ultimately into cities. This development was accompanied by increased division of labor as represented by craftspeople, traders, religious specialists, midwives, bureaucrats, soldiers, noblemen and noblewomen, and others. As more and more states emerged over time, their elites began to control and exploit peasants and artisans while often engaging in warfare with each other. Ordinary peasants enjoyed only limited rights and were often subjugated by elites such as the hereditary members of the nobility. Conquered peasants and others were sometimes turned into slaves, while young women were forced to satisfy the sexual demands of their male conquerors. In the modern world, peasantry survives especially in the poorer countries where, however, outside influences and migration to urban areas are becoming more important.

In many peasant societies, complex and tightly defined kinship systems regulate gender roles, collectivistic forms of childrearing, and rules of inheritance. Extended families and clans are common because they are useful for controlling land and its inheritance. Families tend to have numerous children whose work frequently contributes to family welfare from their early years onward. In the larger peasant societies, the clans and families are mostly based on patrilineal and patrilocal kinship systems together with specialized and unequal gender roles. A wife proves her worth by having many children, among whom boys are favored because the daughters are likely to leave and become members of some other family. The oldest son is often regarded as the main inheritor of the family name and, as such, is expected to provide support for his aging parents. Remote clan members may exert considerable pressure on other male members to provide them with economic and other forms of support. The children of landless laborers and poor peasants, however, tend to grow up in nuclear families that control little, if any, land. Given their family's poverty, their lives tend to be especially difficult during times of war, famines, and local conflicts.

C. Large Digital Information Societies and Their Family Systems

During recent decades, the earlier industrial societies have been rapidly evolving into digital information societies in Europe, North America, and East Asia. Their basis has been shifting from a manufacturing economy to a knowledge economy. Typically, their size is large to extremely large, and they are heavily urbanized. Their social class system relies on a very great variety of occupations based on specialized and constantly changing forms of knowledge. Information societies usually include expanding educational institutions, information and

66   Handbook of Advances in Culture and Psychology

service industries, varied forms of manufacturing, national and multinational corporations, and intensive internal and external trade. Thanks to highly mechanized farming techniques, their agricultural sectors tend to employ only a small percentage of a country's population. Almost all children and most adolescents are attending educational institutions. Increasingly, their attendance begins in their pre-kindergarten years and continues into their early adulthood years. Adolescents and emerging adults in particular are exposed to new forms of knowledge that may be unknown to most of their elders. The influence of social media has increased especially among younger people based on the rapid expansion of information technology. Modern life depends increasingly on intertwined economic, information, and social networks operating across long distances. Information societies include moderately sized societies such as South Korea but also the world's leading powers such as China's large-scale, totalitarian, collectivistic, and rather tightly organized society as well as the democratic, individualistic, and loose society of the United States.

Gender roles are changing rapidly, professional opportunities for women have increased, women's access to modern forms of birth control are improving their ability to regulate their sexual lives, marriage rates and TFRs are declining except among some special religious groups, and small nuclear families are replacing extended families. Upon marriage, the new couple often moves to a neolocal residence. Monogamy is widespread and predominates even in many large Islamic societies such as Indonesia, Pakistan, and Egypt. Because technological and social changes are occurring so rapidly, cultural and educational differences between generations are becoming more prevalent and may undermine the cohesion of families. Having children outside marriage and getting divorced have been on the increase in many societies, for instance, Sweden and the United States. Whereas in former years, families in peasant societies performed many economic functions and were more or less self-sufficient, today's family members tend to perform highly specialized activities while otherwise relying on extensive service industries operating in complex urban settings. Quite a few families or at least some of their members are moving from the countryside to urban areas, which can create difficult economic, personal, and educational situations for the family members.

D. Growing Up in Small but Changing Pedestrian Foraging Bands

Table 2.2 compares how children and youth grow up in small foraging bands, peasant societies, and digital information societies. Because it attempts to

TABLE 2.2: **Children and Youth in Three Types of Society**

	Small-Scale Foraging Bands	Peasant Societies	Digital Information Societies
Children			
Child mortality rates and life expectancies	Very high child mortality rates and low life expectancies due to diseases, hunting accidents, attacks by animals, warfare	High (but declining) child mortality rates and low life expectancies due to diseases, malnutrition, famines, wars	Lowest child mortality rates and highest life expectancies in history due to modern medicine and life conditions
Infancy: breastfeeding and co-sleeping	Frequent on-demand breastfeeding for several years; extensive skin-to-skin contact and co-sleeping	Breastfeeding may last 2–4 years; co-sleeping is common	Breastfeeding often for less than 1 year; variable skin-to-skin contact; variable and time-limited co-sleeping
Early childhood	Considerable freedom to explore non-dangerous environments; considerable autonomy and self-reliant behavior; little physical punishment; multiple caregivers	Increasingly structured, especially for girls; physical punishment is rather common, especially for boys; emphasis on children's obedience and learning of responsibilities	Children's environments are often regulated yet increasing emphasis on self-esteem and self-determination; decreasing outdoor exploration in cities
Attendance of preschools, day-care centers	None: Children learn by observation, play, practice, and from everybody	Uncommon: Children learn by observation, play, practice, and from siblings	Expanding attendance; emphasis on early learning
Obedience and responsibility training	Limited emphasis	Pronounced, especially for girls who tend to be more obedient and responsible	Variable and decreasing; parents may encourage children's assertiveness and questioning behavior
Child work in middle childhood	Children acquire adult skills in semi-playful and non-competitive ways; limited emphasis on rigid work activities	Most children work at home; exploitative child labor is rather common	Little pre-teen child work; part-time jobs for some teenagers

(*continued*)

68 Handbook of Advances in Culture and Psychology

TABLE 2.2: **Continued**

	Small-Scale Foraging Bands	Peasant Societies	Digital Information Societies
Age segregation of children and adolescents	Very limited segregation; mixed-age groups common in early childhood	Moderate; adolescent age-sets common in parts of Africa	Considerable (both voluntary and due to schooling)
Number and influence of siblings	Moderate number of siblings who exert moderate influence on younger children	Many siblings; girls often involved in childrearing duties; early responsibility training by older siblings is common	Few siblings; often limited sibling influence (but more in poor families); individualistic childrearing approaches
Schooling and literacy	Traditionally none; teaching and learning embedded in everyday contexts	Illiteracy and semi-literacy were widespread among peasant children (especially girls) but are now declining; girls' education contested in some Islamic societies	Universal schooling for both boys and girls; most teenagers enrolled in school; tertiary education expanding; learning about remote events, activities, and places is common
Social relations with kin and strangers	Long-term relations with kin and in-group members; limited exposure to strangers	Long-term relations with kin and in-group members; exposure to strangers limited but increasing	Emphasis on nuclear family; numerous interactions with strangers and semi-strangers
Privacy for children and adolescents	Little privacy; life takes place in the open	Often limited or no privacy	Increasing privacy. especially for adolescents in individualistic societies
Adolescents and youth			
Length of adolescent period, time of menarche	Brief period especially for girls; late menarche	Variable but brief or barely existing for many girls; late menarche; variable for boys but prolonged in African age-graded societies	Early menarche; extended adolescence often followed by "emerging adulthood" period (18–26 years)

Worldwide Changes in the Lives of Children and Youth **69**

TABLE 2.2: **Continued**

	Small-Scale Foraging Bands	Peasant Societies	Digital Information Societies
Puberty and adulthood rites	Less common in smaller groups but frequent among larger groups of Australian Aborigines	Common, often painful and dramatic for boys; male and female circumcision common in Middle East and Africa	Selective, voluntary, restricted, less common and less painful rites (e.g., quinceañera); religious rituals common
Age of marriage for girls	Low to fairly low	May be very low (10–20 years) but sometimes late in preindustrial Europe; now later due to global spread of schooling	Increasing (mean = 24–30 years); more ambivalence about marriage; motherhood less emphasized
Are marriages arranged or semi-arranged?	Variable	Mostly yes	Mostly not, some go-betweens
Value of premarital chastity for girls	Often low; sexual play in childhood rather common	Very high in Middle Eastern, Muslim, Hindu (*purdah*), Confucian-heritage societies; girls kept close to home; variable in sub-Saharan societies	Rapidly declining in most Western societies (e.g., Scandinavia) and increasingly so in some East Asian societies
Age of marriage for boys	Low but variable	Variable but increasing; higher in many polygamous societies and in preindustrial Europe	Late marriages; more ambivalence about marriage institution
Knowledge and value differences between generations	Formerly few differences	Limited differences but increasing due to schooling, modernization, global influences	Pervasive differences, especially in the knowledge areas, less so for basic values
Peer group influence	Low to moderate	Moderate (although strong for males in some age-graded African societies)	Pervasive for both males and females

(continued)

70 Handbook of Advances in Culture and Psychology

TABLE 2.2: **Continued**

	Small-Scale Foraging Bands	**Peasant Societies**	**Digital Information Societies**
Adolescents' exposure to mass media	Traditionally none	Was limited (especially for girls) but now common	Pervasive
Adolescent subcultures	Uncommon	Common in age-graded societies; otherwise emerging in schools and the bigger cities	Widespread and increasingly influenced by social and mass media
Impact of global teenage culture(s)	Originally none but now expanding	Growing via media influence and leading to more glocal identities	Powerful: Many adolescents are becoming semi-multicultural
Impact of consumerism on adolescents' lifestyles	Originally none but now emerging	Struggle for survival limits consumerism for the poor; otherwise increasing	Strong impact on adolescent lifestyles and identities
Adolescent self: more individualistic or more collectivistic?	Moderately individualistic; strong emphasis on self-reliance	Collectivistic self is embedded in kin and other face-to-face social networks; more individualism in cities	Individualistic self is linked to personal preferences and lifestyles, especially in Western societies; individualism increasing worldwide
Societal threats to children's and adolescents' welfare	Some infanticide; poor understanding of childhood diseases, internal fighting inside and between larger groups	Infanticide; serfdom, slavery; excessive child labor; very early marriage for girls; sexual abuse and forced prostitution for poor girls; extreme poverty; dangerous slums	Sexual abuse of girls and some boys; parental negligence; poverty and some dangerous slum environments; increasing obesity lowers life expectancies

summarize extensive information about numerous societies of the past and present, the reader is asked to review it in some detail.

In traditional foraging bands, only about 57% of all children survive to the age of 15 years. The others die because of diseases, hunting accidents, attacks by animals, and occasional infanticide (Gurven & Kaplan, 2007). At the same time, many of them are well taken care of in their early years. They are typically breastfed for several years and enjoy extensive bodily contact with their mothers and other women both during the day and at night (Tronick et al., 1992). As younger children, they are granted considerable freedom to explore nearby and non-dangerous environments in small groups and to develop a sense of autonomy. At the same time, they are consistently encouraged to share with others. Because their band is likely to include only a relatively small number of children, contact between boys and girls of roughly similar ages tends to be common. They acquire much of their knowledge and skills in non-competitive ways through play, observation, practice, and guidance by more experienced peers and adults (B. S. Hewlett & Lamb, 2005).

As they approach the time of their menarche at an average age of about 15–18 years, some of the girls may have already been exposed to sexual contact and knowledge given that life among traditional hunter–gatherer bands is fluid while taking place mostly in the open (see Konner, 2005, for the !Kung San of Botswana). Among the Aka of the Congo basin, adolescence is the time when "mating skills, how to hunt large game, and knowledge about special medicine and the supernatural" are acquired (B. L. Hewlett & Hewlett, 2013, p. 82). In some of the more unequal societies, such as among certain groups of Australian Aborigines, young girls have little influence on whom they marry because they have already been promised at an early age to one of the older and more influential males. In contrast, among some African hunter–gatherers such as the !Kung San, more equality and greater freedom of choice exist between men and women.

Today, the life of traditional hunter–gatherers is changing rapidly because they are becoming embedded in much larger and more powerful societies. This may be seen, for instance, in Australia where for some 60,000 years the Aborigines had pursued their lives as hunter–gatherers while having only very limited contact with the outside world. This began to change in 1788, when a group of British convicts was forced to settle in Australia's southeastern area. For the natives, their contact with the British as well as other settlers turned into a series of disasters over the following two centuries. Still, in some areas, such as Arnhem Land in northern Australia, some Aborigines were able to pursue a fairly traditional life until the 1960s (Hamilton, 1981). Today, however, as indigenous Australians attempt to combine their traditional way of life and culture with a more mainstream approach, the results frequently turn out to be calamitous. For instance, a recent study reported unusually high suicide rates for male indigenous youth (Institute for Economics and Peace, 2016). Additional research summarized by Gielen and Kim (2019) points to high rates of alcohol abuse, sniffing petrol, and unemployment, together with low rates of school attendance and a paucity of clear plans for the future. Children living in very remote areas face the greatest disadvantages (Daly, 2005). Although the number of indigenous people and their children has increased considerably in recent years thanks to better medical care, it remains unclear what their place will be in the larger Australian society.

E. Growing Up in Peasant Societies

In most peasant societies of the past, some 80%–90% of all males worked as peasants, farmhands, laborers, servants, and sometimes slaves in the countryside. Their wives were expected to give birth to numerous children, of whom an average of 50%–65% would survive into adulthood. Few, if any, of the rural girls and at best a modest percentage of the boys could read. Most of the children grew up in modest circumstances and began to work from early on. Older sisters took care of their younger siblings, helped their mothers run the household, and worked numerous hours washing clothes, preparing meals, cleaning the kitchen, and taking care of small gardens. If their fathers were farmhands and laborers, their teenage daughters not rarely worked as domestics for the families of landowners and sometimes became the victims of sexual seduction and exploitation. Given that many children were poorly nourished, girls experienced their menarche at an average age of around 15–17 years. Because their lives were governed by their elders, they struggled less with basic questions of identity. Adolescence as a definite social stage tended to be brief or non-existent, while their marriages were frequently based on economic considerations rather than love (for modern Indian examples, see Saraswathi, 1999).

For the boys, life might be a bit freer, yet economic necessity tended to exert a great impact on them as well. From a fairly early age, boys began to accompany their older brothers or fathers to the fields that either their family or their family's employer owned. As they grew older, the fate of boys would in part depend on their society's prevailing inheritance system. Quite a few European societies practiced *primogeniture*, a custom or law stating that the first legitimate son would inherit the family's main estate. In other societies, several or all children would share inheritance. When primogeniture prevailed, younger sons might more or less voluntarily leave their family. For instance, their family might tell them to become an apprentice in a carpenter's business or a hatmaker's shop. Others might get drunk, visit one of the many brothels in a nearby town, gamble away the little money they owned, and then sign a document obligating them to join their king's army. For most children and adolescents in traditional peasant societies, life was, and remains to this day, tough and demanding. Older children and teenagers make crucial contributions to the rural economy, as may be seen, for instance, in Dyson's (2014) ethnography of children who during 2003–2004 were residing in a Himalayan village in India. At the same time, these children were enrolled in a school whose curriculum had been mostly created in India's big cities. During recent years, young people in the world's changing peasant societies have begun to own cell phones, to watch soap operas or soccer games on TV, and to be increasingly aware of both their local world and the digitalized world-at-large. They may consider migration for economic and educational reasons or because life in the cities seems more promising, interesting, and varied to them.

F. Growing Up in Digitalized, Urbanized, and Globalized Information Societies Rather Than in Peasant Societies

Coming of age in today's digital information societies such as South Korea, the United States, Germany, and China would appear to be quite different from growing up as a child of hunter–gatherers or peasants, especially in the days before the Industrial Revolution. Growing up in a tiny camp for foragers or a modest agricultural village enveloped children in a mostly local culture. Surrounded by their natural environment and many siblings, they learned their society's way of life by observation and almost by osmosis. Many adolescents participated in religious celebrations, for instance, identity-defining and at times quite painful puberty rituals in various African societies.

In comparison, growing up in today's information societies has many advantages. Today's children almost always survive their early childhood, while malnutrition, hunger, and pronounced poverty have become uncommon especially outside the United States (Kristof & WuDunn, 2020). Children in the more individualistic societies are encouraged to ask questions and to develop self-esteem. Those living in urban environments are likely to encounter a broad variety of people who may differ from them in their primary language or dialect, religious or non-religious belief systems, ethnic–racial background, social class, gender identity, preferred ways of dressing, and many other ways. While their school attendance is taken for granted, very few of the younger children are forced to work full-time. They live in a world where science has destroyed many earlier misconceptions and superstitions, while information about an endless number of topics and events has become readily accessible to everybody. However, many children in the West grow up in one-parent homes or are exposed to serious family disagreements that may lead to their parents' divorce. Growing up without a father can be especially difficult for boys since they lack a male figure with whom to identify.

Because of very low levels of malnutrition and hunger, puberty nowadays tends to occur very early. In addition, long years of schooling are accompanied by lengthy periods of adolescence that are frequently followed by a period of "emerging adulthood" (Arnett, 2014). During this time, many young adults remain unmarried. Whereas in former years, being an adult meant being married and having children, today most youth defer such commitments to their later 20s, early 30s, or forever. In contrast, the importance of virginity for young women has been declining in many information societies. This holds true in otherwise quite different countries such as Japan, Sweden, and Canada. At the same time, information societies such as Sweden and Finland support more permissive and relaxed forms of childrearing when compared to the more structured and demanding forms that can be observed in South Korea, China, France, and Switzerland. Doepke and Zilibotti (2019) have suggested that because the Scandinavian countries display relatively low levels of economic inequality, they also support egalitarian childrearing and educational practices.

In the past, few, if any, societies changed as rapidly in their basic sociological structure as holds true for today's information societies. A steady stream of technological and scientific innovations means that adolescents and young adults must prepare themselves for a future where the knowledge necessary for mastering specific occupations and professions, basic means of communication, and exposure to foreign ways of doing and information from abroad change rapidly. Such processes can be exciting, but they are also bound to be challenging for a person's understanding of the world and their place in it. For many young people the only constant in their evolving lives is change. Moreover, many young people in the rural areas of the United States (Kristof & WuDunn, 2020), China, South Korea, and elsewhere are under the threat of falling behind their urban peers.

IV. ISSUES IN THE DEVELOPMENT OF CHILDREN AND ADOLESCENTS IN CHINA AND SOUTH KOREA

In this section, we discuss selected aspects of the lives of children and youth in China and South Korea. We chose those East Asian societies because over the last six to seven decades the lives of their children and adolescents have changed dramatically. While as late as the 1950s–1960s, both societies were quite poor and dependent on agriculture, today they have become leaders of the world's movement toward a digitalized future. For many of their children and youth that development is intertwined with a powerful emphasis on succeeding in a highly competitive educational system. Moreover, they or some of their family members are often moving from the rural areas to the bigger cities, which can lead to difficult personal and educational situations for the young people. Given that the two societies are governed by very different political systems, they are trying to meet difficult challenges for their youth in politically and culturally unique but not always successful ways.

A. China's Rural-to-Urban Migration, the *Hukou* System, and Its Effects on Students

In today's world, internal migration—living in a place other than one's birthplace or hometown—has become a widespread phenomenon. UNESCO (2018) estimated that in 2016 the percentage of the global population that had changed their place of residence during the past 5 years as about 20%, which meant more than 1.2 billion persons. Among them, Chinese society included the largest number of migrants. They constituted about 21% of its population or 282 million workers who were aiming to find a better job in the cities (UNESCO, 2018).

Between 1990 and 2019, China achieved rapid economic progress, but it is mostly residents in the urban areas who have experienced higher living standards such as increased income and social benefits (Li & Chui, 2011; Xi, 2006). Consequently, most of China's internal migrants are rural-to-urban migrant workers.

In 2014, almost half, or 132 million, of these migrant workers left their families behind in rural hometowns, which meant that 35% of all rural children were living with either a single parent or one or two grandparents (UNESCO, 2018). China's household registration system, *hukou*, is the primary reason that the adult migrants left their families, and specifically their children. According to *hukou*, Chinese children and adolescents could only attend schools in their hometowns. Moreover, many social benefits, such as various insurance contracts and incentives, were unavailable for those migrants living in urban hosting cities (J. Chen et al., 2016; Li & Chui, 2011; Ma & Wu, 2019). Beginning in 2003, the Chinese government tried to promote "social harmony" by, for instance, requiring local urban governments to provide migrant children from rural areas with the compulsory 9 years of education—from elementary to junior high (Li & Chui, 2011). Since then, a significant number of children ranging from early childhood to middle adolescence have been staying in urban areas together with their migrant parents.

The combination of rapid economic growth, urbanization, the *hukou* system, and the governmental policy of enhancing social development with a better balance between rural and urban areas has created three groups of Chinese children and adolescents born in rural communities but experiencing different circumstances. These youths include (1) migrants who moved to urban areas together with their parents, (2) those left behind with a single parent or grandparent(s), and (3) those who returned from urban areas to enter a senior high school located in their rural hometowns. Unfortunately, all these children and adolescents face various challenges and issues despite the central government's efforts to improve their overall situation (Y. Shen, 2017).

Migrant children to urban areas must go through a harsh process of applying for and registering at a desirable school. Many local city governments have found it difficult to serve rural migrant children, although the Chinese central government commands the public schools in the cities to accept those children. For example, Shanghai, one of China's largest and most prosperous cities, still struggles to secure sufficient financial support for its schools, hire the necessary number of schoolteachers and staff members, and increase the city's number of classrooms (Y. Zhou & Wang, 2016). In Beijing, Guangzhou, and Shenzhen, public schools require migrant parents to submit several certificates of social insurance enrollment, compliance with China's birth planning policy, health conditions in the family, and so on (Li & Chui, 2011; Ma & Wu, 2019). The problem is that rural migrant workers cannot freely access the social welfare system of urban areas because of *hukou*, thus making the acquisition of those certificates in hosting cities difficult or impossible for them (Jan et al., 2017; Li & Chui, 2011). As a result, more than half of all migrant children either attend public schools of low quality that are in urban industrial zones or else private schools—so-called migrant schools—that are designed only for migrant students and mostly unauthorized (Ma & Wu, 2019).

Many migrant children who attend schools in the hosting cities experience other kinds of hardships, such as discrimination, loneliness, and feeling unsupported. For instance, public-school teachers in Shanghai frequently ignored the students from rural areas or kept reminding them that if they wished to attend a high school, they would have to return to their hometown (Yiu, 2016). Rural migrant children in Changshu, a mid-size city in Jiangsu Province, showed lower levels of satisfaction in several areas of their life related to friendship, family, school, freedom, and environment (Zhang, 2018) than their counterparts. These results were mainly associated with a weaker social support system in which migrant children reported that their family moved frequently and that they had a smaller number of friends than non-migrant children. They also were less likely to believe that their neighbors cared about them.

There also exists a disparity in educational outcomes between rural migrant students residing in urban areas and their non-migrant peers (Ma & Wu, 2019). In the nationally representative China Education Panel Survey, migrant students received lower academic aptitude scores related to language, geometry, and calculation. School quality was one of the most important factors influencing the educational outcomes of both migrant and non-migrant youth (Ma & Wu, 2019). Given that more than half of all migrant students in large cities attend low-quality schools, we can conclude that the *hukou* system is the primary source of the social inequality in education between migrant and local children and adolescents.

Because of these challenges, quite a few rural migrant workers decide to leave their children and family members in their hometowns when they move to a city. While 35% of all children in China's rural areas apparently were left behind, in some provinces that are key sources of migrant workers, their proportion was up to 44% in 2014 (Hannum et al., 2018). The total number of left-behind children was estimated at around 40 million in some studies (UNICEF, 2018), but at 60–70 million in some others (Ge et al., 2019; Yiu & Yun, 2017).

These children have been found to display psychological, academic, and health-related problems. In one study, about 18% of all left-behind middle-school students displayed poor nutritional behaviors, high levels of inactivity, substance use, and suicidal ideation (Gao et al., 2010). In another study, left-behind children and adolescents who were living without both of their parents showed higher rates of depression and anxiety, performed less well academically, and experienced lower levels of social support than their counterparts (M. Shen et al., 2015). In a longitudinal study, left-behind children also revealed higher levels of loneliness and lower levels of happiness, as well as lowered life- and school-related satisfaction, compared to those living with their parents (Su et al., 2017).

Similarly, Y. Shen (2017) found that left-behind children were receiving unreliable and insecure support to commute to and from their schools. About 70% of the left-behind students had no one to supervise or check their homework at home. Moreover, left-behind children were susceptible to various threats as well as physical, verbal, or sexual abuse or assaults by a guardian or a teacher. Teachers were less likely to pay attention to left-behind students regarding their academic performance and life circumstances (Y. Shen, 2017).

The status of being left behind, however, seems to have led to inconsistent consequences in various studies of children's academic performance. First, due to the disadvantages in their psychological and health-related environment and outcomes, left-behind children were academically less competent and slower in educational developments than those not left behind (Y. Lu, 2012). Those left behind with no parent or with their fathers not only performed less well in school (Wen & Lin, 2012) but also tended to drop out of school more frequently than their counterparts (S. Lu et al., 2016).

However, there have been quite a few findings pointing to counterintuitive educational outcomes for left-behind children. One study reported that left-behind and non-left-behind children did not differ in their "high school entrance exam, dropout rates, and plans to attend vocational college" (Sui & Song, 2017, p. 350). In a large-scale study that aggregated 27 different surveys across 10 provinces from 2009 to 2013 with a total of about 141,000 children, those left behind did not underperform in mathematics, Chinese, and English compared to children living with both parents (C. Zhou et al., 2015).

Some researchers even found that left-behind children educationally outperformed the other children. In the study conducted by Y. Shen (2017), left-behind children were more likely than those not left behind to be among the top 10 in their class rank. Another study reported that the chances of staying in school, rather than dropping out, for left-behind children were 30% better than those of students living with their parents (Yang & Duan, 2008). The researchers' plausible interpretation of these unexpected results was that the parents' migration and their improved income level might help them to increase educational spending for their children. Indeed, a study showed that fathers' migration is associated with an increased amount of educational spending by the family (Ge et al., 2019). In turn, those students living with their mother received higher scores in school than those living with both parents or only with their fathers.

Another group of disadvantaged adolescents includes those who returned to their rural hometowns from the urban areas where their parents had migrated (Ling, 2017a). Usually, these teenagers move back to take the high school entrance exam, and later, they would prepare themselves for taking the national university entrance exam. They do so because the *hukou* system requires all students to take the high school exam at their birthplace where they are registered. Although some observers consider this positively and see it as "going back to the old home," the adolescents themselves experienced it as "discomfort, disorientation, and even despair" (Ling, 2017b, p. 737). Even if some of them are academically proficient, these returned students may have to face an unfairly harsh competition to enter various top universities because the quota system is tighter for rural applicants than for urban competitors. Many other students who do not think of themselves as being academically very competent or who decide not to attend higher educational institutions return to the urban areas where they had spent their childhood to find a job or attend vocational training programs. This reality has been a primary reason for the systematic inequality that hinders children and adolescents born in the countryside from desiring the upward social mobility they otherwise could obtain through higher education (Ling, 2017b).

Recently, the central government of China declared that it would eliminate the *hukou* system in smaller cities of fewer than 3 million inhabitants, while making it simpler or "looser" in mid-size cities where 3–5 million people reside. The main goal is to promote free movement by families ("China Vows Freer Movement for Workers," 2019). For at least two reasons, the overall effectiveness of this new policy requires future analysis and evaluation: (1) The government excluded the 10 most prominent cities from this amendment such as Beijing, Shanghai, and Guangzhou, where many rural migrant workers and their families have moved and (2) because so far they have not announced more detailed changes, it remains uncertain what actual changes are going to follow from the new policies.

B. Will South Korea Fall off Its Demographic Cliff?

One of the most severe challenges for South Korea's society is the prospective "demographic cliff" (Dent, 2014), the anticipated crisis in its population size due to the country's very low and still declining TFR, which has been reported to be 0.98 for 2018 (Statistics Korea, 2019a). Whereas the total number of newborn babies in 1971 was more than 1 million, this number decreased to around 327,000 in 2018. The government projects that senior citizens (65 years or older) will make up about 40% of the entire population in 2050, while those 14 years and younger will represent only about 9% (Noh, 2019).

Many provinces in South Korea that are located far from the metropolitan area of Seoul already reflect various troublesome consequences of such population trends. For example, several small countryside towns (e.g., Uiseong and

Yeongcheon) about 120 miles away from Seoul have about 35%–39% of their population as aging residents (65 years or older). The middle school of one town closed in 2007, while the playground was turned into a farming area. The largest hospital in the town also moved out in 2016, and instead, a new nursing home and a convalescent hospital opened 3 years later in the building for older patients. Although the local government operates a financial promotion program through which a family with a newborn baby can get about $5000 (USD), the overall demographic situation has not changed (Noh, 2019).

In another small rural town some 80 miles from Seoul, the elementary school recently held its last graduation ceremony, for only two graduating students. The school, whose number of remaining students will be three in 2020, is going to be merged into another elementary school located in the next town. This trend is pervasive across many rural communities. In the province of Gangwon, a total of 38 schools were closed since 2012 due to their declining student populations (Yang, 2019).

The South Korean government has developed various policies to solve this critical issue and for this purpose spent about $85 billion (USD) of the national budget since 2007. As of 2018, the policies had shown virtually no effect (Jung, 2018). Policy-driven efforts to enhance maternity and paternity leaves at workplaces, for example, have not made a big difference because employers do not like to offer them. The government has established public day-care centers to provide secure and affordable childcare services for workers with young babies or children, but every center has a long waiting list of applicants, which indicates that the effort is insufficient (Jung, 2018).

The primary reason why South Korea has one of the world's lowest birth rates is *education fever*—the extreme competition for academic excellence (Gielen & Kim, 2019; Seth, 2002). Not only school-aged children and adolescents but also their parents, teachers, and even schools are participating in this competition. This kind of tight and stressful competition throughout K–12 education and beyond leads most young adults to ask themselves whether they will be able reach their educational and career goals. In this context, they think of potential future events in their life, such as marriage and childrearing, as sources of burdens and responsibilities rather than happiness (Gielen & Kim, 2019). Therefore, a rapidly shrinking number of people of marriageable age consider getting married or creating a family of their own (Choi, 2019).

The massive drive for academic success has led to the country's rapid urbanization together with its consequences, such as the sharp decline of rural communities. This urbanization began already in the 1950s, reached its peak in the 1960s–1970s, and was intertwined with the process of industrialization (Kwon, 2001). Since education fever has been regarded as the primary engine for South Korea's dramatic economic growth and industrialization, it can be said that the drive for educational achievements fueled both urbanization and industrialization (Korea Research Institute for Human Settlements, 1980; also cited in Kwon, 2001).

The long-lasting urbanization of South Korea, together with the traditional preference for boys, has led to a distinct lack of females of marriageable age in almost all rural areas. Since 2000 in particular, the lack has induced rural males in their 30s and 40s to look for spouses in other Asian countries, such as China, Vietnam, Thailand, and the Philippines (The Korea Herald, 2019; Statistics Korea, 2013, 2019b). This phenomenon has challenged Korean society to come to terms with various issues related to multiculturalism.

From 2009 until 2018, the proportion of newborn babies in multicultural families was 4.4%–5.5% among all the country's newborns, or around 18,000–23,000 per year (Statistics Korea, 2019b). In 2015, the ratio of K–12 students from multicultural families increased to 10% in the rural areas (J. W. Hwang, 2016). These students and college-aged young adults, however, appear to experience difficulties in their development and education. For instance, they had significantly lower rates of advancing to the next level of education: About 93% advanced from elementary to middle schools, 88% advanced from middle to high schools, and a mere 49.6% became college students (Ministry of Gender Equality and Family, 2019). These rates are problematic (particularly the low rate of such students getting a higher education) when compared to the very high rates for traditional Korean students: Among all elementary students, 100% have been advancing to middle schools, 99.7% of the middle-school students proceeded to high schools, and about 70%–80% of the high school students ended up in college during the years 2010–2019 (Department of Education, 2019).

There are three primary reasons why students from a multicultural background are suffering in their schoolwork. First, the income levels of their families tend to be lower than those of many other Korean families, with about 85% of all multicultural families earning less than the annual income of average families (Kyung Hee Cyber University, 2017). This means that the parents cannot easily afford various educational expenses for their children, such as fees for private tutoring. Furthermore, immigrant parents—particularly mothers—face their own barriers due to linguistic and cultural differences, and children find it difficult to get help with their homework or in regard to other school-related administrative needs from their parents or others (D. E. Hwang, 2016). According to a survey, the number one reason why these parents experience difficulties in raising their children is expensive educational costs (49.6%), while the second one is the language barrier (25.6%) (Kyung Hee Cyber University, 2017).

As for the multicultural students, their after-school activities are far less academic in nature than those of their counterparts: They are more likely to watch TV or take naps and less likely to do homework or to attend a cram school. The chance of dropping out of school for these students was at least 2.5–4.5 times higher than that for students from typical families from 2012 to 2014. These students often find it difficult to develop a sense of belonging to their school community and to adapt themselves to the Korean culture of emphasizing academic success. This is so because they experience difficulties in making friends and getting along with teachers. Their parents cannot financially support their needs (e.g., to attend highly popular but expensive cram schools or getting tutoring lessons). They lose interest in studying school subjects and find it difficult to learn the Korean language, if their mothers came from a foreign country (Kyung Hee Cyber University, 2017).

In these situations, one can imagine various lifestyle changes and challenges with respect to the developmental outcomes and well-being of children and adolescents in South Korea. Because of the decreasing number of school-aged children and adolescents, as well as college-aged young adults, quite a few schools in the rural towns have already vanished or else will soon disappear, as are a significant number of private colleges or universities (Gielen & Kim, 2019). Children and teenagers residing in the countryside live their school life with a much smaller group of peers or classmates than had been true for the older generations. Many local communities consider merging several schools into one, which can have a negative impact on their members (Yang, 2019), such as longer commuting routes and times for students as well as losing jobs for teachers.

Many rural colleges and universities with an uncertain future due to the dramatic projected decline of enrollees and new applicants have recently admitted many students from other Asian countries, such as China and Vietnam. In 2019, the number of foreign students was estimated at more than 160,000, meaning that it had doubled during the previous 5 years. The new trend appears to help those rural institutions to cope with financial pressures. The quality of the courses and the learning progress of the students, however, are in doubt because the students' Korean-language skills are often insufficient. Indeed, the colleges and universities in South Korea had no time to develop an effective way to check the Korean-language proficiency of their applicants from abroad. Since international students cannot meaningfully contribute to group projects or class discussions, instructors face challenges and dilemmas that they never imagined or experienced in the past. Moreover, native Korean students complain about the lowered quality of their classes and feel uncomfortable about the whole situation (Park & Jung, 2019).

Koreans strongly believe that they are ethnically and culturally homogeneous (A. Kim, 2018; S. K. Kim & Kim, 2012; Lie, 2014). This belief, however, not only makes them reluctant to accept or promote diversity but also supports their being prejudiced and discriminating against people from different cultures. Seen in this context, it seems natural that the Korean government has been inefficient and ineffective in developing policies to embrace children and students from multicultural families and to help them find solutions to their challenges with respect to language barriers and socioemotional-cultural isolation and discrimination (A. Kim, 2018).

Making the entire society and its members open-minded to human diversity so that they can enjoy their multicultural fellow Koreans is unlikely to happen for a good number of years. Moreover, the developmental and educational issues of children and adolescents from multicultural families are paired with their parents' socioeconomic status, something that requires more attention in the broader context of social and governmental efforts (A. Kim, 2018).

Nevertheless, several direct approaches could have some immediate positive results for local communities, multicultural families, and their children. For example, South Korean education is almost exclusively based on textbooks that the government edits or permits. Many textbooks still perceive topics and subjects primarily through the lens of ethnocentrism, while introducing misleading images of people from other cultures or countries (S. K. Kim & Kim, 2012). Changing the direction of the discourse in the textbooks by welcoming and respecting cultural diversity would be a first practical step toward developing a more embracing social climate.

For another example, the sociocultural disparities between native Korean and multicultural families are strongly influenced by the varying employment status, income levels, and educational attainments of the parents. The parents of multicultural families are more likely to be jobless and, in turn, low-income because many of them have not completed their secondary education

(A. Kim, 2018). Providing additional educational support for these parents, such as teaching the Korean language and the necessary social or job skills to mothers in otherwise closing rural schools, could be as useful as "killing three birds with one stone": (1) It would help the parents overcome their language barrier, (2) it could get them educated for a potential job, and (3) it would help those schools to secure some governmental money and thereby keep them from closing their doors.

V. CHILDHOOD AND YOUTH: WORLDWIDE CHANGES AND THE BROAD SWEEP OF HISTORY

We have briefly sketched some interrelated changes in childhood, adolescence, and beginning adulthood that have accompanied humanity's socioecological and sociocultural evolution from small foraging societies to peasant societies and finally to today's digital information societies. In addition, we analyzed in more detail the impact of rural–urban differences and patterns of migration on families and their children in modern China and South Korea. This discussion forms a useful background for reviewing and illustrating an intertwined group of 14 notable global trends that have been and will be shaping the lives of the world's children and youth (cf. Gielen, 2016; Lancy, 2015, pp. 400–410). The majority of today's children are residing in evolving societies where traditional groups of foragers have largely disappeared, while their rural populations are increasingly influenced by economic and sociocultural developments occurring in nearby cities and abroad.

A. The World's Population Has Been Expanding at a Rapid Pace and Will Do So in the Forthcoming Decades: The Population of the Poorest Continent, Africa, Is Increasing the Most Rapidly, While the Populations of Several Information Societies Have Begun to Shrink

The world's population explosion represents a fundamental change in human history. On the eve of the agricultural and pastoral revolutions some 10–12 millennia ago, the hunting and gathering way of life was only able to sustain a population of about 4 million around the world. Once humanity discovered how to plant wheat, millet, corn (originally in Mexico), and subsequently rice, many of its members began to settle down in villages and towns. After further expansion, and beginning about 5800 years ago, parts of humanity began to live in growing city-states in West Asia, China, and the Indus Valley. Over time, the states expanded into large-scale nations depending mostly on agriculture and agropastoralism. By the year 1800, when the Industrial Revolution was beginning to permanently transform the originally agriculture-based nations of the West, the world's population had grown to an estimated 990 million; and by the year 2019, it was surpassing 7.7 billion—roughly 1930 times the population of 12,000 years earlier.

Figure 2.2 depicts global population estimates and predictions for the years 1800–2100. The estimates are based on Roser, Ritchie, and Ortíz-Ospina (2019). While they are subject to some error, especially for the earlier years, they nevertheless summarize humanity's most powerful story. The predictions about future trends assume that there will be no major unforeseen circumstances such as nuclear war, new monstrous diseases, or large-scale environmental disasters.

Different continents account for very different portions of today's global population. In mid-2019, 59.6% of all people lived in Asia, 17% in Africa, 9.7% in Europe, 5.5% in South America, 4.8% in North America, and 0.6% in Oceania (Duffin, 2019). Because many of Africa's poor sub-Saharan countries such as Niger, Chad, Mali, and Nigeria have very young populations together with some of the world's highest fertility rates, the continent's overall population is expected to double in the next 30 years. Thus, while in 2019 Africa included 17% of the world's population, this number is projected to rise to 25% or 2.53

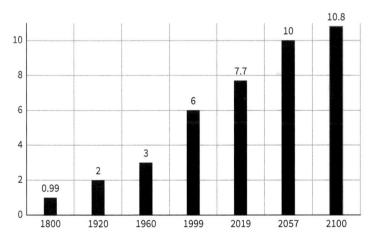

FIGURE 2.2: World Population 1800–2100 (in Billions)
Source of data: Roser, Ritchie, & Ortíz-Ospina (2019).

billion persons by 2050. Some 80%–90% of Africa's additional children are likely to end up in its growing slums. In that year, Asia's population is projected to reach 5.26 billion. By then, India will have become the world's most populous country with an estimated 1.71 billion people, whereas China's population is expected to decline slightly to 1.34 billion. It is likely that the aging populations of East Asian countries such as Japan, South Korea, and Taiwan will be lower than today, given their very low birth rates together with their societies' ambivalent though changing attitudes about immigration. Given Europe's very low fertility rates, its population is projected to decline to 707 million by 2050.

B. Children's Global Mortality Rates Have Declined Dramatically

Figure 2.3 depicts estimated global child mortality and survival rates between 1800 and 2017. Because children are especially likely to die in infancy and the early stages of childhood, the figure depicts below-5 mortality rates (Roser & Ortíz-Ospina, 2019). The dramatic decline seen in the graph constitutes one of history's most inspiring tales: As late as 1800, an estimated 43.3% of the world's children did not reach their fifth birthday, yet by the year 2017 that percentage had declined to 3.9%. These declines occurred in numerous, culturally diverse countries. For instance, between 1890 and 2015, under-5 child mortality rates declined from 48.7% to 2.2% in Mexico, from 47.4% to 0.9%

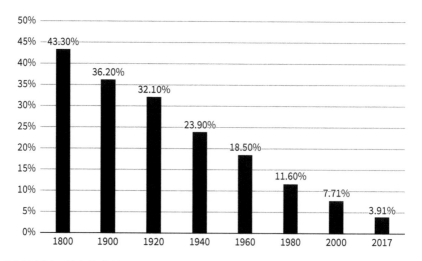

FIGURE 2.3: Global Child Mortality (Below 5 Years)
Source of data: Our World in Data: https://ourworldindata.org/grapher/global-child-mortality-timeseries

in Russia, and from 44.4% to 2.8% in Indonesia. Moreover, even in Africa's poorest countries such as Chad (13.85% in 2015) and Niger (11.21% in 2015), the respective percentages—though still disproportionately high—have nevertheless declined to a fraction of what they had been just a few decades earlier. In countries with progressive public healthcare systems such as Ireland, Germany, Japan, South Korea, and the Scandinavian countries, today's child mortality rates hover around 0.3%. In comparison, the US rate of 0.7% points to a less optimal healthcare system and a more unequal socioeconomic system, yet even that rate would have been considered unthinkably low in 1890 when the rate was 26.8%.

Children used to die in large numbers because of preterm pregnancy problems, birth complications, pneumonia, diarrhea, the measles, smallpox, malaria, and malnutrition. Many common diseases spread because of unclean water, scarcity of modern toilets (e.g., in parts of South Asia), lack of vaccinations, city rats that sporadically spread the devastating black plague (pestilence), European intruders that brought devastating diseases to the New World, and a general lack of insight into the basic nature of diseases and how both laypersons and medical doctors can transmit them. Instead, a rich array of supernatural forces were thought to be at least partially responsible for children's survival or death. Sporadic famines—triggered by unfavorable climatic conditions but sometimes also by military conflicts—sent large numbers of children and adults to their often obscure and nameless burial places. In addition, in many preindustrial societies, a considerable number of infants were abandoned or else ended up in poorly supported orphanages or foundling homes with extremely high death rates (Levene, 2007).

Today, poverty and low levels of mothers' education remain important direct and indirect causes of (relatively) high child mortality rates. That holds true both across and within countries and regions. Poor people have less access to optimal prenatal care, are on average less exposed to basic knowledge about healthcare, may not have access to vaccination programs or else are misinformed about such programs, are exposed to unclean water supplies, and are more likely to have malnourished children susceptible to potentially deadly childhood diseases. Nomadic and isolated mothers living in the countryside, for instance, are more likely to give birth on their own or with the help of untrained grandmothers, have less access to primary care systems and clinics, and know less about immunization programs. Moreover, Gakidou et al. (2010) have provided extensive global evidence that increased educational

Handbook of Advances in Culture and Psychology

attainment by women of reproductive age leads to sharply reduced rates of child mortality. This suggests that if you help poor countries to send their girls to school, you will improve their "human capital" while saving the lives of some of their future children.

C. Because Poverty Has Decreased in Many Countries, the World's High Levels of Young Children's Malnutrition Have Been Declining in Recent Decades; However, Malnutrition Remains a Potent Danger Especially in Sub-Saharan Africa, Parts of Oceania, and South Asia

In the past, most children grew up in families that were involved in subsistence economic activities and lived in poverty or near poverty. Periodic famines killed huge numbers of children and adults in Europe, China, and elsewhere. Child labor both inside and outside the context of families was frequently accompanied by malnutrition. Today, most families in the high-income countries have abandoned those subsistence activities, while their children's tendency to be overweight is steadily increasing. In low-income countries, however, insufficient nutrition remains a major danger for numerous children.

Good nutrition is crucial to the health of children, with severe malnutrition in the early years resulting in frequently devastating consequences for children's brain development and survival chances. Severe malnutrition by children and their mothers is responsible for more ill health than any other cause. A combined report issued by UNICEF, the World Health Organization, and the World Bank Group (2017) distinguishes between three forms of malnutrition. *Stunting* refers to a child who is too short for their age, *wasting* occurs when a child is too thin for their height, and *overweight* refers to a child who is too heavy for their height. In 2016, 22.9% or 154.8 million of the world's children below the age of 5 were stunted, 7.7% or close to 52 million children exhibited signs of wasting, and 6.0% or 40.6 million were seriously overweight. South Asia, sub-Saharan Africa, and parts of Oceania were the centers of insufficient nutrition. For instance, 15.4% of all children in South Asia were in jeopardy because of wasting alone. Although the percentage of stunted and wasted children did decline between the years 2000 and 2016 in Asia, little or no progress was made in sub-Saharan Africa and Oceania, apart from Australia and New Zealand. Dettwyler's (2014) ethnography provides a difficult-to-forget description of small and malnourished "dancing skeletons" in the West African country of Mali. In contrast, overweight and obesity have become growing problems among the children and adults of many culturally diverse countries such as the United States, Argentina, and various Pacific island nations.

D. Children's Lives Improved in 173 out of 176 Countries Between 2000 and 2017

Relying on its multifaceted End of Childhood Index for 176 countries, Save the Children (2019, p. 1) asserts that "children born today have a better chance than at any time in history to grow up healthy, educated and protected." The index combines eight national indicators measuring the overall care of children. They include under-5 mortality rates; prevalence of child stunting; the percentage of out-of-school children, adolescents, and youth; the percentage of children involved in child labor; the percentage of adolescents currently married or in union; the birth rates of adolescent mothers; the percentage of a nation's population displaced by conflict; and national child homicide rates. Most of the relevant data for the index have been drawn from the reports of various UN agencies. (For a more broadly based and more complex Sustainable Child Development Index, see Chang et al. [2018].)

The 10 countries receiving the highest scores and rankings because they are protecting childhood well include eight European countries and two Asian countries. They are Singapore (ranked highest), Sweden, Finland, Norway, Slovenia, Germany, Ireland, Italy, South Korea, and Belgium (number 10). In contrast, the 10 countries ranked lowest are all located in sub-Saharan Africa and include Burkina Faso, Democratic Republic of Congo, Guinea, Nigeria, Somalia, South Sudan, Mali, Chad, Niger, and Central African Republic (ranked lowest among all countries). The world's three most powerful countries, China (ranked 36), United States (also ranked 36), and Russia (ranked 38) received unimpressive rankings and ratings. Given that the United States is the richest among these three countries, its mediocre showing reflects relatively high rates of poverty and economic inequality (Wilkinson & Pickett, 2011), high homicide rates, a non-optimal health system, and the kind of slums or semi-slums that do not exist in the Scandinavian countries or in Singapore.

At the same time, 173 of the 176 countries did a better job supporting children's health, education, and protection status in 2017 (or an adjacent year) when compared to the year 2000. Although sub-Saharan countries and next South Asian countries received the lowest scores in both years, they nevertheless did show considerable improvements over time in protecting their children. Indeed, the End of Childhood Index improved in all regions of the world.

Since the 10 highest-ranked countries are wealthy countries and the 10 lowest-ranked countries are poor countries located in sub-Saharan Africa, we computed a correlation coefficient between the average gross domestic product (purchasing power parity) per capita of 168 countries in 2017 (Statistics Times, 2019) and the same countries' 2017 End of Childhood Index ratings. The yearly per capita income was adjusted for differences in prices between the countries and varied enormously from $700 (Burundi) to $124,122 (Qatar). The correlation coefficient reached $r = .63$ ($p < .0001$), indicating that children's lives and their welfare are strongly and positively influenced by a country's average income.

Some skeptics might argue that the End of Childhood Index is biased and unfairly favors well-to-do children and youth attending educational institutions over children who begin to work earlier in life (cf. Bourdillon & Mulumbwa, 2014; Evans & Skovdal, 2015). They might point out that for thousands of years girls have married and become mothers in their middle and later teenage years. Today, however, many of them are still not allowed to decide when and whom they would like to marry and whether and how long they are allowed to attend school. Moreover, high childhood mortality rates, high rates of children's malnutrition, high child homicide rates, and excessive and/or dangerous work by children should be regarded as unequivocal evils.

E. Women's Fertility Rates Have Been Declining Sharply, Especially in the Digital Information Societies

In most societies and throughout much of history, families had an average of about 5–8 children. In the year 1800, for instance, the average Caucasian family in the United States included about 7.1–7.5 children, of whom close to half did not survive into adulthood (Haines, 1994; "1800 United States Census," 2018). Ninety-three percent of those families lived in rural areas and small towns. Today, the country's average TFR has declined to 1.85, more than 99% of all newborns survive into middle childhood, and the majority of children are growing up in small families. Increasingly, they reside in urban rather than rural areas, where they come into contact with many children and adults otherwise unknown to them. Similar trends can also be found in other economically developed nations.

At the global level, the TFR declined from 4.73 in 1970 to 2.49 in 2015 (Roser, 2017). A good part of this rapid decline reflects the second demographic transition (Lesthaeghe, 2011), which in almost all digital information societies (except for Israel) has resulted in fertility declines below the "fertility replacement level" of 2.1. In other words, when in a modern society the average TFR per woman per lifetime sinks below 2.1, its population will decline unless very high levels of immigration counteract this trend. While some societies such as Canada (TFR = 1.60) have successfully prevented such tendencies by supporting very high levels of immigration, many members of collectivistic East Asian societies such as Japan (TFR = 1.43) and South Korea (TFR = 1.05 and now shrinking below 1.00) have felt uneasy about immigration for nationalistic reasons. As a result, Japan's population has been declining since 2007, while the population of South Korea is expected to do so rapidly in the coming years.

Overall levels and changes in TFRs differ dramatically between countries depending on a country's changing level of economic development. Based on a combination of data supplied by the Central Intelligence Agency's (2018) *World Factbook*, Wikipedia (see "List of Sovereign States," 2020), and the World Bank (2019), here are a few examples comparing, for each country, TFRs in 1960 and 2017: Brazil, TFR = 6.07 in 1960 and 1.71 in 2017; India, TFR = 5.91 in 1960 and 2.30 in 2017; Japan, TFR = 2.17 in 1960 and 1.42 in 2017; South Korea, TFR = 6.10 in 1960 and 1.05 in 2017; Niger, TFR = 7.45 in 1960 and 7.18 in 2017; Nigeria, TFR = 6.35 in 1960 and 5.46 in 2017. One may, for instance, compare Brazil's striking decline in TFRs versus the far smaller declines that did occur in Niger and Nigeria during the same 57 years. Brazil's decline reflects its moderate economic development, whereas the two African countries have remained economically underdeveloped, predominantly agrarian, and pronatalist nations favoring high birth rates. In 1960, South Korea was a very poor country and had a high TFR comparable to the levels of Brazil, India, and Nigeria. By 2017, however, the information society of South Korea reported one of the world's lowest TFRs. Across 152 countries, the correlation between their average TFRs and their price-adjusted per capita incomes was $r = -.51$ $(p < .001)$ in 2017. This indicates that women in the poorer countries tended to have the most children. Moreover and across 152 countries, the correlation between the countries' average End of Childhood Indices and their average TFRs was $r = -.85$ $(p < .0001)$. This very high negative correlation indicates that nations with very high national fertility rates generally have very low End of Childhood Indices.

The major declines in a nation's TFR are strongly influenced by that nation's technological and economic development including the spread of reproductive technologies and birth control practices. They are also intertwined with powerful changes in family structures; gender roles and forms of gender identity; marriage arrangements; women's competing preferences for having careers, being married, and having children; women's and men's respective outlooks on divorce, cohabitation, and childlessness; average marriage age; changing preferences for chastity versus premarital sexual relationships; sibling relationships and responsibilities; an increasing emphasis on individualistic life goals and childrearing practices; young people's prolonged attendance of educational institutions; other general changes in residence patterns and lifestyles; and nationwide discussions about the necessity and desirability of immigration. There exists an important trade-off between the sharp decline of fertility rates and the ongoing changes in gender roles, especially in the non-Islamic information societies. This trade-off has been insufficiently discussed, yet as the earlier example of South Korea demonstrates, sharp declines in a country's TFR can have major destructive consequences.

F. Around the World, Children, Youth, and Especially Girls Are Increasingly Attending Educational Institutions and Becoming Literate

Prior to the early 1800s, the large majority of the world's children, especially outside northern and western Europe as well as parts of North America, did not attend educational institutions at all—or else they did so only for a few years. While in 1820 an estimated 88% of the world's population were illiterate, by 2016 that percentage had shrunk to 14% (see Figure 2.4). Today, for most children living in digital information societies, attendance of educational institutions has become their central activity, while learning from family members such as siblings is less crucial than before. Even in many of the world's low-income nations, school attendance is now legally required and increasingly expected, although quite a few children from poor families are still unable to do so.

Based on Roser and Ortíz-Ospina (2018b). Figure 2.4 depicts worldwide changes in estimated literacy rates between 1820 and 2016. Literacy levels are difficult to ascertain and subject to different definitions. Historians, for instance, may calculate their estimates by ascertaining how many people were able to sign official documents in the past. Other researchers rely partially on school attendance rates, although in a good many countries, various children are taught in languages that they do not hear at home and they therefore find difficult to understand. They, as well as a good many very poor children, are likely to drop out of school, to attend it only sporadically, and to be semi-literate

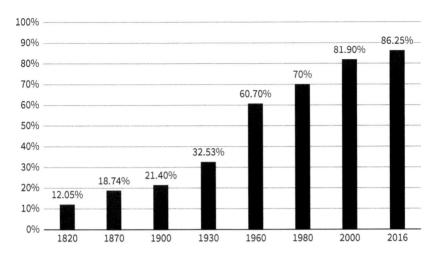

FIGURE 2.4: Literate World Population (15 Years and Older)
Source of data: Roser and Ortíz-Ospina (2018b).

at best. Nevertheless, the estimates depicted in Figure 2.4 tell a dramatic and highly encouraging story even if some of them could be somewhat optimistic.

In 2016, 13.6% of the world's 750 million illiterate persons were youth aged between 15 and 24 years (UNESCO Institute for Statistics, 2017, Table 1). Altogether, 93% of all male youth and 90% of all female youth were literate. Literacy rates were lowest in sub-Saharan Africa, namely 79% for male youth and 72% for female youth. School attendance, especially by girls, remains a major problem in some of the world's poorest and sometimes Islamic countries such as Niger, Chad, Afghanistan, and Nepal (a predominantly Hindu country). There, quite a few parents are unable to pay for their children's textbooks or school uniforms, while others require their children to work at home, in the fields, or by guarding animals. At times, they may be opposed to schooling for girls for religious reasons. At the same time, global school attendance has climbed much faster for girls than for boys. For instance, in 1900, boys in sub-Saharan Africa were over 10 times more likely to attend school than girls. By 2010, the gender ratio between boys and girls had surpassed 80%: In other words, more than 80 girls in sub-Saharan Africa attended school for every 100 boys (J.-W. Lee & Lee, 2016). By 2009, in 87 countries, the educational attainment of women aged 25–34 years had already surpassed that of their male peers (Gakidou et al., 2010). Similarly, in various digital information societies such as the United States, more women than men are now graduating from tertiary educational institutions. Frequently, girls and young women like school more, drop out less frequently, and get superior grades when compared to boys. They do not want to get stuck at home, are less impulsive and act out less often, but may be subject to more internalizing disorders such as social anxiety and depression.

G. While Formal School Learning Undermines Prosocial Learning Based on Observing and "Pitching In," It Improves Children's Overall Intelligence

Because children in many traditional peasant societies spend few, if any, years in school, much of their learning is (or was) based on observing, doing things, and "pitching in" (Coppens et al., 2014; see also Rogoff [2014] for some Central American societies). From their early childhood years on, young learners contribute to family and community endeavors. Eager to belong and to acquire a sense of competence, young girls, for instance, learn how to take care of younger siblings and how to do routine housework by observing their mothers, grandmothers, and same-sex elder siblings. Children who regularly babysit tend to support others and become more nurturant (Whiting & Edwards, 1988). When boys and girls receive guidance from others, it is frequently in the context of performing specific activities. They also learn various skills and acquire cultural knowledge by helping adults with their fieldwork and elsewhere. In addition, they practice role-playing while entertaining themselves via various physical games, listen to narratives and gossip told in their families and neighborhoods, and participate in cultural and religious rituals and festivals. In this way, they develop into knowledgeable and capable carriers of their culture. Children's work at home, in the fields, in crafts, or in shops is often seen as a crucial part of their education as responsible human beings, although some of these children will simply be exploited. Learning by observing, assisting, and collaborating often creates prosocial children; but in modern societies, a disproportionate emphasis on school learning undermines this process.

With the advent of formal schooling, children are increasingly exposed to more organized, hierarchical, and test-oriented forms of learning that are taught outside their families (Cole, 2005). Much of the knowledge and the skills children acquire in school may be unrelated to their immediate life circumstances, yet those skills prepare them for their future occupations. By attending pre-K, kindergarten, and primary and secondary schools, children learn to think in more systematic, analytic, and abstract ways; develop their numeracy; are exposed to scientific ways of thinking; are informed about outside worlds they know little or nothing about; and become aware of expanding options for their future lives (e.g., LeVine et al., 2012). Extensive evidence suggests that average IQ scores have been increasing for decades in a broad range of societies, a phenomenon known as the *Flynn effect* (Flynn, 1999). The global IQ increased by 28.37 points between 1923 and 2013, while Asia's increase between 1951 and 2013 was an impressive 36.75 IQ points (Pietschnig & Voracek, 2015). A major portion of these increments reflects improvements in systematic abstract thinking and not only increases in general information. In contrast, the thinking of unschooled children and adults is more practice-oriented. At the same time, it is important to keep in mind that IQ tests are not designed to measure complex processes of adaptive cultural learning, moral wisdom, or creativity.

H. Perceived Parental Warmth and Acceptance, Rather Than Rejection and Neglect, Inspire Children and Adolescents to Develop Positive Worldviews, to Become Socially Responsible and Connected to Others, and to Experience Feelings of Being Cared for, Self-Worth, and Self-Adequacy

Rohner (2016) has developed a broadly conceived and evidence-based interpersonal acceptance-rejection theory designed to predict the psychological correlates and consequences of interpersonal acceptance and rejection. Extensive pancultural research evidence suggests that when applied to parent/caregiver–child relationships, his theory is able to predict many correlates, effects, and causes of children's perceptions of parental acceptance as opposed to feelings of rejection and neglect.

In order to better understand the cross-cultural implications of Rohner's approach, let us take a brief look at the combined results of more than 120 studies that have been conducted in the Arab world. As summarized by Ahmed et al. (2016), these studies have explored various adaptations of Rohner's measures, the antecedents of perceived parental acceptance–rejection, and its mental health and educational consequences for adolescents, youth, and children. Given that many of these studies are reported in master's theses and dissertations written in Arabic, they remain mostly unknown to the international community of cross-cultural psychologists. At the same time, test–retest studies and factor analyses of the various Parental Acceptance-Rejection Questionnaire scales in Arabic, together with other empirical approaches, suggest that the scales can serve as reliable and valid measures of perceived parental warmth in a variety of Arab countries.

Many of the Arab findings make psychological sense when considered within Rohner's framework. For instance, Egyptian, Kuwaiti, and other Arab youths reporting harsh physical punishment by parents also tend to report more feelings of parental rejection. In several studies, perceptions of parental rejection and neglect were associated with low levels of psychological well-being; feelings of depression, anxiety, and loneliness; social phobias; and experiences of rejection and bullying by peers. Perceived rejection and parental neglect were sometimes associated with adolescents' self-reported internalizing behavior, while other rejected adolescents engaged in externalizing behaviors such as impulsivity, interpersonal aggressiveness, and delinquency. In contrast, higher levels of perceived parental acceptance tended to go hand in hand with less aggressive and bullying behavior but higher levels of scholastic achievement, achievement motivation, emotional intelligence, creativity, self-reported social responsibility, and political participation. Children living in small urban families, those with non-working mothers, and those supported by better socioeconomic circumstances perceived their parents as more accepting and less aggressive when compared to those growing up in semi-nomadic and poorer families. Perhaps surprisingly, more girls than boys felt accepted by their fathers, although Arab families tend to be patrilineal and patrilocal.

Altogether, studies on the association between children's and adolescents' reports of parental behavior and their psychological development and mental health have been conducted in more than 60 nations located around the world (Rohner, 2016). Their results are often compatible with those reported for Arab countries. At the same time, cultures vary in the degree to which parents are expected to exert control over their children's behavior. In more collectivistic societies embracing extended family systems, children and youth may accept their elders' extensive and long-term guidance as long as they remain convinced that they have their best interests in mind. More generally, juvenile perceptions about parental acceptance are influenced by societal norms spelling out the nature of good parenting, as are juvenile perceptions about how well their parents or other caretakers meet those norms. For instance, "good parenting" in modern Western societies and cultures tends to be more permissive, open-ended, and time-limited when compared to how many traditional Asian societies and Asian Americans evaluate "good parenting." Thus, many young South Asian adults and immigrants to the United States expect their parents and other family members to play an important role in arranging their marriages, but young adults from other ethnic groups mostly favor love marriages based on their own preferences (Segal, 2012). At the same time, Asian American couples (including South Asian couples) have low divorce and separation rates compared to the major non–Asian American groups (Angier, 2013).

I. Gender Roles and Associated Family Systems Are Changing in Many Countries

While gender roles have existed in all known cultures, their nature and ideological justifications have shifted over the course of time. In many preindustrial societies and from their early years onward, girls were expected to take care of younger siblings while also learning how to prepare food, wash clothes, take care of small gardens and some of the smaller animals, and develop an evolving identity as an "I-will-soon-be-a-mother." In contrast, many girls in today's information societies spend more time playing and attending educational institutions rather than helping out in the family. Their future identities are less predetermined and much more variable than those of their peers in the preindustrial societies.

Similarly, many boys originally became adult males by observation, imitation, practice, admonition, listening to advice and corrections by family members, becoming an apprentice, and engaging in work already in their middle childhood. The physically more demanding occupations (e.g., controlling big draft animals while plowing) were mostly performed by males rather than by females. In today's high-income societies, however, book learning has become the most important type of learning. Over time, this tends to weaken traditional gender roles since physical strength has become irrelevant for many highly paid professions. However, occupation-related gender roles are not disappearing. For instance, 94% of all American truck drivers are males, while most preschool teachers are females.

In peasant societies, the bearing and raising of many children as well as the running of a household were demanding, time-consuming, and central activities for most women. Moreover, being pregnant, breastfeeding each of their children for 2 or 3 years, taking care of small children, and the possibility of being the victim of sexual violence restricted their ability to get involved in potentially dangerous activities that took them far away from their village. These practical considerations supported the traditional role division between mothers serving as housewives and (more or less) part-time garden and fieldworkers versus fathers who often worked either inside or outside their home as full-time breadwinners. In some form, this division prevailed for a long time in most peasant societies. At the same time, girl children and mothers typically worked longer hours than did boy children and fathers. Today, traditional gender roles remain in force in many rural communities in Africa, Asia, the Middle East, and Latin America, where religious and other cultural traditions support them.

In addition, men and male youth usually dominate military as well as illegal activities involving physical violence and threats of physical violence. For instance, Daly and Wilson (1988) examined criminological records in a variety of societies and historical periods. In their study, the ratio of male to female homicides was approximately 9:1. In many traditional societies including those based on pastoralism and agriculture, periodic threats of conflict and war were common and helped to reinforce male preoccupations revolving around notions of toughness, male glory, honor, and the avoidance of shame. For instance, the Pashtunwali code ("Way of the Pashtuns") has for centuries been endorsed by Pashtun tribes residing in various mountainous areas of Afghanistan and Pakistan. Originally transmitted orally, the code emphasizes male courage, fearlessness, stoicism, chivalry, fierce independence, family honor, vengeance and blood revenge, and hospitality. The code remains popular especially in the countryside and the mountains, where men must defend the honor and reputation of their women or else be subject to public contempt (Rzehak, 2011). The first author encountered this code in 1964 when he was hitchhiking through Afghanistan and northwestern Pakistan. He greatly appreciated the natives' prevailing hospitality but also witnessed the shooting of a European visitor who had photographed a woman working in the fields.

The Hellenic (Greek) warriors in Homer's *Iliad* would have readily understood the non-Islamic aspects of this honor code since their Mediterranean culture revolved around related notions of glory, honor, and dishonor. Honor codes emphasizing fiercely demanding forms of manhood tend to flourish in societies surrounded by harsh and threatening environments that offer scarce resources (Gilmore, 1990). Because digital information societies create softer physical, economic, and sociocultural environments, they are also favoring softer and more diffuse versions of ideal manhood. Whereas information technology workers and accountants do not need a fierce honor code, many herders of animals and peasants surviving in the rough mountains of Afghanistan continue to find it meaningful and adaptive.

J. Changes in Gender Roles Are Accompanied by Shifts in Gender-Related Ideologies

In today's information societies, reliable forms of birth control tend to be available; housework takes less time because of inventions such as washing machines, refrigerators, and convenient heating systems; and children spend many hours and years in school. Increasingly, women's desire to have several children is competing with their dedication to extended years of schooling, their subsequent careers, and their economic welfare and independence. Because it is expensive to bring up children in digital information societies, children tend to be few in number (Kağitçibaşi, 2007); and they are often born relatively late in their mother's life. Cohabitation, late marriages, and divorce have become common practices in Western societies. Pre-existing family systems in many modern Western societies have deteriorated since the 1970s, with many babies nowadays being born to unmarried mothers. Other adults prefer to remain childless in countries as culturally and religiously diverse as Italy, Japan, Morocco, and South Korea. Although religious prescriptions and practices sometimes reinforce traditional gender roles in today's North America, East Asia, and Europe, the general influence of various religious traditions is weakening in many information societies together with their impact on gender roles. In East Asia, the traditional Confucian emphasis on patrilineal, extended family systems has been replaced by the spread of small families together with very low birth rates. While the traditional Confucian preference for boys and for sharply defined, highly unequal gender roles has not disappeared, it is becoming more controversial and less adaptive (Jankowiak & Moore, 2017; see also Brown et al. [2017] for a review of how women's roles are evolving in a variety of countries).

Whereas in the agricultural and herding societies of the past, gender roles tended to be hierarchically structured and anchored in patriarchal and sacred traditions, modern feminist ideologies emphasize that gender roles are human-made and changeable and that they should be egalitarian in nature. In a similar vein, diverse forms of sexual orientation, gender identities, and types of marriage are now legal and considered more or less acceptable, especially in the more individualistic and liberal societies. Consequently, many predominantly liberal psychologists and their professional associations argue that children should be brought up to respect a variety of gender identities and forms of sexual orientation. In contrast, sexual intercourse among members of the same sex remains a criminal activity in more than 70 nations, most of them Muslim countries or former British colonies (Kyama & Perez-Pena, 2019). Similarly, many religiously oriented and conservative adolescents in liberal societies find it difficult to fully embrace liberal teachings about the moral acceptability of diverse sexual orientations and gender identities. Select Christian and Jewish subgroups in Western societies continue to uphold their sacred traditions together with an emphasis on preserving traditional forms of family life based on traditional gender roles. God's blessings become manifest to the Amish, Hassidim, Hutterites, Mennonites, and Mormons when they are having many children.

Ironically, while the members of many Evangelical and other religious groups oppose evolutionary theory, their emphasis on having several children supports their inclusive fitness. The same held true for the religiously as well as practically motivated behavior of child-rich American parents in earlier centuries. They frequently considered evolutionary theory to be of dubious validity, or else it was unknown to them. In contrast, quite a few of today's not so religious social scientists and (female or male) feminists subscribe to evolutionary theory because of its scientific character, yet their ideological commitments and their behavior fail to maximize their inclusive fitness. Their behavior may be contrasted with the practices of polygamous Muslim men in predominantly agricultural countries such as Niger and Mali who maximize their inclusive fitness by having 10–20 (or even more) children with several wives. Each of these wives is expected to have an average of about 6–7 children. No wonder then that the population of sub-Saharan Africa is likely to double by about 2050!

Adopting a historical perspective in this context, one may ask, how would most American women and men of the past have judged their 21st-century descendants' individualistic, divorce-prone, gender-flexible, low-fertility behavior together with their efforts to legalize abortion? Would they not have considered such behavior to be self-centered, sinful, and in contradiction to God's sacred revelations and commandments in the Bible? In this context, it should be kept in mind that in those early days American women tended to occupy a higher moral but lower political status than their frequently violent men. This held especially true if they dressed conservatively and became faithful wives dedicated to the welfare of their many children and their family.

K. Adolescence and Beginning Adulthood Are the Stages of Life Most Likely to Change in the Face of Sociocultural Evolution, Rapid Social Change, and the Forces of Globalization, Especially for Young Women

In many, but not all, rural and preindustrial societies such as non-urban India, adolescence lasted or lasts only a short period, especially for girls (Saraswathi, 1999). Most of their marriages were arranged while they were still young. In the largely patrilineal and patrilocal societies of traditional China and India, girls were considered to be temporary "guests" in their families of origin, were married and traded off to families often living in other villages, and were expected to become pregnant in their teenage years (see Wolf [1972] for a realistic depiction of women's lives in rural Taiwan). Their husbands were frequently older, enjoyed higher status, and possessed more power. Many teenage mothers hoped that some of their children would be boys since that would increase their initially low status in their husband's extended family. In China, many of them were looking forward to becoming grandmothers who, as honored "old dragons," could tell their daughters-in-law what to do. In information societies, however, adolescence for highly educated girls and boys begins early, tends to be prolonged, and is followed by a period of emerging adulthood. Given that gender roles for adolescents and youth have become less distinct and more controversial, this extended period is likely to be especially difficult for those struggling with basic questions of gender identity and sexual orientation.

In traditional agricultural societies, children and adolescents were expected to learn from their elders and from the community that surrounded them. Such societies tended to endorse a collectivistic and tight emphasis on children's and adolescents' obedience, respectfulness, manners, and sense of responsibility (Barry et al., 1959). They supported the construal of an interdependent rather than independent self (Markus & Kitayama, 1991). In contrast, today's rapidly changing information societies are moving toward a greater appreciation of children's and especially adolescents' independence, individuality, self-expression, and self-actualization. Although Western and Westernized Latin American societies emphasize such expectations the most, they have also been emerging among urban middle-class families and youth of various East Asian and South Asian societies. In general, individualism has been on the increase around the world (Santos et al., 2017). While earlier peasant societies emphasized the desirability of having knowledgeable and authoritative parents in full control of their children's behavior, today's parents and grandparents may need to acquire new skills and ideas from their technology-savvy adolescent children. While in the past most youth adopted the lifestyles of their parents and elders, today's youth often choose occupations and lifestyles that differ markedly from those of their parents. They know that they must prepare themselves for a world that will be undergoing constant yet difficult-to-predict change due to new digital, robotic, and 3D technologies.

L. Migration Both Within and Between Countries Is Shaping the Lives of Numerous Children and Youth: As a Part of This Process, Many of Their Families Are Moving From the Countryside to Urban Areas

In varied countries such as Brazil, China, India, Mexico, Morocco, and South Korea, many rural families or at least some of their members migrate internally for economic or educational reasons. Between 1950 and 2019, the percentage of the world's population living in urban areas increased from approximately 30% to over 55%. About one-third of today's urbanites are slum dwellers in the poorer countries (Ritchie & Roser, 2019). Many additional people reside in the semi-urban outskirts of towns and cities. At the same time, child labor is common, for instance, in many urban and rural Latin American areas such as northeast Brazil, where about half of the population lives in poverty. There, urban children work at home, wash cars, shine shoes, and hunt for recyclables under sometimes dangerous circumstances (Kenny, 2007). In sub-Saharan and South Asian countries, more and more families and their children are expected to move to low-income urban areas and slums during the coming decades. In contrast, in the well-to-do countries, slums are uncommon. In those countries, when young internal and transnational migrants are moving to such big cities as London, Berlin, and Sydney, they often consider their new lives to be both challenging and exciting.

However, in some Central American countries featuring high homicide rates, such as San Salvador, Honduras, and Guatemala, urban boys are frequently forced to join violent gangs. At the same time, many poor urban children across the world—although not always in China—are spending more years in primary and secondary schools than they would have been able to had they remained in the countryside. In this context, they may have a better chance of becoming fully literate and numerate, which may secure them a stable job in a competitive environment. Although living conditions in poor slums can be shocking, it should be kept in mind that such conditions may be worse, though less visible, in some otherwise beautiful-looking rural areas. That is often the reason why very poor South Asian and African families are moving from their rural homes to potentially dangerous slums.

In 2019, the worldwide number of international migrants between countries reached 272 million persons or 3.5% of the world population (United Nations, Department of Economic and Social Affairs, Population Division, 2019). In addition to voluntary immigrants, they included 25.9 million refugees and 3.5 million asylum seekers. They mostly lived in northern Africa and western Asia (46% of them) and sub-Saharan Africa (21%). Of the world-wide migrants, 38 million were below the age of 20 years. They accounted for 32% of all migrants in the fertile low-income countries, 18% in middle-income countries, and 11% in high-income countries. Among the often miserable refugees and asylum seekers, however, some 14.7 million or 50% were younger than 18 years (Kaplin, 2019).

International migration exerts a major influence on the identities, patterns of school attendance, and economic prospects of children and adolescents. When young children migrate, they tend to learn the language of their host country in their new schools and from their peers, a process that is likely to shape important aspects of their identities. In contrast, immigrants and temporary workers arriving during their later teenage years are more likely to prefer the language spoken in their country of origin and identify more closely with their parents' culture (Gielen & Palumbo, 2021; Ho & Gielen, 2016). Moreover, major religious and cultural differences between an adolescent's host country and their country of origin can lead to political tensions and undermine the person's identification with their new country and its culture. This proves to be the case, for instance, in France where many Muslim immigrants from Africa are reluctant to identify with the country's nationalistic and secular ideology, although they are expected to do so by many French nationals who falsely claim to be non-racist (Beaman, 2017). On the whole, those immigrants able to develop a bicultural identity are most likely to adapt successfully (Berry et al., 2006). This holds especially true in major immigration countries such as Canada, Australia, and the United States. Moreover, highly educated immigrants such as most East Indian immigrants in Canada and the United States tend to be successful in economic terms and as a group outperform native citizens by substantial margins (Budiman et al., 2019/2022).

Well-educated immigrants and their families tend to end up in cities rather than in villages and small towns. Consequently, sustained migration to high-income countries has led to the formation of major international cities such as New York, London, São Paulo, Toronto, Sidney, Singapore, and Amsterdam. In several of these cities, one can find schools where a majority of the students were born abroad. Attending such schools, quite a few immigrant children feel at ease, form bonds with fellow students from a variety of cultural backgrounds, develop multicultural identities based on their interactions with both their immigrant parents and their peers, and are able to compete in educational terms as soon as they have fully mastered the language of their

104   Handbook of Advances in Culture and Psychology

host country (Chuang & Gielen, 2009; Gielen & Palumbo, 2021). In spite of various tensions, traditional immigration societies such as Canada, Australia, and the United States have in recent decades been more successful at integrating non-Western immigrant children and youth compared to European societies such as France and Germany. In many European countries, political opposition by conservative parties against culturally and religiously different immigrants has intensified in recent years.

M. The Number of Forcibly Displaced and Refugee Children Has Increased in Recent Years

While voluntary migrants tend to move from medium-income countries to high-income countries, most of the world's forcibly and internationally displaced minors live in medium- or low-income countries, such as Turkey, Lebanon, Colombia, Kenya, Pakistan, and Bangladesh. These countries often border on countries experiencing violent conflict, such as Syria, Afghanistan, and South Sudan. Frequently residing in unsafe and crowded camps, the refuge- and asylum-seeking children are often unaccompanied and traumatized and may have insufficient access to food and medicine. Many of them enjoy few legal rights, may or may not be allowed to attend school, face discrimination and indefinite detention, are socially isolated, and face an uncertain and discouraging future (Connor & Krogstad, 2016). For these children, both their past traumatic experiences such as the death of family members as well as their current highly stressful and disappointing "post-migration" experiences undermine their resilience and contribute to their high rates of mental health problems (Miller & Rasmussen, 2014). While in 2017, refugees and asylum seekers in low-income countries made up 41.9% of all international migrants, they constituted a mere 2.7% in the high-income countries (United Nations, Department of Economic and Social Affairs, Population Division, 2019). Most rich nations are very reluctant to accept and integrate more than a limited number of refugees into their respective societies.

About two-thirds of all children who are displaced due to armed conflict or human rights violations are "internally displaced" within their own countries. The first author, for instance, lived in an apartment in Berlin, Germany, during World War II. Prior to reaching his fourth birthday, the apartment was partially destroyed in an Allied bombing raid. Thereupon, the Nazi government sent his mother and her three children to a small town that today is located in Poland. When the Soviet army was close to conquering that town, his mother was seized by a deeply rooted and realistic fear that she might be violently raped by multiple Soviet soldiers. Fortunately, the family was able to escape under dramatic circumstances and ended up as internally displaced persons in a tiny village high up in the Bavarian Alps. There the family shared a room in a peasant's house, while a little bit later his mother began to work as a maid for the American occupation forces. Four years later, after a further move to the ancient island town of Lindau, things began to improve because the family was finally able to live in "normal poverty"—as did quite a few of the other 12–14 million German refugees/internally displaced persons/victims of ethnic cleansing (Douglas, 2012).

As also holds true for many of today's displaced and refugee children, the author's life was at times ruled by chance. It included several near misses in very dangerous situations. While his family and he were quite lucky given the circumstances, today's world remains a brutal place for far too many displaced children. Refugee children traveling alone are especially vulnerable to serious abuse. Moreover, 3.7 million refugee children of various ages are out of school including 76% of those at the secondary school level (UNHCR: The UN Refugee Agency, 2019). Those of us residing in wealthy countries and leading comparatively easy lives need to listen to the voice of our conscience, urge our reluctant politicians to welcome more refugee and asylum-seeking children together with their families, and support international organizations designed to help refugees, asylum seekers, and other forcibly displaced children.

N. Local Forces, Societal Changes, and Globalization Are Jointly Influencing the Lives and Identities of Many Teenagers and Young Adults: Immigrant and Minority Group Adolescents Are Especially Likely to Be Exposed to Competing Cultural Expectations and Pressures, Together With Various Forms of Tribalism and Nationalism

Many modern youths are fascinated with social media and mass media, together with the ubiquitous information and entertainment they find on the web. In addition, their involvement in rapidly changing adolescent subcultures tends to influence their outlook on life. These diverse subcultures often reflect the simultaneous influence of potentially conflicting local, national, and global expectations and prescriptions. Digitalization, the growth of internal and external migration, the increase of intercultural families, and the powerful forces of economic globalization are supporting the emergence of complex, glocal, hybrid, and transnational identities and sub-identities (Rao et al., 2013).

Nevertheless, various opposing forms of tribalism, nationalism, and religious intolerance have existed for a very long time and are not about to disappear from this earth. They are especially likely to emerge in times of economic and political tensions and are strengthened by linguistic, cultural, religious, and ethnic or racial differences between societies. Trying to reinforce their cultural unity and identity, collectivistic and tightly run societies are often opposed to immigration while rejecting the desirability of multicultural and globally anchored forms of identity. While the forces of globalization have been influencing the lives of adolescents in numerous low-, medium-, and high-income countries, many of them are also embracing various forms of nationalism. In mainland China, for instance, many children and teenagers like to visit the new and large-scale Disneyland near Shanghai, yet they are also exposed to an educational system that is attempting to reinforce age-old, patriotic notions about the superiority of Chinese (= Han) culture. In India, the world's largest democracy, global influences are exerting a powerful impact on the lives of English-speaking mainstream teenagers, but many among them are also drawn to Prime Minister Narendra Modi's nationalistic and Hindu-centric vision of India as the newly emerging global power. Others, however, are protesting the legal changes that go hand in hand with Modi's religiously motivated vision. India includes 617 million young persons, 0–24 years old, who are bound to have a worldwide influence in the coming decades (e.g., Kapadia, 2017).

VI. A LOOK INTO THE FUTURE: THE CRC, THE PROMOTION OF CHILD WELFARE, AND THE INTERNATIONALIZATION OF PSYCHOLOGY

While there exist many behavioral, sociocultural, and moral differences between the frequently contentious members of humanity across different countries and cultural boundaries, the world's nations have in recent decades been able to agree on how to improve the lives of numerous children and families around the globe. Originally, in 1946, the UN General Assembly helped found UNICEF. Its mandate is to advocate for the protection of children's rights, help meet their basic needs, and expand their opportunities to reach their full potential. The organization has a worldwide presence and emphasizes the importance of community services to promote the interests of children, especially in the poorer countries. UNICEF also helped to bring into existence the CRC (UNICEF, 1989), which was ratified in 1989 and became active in 1990. It soon became the most widely affirmed human rights treaty in the history of humanity, and today, 192 of the UN's 193 member states have ratified it. The one glaring exception is the United States. And so, in spite of their many economic, political, cultural, and religious differences, the world's nations have actually achieved a fairly broad consensus regarding which children need help the most, how their dignity might be buttressed, and how to support them on their developmental journeys. At the same time, many challenges arise when nations and organizations are trying to implement the broad goals as well as the specific prescriptions contained in this unique document (Gielen & Almanzar, 2020).

Applying to children prior to the age of 18 years or else their country's official age of majority, the CRC outlines a broad range of social, economic, cultural, civil, and political rights. In the past, children were at times treated like property (Lancy, 2015). They had few, if any, rights in most societies, although their families attempted to take care of and love them. The CRC, however, emphasizes that above all children's dignity must be protected (Melton, 2005). To do so, governments need to create a positive environment and a standard of living for all children that can support their physical, social, mental, spiritual, and moral development. Regardless of their gender, religion, race, or ethnicity, children have a right to equal treatment within the context of a protective and caring social environment that assures them of a personal and cultural identity. Thus, the CRC does not embrace the emphasis on pervasive cultural and sociomoral differences that many cultural anthropologists like to emphasize. Instead, it implicitly enjoins governments and child-oriented organizations to apply the golden rule to the lives and welfare of children. It is hoped that they will do so even when age-old but destructive customs, such as sex-selective abortion, infanticide, hazardous and exploitative child labor, premature child marriage, recruiting children to become soldiers, and genital cutting in the case of girls, contradict it.

The extreme, pharaonic custom of genital cutting, for instance, can be traced back to the ancient Egypt of the pharaohs (Ahmed & Gielen, 2017), yet endorsing the CRC implies that this long established practice should be abandoned in northeast Africa as well as anywhere else. When applied to this custom, both the golden rule (Jesus of Nazareth: "Do onto others as you would have them do unto you", see Matthew 7:12), and its cousin, the silver rule (Confucius: "Do not do to others what you would not want done to yourself", as reported in *The Analects*, see Watson, 2007) convey to us that since we would not like to experience genital cutting ourselves and since it does not serve any health-related purposes, it should be abolished. At the same time, the golden and silver rules have been recognized as moral ideals across time and by some representatives of otherwise quite diverse religions and cultural traditions. This holds true even though other followers of the same traditions either ignore or do not fully understand the golden and silver rules. They may not wish to apply the rules to those differing from themselves with respect to gender (e.g., Confucius), religion, race or ethnicity, caste or social class, and so on. They may seek to deny some of the implications of these rules if that should serve their self-interest or the collective interests of their in-group. Pursuing demanding moral ideals comes at a cost, so many people (including ourselves) sometimes pay lip service to them. In such situations our moral consciousness undergoes a process of segmentation.

A. Promoting the Goals of the CRC and Overcoming Crucial Challenges in Children's Lives

Since 2002, UNICEF (2005) has been advocating a plan of action that aligns with the goals of the CRC. The goals pertain to children's health, education, labor, involvement in armed conflict, sexual exploitation, and child trafficking. Following the UN's adoption of 17 updated Sustainable Development Goals (SDGs) for the years 2015–2030 (United Nations, 2015), this redefined plan of action has become intertwined with worldwide efforts to reduce poverty, create a more just world, and improve the lives of children (Gielen & Almanzar, 2020; Save the Children, 2019). Poor countries tend to find it especially difficult to live up to the ambitious goals of the CRC. Therefore, the 2030 Agenda for Sustainable Development emphasizes that "eradicating poverty in all its forms . . . is an indispensable requirement for sustainable development" (United Nations, 2015). This emphasis agrees well with the previously reported high correlation we found between national per capita incomes and high national scores on the End of Childhood Index. At the same time, most of the CRC goals have also been included in the African Charter on the Rights and Welfare of the Child, which has been ratified by 49 of the African Union's 55 member states (African Committee of Experts on the Rights and Welfare of the Child, 2019). Like the CRC, the charter includes goals that are at variance with traditional customs practiced in some of these nations.

Crucial challenges for many children growing up in the world's poorer countries include the following.

1. Their conception and birth were unplanned because family planning was unknown or inaccessible to their mother.

2. Many children have neither their birth nor their name registered, which may result in major problems for them since they officially do not exist and are thus "nobodies." This can be, for instance, a major problem for refugee and displaced children.
3. Their families are living in poverty and have inadequate access to trained healthcare personnel, proper prenatal care, and immunization services.
4. Common childhood diseases such as diarrhea and pneumonia, child mortality, and malnutrition and stunting continue to threaten many children and their lives.
5. Many children and youth are involved in long hours of exhausting and potentially dangerous child labor (Kak & Pati, 2016).
6. Children (mostly girls) are being trafficked for sexual purposes or so that they can be exploited as slave-like laborers. Other girls voluntarily, though reluctantly, engage in sex work to support their families.
7. Quite a few boys are being recruited or forced to become child soldiers. They and many of their hapless peers may end up as victims of armed conflict, especially in the Middle East and parts of Africa, while others become displaced persons inside or refugees outside their countries of birth.
8. A good number of children are part of a child-headed household because their parents died of diseases such as HIV/AIDS, which is especially common in parts of southern Africa.
9. Numerous girls are married off and become pregnant during their middle teenage years, a frequent fate for girls living in poor African and South Asian nations or in conflict-ridden countries such as Yemen (Ali & Minoui, 2010). Many of them have little or no access to contraception that would enable them to space the births of their children.
10. Large numbers of girls undergo one of several forms of genital cutting that are practiced in many African and Middle Eastern and North African countries such as Mali and Sudan.
11. Several hundred million children receive little or no formal education or else are enrolled in corrupt and inadequate educational institutions (Save the Children, 2018a, 2018b; UNICEF, National Working Committee on Children and Women, & National Bureau of Statistics, 2018).

The CRC challenges governments and child-oriented organizations to develop and set into motion effective programs that can reduce the pervasive negative impact that these all-too-common situations have on the welfare of hundreds of millions of children. This includes reducing the overall poverty of societies and families. Since many of the aforementioned threats to children's welfare are quite specific and concrete in nature, even outsiders living in well-to-do countries should be able to grasp their often devastating impact. Other outsiders may wake up when they encounter a dramatic case in their everyday lives or see it vividly depicted in the mass media. To support this process, academics may wish to show their students a concise, prize-winning documentary depicting how four children are trying to survive in one of India's brutal and unsafe slums (The Street Kids of Mumbai, 2010). Several of our middle-class students have told us that they had no idea what life has in store for children such as these. They also began to understand more clearly how privileged their own lives might be.

Several thousand non-governmental and international organizations are represented in various ways at the United Nations. Many of them support the CRC and have engaged in admirable efforts to improve the welfare of families and children around the world. Besides UNICEF, we may in this context mention Save the Children, SOS Children's Village, Oxfam, The Bill and Melinda Gates Foundation, the Bernard van Leer Foundation, The Smile Train, and the International Labor Organization. They all are worthy of receiving contributions. Although psychologists have become active in quite a few of these organizations and at the UN, their overall role and contributions could and should be expanded (Congress et al., 2020).

B. Adding Global Perspectives to Western Psychology

Many western academic psychologists evince limited interest in the lives of children in the poorer countries of the world and could fruitfully introduce more global perspectives into their teaching and research activities (Gielen & Rich, 2017; Nielsen et al., 2017). For instance, how many American developmental textbooks describe and discuss the lives of Bangladeshi (and numerous other) children working 50–60 hours a week on a farm or in a factory or the 18% of India's young women who were married off before the age of 15 (UNICEF, 2017)? How many psychologists have heard about the unique abilities of courageous Tibetan nomadic boys in their mid-teenage years who have learned to defend yaks and sheep against wolves, snow leopards, and bears with the help of simple, self-made slingshots (Gielen & Kim, 2019;

Hermanns, 1959)? And how about 10-year-old girls from Lesotho who take care of their siblings because their parents died of HIV/AIDS, the survival strategies of Brazilian street children in the face of brutal police tactics, or the growing number of children who make a living by collecting garbage and throw-away food in South Asia's and Africa's highly polluted slums (Boo, 2012)? Similarly, many mainstream developmental psychology textbooks fail to inform their readers about the CRC, its worldwide impact on the lives of numerous children, and why and how the world was able to agree on the CRC's basic goals.

Although American psychologists are nowadays paying more attention to contributions from international psychologists and to cultural comparisons than a few decades ago, the overall field remains Western-oriented in its basic outlook (Navarrete-Cortes et al., 2010; Stevens & Gielen, 2007). Above all, it needs to incorporate the perspectives and empirical studies of non-Western psychologists and other social scientists including those from poorer countries (e.g., Bhatia [2018] and Saraswathi et al. [2018] for child development in India; Comunian & Gielen [2000]; Gielen & Rich [2017], and Gielen & Roopnarine [2016] for developmental psychology). For more general suggestions about how to do this, consult Rich, Gielen, & Takooshian (2017); Takooshian, Gielen, Plous, et al. (2016); and Takooshian, Gielen, Rich, and Velayo (2016). Western psychologists could also contribute more to the world's not so successful efforts to slow down population growth in the poorer countries in order to limit environmental destruction, global warming, and the danger of international conflicts. At the same time, it is the rich countries such as Saudi Arabia and the United States that contribute the most to global warming on a per capita basis. More generally, developmental and other psychologists need to remain focused on the big global picture from both a historically informed and a future-oriented point of view, aim to improve the lives of today's 2.3 billion children below the age of 18, and move beyond their preoccupation with children and adults living in their own well-to-do countries (Kristof, 2019). After all, most children and adults needing help do not live there.

VII. CONCLUSION

The main goal of this chapter has been to analyze the changing nature of childhood and youth from a long-term, socioecological, and global perspective. Although today the members of hunting–gathering societies make up less than 0.01% of the world's population and many of their adolescents are struggling to reconcile old traditions with the expectations, temptations, and threats of the modern world, cross-cultural psychologists should not forget that an analysis of their lives does tell us something important about the evolution of human nature. For many social scientists in the non-Western world, however, the difficult struggles of peasant and transitional societies to evolve step by step into economically better-off digital information societies are closer to their hearts. They know that in their low- to medium-income countries, intertwined economic and political problems leave a powerful imprint on the daily lives of numerous children and youth, especially in parts of Asia, Africa, Latin America, Oceania, and the Caribbean. Similar to India, children living in other countries' poor rural areas and slums often lead very harsh lives, whereas the lives of middle-class children tend to be closer to those led by children in Western societies (Kapadia, 2017). In societies such as China and South Korea, however, extreme poverty has largely disappeared, while the lives of many children and adolescents are governed by pressures stemming from the countries' powerful educational systems. The economic demands and time-intensive parenting required by such systems tend to have powerful negative effects on fertility rates and family systems.

Given the pronounced sociocultural variability among the societies of the past and the present, anthropologists such as Margaret Mead (1954) consider(ed) human behavior to be highly malleable and therefore feel tempted to embrace some form of cultural-moral relativism. In this context, they have been skeptical about the general validity of the seemingly ethnocentric, contradictory, and unique value systems of the West. In contrast to such notions, this chapter relies on a socioecological approach in order to understand how societies and their children have evolved in both similar and different ways over time. In addition, the almost universal endorsement of the 1989 CRC is taken to suggest that humanity does share some important moral notions regarding what lives children and youth should ideally lead. Fortunately, various problematic aspects of children's lives in many societies have been on the decline prior to 2020. These include growing up surrounded by extreme poverty, malnourishment and childhood stunting, very high child mortality rates, exploitative and at times dangerous child labor, near enslavement of children and their parents, inferior status for females, child marriage, illiteracy, and lack of formal education. This shows that the world has been becoming a better place for many children, youth, and their families (Pinker, 2017). As societies modernize and develop economically, they are able to offer improved lives to their children even if globalization does not constitute an unmitigated blessing for them. However, far too many other children continue to struggle with difficult circumstances.

Will the world continue to actively support the 17 SDGs that the UN has adopted for 2015–2030? Those goals are compatible with the overall perspective and findings represented in this chapter, yet between 2015 and 2019 the world made only very slow progress toward meeting them (UNICEF, 2019a). Many nations have failed to mainstream the SDGs into national and local government plans. Moreover, recent political trends have been undermining the moral and political dedication to UN goals that the United States had displayed in earlier decades. In addition, the world's population explosion, the intensification of global warming and environmental degradation (Intergovernmental Panel on Climate Change, 2018), the erosion of multilateralism, and various political conflicts leading to a worldwide increase of refugees and displaced families and their suffering children represent powerful threats to the future welfare of children and youth. For instance, by 2019, the number of displaced and frequently traumatized children was approaching 50 million (UNICEF, 2019b). For cross-cultural psychologists, other social scientists, and all of us as simple human beings, the overall message should be clear: The world's children and their families badly need our active engagement. That holds true above all for the world's 706 million destitute children, women, and men (Alkire & Robles, 2017). More of us must embrace an identity as global citizens (Reysen & Katzarska-Miller, 2013) and develop the foresight, determination, and strength needed to build a better future for the children who will inherit this endangered world. This is especially true when the coronavirus crisis threatens to undo much of the progress the world did achieve in the decades prior to 2020. The crisis will also make it more difficult for organizations such as Oxfam to raise money for their idealistic activities in the Global South.

ACKNOWLEDGMENTS

Ghazala Afzal, Elaine Congress, Michele Hirsch, and Daniel Kaplin kindly agreed to read earlier draft manuscripts of this chapter. We are deeply grateful to them for making important suggestions for improvements.

REFERENCES

African Committee of Experts on the Rights and Welfare of the Child. (2019). *African charter on the rights and welfare of the child*. Retrieved December 22, 2019, from acerwc.africa/acrw-full-text/

Ahmed, R. A., & Gielen, U. P. (2017). Women in Egypt. In C. Brown, U. P. Gielen, J. L. Gibbons, & J. L. Kuriansky (Eds.), *Women's evolving lives: Global and psychosocial perspectives* (pp. 91–116). Springer.

Ahmed, R. A., Rohner, R. P., Khaleque, A., & Gielen, U. P. (2016). Interpersonal acceptance and rejection in the Arab world: How do they influence children's development? In U. P. Gielen & J. L. Roopnarine (Eds.), *Childhood and adolescence: Cross-cultural perspectives and applications* (2nd ed., pp. 121–150). Praeger.

Ali, N., & Minoui, D. (2010). *I am Nujood, age 10 and divorced*. Three Rivers Press.

Alkire, S., & Robles, G. (2017). *Global multidimensional poverty index 2017* (OPHI briefing 47). Oxford Poverty & Human Development Initiative.

Angier, N. (2013, November 26). The changing American family. *New York Times*.

Arnett, J. J. (2014). *Emerging adulthood: The winding road from the late teens through the twenties* (2nd ed.). Oxford University Press.

Barry, H., III, Child, I. L., & Bacon, M. K. (1959). Relation of child training to subsistence economy. *American Anthropologist, 61*(1), 51–63.

Beaman, J. (2017). *Citizen outsider: Children of North African immigrants in France*. University of California Press.

Berry, J. W., Phinney, J. S., Sam, D. L., & Vedder, P. (2006). Immigrant youth: Acculturation, identity, and adaptation. *Applied Psychology: An International Review, 55*(3), 303–322.

Bhatia, S. (2018). *Decolonizing psychology: Globalization, social justice, and Indian youth identities*. Oxford University Press.

Bongaarts, J., & O'Neill, B. C. (2018). Global warming policy: Is population left out in the cold? *Science, 361*(6403), 650–652.

Boo, K. (2012). *Behind the beautiful forevers: Life, death, and hope in a Mumbai undercity*. Random House.

Bourdillon, M., & Mulumbwa, G. (Eds.). (2014). *The place of work in African childhoods*. CODESRIA.

Brown, C. M., Gielen, U. P., Gibbons, J. L., & Kuriansly, J. (Eds.). (2017). *Women's evolving lives: Global and psychosocial perspectives*. Springer International Publishing.

Budiman, A., Cilluffo, A., & Ruiz, N. G. (2019–2022). *Key facts about Asian origin groups in the U.S.* Pew Research Center. (Originally consulted in December 2019) https://www.pewresearch.org/fact-tank/2021/04/29/key-facts-about-asian-americans/

Central Intelligence Agency. (2018). *The world factbook*. https://www.cia.gov/the-world-factbook/ (Originally consulted in 2018)

Chagnon, N. A. (2012). *The Yanomamo* (6th ed.). Wadsworth Cengage Learning.

Chang, Y.-J., Lehman, A., Winter, L., & Finkbeiner, M. (2018). The Sustainable Child Development Index (SCDI) for countries. *Sustainability, 10*, Article 1563.

Chen, J., Wang, D., & Zhou, Y. (2016). Education for population control: Migrant children's education under new policies in Beijing. In Y.-K. Cha, J. Gundara, S.-H. Ham, & M. Lee (Eds.), *Multicultural education in global perspectives: Policy and institutionalization* (pp. 153–168). Springer.

China vows freer movement for workers by relaxing "hukou" system. (2019, December 26). Bloomberg News. https://www.bloomberg.com/news/articles/2019-12-26/china-vows-freer-movement-for-workers-by-relaxing-hukou-system

Choi, J. Y. (2019, March 22). Can scolding the young generation for having no baby make a difference? There should be a change at the societal level [In Korean]. *Seoul Shinmun* https://www.seoul.co.kr/news/newsView.php?id=20190322028001

Chuang, S., & Gielen, U. P. (2009). On new shores: Child development, family dynamics, and relationships among immigrant families around the world [Special issue]. *Journal of Family Psychology, 23*(3).

Cole, M. (2005). Cross-cultural and historical perspectives on the developmental consequences of education. *Human Development, 48,* 195–216.

Comunian, A. L., & Gielen, U. (Eds.). (2000). *International perspectives on human development.* Pabst.

Congress, E., Takooshian, H., & Asper, A. (2020). *Behavioral science in the global arena: Addressing timely issues at the United Nations and beyond.* Information Age Publishing.

Connor, P., & Krogstad, J. M. (2016). *Key facts about the world's refugees.* Pew Research Center.

Coppens, A. D., Silva, K. G., Ruvalcaba, O., Alcalá, L., López, A., & Rogoff, B. (2014). Learning by observing and pitching in: Benefits and processes of expanding repertoires. *Human Development, 57,* 150–161.

Daly, A. (2005). Indicators of risk to the wellbeing of Australian indigenous children. *Australian Review of Public Affairs, 6*(1), 39–57.

Daly, M., & Wilson, M. (1988). *Homicide.* Aldine.

Dent, H. (2014). *The demographic cliff: How to survive and prosper during the great deflation of 2014–2019.* Penguin.

Department of Education. (2019). *Admission rate to the next level of education.* National Index System. Retrieved from http://index.go.kr

Dettwyler, K. A. (2014). *Dancing skeletons: Life and death in West Africa* (rev. ed.). Waveland Press.

Doepke, M., & Zilibotti, F. (2019). *Love, money, and parenting: How economics explains the way we raise our children.* Princeton University Press.

Douglas, R. M. (2012). *Orderly and humane: The expulsion of the Germans after the Second World War.* Yale University Press.

Duffin, E. (2019, September 20). *Distribution of the global population 2019, by continent.* Statista. Retrieved September 25, 2019, from https://www.statista.com/statistics/237584/distribution-of- the-world-population-by-continent/

Dyson, J. (2014). *Working childhoods: Youth, agency and the environment in India.* Cambridge University Press.

1800 United States Census. (2018). In *Wikipedia*. Retrieved June 7, 2018, from https://en.wikipedia.org/wiki/1800_United_States_Census

Evans, R., & Skovdal, M. (2015). Defining children's rights to work and care in sub-Saharan Africa: Tensions and challenges in policy and practice. In K. P. Kallio, S. Mills, & T. Skelton (Eds.), *Politics, citizenship and rights* (pp. 3–20). Springer.

Flynn, J. (1999). Searching for justice: The discovery of IQ gains over time. *American Psychologist, 54,* 5–20.

Gakidou, E., Cowling, K., Lozano, R., & Murray, C. J. L. (2010). Increased educational attainment and its effect on child mortality in 175 countries between 1970 and 2009: A systematic analysis. *Lancet, 376,* 959–974.

Gao, Y., Li, L. P., Kim, J. H., Congdon, N., Lau, J., & Griffiths, S. (2010). The impact of parental migration on health status and health behaviours among left behind adolescent school children in China. *BMC Public Health, 10,* Article 56.

Ge, Y., Song, L., Clancy, R. F., & Qin, Y. (2019). Studies on left-behind children in China: Reviewing paradigm shifts [Special issue]. *New Directions for Child and Adolescent Development, 2019*(163), 115–135.

Gelfand, M. (2018). *Rule makers, rule breakers: How tight and loose cultures wire our world.* Scribner.

Gielen, U. P. (2016). The changing lives of 2.2 billion children: Global demographics trends and economic disparities. In U. P. Gielen & J. L. Roopnarine (Eds.), *Childhood and adolescence: Cross-cultural perspectives and applications* (2nd ed., pp. 63–95). Praeger.

Gielen, U. P., & Almanzar, Y. (2020). Child welfare and child well-being around the world. In E. Congress, H. Takooshian, & A. Asper (Eds.), *Behavioral science in the global arena: Addressing timely issues at the United Nations and beyond* (pp. 31–43). Information Age Publishing.

Gielen, U. P., & Kim, S. (2019). *Global changes in children's lives.* Cambridge University Press.

Gielen, U. P., & Palumbo, J. (2021). Growing up between two cultures: Young Chinese Americans in New York City. In S. S. Chuang, R. Moodley, U. P. Gielen, & S. Akram-Pall (Eds.), *Asian families in Canada and the United States: Implications for mental health and well-being* (pp. 65–94). Springer.

Gielen, U. P., & Rich, G. (2017). A global perspective on lifespan psychology. In G. J. Rich, U. P. Gielen, & H. Takooshian (Eds.), *Internationalizing the teaching of psychology* (pp. 315–329). Information Age Publishing.

Gielen, U. P., & Roopnarine, J. (Eds.). (2016). *Childhood and adolescence: Cross-cultural perspectives and applications* (2nd ed.). Praeger.

Gilmore, D. D. (1990). *Manhood in the making.* Yale University Press.

Gurven, M., & Kaplan, H. (2007). Longevity among hunter–gatherers: A cross-cultural examination. *Population and Development Review, 33*(2), 321–365.

Haines, M. R. (1994). *The population of the United States, 1790–1920* [Working paper 0056]. National Bureau of Economic Research.

Hamilton, A. (1981). *Nature and nurture: Aboriginal child-rearing in north central Arnhem Land.* Australian Institute of Aboriginal Studies.

Hannum, E., Hu, L.-C., & Shen, W. (2018). *Short- and long-term outcomes of the left behind in China: Education, well-being, and life opportunities* [Paper commissioned for the 2019 Global Education Monitoring Report, *Migration, displacement and education: Building bridges not walls,* Background paper prepared for the 2019 Global Education Monitoring Report]. UNESCO.

Hermanns, M. (1959). *Die Familie der A mdo-Tibeter* [The family of the A mdo-Tibetans]. Verlag Karl Alber.

Hewlett, B. L., & Hewlett, B. S. (2013). Hunter–gatherer adolescence. In B. L. Hewlett & B. S. Hewlett (Eds.), *Adolescent identity: Evolutionary, cultural, and developmental perspectives* (pp. 73–104). Routledge.

Hewlett, B. S., & Lamb, M. F. (Eds.). (2005). *Hunter–gatherer childhoods: Evolutionary, developmental, and cultural perspectives.* Aldine/Transaction Publishers.

Ho, J., & Gielen, U. P. (2016). Chinese American adolescents and emerging adults in New York City: Striving for a place in the sun. In U. P. Gielen & J. L. Roopnarine (Eds.), *Childhood and adolescence: Cross-cultural perspectives and applications* (2nd ed., pp. 347–376). Praeger.

Hwang, D. E. (2016). *Children from a multicultural family* [In Korean]. https://walkingwithus.tistory.com/277

Hwang, J. W. (2016). The trend of students from multicultural families [In Korean]. *Education Development, 197.* Retrieved from http://kess.kedi.re.kr

Institute for Economics and Peace. (2016). *Australian Youth Development Index: A jurisdictional overview of youth development.* Victoria University.

Intergovernmental Panel on Climate Change. (2018). Global warming of 1.5 Celsius. https://www.ipcc.ch/sr15/

Jamieson, D. (2014). *Reason in a dark age: Why the struggle against climate change failed—And what it means for our future.* Oxford University Press.

Jan, C., Zhou, X., & Stafford, R. S. (2017). Improving the health and well-being of children of migrant workers. *Bulletin of the World Health Organization, 95,* 850–852.

Jankowiak, W. R., & Moore, R. L. (2017). *Family life in China.* Polity Press.

Jung, H. S. (2018, January 16). In spite of spending 100 billion KRW, "the demographic cliff" has been severed [In Korean]. *Kookmin Ilbo.* http://m.kmib.co.kr/view.asp?arcid=0923884992

Kağıtçibaşi, Ç. (2007). *Family, self and human development across cultures: Theory and applications* (2nd rev. ed.). Erlbaum.

Kak, S., & Pati, B. (Eds.). (2016). *Enslaved innocence: Child labour in South Asia.* Primus Books.

Kapadia, S. (2017). *Adolescence in urban India.* Springer.

Kaplin, D. (2019). Framing the issue: An introduction to various types of international migrants, latest figures, and the central role of the United Nations. *Journal of Infant, Child, and Adolescent Psychotherapy, 18*(4), 313–318.

Kenny, M. L. (2007). *Hidden heads of households: Child labor in urban northeast Brazil.* University of Toronto Press.

Kim, A. (2018). Social exclusion of multicultural families in Korea. *Social Sciences, 7*(4), 63. https://doi.org/10.3390/socsci7040063

Kim, S. K., & Kim, L. H. (2012). The need for multicultural education in South Korea. In D. A. Urias (Ed.), *The immigration and education nexus: A focus on the context and consequences of schooling* (pp. 243–253). Sense Publishers.

Konner, M. (2005). Hunter–gatherer infancy and childhood: The !Kung and others. In B. S. Hewlett & M. F. Lamb (Eds.), *Hunter–gatherer childhoods: Evolutionary, developmental, and cultural perspectives* (pp. 19–64). Aldine/Transaction Publishers.

Korea Research Institute for Human Settlements. (1980). *Ad hoc survey on the behavior of residential location in Seoul* [Unpublished report, in Korean].

Kristof, N. D. (2019, September 12). Our children deserve better. *New York Times.*

Kristof, N. D., & WuDunn, S. (2020). *Tightrope: Americans reaching for hope.* Alfred A. Knopf.

Kwon, W.-Y. (2001). Globalization and the sustainability of cities in the Asia Pacific region: The case of Seoul. In F. Lo & P. J. Marcotullio (Eds.), *Globalization and the sustainability of cities in the Asia Pacific region* (pp. 140–166). United Nations University Press.

Kyama, R., & Perez-Pena, R. (2019, May 25). Kenya's high court upholds colonial-era ban on gay sex. *New York Times.*

Kyung Hee Cyber University. (2017). *Counseling for multicultural families: Characteristics and trends of South Korean multicultural families* [Unpublished manuscript, in Korean]. contents2.kocw.or.kr/KOCW/data/edu/document/khcu/kangtaein1205/15.pdf

Lancy, D. F. (2015). *The anthropology of childhood: Cherubs, chattel, changelings* (2nd ed.). Cambridge University Press.

Lee, J.-W., & Lee, H. (2016). Human capital in the long run. *Journal of Development Economics, 122,* 147–169.

Lee, R. B., & Daly, R. H. (Eds.). (1999). *Cambridge encyclopedia of hunters and gatherers.* Cambridge University Press.

Lesthaeghe, R. J. (2011). The "second demographic transition": A conceptual map for the understanding of late modern demographic developments in fertility and family formation. *Historical Social Research, 36*(2), 179–218.

Levene, A. (2007). *Childcare, health and mortality at the London Foundling Hospital, 1741–1800*. Manchester University Press.

LeVine, R. A., LeVine, S., Schnell-Anzola, B., Rowe, M. L., & Dexter, E. (2012). *Literacy and mothering: How women's schooling changes the lives of the world's children*. Oxford University Press.

Li, Y., & Chui, E. (2011). China's policy on rural–urban migrants and urban social harmony. *Asian Social Science*, 7(7), 12–22.

Lie, J. (2014). Introduction: Multiethnic Korea. In J. Lie (Ed.), *Multiethnic Korea? Multiculturalism, migration, and peoplehood diversity in contemporary South Korea* (pp. 1–27). Institute of East Asian Studies, University of California, Berkeley.

Ling, M. (2017a). Precious son, reliable daughter: Redefining son preference and parent–child relations in migrant households in urban China. *The China Quarterly*, *229*, 150–171.

Ling, M. (2017b). Returning to no home: Educational remigration and displacement in rural China. *Anthropological Quarterly*, *90*(3), 715–742.

List of sovereign states and dependencies by total fertility rate. (2020). In *Wikipedia*. Retrieved January 23, 2020, from https://en.wikipedia.org/wiki/List_of_sovereign_states_and_dependencies_by_total_fertility_rate

Lu, S., Lin, Y.-T., Vikse, J. H., & Huang, C.-C. (2016). Well-being of migrant and left-behind children in China: Education, health, parenting, and personal values. *International Journal of Social Welfare*, *25*, 58–68.

Lu, Y. (2012). Education in children left behind in rural China. *Journal of Marriage and Family*, *74*(2), 328–342.

Ma, G., & Wu, Q. (2019). Social capital and educational inequality of migrant children in contemporary China: A multilevel mediation analysis. *Children & Youth Services Review*, *99*, 165–171.

Markus, H. R., & Kitayama, S. (1991). Culture and the self: Implications for cognition, emotion, and motivation. *Psychological Review*, *98*, 224–253.

Mead, M. (1954). Research on primitive children. In L. Carmichael (Ed.), *Manual of child psychology* (2nd ed., pp. 735–780). John Wiley & Sons.

Melton, G. B. (2005). Building human communities respectful of children. The significance of the Convention on the Rights of the Child. *American Psychologist*, *60*, 918–926.

Miller, K. E., & Rasmussen, A. (2014). War experiences, daily stressors and mental health five years on: Elaborations and future directions. *Intervention*, *12*(Suppl 1), 33–42.

Ministry of Gender Equality and Family. (2019). *National study: Investigation of multicultural families in 2018*. http://www.mogef.go.kr/kor/skin/doc.html?fn=95571c9ad0c84d67af608f610afca498.pdf&rs=/rsfiles/202201/

Navarrete-Cortes, J., Fernández-López, J. A., López-Baena, A., Quevedo-Blasco, R., & Buela-Casal, G. (2010). Global psychology: A bibliometric analysis of web of science publications. *Universitas Psychologica*, *9*(2), 553–581.

Nielsen, M., Haun, D., Kärtner, J., & Legare, C. H. (2017). The persistent sampling bias in developmental psychology: A call to action. *Journal of Experimental Child Psychology*, *162*, 31–38.

Noh, K. M. (2019, November 4). South Korea in 2050: An anticipated wave of the disaster in population [In Korean]. *Korean Economy*. https://www.hankyung.com/economy/article/2019110436571

Nolan, P., & Lenski, G. (2014). *Human societies: An introduction to macrosociology*. Oxford University Press.

Ozer, S., Bertelsen, P., Singla, R., & Schwartz, S. J. (2017). "Grab your culture and walk with the global": Ladakhi students' negotiation of cultural identity in the context of globalization-based acculturation. *Journal of Cross-Cultural Psychology*, *48*, 294–318.

Ozer, S., Meca, A., & Schwartz, S. J. (2019). Globalization and identity development among emerging adults from Ladakh. *Cultural Diversity and Ethnic Minority Psychology*, *25*(4), 515–526. http://dx.doi.org/10.1037/cdp0000261

Park, J. K., & Jung, U. J. (2019, October 20). The business of college campuses with foreign students: Those who cannot communicate in Korean [In Korean]. *Korean Economy*. Retrieved from https://www.hankyung.com/society/article/2019102072451

Pietschnig, J., & Voracek, M. (2015). One century of global IQ gains: A formal meta-analysis of the Flynn effect (1909–2010). *Perspectives on Psychological Science*, *10*(3), 282–306.

Pinker, S. (2017). *Enlightenment now: The case for reason, science, humanism, and progress*. Penguin Books.

Rao, M. A., Berry, R., Gonsalves, A., Hastak, Y., Shah, M., & Roeser, R. W. (2013). Globalization and *identity remix* among urban adolescents in India. *Journal of Research on Adolescence*, *23*(1), 9–24.

Reysen, S., & Katzarska-Miller, I. (2013). A model of global citizenship: Antecedents and outcomes. *International Journal of Psychology*, *48*(5), 858–870.

Rich, G., Gielen, U. P., & Takooshian, H. (Eds.). (2017). *Internationalizing the teaching of psychology*. Information Age Publishing.

Ritchie, H., & Roser, M. (2019). *Urbanization*. Retrieved December 15, 2019, from https://ourworldindata.org/urbanization#citation

Rogoff, B. (2014). Learning by observing and pitching in to family and community endeavors. An introduction. *Human Development*, *57*, 69–81.

Rohner, R. P. (2016). Introduction to interpersonal acceptance–rejection theory (IPARTheory) and evidence. *Online Readings in Psychology and Culture*, *6*(1). https://doi.org/10.9707/2307-0919.1055

Roser, M. (2017). *Fertility rate*. Our World in Data. Retrieved May 18, 2018, from https://ourworldindata.org/fertility-rate

Roser, M. (2019). *The short history of global living conditions and why it matters that we know it*. Our World in Data. Retrieved November 6, 2019, from https://ourworldindata.org/a-history-of-global-living-conditions-in-5-charts

Roser, M., & Ortíz-Ospina, E. (2018a). Child mortality share of children, born alive, dying before they are five years old. Retrieved on May 17, 2018, from https://ourworldindata.org/search?q=+Child+Mortality+

Roser, M., & Ortíz-Ospina, E. (2018b). *Literacy*. Our World in Data. Retrieved May 18, 2018, from https://ourworldindata.org/literacy

Roser, M., & Ortíz-Ospina, E. (2019). *Child and infant mortality*. Our World in Data. Retrieved May 17, 2018, from https://ourworldindata.org/child-mortality

Roser, M., Ritchie, H., & Ortíz-Ospina, E. (2019). *World population growth*. Our World in Data. Retrieved October 31, 2019, from https://ourworldindata.org/world-population-growth

Rzehak, L. (2011). *Doing Pashto: Pashtunwali as the ideal of honourable behavior and tribal life among the Pashtuns*. Afghanistan Analysts Network. Retrieved January 6th, 2022 from https://www.afghanistan-analysts.org/wp-content/uploads/downloads/2012/10/20110321LR-Pashtunwali-FINAL.pdf

Santos, H. C., Varnum, M. E. W., & Grossmann, I. (2017). Global increases in individualism. *Association for Psychological Science*, 28(9), 1228–1239.

Saraswathi, T. S. (1999). Adult–child continuity in India: Is adolescence a myth or an emerging reality. In T. S. Saraswathi (Ed.), *Culture, socialization and human development: Theory, research and applications in India* (pp. 213–232). Sage.

Saraswathi, T. S., Menon, S., & Madan, A. (Eds.). (2018). *Childhoods in India: Traditions, trends and transformations*. Routledge.

Save the Children. (2018a). *The many faces of exclusion: End of childhood report 2018*. Retrieved April 28, 2019, from https://reliefweb.int/report/world/many-faces-exclusion-end-childhood-report-2018

Save the Children. (2018b). *Stolen childhoods*. Retrieved May 5, 2018, from https://resourcecentre.savethechildren.net/pdf/endofchildhood_report_2017_english.pdf

Save the Children. (2019). *Changing lives in our lifetime: Global childhood report 2019*. Retrieved November 6, 2019 from https://www.savethechildren.org/content/dam/usa/reports/advocacy/global-childhood-report-2019-pdf.pdf

Schlegel, A., & Barry, H. (1991). *Adolescence: An anthropological inquiry*. Free Press.

Segal, U. A. (2012). The Indian American family. In R. Wright, C. H. Mindel, R. W. Habenstein, & T. V. Tran (Eds.), *Ethnic families in America* (Vol. 5, pp. 288–319). Prentice Education.

Seth, M. J. (2002). *Education fever: Society, politics, and the pursuit of schooling in South Korea*. University of Hawaii Press.

Shen, M., Gao, J., Liang, Z., Wang, Y., Du, Y., & Stallones, L. (2015). Parental migration patterns and risk of depression and anxiety disorder among rural children aged 10–18 years in China: A cross-sectional study. *BMJ Open*, *5*, e007802.

Shen, Y. (2017). "Migrating" or being "left behind": The education dilemma of rural children in mainland China. *Chinese Education & Society*, *50*, 217–244.

Statistics Korea. (2013). *Statistics of the trend for the multicultural population in 2012* [In Korean].

Statistics Korea. (2019a). *Final results of birth statistics in 2018* [In Korean].

Statistics Korea. (2019b). *Statistics of the trend for the multicultural population in 2018* [In Korean].

Statistics Times. (2019). *GDP (PPP) per capita 2017* [International Monetary Fund data]. Retrieved on November 14, 2019, from https://data.worldbank.org/indicator/NY.GDP.PCAP.CD

Stevens, M. J., & Gielen, U. P. (Eds.). (2007). *Toward a global psychology: Theory, research, intervention, and pedagogy*. Erlbaum.

Su, S., Li, X., Lin, D., & Zhu, M. (2017). Future orientation, social support, and psychological adjustment among left-behind children in rural China: A longitudinal study. *Frontiers in Psychology*, *8*, Article 1309. https://doi.org/10.3389/fpsyg.2017.01309

Sui, H., & Song, Y. (2017). Does the left-behind experience affect the exam behavior, drop-out behavior, and intention to colleges of secondary vocational students? Based on longitudinal data from Zhejiang and Shaanxi provinces. *Chinese Education & Society*, *50*, 350–367.

Takooshian, H., Gielen, U. P., Plous, S., Rich, G. J., & Velayo, R. (2016). Internationalizing undergraduate psychology education: Trends, techniques, and technologies. *American Psychologist*, *71*(2), 136–147.

Takooshian, H., Gielen, U. P., Rich, G. J., & Velayo, R. S. (Eds.). (2016). *International psychology* (Oxford Bibliographies in Psychology). Oxford University Press.

The Korea Herald. (2019, November 12). Multicultural children [Editorial]. http://www.koreaherald.com/view.php?ud=20191112000276

The Street Kids of Mumbai [Video]. (2010). YouTube. Retrieved on January 6, 2022, 2019, from https://watchdocumentaries.com/the-street-kids-of-mumbai/

Triandis, H. C. (2009). Ecological determinants of cultural variation. In R. Whyte, C. Chiu, & Y. Hong (Eds.), *Understanding culture: Theory, research and application* (pp. 189–210). Psychology Press.

Tronick, E. Z., Morelli, G. A., & Ivey, P. K. (1992). The Efe forager infant and toddler's pattern of social relationships: Multiple and simultaneous. *Developmental Psychology*, *28*(4), 568–577.

UNESCO. (2018). *Global education monitoring report 2019: Migration, displacement and education—Building bridges not walls*.

UNESCO Institute for Statistics. (2017). *Literacy rates continue to rise from one generation to the next* [Fact sheet 45, FS/2017/LIT/45]. Retrieved June 18, 2018, from uis.unesco.org/sites/default/files/documents/fs45-literacy-rates-continue-rise- generation-to-next-en-2017_0.pdf

UNHCR: The UN Refugee Agency. (2019). *Stepping up: Refugee education in crisis.* Retrieved January 6, 2020, from www.unhcr.org/steppingup

UNICEF. (1989). *Convention on the Rights of the Child.* Retrieved December 18, 2019, from https://www.unicef.org/sites/default/files/2019-04/UN-Convention-Rights-Child-text.pdf

UNICEF. (2005). *State of the world's children 2005.* Retrieved November 6, 2019, from https://www.unicef.org/reports/state-of-worlds-children

UNICEF. (2017). *The state of the world's children 2017: Children in a digital world.* Retrieved November 6, 2019, from https://www.unicef.org/reports/state-worlds-children-2017

UNICEF. (2019a). *Progress for every child in the SDG era. The situation in 2019.* Retrieved January 20, 2020, from https://www.unicef.org/reports/progress-for-every-child-in-the-sdg-era-2019

UNICEF. (2019b). *Child refugees and migrants.* Retrieved May, 25, 2019, from https://www.unicefusa.org/mission/emergencies/child-refugees

UNICEF, National Working Committee on Children and Women, & National Bureau of Statistics. (2018). *Children in China: An atlas of social indicators.* UNICEF China.

UNICEF, World Health Organization, & World Bank Group. (2017). *Levels and trends in child malnutrition.* Retrieved November 2, 2019, from data. https://www.who.int/nutgrowthdb/jme_brochoure2017.pdf

United Nations. (2015). *Transforming our world: The 2030 agenda for sustainable development* (A/RES/70/1). Retrieved November 2, 2019, from https://sustainabledevelopment.un.org/post2015/transformingourworld

United Nations, Department of Economic and Social Affairs, Population Division. (2019). *International Migration 2019: Report* (ST/ESA/SER.A/438).

Wallace-Wells, D. (2019). *The uninhabitable earth: Life after warming.* Tim Duggan Book

Watson, B., translator (2007). *The Analects of Confucius.* Columbia University Press.

Wen, M., & Lin, D. (2012). Child development in rural China: Children left behind by their migrant parents and children of nonmigrant families. *Child Development, 83*(1), 120–136.

Whiting, B. B., & Edwards, C. P. (1988). *Children of different worlds: The formation of social behavior.* Harvard University Press.

Wilkinson, R., & Pickett, K. (2011). *The spirit level: Why greater equality makes societies stronger.* Bloomsbury.

Wolf, M. (1972). *Women and family in rural Taiwan.* Stanford University Press.

World Bank. (2019, December). *The World Bank in China: Overview*. Retrieved from https://www.worldbank.org/en/country/china/overview

Xi, J. (2006). Introduction to Chinese youth. In J. Xi, Y. Sun, & J. J. Xiao (Eds.), *Chinese youth in transition* (pp. 79–105). Ashgate Publishing.

Yang, J. W. (2019, December 31). "My school is going to disappear." A sad graduation ceremony of a rural elementary school [In Korean]. *Yonhap News Agency*. Retrieved from https://www.yna.co.kr/view/AKR20191231089400062

Yang, J., & Duan, C. (2008). A comparative analysis of educational opportunities for migrant, stay and other children in rural China. *Population Research*, *32*(1), 11–20.

Yiu, L. (2016). The dilemma of care: A theory and praxis of citizenship-based care for China's rural migrant youth. *Harvard Educational Review*, *86*(2), 261–309.

Yiu, L., & Yun, L. (2017). China's rural education: Chinese migrant children and left-behind children. *Chinese Education & Society*, *50*, 307–314.

Zhang, J. (2018). Comparative study of life quality between migrant children and local students in small and medium-sized cities in China. *Child and Adolescent Social Work Journal*, *35*, 649–655.

Zhou, C., Sylvia, S., Zhang, L., Luo, R., Yi, H., Liu, C., Shi, Y., Loyalka, P., Chu, J., Medina, A., & Rozelle, S. (2015). China's left-behind children: Impact of parental migration on health, nutrition, and educational outcomes. *Health Affairs*, *34*(11), 1964–1971.

Zhou, Y., & Wang, D. (2016). Understanding the constraints on the supply of public education to the migrant population in China: Evidence from Shanghai. *Journal of Contemporary China*, *25*(100), 563–578.

CHAPTER 3

On the Causes and Consequences of Cross-Cultural Differences

An Economic Perspective

NATHAN NUNN

Abstract

This review summarizes a recent body of research within economics that seeks to explain contemporary cross-societal differences in culture. One line of research traces the effects of determinants in the distant past and studies how they affect the evolution of cultural traits and their transmission across multiple generations. Another line takes a shorter-term and more micro-level perspective to study how events faced by an individual or group affect their culture. Most recently, this line of inquiry has turned to the question of how cultural traits interact with economic factors, in particular how cultural differences can inform the optimal design of economic and social policy and how such policies can, in turn, shape the evolution of cultural traits.

Key Words: culture, value, norm, historical determinant, economics

---

I. INTRODUCTION

It is now widely recognized that there is important and sizeable variation across societies in their traditional practices, cultural traits, values, and beliefs (Henrich et al., 2010b). Although societies exhibit significant within-group differences, there are also important differences across societies (Desmet et al., 2017). Importantly, when studying *culture*, defined as values, beliefs,

---

Nathan Nunn, *On the Causes and Consequences of Cross-Cultural Differences* In: *Handbook of Advances in Culture and Psychology*. Edited by: Michele J. Gelfand, Chi-yue Chiu, and Ying-yi Hong, Oxford University Press.
© Oxford University Press 2022. DOI: 10.1093/oso/9780197631669.003.0003

and knowledge that are transmitted between individuals, it is found that Western societies are not typical (Henrich et al., 2010b). The characteristics of these societies (Western, educated, industrialized, rich, and democratic) are exceptional and tend to be very different from most of the rest of the world.

This review examines recent research within economics that attempts to better understand this cross-cultural variation. In doing this there are two sets of questions that the literature has attempted to make progress on. The first set is related to the issue of the origins of this variation. Where do the differences come from, and can existing variation be explained by systematic historical and evolutionary processes? If the determinants are historical, how far back in time do they go? Do short-run factors also affect culture, and how easy is it to affect these traits? The second set of questions relates to the consequences of cultural variation. What are the effects of these differences? Do they matter for economic well-being, and what do they imply for policy?

This review will consider the progress made on these issues within the field of economics over the past decades. While it is clear that much progress has been made outside of economics and that the field regularly draws inspiration and insights from other fields, the focus here will be on the literature that has had influence in the field. While I do not think that what has been learned is greater or more important in any way than insights gained in other fields, I do think that readers will be less familiar with this line of research, and it is what I know best. I have found that economists and those in other disciplines are often working on the same questions that seek to better understand human behavior and the nature of societies generally. This chapter provides a summary of the research coming out of the economics discipline that attempts to understand the origins of global differences in culture and their consequences today.

II. CONCEPTUAL FRAMEWORK

Before turning to an overview of the empirical research on the determinants of cross-societal differences in cultural traits, particularly those that affect economic behavior, I pause to provide a conceptual and theoretical framework that will help in interpreting the empirical evidence that I review.

The starting point is a recognition of the fact that human beings have cognitive limits. Acquiring and processing information has an opportunity cost. The time and effort could be directed toward other productive activities. In the face of these limits, we have developed heuristics or shortcuts that aid in our decision-making. These are "fast and frugal" (Gigerenzer & Goldstein,

1996; Gigerenzer et al., 1999). It is these shortcuts that I view as comprising an important part of culture.

The (mathematical) theory behind this has been well developed, beginning decades ago with Boyd and Richerson (1985) and Rogers (1988), among others. The theories model a situation where a decision must be made, with some choices being better than others. The environment is variable, so the optimal choice is not easily known with certainty. Individuals can either collect information and figure out the optimal action on their own or rely on the culture/norms/traditions/etc. that have evolved over time. This is done by simply copying the action of a representative (i.e., randomly chosen) person from the previous generation. This effectively models the process of transmission of cultural traits across generations. The theory shows that, under very general conditions, there will always be some proportion of the population that relies on the cultural traditions of the previous generation (e.g., Aoki & Feldman, 1987; Boyd & Richerson, 1985, 2005; Feldman et al., 1996; Rogers, 1988).

The logic of these models provides a foundation for understanding why culture exists, how and why it affects economic decisions, and why it tends to be sticky over time. In the models, a change in the environment and the action that is optimal in that setting will cause the transmitted behavior to change over time, but this does not occur instantaneously. The traits evolve based on their net benefit relative to other traits in the population. Thus, the models predict that, under fairly general conditions, we should observe the existence of types that rely on decision-making heuristics like accumulated culture, norms, or traditions. This is because they allow for quick and easy decision-making heuristics, which are shaped through evolutionary forces over time as they are transmitted from one generation to the next.

There are many real-world examples of functional norms or traditions evolving and being followed despite the population not knowing their benefits. My favorite example is the alkali processing of maize, which is the traditional method of preparing maize in Latin America. During the process, dried maize is boiled in a mixture of water and either limestone or ash, before being mashed into dough, which is then eaten. Although it was unknown at the time, putting limestone or ash in the water before boiling prevents pellagra, a disease resulting from niacin deficiency, which occurs in diets that consist primarily of maize. This is because the alkaline solution that results from the inclusion of limestone or ash increases the body's absorption of niacin (Katz et al., 1974).[1]

The theory highlights an important benefit of culture: It allows individuals to accumulate knowledge either over generations through vertical or oblique transmission or across individuals within the same generation through horizontal transmission. Through such processes, individuals are able to learn by relying on the accumulation of knowledge. Culture provides an effective shortcut to decision-making that is cheap and effective.

A corollary of the theory is that the historical environment, through evolutionary forces, can affect culture today. In particular, historical shocks, even when temporary if they are large enough, can leave their imprint on modern cultural traits. A sizeable literature within the field of economics has sought to test which factors affect cultural evolution. As we will discuss, ample evidence has been put forth that many important historical events—such as Africa's slave trades, preindustrial agriculture, colonial missions, or ancient kingdoms—have detectable effects today. Further, studies also find that long-run historical factors are not all that matters. Events within one's lifetime—such as economic or social conditions within one's childhood or youth—have been shown to also affect culture. Before turning to an examination of this line of research, we pause to discuss the fundamental question of the measurement of cultural traits in the economics literature.

III. GLOBAL VARIATION IN CULTURAL TRAITS

I now turn to a discussion of the patterns of variation in cultural traits globally. An extensive body of research has developed documenting cultural and psychological variation outside of economics (Gelfand et al., 2011; Hofstede, 2001; House et al., 2004; Schwartz & Sagiv, 1995). While this body of work has clearly been extremely influential, my review will focus on progress that has been made within the field of economics, in part because this area of research is likely to be less well known to the reader.

Many strategies have been developed to measure cultural traits. One is to use survey questions. However, there are several potential concerns with this strategy. First, there is typically little at stake when survey respondents answer questions. Second, it is difficult to assess whether the variation in answers is being driven by cultural differences or whether it is driven by differences in the environment that respondents live in. For example, variation in the standard trust question could be due to cultural differences in how trusting groups are, but it could also be due to differences in the institutional or legal environment which affects whether individuals behave in a trustworthy manner or not. More generally, when looking across individuals or societies, a lot of other factors also vary. In the face of this difficulty, experimental methods are often used. Here, artificial situations are constructed, where all individuals face the same external environment, including the same set of players, material payoffs, and available actions. Since everything else is being held constant, one can be more confident that any variation in behavior that is observed is due to differences in culture.

Over the past decades, a greater effort has been made to bring standardized experimental "games"—the common ones being the dictator, ultimatum, public goods, and trust games—to wide societies across the globe. One of the best-known early studies of this type was Joseph Henrich's (2000) study, which implemented the ultimatum game among the Machiguenga, a small-scale horticultural society living in the Peruvian Amazon. In the ultimatum game, a fixed amount of money or resources is divided between two players (Player 1 and Player 2). Player 1 first offers a division of the resource. Player 2 then can accept or reject this offer. If Player 2 accepts the offer, then the players get the division proposed by Player 1, and the game ends. If Player 2 rejects the offer, then both players get zero, and the game ends. The behavior of the Machiguenga was compared to behavior from a population of University of California Los Angeles students, as well as behavior from previous studies, which included populations from Jerusalem, Yugoslavia, Pittsburgh, and Tokyo (Roth et al., 1991); Indonesia (Cameron, 1999); and Tucson (Hoffman et al., 1994). Within this set of groups, the Machiguenga were unique in their behavior. While, in nearly every other population, the modal offer made by Player 1 in the ultimatum game was for Player 2 to have 50% of the total, among the Machiguenga, this offer was only 15%. Interestingly, the only other population to deviate from 50% was the population from Indonesia, whose modal offer to the other player was 40%.

The findings from Henrich (2000) suggested that the Machiguenga were somehow unique or peculiar. In subsequent studies, undertaken by Henrich and coauthors, the same experiments were implemented in a larger set of populations. In Henrich et al. (2001), the ultimatum game was implemented in 15 small-scale societies. As with the case of the Machiguenga, there were many groups with modal offers to the other player that were significantly different from 50%, including the Hadza (Tanzania), Tsimane (Bolivia), Qichua (Ecuador), Torguud (Mongolia), Khazax (Mongolia), Mapuche (Chile), Aug (Papua New Guinea), Gnau (Papua New Guinea), and Ache (Paraguay). In fact, roughly as many populations had model offers significantly lower than 50% as had 50%. This basic finding was replicated in Henrich et al. (2005) and Henrich et al. (2010a), both of which compared variation between new sets of societies. Again, significant deviations from the 50–50 split were common in approximately half of the locations sampled. Thus, the subsequent research showed that the Machiguenga no longer appeared exceptional. In Henrich (2000), the Machiguenga were the only population from a less developed (unindustrialized) society. Once one began to include a more complete range of populations, it became clear that the industrialized western European samples are not typical but appear to be the outliers. This is a point that is made clear by Henrich et al. (2010b).

A number of studies have found that behavior in experimental games does correlate with the same or relative behavior in real life, thus providing support for their use as a tool to measure cross-cultural variation. For example, there are games that measure the extent to which individuals cheat or engage in dishonest behavior by asking individuals to roll a die or dice (in some versions participants flip a coin) and then report what they roll, which determines their payoff. This provides an opportunity for them to gain money by being dishonest. In the experiments, it generally isn't possible for the experimenter to know if an individual lied at any point in time; but with larger groups of individuals, it is possible to detect lying statistically since the distribution of outcomes will differ from what is expected. Several studies have found that cheating behavior in these games correlates strongly with cheating in real life, as measured by misbehavior in school by Swiss students (Cohn & Marechal, 2016), absence from work by government nurses in India (Hanna & Wang, 2017), dilution of milk by small-scale milk sellers in India (Kroell & Rustagi, 2019), or misconduct of inmates in a maximum-security prison in Switzerland (Cohn et al., 2015).

One concern with experiments is that participants know they are in an artificial experiment, and their behavior may be driven by this fact. Of particular concern is that what participants think the experimenter wants them to do influences behavior. This concern has led a number of studies to measure culture using "natural experiment" or "lab-in-the-field" experiments. For example, Miguel and Fisman (2007) used the number of accumulated unpaid parking tickets by diplomats in Manhattan as a measure of a culture of corruption in the diplomat's home country. Along similar lines, Miguel et al. (2011) used the number of accumulated yellow and red card fouls by international European professional soccer players. They interpreted this as a measure of a culture of violence and showed that it correlates with the prevalence of civil war in the country when the player was growing up.

An example of a recent lab-in-the-field experiment is found in the recent study by Cohn et al. (2019) that attempted to obtain credible and comparable measures of civic honesty across the globe. To do this, they dropped 17,000 wallets in 355 cities in 40 countries across the globe. The wallets, one of which is shown in Figure 3.1, were transparent so that all contents could be easily seen. Each wallet contained business cards, a shopping list, money, and a key. The exact amount of money was varied in different versions of the experiment. The authors used the rate at which the wallets were returned as a measure of civic honesty. Country-level averages are reported in Figure 3.1. One perhaps surprising finding from the study, which is also shown, is that, in nearly all settings, honesty was greater when the wallets had money in them.

While experiments remain a credible and convincing way to measure cultural traits, they are costly and logistically difficult to implement. A number of recent studies confirm that surveys provide a reliable alternative when experiments are not feasible. Johnson and Mislin (2011) compared trust game behavior from 23,000 participants in 162 experiments with survey data from standard trust questions across 162 countries. The authors found that self-reported trust correlates very strongly with how much money one sends to Player 2 in the trust game (i.e., how much Player 1 trusts Player 2). Falk et al. (2016) studied 409 participants and assessed the comparability of experimental behavior and survey questions that measure risk aversion, time discounting, trust, altruism, positive reciprocity, and negative reciprocity. They found that behavior in the experiments correlates very highly with survey measures aimed at capturing the same traits.[2] Recent evidence also seems to indicate that an individual's response to survey questions may be more stable over time relative to behavior in experiments (Chuang & Schechter, 2015).

A number of studies have attempted to gain an understanding of the global variation in cultural traits at a very micro level using individual-level survey data. Desmet et al. (2017) studied within– and between–ethnic group variation using measures of cultural traits distilled from the World Values Survey. They found that within countries the variation within ethnic groups is much greater than the average differences between ethnic groups. According to their calculations, less than 2% of the total variation in their cultural measures is explained by average differences between ethnic groups. Interestingly, when the same exercise was performed but for countries rather than ethnic groups, they found that about 12% of the total variation was explained by average cross-country differences, which is a sizeable proportion. In a follow-up study, Desmet and Wacziarg (2019) undertook a similar exercise but looked

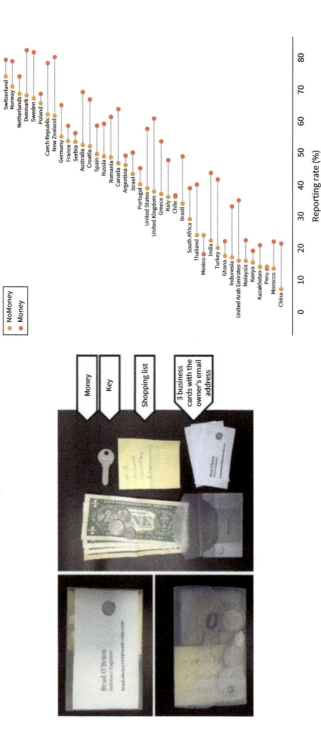

FIGURE 3.1: Wallet used to measure civic honesty around the world (left) and country-level averages in the return rate for wallets without and with money (right).

at different groups within the United States using the General Social Survey. They created 11 different groups based on different attributes, such as gender, religion, race, income, region, and education. They also found that the between-group differences were small when compared to within-group variation. They also examined between-group differences over time and found that, in general, they fell from 1972 until the late 1990s and then rose thereafter (Desmet and Wacziarg, 2019).

The findings, while interesting, are somewhat hard to assess since there is so much idiosyncratic variation (i.e., noise) in the survey measures. As Falk et al. (2016) have shown, even experimental measures of cultural traits can be very different when using the same person but at different points in time. The same is also true for survey questions. Survey questions that measure the same cultural trait are often weakly correlated with one another (Falk et al., 2018). All of this suggests that our measures of traits, whether surveys or experiments, likely contain a significant amount of noise, which, if Gaussian, will tend to increase variation across individuals and not across groups. Thus, it is hard to assess how much of the variation that we see across individuals is due to true differences and how much is due to imprecision in measurement.

The findings from Falk et al. (2018), which are taken from their recent Global Preferences Survey (GPS), contrast those of (Desmet and Wacziarg, 2019). The GPS is an experimentally validated survey module that reports individual-level measures (based on principal components) for patience, risk-taking, positive reciprocity, negative reciprocity, altruism, and trust. Falk et al. (2018) found that their measured traits "vary substantially across countries" (p. 1663). They report that for each trait cross-country differences tend to be statistically significant—that is, about 80% of pairwise comparisons are significant. It is difficult to compare this to the 12% figure from Desmet et al. (2017) because Falk et al. (2018) did not examine variation across ethnic groups. The cross-individual within-group variation documented by economists dovetails nicely with recent research in psychology on the "tightness" of cultural norms—that is, the extent to which norms are well defined and deviation from them isn't tolerated in a society (see Gelfand, 2018). Given that values, beliefs, and norms are not everywhere perfectly "tight," then we would expect some individual-level variation within groups. What hasn't yet been done is the examination of whether the within-group variation measured in these studies lines up with existing measures of cultural tightness, across either countries, time, or states within the United States (Gelfand et al., 2011,

134 Handbook of Advances in Culture and Psychology

Harrington & Gelfand, 2014). One would expect greater within-group variation in cultural traits to be negatively correlated with the tightness of norms.

Although these findings are purely descriptive, they do raise some interesting questions. It appears that country-level factors may have some effect on cultural values. This likely arises due to national laws, institutions, policies, and shared historical factors being important determinants of cultural values. The evidence for such determinants will be described next.

IV. LONGER-RUN DETERMINANTS

Given the variation that we observe in cultural traits globally, the natural next question to ask is what explains these differences. The early research, which used experiments to study cross-cultural variation in cultural traits, took initial steps toward answering this question. For example, Henrich et al. (2001, 2005, 2010a) document that a higher offer in the ultimatum game is associated with the extent to which consumption within the society occurs through market exchange and interactions with non-kin. Henrich et al. (2010a) also show that this behavior is correlated with the presence of world religions that feature a moralizing high God.

Since these first studies, there has been an explosion of research within economics that has taken additional steps to better understand the origins of the differences in cultural traits that we observe in the world today. There are several noteworthy characteristics of this body of research. First, studies tend to involve the construction of new historical data sets often from archival or other primary sources. These data allow researchers to examine deep historical determinants and to study how they affect the subsequent evolution of cultural traits. Examples of these include historical state formation, colonial policies, missionary activities, warfare, subsistence activities, migration, and trade. Second, the studies have been particularly successful at making progress on the issue of causality. As is well known, just because there is a statistical relationship between a historical factor and a cultural trait does not mean that the factor caused the trait. The determinant could have been caused by the cultural trait and not the other way around (i.e., reverse causality). It is also possible that both the trait and the determinant are caused by other factors (i.e., omitted variables bias). The studies in this literature share a common attempt to, as much as is possible, gain confidence in whether the factors being studied are truly causal determinants or not. This is done through several statistical strategies, including the use of natural experiments, instrumental variables, regression discontinuity, difference-in-difference estimates, or randomized control trials.

Table 3.1 provides a brief overview of some of the most prominent studies from the economics literature. The table indicates the citation, with the full reference reported at the end of the chapter, the cultural trait being explained, the long-run determinant being studied, the unit of analysis (e.g., individuals, ethnic groups, countries), the scope of the sample used in the analysis, and the statistical identification strategy employed in the study to obtain casual estimates. A description of the different identification strategies is provided in the table notes.[3]

From the table, it is clear that the literature being summarized is very young. The oldest reported study is from 2007, and the vast majority of studies are from the last decade. The dearth of earlier studies reflects the previous reluctance of the discipline to acknowledge real deviations from a narrow definition of rationality and to study other determinants of behavior like values, beliefs, and morals. It is no coincidence that the recent increase in research seeking to better understand culture, including its historical origins, follows on the heels of the rise of behavioral economics and its movement into the mainstream in the profession.

The literature, especially early on, focused on some of the largest shocks that have occurred historically and their most likely consequences. An early example of such research is a study with Leonard Wantchekon that examined the consequences of the trans-Atlantic and Indian Ocean slave trades (Nunn & Wantchekon, 2011). The trades were responsible for the shipment of over 20 million people from the African continent over nearly five centuries (Nunn, 2008). Many more were either killed or adversely affected in a very significant way by the slave trades. The study built on an earlier study of mine that showed that these slave trades (in addition to the continent's trans-Saharan and Red Sea slave trades) had adverse long-term economic effects (Nunn, 2008). Looking into micro-level historical accounts of the manner that slaves were captured, we found that a large proportion of the slaves were taken by those close to them such as fellow villagers, neighbors, friends, and even family members. An example of such evidence is reported in Table 3.2. The underlying data are from interviews conducted as part of a mid-19th-century study by the German linguist Sigismund Koelle (1854). The statistics in the table are consistent with the many accounts of children being kidnapped and sold into slavery or of friends or family turning on one another and selling each other into slavery due to disagreements or disputes. A well-known description is

TABLE 3.1: **Overview of the Economics Literature on the Long-Term Determinants of Cultural Traits**

Study	Trait Being Explained	Determinant Being Tested	Unit of Observation	Scope of Sample	Statistical Strategy
Alesina & Fuchs-Schundeln (2007)	Preferences for government redistribution	Communism	Individuals	East and West Germany	Natural experiment, OLS
Alesina et al. (2013)	Gender roles and gender attitudes	Plow agriculture	Individuals, ethnicities, countries	Global	OLS, IV
Alesina et al. (2018)	Male–female sex ratio if children	Plow agriculture	Countries	Global	OLS, IV
Alsan & Wanamaker (2018)	Trust of medical system	Tuskegee experiment	Individuals	United States	DD
Andersen et al. (2016)	Work ethic	Catholic Order of Cistercians	Counties	England	OLS
Ang & Fredriksson (2017)	Individualism	Labor-intensive agriculture	Countries, ethnicities	Global	OLS
Ang & Fredriksson (2017)	Strength of family ties	Wheat agriculture	Individuals, districts, countries	United States and global	OLS
Baranov et al. (2018)	Attitudes about gay marriage	19th-century sex ratios	Individuals, counties	Australia	OLS, IV
Bazzi et al. (2018)	Individualism/collectivism	Frontier experience	Counties	United States	OLS, DD, IV
A. Becker (2019)	Female genital cutting	Pastoralism	Individuals, ethnic groups	Africa, global	OLS, IV

S. O. Becker et al. (2016)	Trust of state bureaucracy	Habsburg Empire	Individuals	Eastern Europe	RD
BenYishay et al. (2017)	Matrilineal inheritance	Presence of coral reefs	Islands and ethnic groups	Global	OLS
Blouin (2018)	Interpersonal trust	Colonial production quotas	Individuals	Rwanda	Natural experiment, OLS
Brodeur & Haddad (2019)	Attitudes toward homosexuality	19th-century gold rush	Counties	United States	OLS, DD
Campa & Serafinelli (2019)	Attitudes toward gender equality	Communism	Women, cohorts	Germany, central and eastern Europe	IV, RD, DD
Campante & Yanagizawa-Drott (2016)	Authoritative parenting style	Father's war experience	Individuals	United States	Natural experiment, IV
Cervellati et al. (2019)	Ethnic affiliation, endogamy	Prevalence of malaria	Individuals, ethnic groups	Africa	OLS
Chaudhary et al. (2019)	Cooperation (contribution to a public good)	Colonial rule (direct vs. indirect)	Individuals, villages	Rajasthan, India	Natural experiment
Cornelson (2018)	African American educational attainment	Role models from Cosby Show	Cities and birth cohorts	United States	DD, IV

(continued)

TABLE 3.1: **Continued**

Study	Trait Being Explained	Determinant Being Tested	Unit of Observation	Scope of Sample	Statistical Strategy
Couttenier et al. (2017)	Homicides	Timing of mineral discoveries	Counties	United States	OLS
Dell et al. (2019)	Cooperation	Dai Viet Kingdom	Villages, individuals	Vietnam	RD
Dell & Querubin (2018)	Attitudes toward the United States	Military bombing	Villages, individuals	Vietnam	RD
Enke (2019)	Universal/limited morality	Strength of kinship ties	Individuals, ethnic groups, countries	Global	OLS, IV
Fernandez et al. (2004)	Gender attitudes	Female wartime employment during World War II	Married women	United States	OLS, DD
Fouka & Schlapfer (2020)	Work ethic	Marginal returns to labor of crop mix	Individuals, districts, countries	Europe	OLS
Galor & Ozak (2016)	Patience	Agricultural suitability of traditional crops	Individuals, countries	Global	OLS, DD
Galor & Savitskiy (2018)	Loss aversion	Climatic volatility	Individuals, ethnic groups, countries	Global	OLS
Gershman (2019)	Supernatural beliefs	Trans-Atlantic slave trade	Individuals, ethnic groups, regions	Africa and Latin America	OLS, IV
Giuliano & Nunn (2013)	Support for democracy	Traditional village leadership	Individuals, countries	Global	OLS

Giuliano & Nunn (2019)	Importance of tradition	Similarity of environment across generations	Individuals, ethnic groups, countries	Global	Natural experiment, OLS
Grosjean (2014)	A culture of honor	Scotch-Irish immigration	Counties	United States	OLS
Grosjean & Khattar (2018)	Attitudes about gender equality	18th-century male-biased sex ratios	Counties	Australia	IV
Guiso et al. (2016)	Self-efficacy, civic mindedness	Medieval independent city-states	Individuals, villages	Italy	IV, DD, OLS
Heldring (2021)	Obedience to state	State formation	Individuals	Rwanda	Natural experiment
Karaja & Rubin (2017)	Interpersonal trust	Habsburg vs. Ottoman/Russian state	Individuals, villages	Region of Romania	Natural experiment
Lowes et al. (2017)	Rule following	State formation	Individuals	Province in the Democratic Republic of the Congo	Natural experiment
Lowes & Montero (2017)	Trust in Western medicine	Colonial medical campaigns	Individuals, districts	French colonial Africa	IV, OLS
Lowes & Montero (2019)	Social cohesion	Forced rubber collection	Individuals, villages	Democratic Republic of the Congo	RD, OLS

(*continued*)

TABLE 3.1: **Continued**

Study	Trait Being Explained	Determinant Being Tested	Unit of Observation	Scope of Sample	Statistical Strategy
Michalopoulos (2012)	Ethnic affiliation	Variation in agricultural suitability	Grid cells	Global	OLS
Michalopoulos et al. (2018)	Adherence to Islam	Trade routes, land suitability	Countries or ethnic groups	Global	OLS
Moscona et al. (2017)	In-group and out-group trust	Traditional segmentary lineage organization	Individuals, ethnic groups	Africa	OLS
Nunn (2010)	Belief in Christianity	Colonial mission stations	Individuals, ethnic groups, villages	Africa	OLS
Nunn & Wantchekon (2011)	Trust	Slave trades	Individuals	Sub-Saharan Africa	IV
Okoye (2017)	Trust	18th-century Christian missions	Individuals, ethnic groups	Nigeria	OLS
Olken (2009)	Social cohesion	Introduction of TV and radio	Villages, individuals	Indonesia	OLS
Ramos-Toro (2019)	Prosociality, in-group bias, trust in medicine	Ancestors being kept in a leper colony	Individuals	Colombia	OLS
Rubin (2014)	Religious beliefs (Protestantism)	Early access to printing press	Cities	Europe	OLS

Rustagi (2019)	Conditional cooperation	Medieval democracy	Individuals, municipalities	Switzerland	OLS, IV
Schulz (2017), Schulz et al. (2019)	Kinship ties	Catholic Church's medieval policies	Cities, regions, countries	Europe and global	DD, OLS
Teso (2019)	Gender roles	Slave trades	Individuals, ethnic groups	Sub-Saharan Africa	OLS, IV
Xue (2018)	Gender roles	Cotton weaving	Counties	China	IV

Note: The statistical strategies in the last column of the table include natural experiments, instrumental variables (IVs), regression discontinuity (RD), difference-in-difference estimates (DD), and randomized control trials. Natural experiments are cases where the determinant of interest occurs in locations or to individuals in an idiosyncratic manner that is close to randomly assigned. Instrumental variables are employed when one can find a variable (i.e., instrument) that is correlated with the determinant and only affects the outcome of interest through the determinant. In such cases, the instrument can be used to obtain a consistent causal estimate of the effect of the determinant on the outcome. Regression discontinuity can be employed when the treatment of interest has strict idiosyncratically determined borders delineating the treated group from the untreated group. In such cases, differences in the outcome of interest can be compared at the boundary, and this provides an unbiased causal estimate of the treatment of interest. Difference-in-difference estimates exploit variation in a treatment over time and estimate effects by looking at how the outcome changes for the treatment group relative to the control group after, relative to before, the treatment occurs. Another strategy is for the researcher to manipulate the implementation of a treatment of interest so that the implementation is done randomly (randomized control trial). This allows the researcher to obtain causal estimates by comparing the randomly chosen treatment group to the randomly chosen control group. Lastly, OLS refers to ordinary least squares, which indicates that the study relies on evidence from conditional correlations.

142 Handbook of Advances in Culture and Psychology

TABLE 3.2: **Manner of Enslavement of Koelle's Informants**

Manner of Enslavement	Percentage
Taken in a war	24.3%
Kidnapped or seized	40.3%
Sold/tricked by a relative, friend, etc.	19.4%
Through a judicial process	16.0%

Note. The data are from Sigismund Koelle's Linguistic Inventory. The sample consists of 144 informants interviewed by Koelle for which their means of enslavement is known.

from the Kong Kingdom, where Duarte Lopes, who was there from 1578 to 1583, described the situation as one where "as a result of the necessity, father sold son, and brother, brother so that each person obtained food in any manner they could" (Heywood, 2009, p. 7).

In such an environment, where one had to be constantly on guard against being sold into slavery even with one's friends and family, it is likely that distrust may have been beneficial and, thereby, spread. In other words, the slave trades may have led to a culture of distrust. Our analysis took this hypothesis to the data, by constructing estimates from shipping records combined with a wide range of primary and secondary historical sources that report the ethnicity of over 100,000 individuals who were captured during the Atlantic and Indian Ocean slave trades. We constructed ethnicity-level measures of the intensity of slave capture, which we used as a proxy for the extent to which an ethnic group experienced the slave trade. These are mapped and shown visually in Figure 3.2.

The ethnicity-level slave export data were combined with contemporary data from household surveys that report a respondent's level of trust of those around them—namely their neighbors, family, coethnics, non-coethnics, and local government. We found strong evidence that the more an ethnic group was affected by the slave trades, the more they distrust those others today. Interestingly, the detrimental effects on trust of those close to an individual, such as family members, neighbors, and coethnics, appears to be stronger than the effect on those further from an individual, such as non-coethnics.

In the analysis, we took special care to address the issue of causality. A concern was that groups that were less trusting initially were more likely to participate in the slave trade and that this low level of trust persists until today. If this were the case, then one would observe a relationship between historical

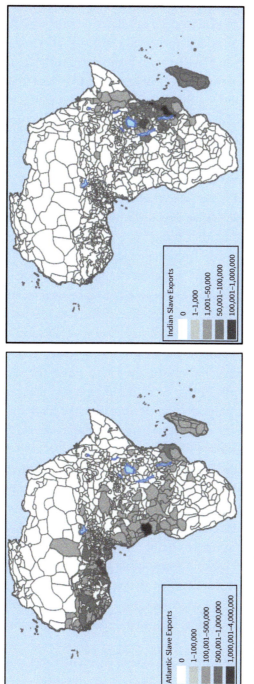

FIGURE 3.2: Map showing the number of slaves taken from a location during the trans-Atlantic and Indian Ocean slave trades.

slave exports and trust today even if the slave trade had no causal effect on trust. To help understand whether the correlation we observed in the data was causal, we used a statistical strategy called *instrumental variables*. The strategy requires the use of a variable (or instrument) that affects slave exports but does not affect contemporary trust (or is correlated with it in any way).

For this, we used the distance of the centroid of an ethnic group's territory from the coast during the period of the slave trades. Since the demand for slaves was external, ethnic groups closer to the coast more intensively experienced the slave trade and tended to export more slaves. We found that the instrumental variable estimates confirmed that the negative relationship between the slave trade and trust is causal.

One concern with the identification strategy is that distance from the coast could potentially have a direct effect on trust today. We checked for this by conducting a falsification test. If one looks within Africa, one observes that ethnic groups farther from the coast have higher levels of trust. This is because those farther inland had a smaller share of the population captured and exported and, therefore, higher levels of subsequent trust. If the distance from the coast matters for trust other than through the slave trade, then if we look outside of Africa, where the slave trades were not present one should also see a relationship. This is the logic of the "falsification test." When we do this, we find no relationship between the distance from the coast and the slave trade. It is only the part of the world that experienced the slave trades where we observe a relationship between distance from the coast and trust.

The last part of the study tested whether cultural evolution is the mechanism behind the estimated relationship between the slave trade and trust. It is possible that the slave trade adversely affected institutional and social structures. Therefore, respondents reported trusting others less not because they are less trusting per se but because others act in a less trustworthy manner because well-functioning institutions that constrain bad behavior are not present. We tested for this alternative mechanism and found evidence that it is also present. We observed worse-quality institutions and an effect of the slave trade on the trustworthiness of others where the slave trade was more intensive. However, when controlling for these factors, the effect of the slave trade on trust remained and was very similar in magnitude and statistical significance.

Several other studies have also examined other historical determinants of contemporary trust levels. S. O. Becker et al. (2016) used a regression-discontinuity identification strategy to examine the effects of the long-term effects of the Ottoman and Habsburg Empires on trust in local institutions. Comparing trust levels of individuals living in eastern Europe near the former Ottoman–Habsburg border, they found that trust in the judicial system (i.e., the police force and courts) was higher in locations that were formerly Habsburg. This appears to be driven by lower levels of corruption in these systems today. To help address concerns of causality, the authors implemented a regression-discontinuity design, where the observations examined were restricted to lie within 200 kilometers of the former border; and observations were only compared if they occurred within the same modern country (either Montenegro, Poland, Romania, Serbia, or Ukraine). The strategy helps to ensure that the observations being compared are as similar as possible. An example within the African context is the study by Okoye (2017), which found that Christian mission stations in Nigeria are associated with lower trust today.

Studies have also examined the determinants of trust in the Western medical system, which is an important contemporary policy issue, in both the developed and developing worlds. There is accumulating evidence that deficient medical policies in the past can have detrimental effects that continue to be felt today. Lowes and Montero (2017) found that colonial medical campaigns in French Equatorial Africa are associated with less trust in Western medicine today, which results in lower vaccination rates and poor performance of foreign health interventions. Ramos-Toro (2019) showed that the descendants of patients forcibly confined to a leper colony that was in operation in Colombia from 1871 to 1950 report less trust in the medical system today. Alsan and Wanamaker (2018) studied the Tuskegee experiments, which were run by the US Public Health Service from 1932 to 1972. The study purposely left infected African American men untreated for syphilis, to learn more about the life cycle of the disease. In return for their participation in the study (comprising medical exams, blood draws, spinal taps, and an autopsy), participants received hot meals and burial payments. The authors found that the experiment and its disclosure in a 1972 magazine article resulted in a decline in trust in the medical system among African American men. In turn, this distrust in the medical system, due to lower rates of utilization of medical facilities, has measurably worsened the health and lowered the life expectancy of this group.

Trust can be viewed as part of a larger set of *prosocial* cultural traits that have been widely studied in the literature. Although there is some imprecision in the definition, such traits typically refer to behavior that may not be individually optimal but that help others and are beneficial for the group or society as a whole. These are commonly measured using a range of experiments, including the dictator game, trust game, ultimatum game, and public goods game. Prosocial behavior has been correlated with a number of factors. A series of early papers showed that the average level of prosociality across societies, measured using behavioral experiments such as the ultimatum game or dictator game, is associated with the level of market development of a society (Henrich et al., 2001, 2005, 2010a). The authors hypothesize that the relationship exists because of the need to have norms of cooperation in exchange. Thus, a more interdependent society increases the benefit to prosocial norms, which in turn leads to a more complex market-oriented production structure.

Other studies have found that institutional development, a factor that we expect to coevolve with market development, also tends to have a positive effect on prosocial cultural traits. Guiso et al. (2008) studied the long-term effects of self-governed medieval city-states, which had more inclusive political systems, in northern Italy and showed that today these locations have higher levels of civic capital, as measured by blood donations, the presence of non-profit organizations, and less cheating in school. Rustagi (2019) looked at medieval self-governed cities in what today is Switzerland and showed that this historical institutional structure is associated with more conditional cooperation today, measured by play in public goods games and survey responses. Tabellini (2010) used data on the extent of democracy across regions of Europe in the 19th century and showed that this is highly predictive of prosocial traits like trust and respect for others, which are measured using survey questions from the World Values Surveys.

While these findings suggest that economic activity leads to greater prosociality, some studies have also found that, surprisingly, conflict can have the same effect (Bauer et al., 2014, 2016). The studies implemented behavioral games that measure prosociality, such as the dictator, ultimatum, and public goods games, and survey questions that measure trust, prosociality, or civic participation. The authors found that all outcomes except for trust were positively correlated with a history of conflict. Also, the effects on prosocial behavior in the experiments were only found when the game was being played with others from the same in-group (e.g., from the same village).

While these studies examined the shorter-run effects of conflict, the same relationships have also been found in the longer run. Employing a regression-discontinuity identification strategy, Lowes and Montero (2019) examined the long-term effects of forced rubber collection in the Congo Free State. They found that the practice, which was violent and deadly, was associated with worse economic and institutional outcomes, such as income, education, infant mortality, access to public goods, and the quality of village chiefs, and that it was also associated with more prosocial cultural traits today such as trust and sharing. The positive effects on prosocial cultural traits contrast with the findings from Nunn and Wantchekon (2011), who showed that another form of violence—slave capture—had long-term detrimental effects on interpersonal trust. It is possible that the differences in the nature of the violence explain the different effects. With civil conflict and with the rubber concessions, the violence was typically perpetrated by those from outside of the community. It is possible that, as in Lowes and Montero (2019), the presence of an external enemy increases social cohesion within the community. By contrast, as Nunn and Wantchekon (2011) document, a sizeable proportion of slaves that were taken during the slave trade were captured by those within the community and very often by friends and even family members. This within-group violence may have had a very different effect and resulted in a deterioration of within-group cohesion. Consistent with this, Nunn and Wantchekon (2011) found larger adverse effects of the slave trade on the distrust of those close to the respondent (e.g., family and neighbors) than on the distrust of those more distant, such as non-coethnics.

Another set of cultural traits that have received significant attention in the literature is those associated with attitudes related to gender. A number of studies have shown how historical factors play an important role in shaping the wide variation in gender attitudes that we see today. In an early study along these lines, I tested a well-established hypothesis that was originally developed by Boserup (1970), about the agricultural origins of contemporary gender attitudes (Alesina et al., 2013). According to her hypothesis, in places with plow agriculture, because of the strength required to use the plow, men tended to work in the fields, while women tended to work in the home only. By contrast, with forms of agriculture that did not use the plow, such as swidden or hoe agriculture, women actively participated in work outside the home. These patterns generated values and beliefs that supported the existing division of labor in society: Plow societies tended to develop norms that women should not work outside the home, while in non-plow societies, such norms did not develop.

The first step we undertook was to look at ethnographic data from the *Ethnographic Atlas* to confirm that societies that used the plow in traditional agriculture did, indeed, have lower rates of female participation in agriculture. We then studied the effects of traditional plow use on gender equality today. This required matching ethnographic information from over 1200 ethnic groups with information on the global distribution of over 7000 languages and dialects spoken around the world today. This provided us information at a fine level of granularity about whether a society's ancestors traditionally engaged in plow agriculture. Looking across countries, districts, and ethnic groups, we found that those with a tradition of plow use have lower rates of female labor force participation, a lower share of female politicians, less female entrepreneurship (measured by firm ownership), and less support for female employment outside the home in the contemporary period. While the analysis incorporated a large set of covariates, for illustration, Figure 3.3 reports the raw cross-country correlations between ancestral plow use and both female labor force participation (left graph) and female firm ownership (right graph). As shown, even in the raw data, one observes a negative and statistically significant relationship.

To gain a better understanding of the causal effect of traditional plow use, we used instruments that affect whether the plow was adopted but are unlikely to directly affect contemporary female labor force participation through other channels. The instruments are based on the suitability of one's ancestral environment for cultivating different crops. Certain crops were particularly suitable for the adoption of the plow, while others were not. The plow requires upfront investment, but it allows a large amount of land to be cultivated during a short period of time. This is particularly beneficial for crops with a short growing season or for those that require a large amount of land to produce a given number of calories. The plow is also less beneficial for crops that can be grown on rocky, sloped, or swampy soils. Motivated by this, we used the average geoclimatic suitability of an

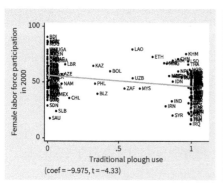 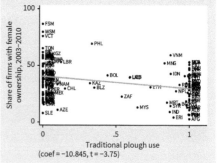

FIGURE 3.3: Graphs showing the relationship between traditional plow use and either female labor force participation (left) or female firm ownership (right).

On the Causes and Consequences of Cross-Cultural Differences **149**

ancestral location for the cultivation of three plow-positive crops (wheat, barley, and rye) and three plow-negative crops (sorghum, pearl millet, and foxtail millet) as instrumental variables. We chose this specific set of crops because they are otherwise quite comparable, each being cereal crops from the Old World. The instrumental variable estimates confirm that the relationship between traditional plow use and gender norms about women's employment today is, in fact, causal.

Other studies have also found that other factors that affected the historical gender division of labor appear to matter for cultural values today. Xue (2018) documented the effect that the 17th-century cotton revolution in China had on gender equality in China. Looking across counties, she found that the prevalence of cotton weaving during the medieval period, which was the primary wage-earning occupation for women at the time, is associated with greater gender equality today, measured using the male–female sex ratio at birth.

Teso (2019) found evidence that the gender imbalance caused by the trans-Atlantic slave trade affected attitudes about gender roles today. The Atlantic slave trade, which was responsible for the enslavement and export of primarily male slaves, resulted in a shortage of men in many parts of the continent. As a result, women were forced into roles that were traditionally held by men, such as employment, political positions, and even warfare. The best-known historical example of this is the female "Amazon" army, which was established by Dahomey at the height of the slave trade in the 17th century and continued until the end of the 19th century. Teso (2019) showed that those parts of Africa that were the most impacted by the trans-Atlantic slave trade have higher rates of female labor force participation today. Interestingly, the same relationship is not found for the Indian Ocean slave trade, which shipped a more equal mix of men and women overseas and therefore did not result in the same shortage of males.

Grosjean and Khattar (2018) studied the consequence of another historical episode of gender imbalance: the early settlement of Australia. During the 18th and 19th centuries, larger numbers of male convicts were sent to Australia, resulting in severely male-biased sex ratios. Looking across Australia, the authors document that in localities with more male-biased sex ratios, women were less likely to participate in the labor force and were less likely to participate in high-ranking occupations. Today, these same places are more likely to have attitudes that reflect less gender equality between men and women. Female labor force participation is lower, particularly in high-ranking occupations. These findings dovetail nicely with those from Teso (2019). Both studies suggest that gender imbalances that induced women into new roles (or prevented them from entering new roles) shaped attitudes and beliefs about the natural role of women in society, which persist and have effects long beyond the temporary episode of the sex imbalance. Because attitudes and beliefs shape the actual roles that women have in society, which in turn shape attitudes and beliefs about what is natural, these effects can be particularly stable and long-lasting. A. Becker (2019) documented a relationship between a historical reliance on pastoralism and cultural practices that control women's sexuality like infibulation. Because pastoralism is associated with prolonged periods of absence of husbands from wives, there is the potential for infidelity. According to her hypothesis and supporting evidence, in response, practices like infibulation developed, which served to control female sexuality by making sex more painful and less pleasurable. She also showed that, more generally, traditionally pastoral societies tend to have more restrictive norms and expectations about women's sexual freedom and to limit women's mobility and freedoms. Campa and Serafinelli (2019) provide compelling evidence that communism, by promoting the employment of women in the workplace, including in many sectors that would otherwise have been male-dominated like heavy manufacturing, created values and beliefs that reflect greater gender equality.

In this section, I have provided a sampling of the type of research studying the historical determinants of contemporary cultural variation. As you can see, this line of research typically combines historical data, often from primary archival sources, with contemporary measures of cultural traits, from surveys or experiments, often implemented by the researchers themselves, to test hypotheses of interest. While challenging given the historical nature of the analysis, the studies used empirical strategies that allow one to identify causal relationships rather than correlations which can be biased due to reverse causality or omitted factors.

V. SHORTER-RUN DETERMINANTS

The findings reviewed in the previous section show that historical factors, even those in the distant past, can have effects that continue to be present today. Another line of research has begun to examine factors that affect culture but ones in the less distant past. This literature is summarized in Table 3.3, which has the same structure as Table 3.1 except that it summarizes the research of studies that estimate the more immediate effects of the factors of

TABLE 3.3: **Overview of the Economics Literature on the Shorter-Term Determinants of Cultural Traits**

Study	Trait Being Explained	Determinant Being Tested	Unit of Observation	Scope of Sample	Statistical Strategy
Alesina & Fuchs-Schundeln (2007)	Changing preferences for government redistribution	Unification of Germany	Individuals	East and West Germany	Natural experiment, OLS
Bau (2019)	Differential child preference	Government pension	Individuals	Indonesia and Ghana	DD
Bauer et al. (2014)	Prosociality and in-group bias	Civil conflict	Individuals	Republic of Georgia and Sierra Leone	OLS
Beaman et al. (2009)	Attitudes about women and politics	Reservation of position for women	Individuals	India	Natural experiment
Bentzen (2019)	Religiosity	Earthquakes	Individuals	Global	Natural experiment, DD
Bergh & Ohrvall (2018)	Trust	Movement to new country	Individuals	Swedish expatriates	Natural experiment, OLS
Booth et al. (2019)	Competitiveness	Growing up under communism	Women	Beijing and Taipei	Natural experiment, DD
Bursztyn et al. (2018)	Attitudes about gender equality	Information provision	Men	Saudi Arabia	Randomized intervention
Campante & Yanagizawa-Drott (2015)	Religiosity and subjective well-being	Ramadan fasting	Individuals	Global	Natural experiment, DD

(continued)

TABLE 3.3: **Continued**

Study	Trait Being Explained	Determinant Being Tested	Unit of Observation	Scope of Sample	Statistical Strategy
Cassar et al. (2013)	Trust	Civil conflict	Individuals	Tajikistan	OLS
Cantoni et al. (2017)	Political beliefs and attitudes	School curricula	Students	China	DD
Clingingsmith et al. (2009)	Attitudes about gender equality	Hajj pilgrimage	Individuals	Global (all visa applicants)	Natural experiment
Della Vigna & Kaplan (2007)	Political preferences (voting)	Access to Fox News	Towns	United States	Natural experiment, DD
Depetris-Chauvin et al. (2020)	National identity vs. coethnic identity	National soccer team victories	Individuals	Africa	RD, natural experiment
Fernandez et al. (2019)	Openness to homosexuality	AIDS epidemic	Individuals	United States	OLS, DD
Fouka (2020)	Cultural assimilation	Language restrictions	Individuals	German immigrants in United States	Natural experiment, DD
Francois et al. (2010)	Trust	Firm competition	Workers, industries	United States	OLS
Francois et al. (2018)	Trust	Banking deregulation, firm competition	Workers, industries	United States, Germany	OLS, DD
Giuliano & Spilimbergo (2014)	Luck vs. effort, preferences for redistribution	Childhood recession	Individuals	United States and 37 countries	DD

Henrich et al. (2019)	Religiosity	War	Individuals	Uganda, Sierra Leone, Tajikistan	OLS
Jakiela & Ozier (2019)	Exposure to election violence	Risk aversion	Individuals	Kenya	Natural experiment, DD, IV
Jensen & Oster (2009)	Gender norms, female empowerment	Cable and satellite television	Villages	India	DD
Kosse et al. (2020)	Altruism, trust, and other-regarding behavior	Mentor program	Children	Germany	RCT
La Ferrara et al. (2012)	Norms about fertility	Television soap operas	Women	Brazil	Natural experiment, DD
Madestam & Yanagizawa-Drott (2011)	Political preferences	Fourth of July festivities	Individuals	United States	Natural experiment, DD
Madestam et al. (2013)	Political preferences	Tea Party protests	Counties	United States	Natural experiment, DD
Mitrunen (2019)	Assimilation and patriotism	Compulsory patriotic acts in schools	Children	United States	Natural experiment, OLS
Qian (2008)	Gender bias (sex imbalance)	Female income	Individuals	China	DD
Rao (2019)	Altruism toward outgroup	School integration policies	Children	Private schools in Delhi, India	Natural experiment, DD

(continued)

TABLE 3.3: **Continued**

Study	Trait Being Explained	Determinant Being Tested	Unit of Observation	Scope of Sample	Statistical Strategy
Riley (2017)	Educational success	Watching inspirational movie	Secondary school students	Schools in Uganda	Randomized intervention

Note. The statistical strategies in the last column of the table include natural experiments, instrumental variables (IVs), regression discontinuity (RD), difference-in-difference estimates (DD), and randomized control trials (RCTs). Natural experiments are cases where the determinant of interest occurs in locations or to individuals in an idiosyncratic manner that is close to randomly assigned. Instrumental variables are employed when one can find a variable (i.e., instrument) that is correlated with the determinant and only affects the outcome of interest through the determinant. In such cases, the instrument can be used to obtain a consistent causal estimate of the effect of the determinant on the outcome. Regression discontinuity can be employed when the treatment of interest has strict idiosyncratically determined borders delineating the treated group from the untreated group. In such cases, differences in the outcome of interest can be compared at the boundary, and this provides an unbiased causal estimate of the treatment of interest. Difference-in-difference estimates exploit variation in a treatment over time and estimate effects by looking at how the outcome changes for the treatment group relative to the control group after, relative to before, the treatment occurs. Another strategy is for the researcher to manipulate the implementation of a treatment of interest so that the implementation is done randomly (RCT). This allows the researcher to obtain causal estimates by comparing the randomly chosen treatment group to the randomly chosen control group. Lastly, OLS refers to ordinary least squares, which indicates that the study relies on evidence from conditional correlations.

interest—namely, effects that are felt within a person's lifetime rather than multiple generations into the future.

An important contribution of this line of research is to help understand the mechanisms behind the findings from the previous studies. While most of the studies of long-run determinants of culture do a good job of identifying convincing causal estimates of the historical factor, they tend to be less strong in identifying the exact mechanisms or paths of the effects being estimated. The empirical literature estimating shorter-run effects provides evidence on mechanisms that are helpful for understanding and interpreting the longer-term effects.

In thinking about mechanisms through which historical events affect outcomes today, one way is to partition them into vertical, horizontal, and oblique transmission. Several studies provide evidence for the importance of horizontal transmission (i.e., cultural transmission between individuals from the same generation). Two recent studies, Madestam and Yanagizawa-Drott (2011) and Madestam et al. (2013), examined the effects of an important avenue for horizontal transmission—socialization activities that involve groups of people. The first paper estimates the causal effects of participating in Fourth of July festivities as a child and adolescent, while the second paper looks at the causal effects of participating in Tea Party protests as an adult. Of course, estimating the effects of these activities is difficult since those who attend the protests likely have different cultural values to start with. In both studies, the authors make progress on this issue by exploiting the fact that the activities all occur outdoors. Thus, they exploit variation in whether it rains on the days of the activities to obtain exogenous variation in the extent to which people participate in them. Attendance at both Tea Party protests and Fourth of July festivities, such as fireworks, barbecues, and parades, is significantly lower (or even canceled) when it rains. Exploiting this source of "exogenous variation," both studies find strong evidence that the socialization activities have important effects. Participation in Tea Party protests is found to move one's political orientation further toward the right. More surprisingly, the same effect is found for Fourth of July festivities. Participating in these activities as a child is associated with more conservative political views (and more conservative voting) as an adult. In addition to the specific findings of the paper, an important takeaway is that socialization activities, like festivals, protests, and holidays, can have important effects.

In a very different setting and using a different empirical strategy to obtain causal effects, Clingingsmith et al. (2009) also found evidence that socialization can affect culture. They estimated the effects of the Hajj—an annual pilgrimage to Mecca made by Muslims—on the values and beliefs of participants. The students exploit the fact that, in Pakistan, participation (namely, travel visas) is limited and allocated randomly by lottery. The authors examine the sample of all applicants comparing those who were randomly selected to those who were not. They found that participation in the Hajj increased religiosity and one's feeling of unity with fellow Muslims, while decreasing perceived differences or inequalities between groups within Islam. It also increased attitudes about gender equality and female empowerment. This is expected since the Pakistani population being studied is much more conservative on this dimension than the modal participant of the Hajj. Thus, attitudes about gender appear to have converged closer to the modal Islamic view after the Hajj. This is likely due to Pakistani participants meeting other Muslims with more liberal gender attitudes than their own.

One of the important findings from Clingingsmith et al. (2009) is that the Hajj can increase group identity and cohesion. Depetris-Chauvin et al. (2020) found that, remarkably, soccer has similar effects. Looking at populations within Africa, they compared people's self-reported attitudes before and after international professional soccer matches in which their national team won and lost. They found that victories increase the extent to which respondents identify with their country and decrease the extent to which they identify with their ethnic group. Thus, this form of shared experience does appear to be important for building a national identity, at least in this particular setting.

Others have studied horizontal transmission that occurs through the media, such as television, and found that this can have sizeable and important effects. Della Vigna and Kaplan (2007) exploited the staggered introduction of Fox News, using a difference-in-differences estimation strategy and found that exposure to the cable news station had large effects on the Republican vote shares in presidential and national Senate elections. According to their best estimates, Fox News was able to change the political views of between 3% and 28% of its viewers (depending on the specification), convincing them to vote Republican. Similarly, large effects from media were also found by La Ferrara et al. (2012), who relied on a similar identification strategy but for Brazilian soap operas (called *novelas*) produced by a company named Rede Globo. They found evidence that the *novelas*, which tend to feature smaller families in their stories, affected norms about desired family size and reduced rates of fertility. Most recently, Cornelson (2018) found evidence that *The Cosby Show*, which was one of the first prime-time sitcoms to feature an educated upper-middle-class African American family, changed attitudes toward education, and actual educational attainment, among African Americans. Since the popularity of *The Cosby Show* is potentially endogenous to pre-existing values, the author used whether a city's NBA basketball team regularly had games at the same time as the show as an instrument. The assumption was that this does not have a direct effect on attitudes but only affects them by reducing the frequency of *Cosby Show* viewing. The study also found that the educational effects of *The Cosby Show* are only found for African Americans and not for those who were White.

Studies have also found evidence for the importance of vertical transmission. Campante and Yanagizawa-Drott (2016) examined the effects of a father's military experience on his son's attitudes. The authors obtained quasi-exogenous variation in the extent to which American fathers served in the military from the fact that one's likelihood of participating in war depends on one's age at the time of the war. They showed that the probability is maximized for those 21 years old at the time of war and decreases as one moves away from this age (either older or younger). They found that there appears to be a form of vertical transmission. They found evidence that a father's wartime service affects the values and beliefs of his sons, making them more likely to also serve during wartime. Another example of a study that shows a similar form of vertical transmission is Fernandez et al. (2004), who examined the intergenerational transmission of attitudes about gender roles. They exploited variation in female employment arising from World War II and showed that if a man's mother was employed while he was growing up, then his wife is also more likely to work. These findings complement those from several studies that examine the behavior of second-generation immigrants to the United States and Europe. Such studies have found that individuals who are born and raised in the United States but with parents born in a different country exhibit behavior that reflects their origin country of their parents. Evidence for vertical transmission has been put forth for a range of cultural traits, including trust (Algan & Cahuc, 2010), gender roles (Fernandez & Fogli, 2009), family living arrangements (Giuliano, 2007), thrift (Costa-Font et al., 2018), and endogamy (Giuliano & Nunn, 2021).

VI. CULTURAL PERSISTENCE AND CHANGE

The empirical evidence reviewed to this point makes clear that cultural traits are malleable and that they evolve in systematic and predictable ways. They are shaped by historical forces and evolve through time. What is less clear is how quickly or how easily a society's culture can change. One of the few studies to touch on these questions directly is Alesina and Fuchs-Schundeln's (2007) study of the speed of cultural convergence following the reunification of East and West Germany. Using survey data, Alesina and Fuchs-Schundeln documented that following reunification, former East Germans remain more supportive of government policies that redistribute income than former West Germans. However, over time, the difference has been declining. According to their estimates, at the current rate, the differences will disappear within 40 years.

Another strategy that has been undertaken to examine the persistence and decay of culture is to compare the culture of immigrants and their off-spring (e.g., Algan & Cahuc, 2010; Fernandez & Fogli, 2009; Giuliano, 2007). Immigration provides a natural experiment where one can examine the extent of cultural persistence and change in a setting that features a significant change in the external environment, including the dominant social norms. Studies have looked at a range of cultural outcomes, including attitudes about gender roles, fertility, living arrangements, endogamy, and trust. They have consistently found that there is a persistence of these values even after multiple generations in the new locations. For example, it is found that individuals who are born and raised in the United States or Europe but have parents and/or grandparents who were born in a foreign country have values and behaviors that resemble those from their ancestral country. Although the continuity of the culture of one's ancestors is by no means perfect (there is decay), it is estimated to be remarkably strong. Algan and Cahuc (2010) studied trust among fourth-generation immigrants to the United States and showed that even for this group, whose parents and grandparents but not great grandparents were born in the United States, the variation in trust closely reflects the level of trust in the origin country of the great grandparents. Thus, even after three generations in the United States, the cultural residue of the origin country remains.

Recent research has turned to the question of whether cultural persistence differs depending on the particular cultural trait being examined. Giavazzi et al. (2019) examined the persistence of a range of different cultural traits among immigrants and their descendants using the US General Social Survey. Their analysis, which studied Mexicans and six different European groups (British, German, Irish, Italian, Polish, and Scandinavian), found that the degree of cultural persistence varies significantly for different cultural traits. Values related to prosociality (e.g., trustworthiness, helpfulness, fairness toward others) tend to be the least persistent. For these traits, the values held by immigrants and their descendants quickly converge to those of the destination location. By contrast, values related to politics, religion, and morality (e.g., the role of government, sexual behavior, abortion) appear to be much more persistent. They also find that attitudes about family and gender (e.g., female employment, women in politics, the obedience of children, divorce) occupy an intermediate position.

In recent research, I have tried to better understand the factors that determine the extent to which a society has cultural traits and cultural traditions that are more fluid and less fixed. In a recent paper with Paola Giuliano, we tested a core prediction that arises from evolutionary models of culture (such as those discussed in Section II): that an environment that is stable (or similar) from one generation to the next results in society placing more importance in upholding the traditions of previous generations, which results in more cultural persistence and less cultural change (Giuliano & Nunn, 2021). In stable settings, the evolved traditions are particularly relevant and beneficial for the current generation. In settings where the environment differs significantly between generations, evolved traditions may have been beneficial in the previous setting but not in the current one.

To test this, we used paleoclimatic data, which are available starting in 500 CE, to create measures of how variable the climate was between generations historically.[4] Such data are available at a 5-degree grid-cell level globally and at a 0.5-degree level for North America. The instability measures that we constructed are shown in Figure 3.4.

We then combined these data with information on the historical location of ethnic groups in the preindustrial period taken from various ethnographic sources. This provides a measure of the cross-generational climatic instability of the ancestors of individuals alive today. We then tested for the importance of tradition and cultural persistence by linking individuals observed today with ancestral groups in the past using language, ethnicity, or location of birth, depending on data availability. The analysis undertook a series of tests which all yielded the same conclusion: Instability of the environment across previous generations is associated with less importance placed on tradition and less cultural persistence today. We looked globally at survey data that report the strength of a person's beliefs about the importance of following a society's pre-existing traditions and customs. The raw bivariate relationship between the average strength of this view in a country and ancestral climatic instability is shown in Figure 3.5a, which is taken from Giuliano and Nunn (2021).

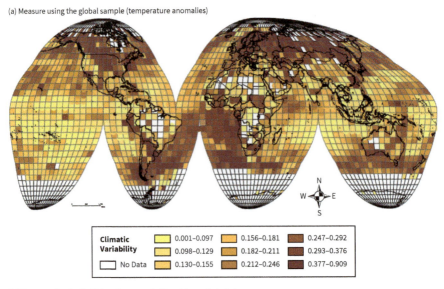

(a) Measure using the global sample (temperature anomalies)

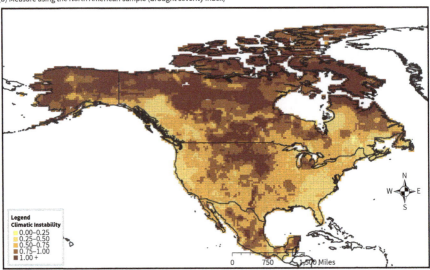

(b) Measure using the North American sample (drought severity index)

FIGURE 3.4: Grid cell–level measures of the instability of the climate across previous generations, 500–1900.

We also used immigrants to the United States as a natural experiment to study the persistence of tradition. We studied the children of immigrants, born and raised in the same locations in the United States but from different cultural backgrounds, and examined the extent to which they continue the traditions of their home country. We find that second-generation immigrants are less likely to marry within their own group or speak their ancestral

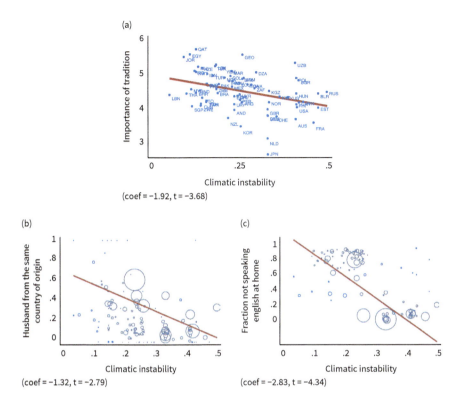

FIGURE 3.5: The bivariate cross-country relationship between average instability of the climate across previous generations and the average self-reported importance of tradition today.
Figures from Giuliano & Nunn (2021).

language at home if they are from a country where the ancestors of the country lived in an environment that was more unstable across generations. The relationships are shown in Figure 5b and c, which report bivariate correlations at the origin-country level. Another strategy that we undertook was to study Indigenous populations living in the United States and Canada and whether they continue to speak their traditional language. We found that Indigenous populations with ancestors who lived in a more variable environment are less likely to know how to speak their traditional language today.

The importance placed on tradition has been studied extensively by economic historian Joel Mokyr (2018) in his book *A Culture of Growth*. In it, he argues that a crucial determinant of the 18th-century Industrial Revolution in western Europe was the new belief that it was acceptable for new generations to question the wisdom of the previous generations (i.e., the "ancients"). This, combined with a resulting cultural belief that it is possible and desirable to understand how the natural world works, led to innovation and knowledge creation, which ultimately created the economic productivity gains of the Industrial Revolution. Mokyr (2018) argues that the presence of this new cultural trait—a weakening of the importance placed on traditional ways of thinking—was present in western Europe but not China, which explains why, despite similar levels of economic development, the Industrial Revolution did not occur in China. He argues that "the heavy hand of the respect for the 'ancients' was felt through much of Chinese history" (p. 298). According to this argument, a weakening of tradition and the resulting cultural change are key determinants of the Industrial Revolution and the world's current economic prosperity.

VII. ECONOMIC CONSEQUENCES OF CULTURAL DIFFERENCES

One line of inquiry that is of particular importance to the cultural economics literature is the economic consequences of cross-cultural differences in the world today. The traditional and mainstream view within economics has been that cultural differences may exist but that they are unlikely to affect anything that economists care about. This was often used as a defense by some to justify the field's traditional neglect of culture. However, a growing body of recent research has sought to test whether cultural differences appear to affect economic outcomes. The answer provided by this line of research is a clear "yes." Cultural factors explain a host of outcomes that are squarely important to economists, like trade, foreign direct investment, innovation, savings, investment, and economic growth. A sampling of the key studies from this body of research is provided in Table 3.4.[5]

One of the first and most widely studied traits is interpersonal trust, which has long been recognized by economists as being a foundation for economic exchange (e.g., Arrow, 1972). Guiso et al. (2009) considered the effect that trust has on exchange in the international context. They were interested in whether the average level of trust of one country toward another affects trade between the two. They measured the trust of one country towards another using measures from the Eurobarometer surveys, which ask about bilateral trust between members of the European Union.

The authors show that these measures of bilateral trust are remarkably strong predictors of the amount of trade between two countries. If a country trusts another country more, then imports from that country are higher. While the authors are not able to pin down the exact channels, an important

TABLE 3.4: **Overview of the Economics Literature on the Consequences of Differences in Cultural Traits**

Study	Outcome Being Affected	Trait Being Examined	Unit of Observation	Scope of Sample	Statistical Strategy
Aghion et al. (2010)	Government regulation	Distrust	Individuals, countries	Global	OLS
Algan & Cahuc (2010)	Economic growth	Generalized trust	Individuals, countries	Global	Natural experiment, IV
Ashraf et al. (2020)	Education	Bride price	Individuals, ethnic groups	Indonesia and Zambia	OLS, DD
Atkin (2016)	Malnutrition	Food preferences	Households	India	Natural experiment, OLS
S. O. Becker & Woesmann (2008)	Female education, gender gap	Religious beliefs (Protestantism)	Counties	Prussia	OLS, IV
S. O. Becker & Woesmann (2009)	Education and economic growth	Religious beliefs (Protestantism)	Counties	Prussia	OLS, IV
Butler et al. (2016)	Income	Generalized trust	Individuals	Global	OLS
Campante & Chor (2017)	Industrial specialization of production	Workplace obedience	Countries and industries	Global	OLS, DD
Campante & Yanagizawa-Drott (2015)	Happiness, economic output	Religiosity due to fasting	Individuals, countries	Islamic countries	Natural experiment
Corno et al. (2020)	Early marriage and fertility differences due to drought	Bride price or dowry	Women	Sub-Saharan Africa and India	OLS

(continued)

TABLE 3.4: **Continued**

Study	Outcome Being Affected	Trait Being Examined	Unit of Observation	Scope of Sample	Statistical Strategy
Dohmen et al. (2018)	Capital accumulation and economic growth	Patience	Countries	Global	OLS
Enke (2020)	Voting in US presidential elections	Universal vs. group-based morality	Counties	United States	OLS
Enke (2019)	Economic growth	Kinship tightness, universal morality	Ethnic groups, countries	Global	OLS
Enke & Rodriguez-Padilla (2019)	Political preferences	Universal vs. group-based morality	Individuals, countries	United States and Europe	OLS
Figlio et al. (2019)	Educational performance	Long-term orientation	Immigrant students in United States	Global	OLS
Gorodnichenko & Roland (2011, 2017)	Economic growth	Individualism vs. collectivism	Countries	Global	OLS, IV
Gorodnichenko & Roland (2015)	Autocratic vs. democratic national government	Individualism vs. collectivism	Countries	Global	OLS, IV
Gorodnichenko et al. (2018)	Foreign outsourcing vs. foreign direct investment	Cultural difference between countries	Country pairs	Global	OLS, DD
Guiso et al. (2009)	Bilateral trade and foreign direct investment	Trust between countries	Countries	European countries	OLS
Jayachandran & Pande (2017)	Childhood stunting	Son preference	Children	India and Africa	OLS

TABLE 3.4: *Continued*

Study	Outcome Being Affected	Trait Being Examined	Unit of Observation	Scope of Sample	Statistical Strategy
Lowes (2018)	Household cooperation, female and child well-being	Matrilineal kinship	Individuals, ethnic groups	Democratic Republic of the Congo	RD, OLS
Moscona et al. (2019)	Conflict	Segmentary lineage systems	Ethnic groups, grid cells	Africa	OLS, RD
Nunn et al. (2019)	Political turnover	Generalized trust	Countries, US counties	Global and United States	DD
Nguyen (2018)	Innovation	Interpersonal trust	CEOs, workers, companies	United States	OLS

Note. The statistical strategies in the last column of the table include natural experiments, instrumental variables (IVs), regression discontinuity (RD), difference-in-difference estimates (DD), and randomized control trials. Natural experiments are cases where the determinant of interest occurs in locations or to individuals in an idiosyncratic manner that is close to randomly assigned. Instrumental variables are employed when one can find a variable (i.e., instrument) that is correlated with the determinant and only affects the outcome of interest through the determinant. In such cases, the instrument can be used to obtain a consistent causal estimate of the effect of the determinant on the outcome. Regression discontinuity can be employed when the treatment of interest has strict idiosyncratically determined borders delineating the treated group from the untreated group. In such cases, differences in the outcome of interest can be compared at the boundary, and this provides an unbiased causal estimate of the treatment of interest. Difference-in-difference estimates exploit variation in a treatment over time and estimate effects by looking at how the outcome changes for the treatment group relative to the control group after, relative to before, the treatment occurs. Another strategy is for the researcher to manipulate the implementation of a treatment of interest so that the implementation is done randomly (randomized control trial). This allows the researcher to obtain causal estimates by comparing the randomly chosen treatment group to the randomly chosen control group. Lastly, OLS refers to ordinary least squares, which indicates that the study relies on evidence from conditional correlations. CEO = chief executive officer.

channel may be that importing requires trust that the reported quality and longevity of the product are what the exporter promises. Since a product's quality may not be revealed for many years into the future, some amount of trust is required at the time of purchase. Consistent with this, they found that trust matters more for products that are more complex and sophisticated, such as consumer electronics, and less for standardized products and commodities, like potatoes or steel, for which the quality and other attributes are more easily verifiable. They also found a similar relationship for foreign direct investment. If a country's level of trust of another country is higher, then foreign investment into that country is also higher. This likely reflects the fact that investing in a country requires not only trust in the local business environment or government but also trust that people will not take advantage of you once your investments in the location have been made. Overall, the findings of Guiso et al. (2009) provide clear evidence that, at least internationally, trust does facilitate economic activity.

Given that trust affects economic exchange, the natural next question is whether it affects overall economic development. This question was tackled by Algan and Cahuc (2010), who found that, indeed, countries with greater trust also have higher levels of economic development. This is consistent with expectations since a sufficient amount of trust is needed to conduct business, especially in the modern economy. A concern with such a relationship is that the causality could be reversed. It might be easier for those in rich countries to trust each other than those in poor countries. The study addressed this by measuring the trust of those from different backgrounds but in the same external environment. In this way, one can be more confident that the measure of trust truly captures the cultural component and not the part of the variable that is affected by external factors like wealth, laws, or institutions. They did this by looking at individuals born and raised in the United States but with parents (or grandparents) who were born in a foreign country. Conditioning on a host of observable characteristics, this can then be used to provide a measure of the inherent culture of trust of individuals from a particular country that is purged of the direct effects that the country's characteristics have on the measure. Undertaking this procedure, the authors find that trust does indeed have a sizeable and significant effect on economic performance. Countries with a higher level of generalized trust are richer.

While the research of Algan and Cahuc (2010) focuses on the relationship between trust and economic well-being at the country level, a related and interesting question is whether the relationship is similar at the individual level as well. One difference is that across individuals one can imagine that if someone is too trusting, then they may be too gullible and cheated. In other words, one might have too much trust. This suggests that the optimal level of trust might take on an intermediate value. Too much trust is not good, and too little trust is not good. A study by Butler et al. (2016) examined individual-level data from the World Values Surveys and showed that, consistent with this, the relationship between trust and income is non-monotonic and hump-shaped. Trust that is too low is associated with low income, but trust that is too high is also associated with low income. Thus, at the group level (e.g., countries) income appears to be monotonically increasing with the level of trust. However, at the individual level, at low and moderate levels of income, more trust is associated with higher income. However, for those at higher levels of income, greater trust is associated with lower income. This difference is interesting and suggests that the highest levels of trust may not be individually beneficial, although they are beneficial for the group as a whole.

Nguyen (2018) also looked at the effects of trust at the individual level but in a very specific context: the trust of chief executive officers (CEOs) in the largest public firms in the United States. She was interested in how variation in the trust of CEOs, arising from differences in ancestry, affects innovative activity within the firm. She hypothesized that when a CEO has higher levels of trust in its research and development staff, they will be more willing to take risks, which results in more innovation. Her analysis, which studied 5743 CEOs, 3598 firms, and over 700,000 patents, looked within firms that had changes in CEOs to identify the effect of CEO trust on innovative activity. She measured CEOs' trust by using their surname to impute ancestry for which we have measures of average trust. She found that the generalized trust of CEOs is positively correlated with innovative activity. A 1–standard deviation increase in CEO generalized trust was associated with 6% more patents in the firm annually. The study then pushed the analysis further by studying whether bilateral measures of trust (i.e., the trust of one group toward another), which are available from Guiso et al. (2009), predict inventor performance. That is, if the ancestry of the CEO has a high level of trust in inventors of a certain background, do those inventors perform better. She found that even when looking at these bilateral measures of trust, higher trust was associated with more innovation. Another cultural trait that has been examined in the economic literature is the distinction between collectivism and individualism (Nisbett, 2003). In a series of papers, Gerard Roland and Yuriy Gorodnichenko documented that more individualistic countries, measured using data from Hofstede (2001), have more innovation and higher levels of income today (Gorodnichenko & Roland, 2011, 2017). They argued that this is because those from individualistic societies tend to place more importance on individual achievement and individual status, which results in higher rates of technological innovation, which fuels economic growth.

While it is true that today countries that are more individualistic are richer, this has not always been the case. Enke (2019) showed that countries that are more individualistic, which he measured using weakness of kinship ties, were not significantly wealthier until after 1700. At the time of the Industrial Revolution, societies that were more individualistic began to experience faster economic growth. The fact that this occurs during the Industrial Revolution is consistent with Roland and Gorodnichenko's evidence showing that innovation is an important mechanism.

While all of the studies examined so far have focused on the economic consequences of cultural traits, recent studies have turned to the question of whether such traits also matter for politics. For example, in a recent study with Nancy Qian and Jaya Wen, we studied the political consequences of differences in generalized trust (Nunn et al., 2019). Looking at the experience of countries in the post–World War II period, we found that generalized trust is an important moderating cultural trait that determines the extent to which national leaders are voted out of office when an economic recession occurs. The statistical analysis examined the determinants of leader turnover using annual data and in a (difference-in-differences) specification that includes country fixed effects and year fixed effects. The key determinant of interest was an interaction between the average level of generalized trust in a country and whether the country experienced an economic recession in the previous year. While recessions lead to a higher probability that leader turnover will occur, this effect is lower if a country has a higher level of trust. We interpret the finding as being due to a society's greater proclivity to believe politicians when they argue that the economic situation is despite their best efforts rather than due to their mistakes. We find these effects are present in countries that have established and regular elections but not in those that do not; this is consistent with politicians being more accountable and more influenced by public opinion in democratic systems than in autocratic regimes. To gain a deeper understanding of the validity of this finding, we also checked for the same effect within the United States for presidential elections. The findings here are the same: Counties with a higher level of trust are more likely to vote for the incumbent party in the face of a recession.

Another example is Gorodnichenko and Roland (2015), who documented that more individualistic countries are more likely to have been democratic between 1980 and 2010. The authors developed a model that shows how such a relationship can emerge if one assumes that collectivist societies are more prone to conformity and have a greater aversion to institutional change. Consistent with this, recent studies find that societies with a greater prevalence of cousin marriage today, which is strongly associated with collectivism (Schulz et al., 2019), tend to have less democratic governance structures (Schulz, 2017) and more corruption (Akbari et al., 2019).

A trait that has been shown to be closely related to the individualism/collectivism distinction is how universal one's morality is (Enke, 2019). In some societies, morality (e.g., altruism, loyalty, allegiance) is only extended to a limited group (e.g., the lineage, clan, or village). Here, it is viewed as normal and correct to treat in-group and out-group members differently. In these societies, which tend to be classified as collectivist, morality is group-specific or limited. In other societies, the belief is closer to the view that all individuals should be treated the same regardless of how distant they are from you. Here, morality is more universal. As shown by Enke (2019), these societies tend to be more individualistic, where the rights of individuals are placed before the rights of the group. Thus, collectivist societies tend to have a more limited group-based morality, while individualistic societies tend to have a more universal morality.

Building on the distinction between group-based and universal morality, Enke (2020) studied its importance for political preferences. He studied the 2016 presidential election and showed that the most important determinant of the election (and previous presidential elections) was the extent of morality. He used text analysis to examine campaign speeches and showed that of all candidates since World War II, Donald Trump's speeches exhibited values that were the least universal and the most group-specific. By contrast, Hilary Clinton's speeches exhibited values that were the most universal and the least group-specific relative to all politicians since World War II. Thus, the two were on polar opposite sides of the spectrum. Using survey data, he then quantified the extent to which the average values in a county are universal or not and showed that counties with less universal values were much more likely to vote for Donald Trump than for Hilary Clinton. He then extended his analysis to all presidential candidates since World War II and showed that this pattern holds more generally. Thus, the extent to which an individual's morality is group-based (rather than universal) appears to be an important determinant of voting during past presidential elections.

The last set of studies that I discuss examines the consequences of traditional customs, which can be seen as a consequence of sets of norms that arise from underlying cultural values, beliefs, and morals. The economic consequences of traditional customs, like kinship practices, marriage customs, food customs, or gender preferences, have recently been examined. For example, in a recent study that I have undertaken with Jacob Moscona and James Robinson, we found that segmentary lineage organization is associated with greater conflict and civil war in sub-Sharan Africa (Moscona et al., 2019). Segmentary lineages are an organizational form, where the economic and political structure of the society is grouped into nested segments and one's position within the lineage dictates one's rights, obligations, and responsibilities. A defining characteristic of segmentary lineage groups is the presence of strong obligations to come to the defense of one's lineage mates in times of conflict. It has been hypothesized that this characteristic results in a great capacity to mobilize fighters for war and therefore generates larger and more frequent conflicts (Evans-Pritchard, 1940; Sahlins, 1961). Our research found that segmentary lineage organization is an important factor explaining the intensity of conflict—including civil wars—within Africa in the modern period.

Other traditional customs have also been studied. Recent studies have found that matrilineal kinship is associated with less household cooperation but more educated and healthier children (Lowes, 2018); male child preference explains much of the prevalence of child stunting in India (Jayachandran & Pande, 2017); food culture explains an important portion of malnutrition among migrants within India (Atkin, 2016); and differences in marriage payments are important determinants of differences in girls' educational attainment and age at marriage (Ashraf et al., 2020; Corno et al., 2020).

VIII. THE INTERPLAY OF CULTURE AND POLICY

With much of the profession now understanding the importance of culture for economic outcomes, research has turned to the natural question of how these insights apply to economic policy. A number of recent studies have attempted to make progress on a better understanding of how accounting for culture can help us design better economic policies.

Lowes and Montero (2017) studied the long-term consequences of medical interventions that occurred during the colonial period in French Equatorial

Africa. The interventions were aimed at eradicating sleeping sickness (try-panosomiasis). The campaigns required villagers, often at gunpoint, to submit to physical exams and tests for sleeping sickness. The only effective test at the time was a spinal tap, an extremely painful procedure. Given this, it was often easier to simply treat whole villages, rather than only those with the disease. The early treatment used was an arsenic-based drug called atoxyl, which, it was later discovered, had the side effect of causing at least partial blindness in approximately 20% of those treated. The parents, grandparents, and great grandparents of those alive today directly experienced the medical interventions, which continued regularly until the end of colonial rule. Stories are told and songs sung of these traumatic historical experiences.

The authors were interested in testing whether these historical experiences and others like them, which occurred throughout the continent, could explain why populations in Africa often refuse or are suspicious of Western medicine. To test the hypothesis, the authors digitized archival documents that reported the frequency with which different locations within French Equatorial Africa were visited by the colonial medical campaigns. With this information, they compared how the historical experience with colonial medical campaigns is associated with the success of contemporary foreign medical interventions. They found that places with more visits in the past have medical interventions that are less successful today. This negative effect was only found for medical projects and is not observed for other types of projects. They also showed that refusal rates for blood tests (for anemia and HIV/AIDS) and vaccines are significantly higher in locations that experienced more colonial medical campaigns historically.

This example illustrates the importance of understanding the historical and current cultural context of a location for contemporary development policy. Once these are known, behavior that might be viewed as irrational and frustrating becomes perfectly understandable. In addition, knowing the origins of this behavior sheds light on potential solutions. The history of these locations suggests that much more needs to be done besides simply showing up and asking individuals to line up for vaccinations or blood tests. Instead, it is likely that significant outreach, communication, and a sensitivity to past experiences with Western medicine are essential.

Another example of how understanding the origins and history behind current cultural differences and how this provides information that is valuable for policy moving forward is provided by the recent study by Alsan and Wanamaker (2018). It documents that much of the elevated mortality that we observe among African American men today has its roots in the Tuskegee study, which after being exposed in 1972, caused a significant increase in distrust of medicine and the medical profession. From a public health perspective, knowing this is potentially important since it allows one to develop policies that tackle the root of the problem, which in this case appears to be distrust. This is exactly what one of the authors, Marcella Alsan, who is also a medical doctor, did in a follow-up study (Alsan et al., 2018). In it, the authors implemented a field experiment in Oakland, California, where 1300 Black men were recruited from local barbershops. The participants were provided vouchers for a free health screening that occurred in mobile medical clinics. Half of the participants were randomly assigned a Black doctor and half a White doctor. The study found that those who were assigned to a Black doctor were more likely to talk about their health problems and more likely to choose to receive additional (free) medical tests and services.

The recent study by Ashraf et al. (2020) provides an example of how an understanding of a society's evolved cultural traits is crucial for policy. Their analysis revisits one of the largest school construction projects in the world, undertaken in Indonesia in 1973. In the 5 years following its launch, more than 60,000 elementary schools were built. Although the school construction project had been shown to increase boys' schooling (Duflo, 2001), on average, it did not affect girls' schooling. Ashraf et al. (2020) showed that this average masks important heterogeneity. Among ethnic groups with the practice of *bride wealth*—a large transfer made at the time of marriage from the husband to the bride's family—school construction increased girls' schooling. However, among ethnic groups without this practice, school construction had no effect. The authors showed that this same pattern is found in Zambia, a country that also had a large-scale school construction project. Having shown that the success of this policy hinges critically on the cultural context, the authors provided an explanation. They showed that the value of the bride wealth received by the bride's parents increases with the daughter's level of education and that this is widely known by local populations. Thus, the marriage custom provides an added monetary incentive for parents to educate their daughters. Groups with this practice are quick to take advantage of the newly constructed schools, while those without it are not. Their findings are significant since they show that the success of important policies can hinge critically on the details of the evolved social customs of the group in question. Thus, understanding the cultural context, and the evolutionary process that generated it, is crucial for understanding the efficacy of economic development policies.

Heller et al. (2017) examined the effectiveness of a series of interventions aimed at improving the outcomes of disadvantaged youth from Chicago. One was a 1-year program (2009–2010) called Becoming a Man (BAM), which was developed by the Chicago nonprofit Youth Guidance. The other was the same program but stretched out over 2 years (2013–2015). The first involved 2740 randomly selected youth and the second 2064 youth. Both versions of the program had significant effects. It reduced total arrests by 28%–35%, arrests for violent crime by 45%–50%, and arrests for other crimes by 37%–43%. One also observes persistent effects on schooling outcomes: Graduation rates increased by 6–9 percentage points. The third program, which had many of the same elements of BAM but was implemented among high-risk juvenile arrestees, was carried out by the Cook County, Illinois, Juvenile Treatment Detention Center.

The authors studied the potential mechanisms that could explain these results. They found that the evidence pointed to one common aspect of the interventions being important. Much of our behavior is driven by automatic impulses—what Daniel Kahneman (2011) calls System 1. This is also true for the youth in the programs, who were from distressed neighborhoods where being aggressive and fighting were often necessary in order to save one's reputation. However, these automatic responses, although generally adaptive to the youths' environment, may not be the best response in many situations, like in school. The programs help students develop the mental tools necessary to switch from an automatic reaction based on System 1 to one that is more thoughtful, taking into account the specifics of the situation, and relies on System 2. The experiments were able to exploit what is known about individual culture and psychology to develop what the authors call "a greater sense of occasion" (Heller et al., 2017, p. 6). This provides an excellent example that illustrates how knowing the cultural roots of behavior helps design policy that can effectively improve the actions and outcomes of those involved.

An important issue when thinking about designing policies in a way that accounts for the specific cultural context of a given setting is whether the policy could have feedback effects and alter the cultural traits. Recent evidence shows that policy can indeed have an effect on culture (Bowles & Polania-Reyes, 2012). A recent study by Bau (2019) directly examined this issue by looking at how the introduction of government pension policies affects the traditional residency practices in Ghana and Indonesia. Examining *matrilocality* (residence with the wife's parents after marriage) in Indonesia and *patrilocality* (residence with the husband's parents) in Ghana, she showed that the introduction of government pension plans (in 1977 in Indonesia and 1972 in Ghana) led to a reduction of residence with parents. Part of the benefit of the cultural tradition is that the children are able to provide old-age support for elderly parents. The introduction of the pension plans reduced this benefit of these traditions. She then showed that the policy and cultural changes also had important effects on educational attainment. She first showed that matrilocality caused parents to educate their daughters more since they would be the ones looking after them in their old age. Similarly, patrilocality caused parents to educate their sons more. As a consequence, the introduction of the pension plans and the resulting weakening of the residence traditions caused a relative decline in the education of daughters and sons in Indonesia and Ghana, respectively. The study thus shows how economic policies can cause cultural change, which in turn affects economic factors.

Another example is the recent study by Gautam Rao (2019), who studied the cultural effects of a 2007 policy change in India that required most elite private schools to offer admission and enrollment to poor students free of charge. The study collected test scores and administrative data for 2362 students from 17 private schools in Delhi, 13 of which were subject to the policy and four of which were not. He implemented experiments among the children to measure the effects of the policy on the generosity and altruism of the wealthy students toward low-income students. These comprised variants of the dictator game, as well as a more elaborate game where students participated in a sports day and chose children of different abilities and wealth backgrounds to be part of their team. The author used this to measure children's willingness to trade off having wealthier but lower-ability teammates with poorer but higher-ability teammates. The study found strong evidence that the policy had real effects. Rich students who were exposed to poorer classmates because of the policy were more willing to interact with poor students, discriminated less against them, and showed more altruism and generosity toward them.

Another line of research has tackled the closely related question of how formal institutions, like governments and the laws they enact, affect the evolution of cultural values.[6] Theoretical work has been done examining the relationship between formal state enforcement of cooperation and the evolution of prosocial values. Tabellini (2008b) shows that the nature of the relationship is ambiguous. Perhaps surprisingly, stronger state institutions can crowd out norms of prosocial behavior. In his model, with more state enforcement, parents optimally choose to devote less effort to instill cooperative values in their children. It is less important for parents to instill cooperative norms because state institutions ensure prosocial behavior. Thus, the behavior of children is similar whether or not prosocial values are taught by the parents. In the model, depending on parameter values, it is possible for state enforcement to also crowd in prosocial values.

The relationship between the presence of state institutions and prosocial values has been studied empirically in a number of papers. Interestingly, the findings, to this point, are mixed. Lowes et al. (2017) studied the effects of a state within central Africa called the Kuba Kingdom on norms of rule-following using behavioral games that allow participants to cheat without being observed. One is only able to observe probabilistically whether large groups of individuals cheat. They found that the state is associated with weaker norms of rule-following. By contrast, Heldring (2021) studied the long-term impact of the precolonial Nyinga Kingdom in Rwanda. He found that a history of living under the state is associated with stronger norms about the importance of being obedient to authority. S. O. Becker et al. (2016) examined the long-term differences between the descendants of the Habsburg Empire and the Ottoman Empire. The former was known for having a particularly well-functioning and effective bureaucracy, while the latter had a more corrupt bureaucracy. Studying individuals in villages on both sides of the historical border but living in the same countries today, the authors found that the Habsburg Empire is associated with more trust and confidence in the courts and police. A subsequent study by Karaja and Rubin (2017) used a similar methodology and found that Habsburg ancestry is associated with higher levels of trust of *outsiders*, defined as people from other villages.

Campa and Serafinelli (2019) also studied the effects of communism on attitudes and norms about female employment. On average, communist countries tended to more actively promote the employment of women outside of the home, even in heavy manufacturing industries. The authors found that those in communist East Germany had more equal attitudes about female participation in the workplace. They found that this appears to be proximately affected by actual female employment and not by communist education or propaganda. They also find this same pattern when looking more broadly across countries in western, eastern, and central Europe, as well as looking at immigrants to the United States from these countries. A benefit of this strategy is that they were able to examine communist and non-communist countries before and after the onset of communism, which provides variation across time and space in communist policies and adds additional credibility to the estimates. Overall, the evidence that communism strongly affected gender norms by altering actual female employment appears extremely convincing.

The finding from Lowes et al. (2017) that institutional or policy pressures move cultural traits in the opposite direction of that which is intended—a kind of backlash effect—has also been found in other settings. For example, Beaman et al. (2009) studied the effects of gender quotas for seats held on Indian village councils. They found that those villagers who have a female village leader due to the quotas exhibit self-reported views that are less favorable about women's participation in politics. Despite this conscious backlash effect, the authors found that individuals' subconscious stereotypes against women participating in politics, as measured by the implicit association test, are improved.

Another example of backlash is Vicky Fouka's (2020) study of the effects of a forced assimilation policy in the United States against Germans following World War I. She found that the policy, which prohibited German from being used in schools, caused Germans to hold on more closely to their culture. As a result of the policy, they became less likely to marry non-Germans, more likely to give their children distinctively German names, and less likely to volunteer for the US Army during World War II. This finding can be contrasted against an (arguably) lighter-touch assimilation policy studied by Mitrunen (2019), where compulsory patriotic acts, such as standardized pledging of allegiance to the flag, were introduced into public schools. In contrast to the findings of Fouka (2020), it was found that this policy caused immigrants, when adults, to marry coethnics less, to give their children less ethnic names, to be more likely to volunteer for military service, and to be more likely to naturalize. These findings suggest that policies with the same intended goals can have very different effects. I view this as an important direction for future research. When do policies crowd in the intended behavior, and when is there a backlash effect where the intended behavior is unintentionally crowded out?

IX. CONCLUSIONS

In this chapter, I have provided an overview of a body of research within economics that seeks to empirically understand the determinants of cross-societal differences in culture. While the issues and questions tackled by this literature—namely, the causes and consequences of differences in cultural traits—are studied in a range of fields, the approach in this literature differs from the general approach taken in other disciplines. The line of research has made particular strides in making use of primary historical data, often from archival sources, and combining this with contemporary data to test theories about the long-term determinants of cultural traits today. This typically involves the linking of very different data sources, through either location or ancestry. There is also a particularly strong emphasis put on identifying causal effects rather than only conditional correlations. When possible, studies attempt to gain traction on causality by exploiting natural experiments or using identification strategies such as instrumental variables, regression discontinuity, or difference-in-differences estimators.[7]

Several conclusions emerge from this literature. The first is that the evidence suggests that cultural traits follow a historical process where relative costs and benefits of traits determine their evolution over time. There is now a vast literature showing that historical factors affect the evolution of traits in expected and logical ways. The second conclusion is that while deeply rooted historical factors shape culture, so do shorter-term factors, such as events that occur within a person's childhood or youth. Given the fluid and evolutionary nature of culture, it is expected that deep historical factors as well as shorter-term factors are both important for shaping cultural traits.

Most recently, research has turned to the question of how a deeper understanding of the nature and origins of the cultural traits of society informs policy. From emerging research, it is clear that these factors are important for policy and can inform their implementation and design. Preliminary evidence also indicates that real-world policies can have sizeable effects on culture and that the nature of these effects is often unexpected and unanticipated by policymakers.

ACKNOWLEDGMENTS

I thank Michele Gelfand, Joseph Henrich, Sara Lowes, Joel Mokyr, and James Robinson for useful discussions, comments, and/or feedback.

NOTES

1. For other examples and additional evidence along these lines, see Henrich (2015).
2. The correlation coefficients are .41 for risk aversion, .59 for time discounting, .67 for trust, .42 for altruism, .58 for positive reciprocity, and .37 for negative reciprocity.
3. The body of research overlaps significantly with a line of research that seeks to understand the long-run effects of historical events and particularly their

importance for contemporary outcomes. For recent reviews of this literature, see Nunn (2009, 2014, 2020) and Spolaore and Wacziarg (2013).

4. Specifically, we calculated the mean of the climate measure for each 20-year generation and then calculated the standard deviation of this across generations.

5. For a review of the early literature documenting the economic consequences of culture, see Guiso et al. (2006).

6. For a recent review of the economic literature about the interplay between culture and institutions, see Tabellini (2008a) and Alesina and Giuliano (2015).

7. A short description of each of these is provided in the notes of Tables 3.1–3.4. Also see Angrist and Pischke (2009) for an excellent introduction to and description of these techniques.

REFERENCES

Aghion, P., Algan, Y., Cahuc, P., & Shleifer, A. (2010). Regulation and distrust. *Quarterly Journal of Economics*, *125*(3), 1015–1049.

Akbari, M., Bahrami-Rad, D., & Kimbrough, E. O. (2019). Kinship, fractionalization and corruption. *Journal of Economic Behavior and Organization*, *166*, 493–528.

Alesina, A., & Fuchs-Schundeln, N. (2007). Good-bye Lenin (or not?): The effect of communism on people's preferences. *American Economic Review*, *94*(4), 1507–1528.

Alesina, A., & Giuliano, P. (2015). Culture and institutions. *Journal of Economic Literature*, *53*(4), 898–944.

Alesina, A., Giuliano, P., & Nunn, N. (2013). On the origins of gender roles: Women and the plough. *Quarterly Journal of Economics*, *128*(2), 469–530.

Alesina, A., Giuliano, P., & Nunn, N. (2018). Traditional agricultural practices and the sex ratio today. *PLoS ONE*, *13*(1), Article e0190510.

Algan, Y., & Cahuc, P. (2010). Inherited trust and growth. *American Economic Review*, *100*(5), 2060–2092.

Alsan, M., Garrick, O., & Graziani, G. (2018). *Does diversity matter for health? Experimental evidence from Oakland* [Working paper]. Stanford University.

Alsan, M., & Wanamaker, M. (2018). Tuskegee and the health of black men. *Quarterly Journal of Economics*, *133*(1), 407–455.

Andersen, T. B., Bentzen, J., Dalgaard, C.-J., & Sharp, P. (2016). Pre-reformation roots of the Protestant ethic. *Economic Journal*, *127*(604), 1756–1793.

Ang, J. B., & Fredriksson, P. G. (2017). Wheat agriculture and family ties. *European Economic Review*, *100*, 236–256.

Angrist, J., & Pischke, J.-S. (2009). *Mostly harmless econometrics*. Princeton University Press.

Aoki, K., & Feldman, M. W. (1987). Toward a theory for the evolution of cultural communication: Coevolution of signal transmission and reception.

Proceedings of the National Academy of Sciences of the United States of America, *84*, 7164–7168.

Arrow, K. (1972). Gifts and exchanges. *Philosophy and Public Affairs*, *1*(4), 343–362.

Ashraf, N., Bau, N., Nunn, N., & Voena, A. (2020). Bride price and female education. *Journal of Political Economy*, *128*(2), 591–641.

Atkin, D. (2016). The caloric costs of culture: Evidence from Indian migrants. *American Economic Review*, *106*(4), 1144–1181.

Bau, N. (2019). *Can policy change culture? Government pension plans and traditional kinship practices* [Working paper]. University of California Los Angeles.

Bauer, M., Blattman, C., Chytilova, J., Henrich, J., Miguel, E., & Mitts, T. (2016). Can war foster cooperation? *Journal of Economic Perspectives*, *30*(3), 249–274.

Bauer, M., Cassar, A., Chytilova, J., & Henrich, J. (2014). War's enduring effects on the development of egalitarian motivations and in-group biases. *Psychological Science*, *25*(1), 47–57.

Bazzi, S., Fiszbein, M., & Gebresilasse, M. (2018). *Frontier culture: The roots and persistence of "rugged individualism" in the United States* [Working paper]. Boston University.

Beaman, L., Chattopadhyay, R., Duflo, E., Pande, R., & Topalova, P. (2009). Powerful women: Does exposure reduce bias? *Quarterly Journal of Economics*, *124*(4), 1497–1540.

Becker, A. (2019). *On the economic origins of restrictions on women's sexuality* [Working paper]. Harvard University.

Becker, S. O., Boeckh, K., Hainz, C., & Woessmann, L. (2016). The empire is dead, long live the empire! Long-run persistence of trust and corruption in the bureaucracy. *Economic Journal*, *126*(590), 40–74.

Becker, S. O., & Woessmann, L. (2008). Luther and the girls: Religious denomination and the female education gap in nineteenth-century Prussia. *Scandinavian Journal of Economics*, *110*(4), 777–805.

Becker, S. O., & Woessmann, L. (2009). Was Weber wrong? A human capital theory of Protestant economic history. *Quarterly Journal of Economics*, *124*(2), 531–596.

Bentzen, J. S. (2019). Acts of god? Religiosity and natural disasters across subnational world districts. *Economic Journal*, *129*(622), 2295–2321.

BenYishay, A., Grosjean, P., & Vecci, J. (2017). The fish is the friend of matriliny: Reef density and matrilineal inheritance. *Journal of Development Economics*, *127*, 234–249.

Bergh, A., & Ohrvall, R. (2018). A sticky trait: Social trust among Swedish expatriates in countries with varying institutional quality. *Journal of Comparative Economics*, *46*(4), 1146–1157.

Booth, A., Fan, E., Meng, X., & Zhang, D. (2019). Gender differences in willingness to compete: The role of culture and institutions. *Economic Journal*, *129*(618), 734–764.

Boserup, E. (1970). *Woman's role in economic development*. Allen and Unwin.

Bowles, S., & Polania-Reyes, S. (2012). Economic incentives and social preferences: Substitutes or complements? *Journal of Economic Literature, 50*(2), 368–425.

Boyd, R., & Richerson, P. J. (1985). *Culture and the evolutionary process*. University of Chicago Press.

Boyd, R., & Richerson, P. J. (2005). *The origin and evolution of cultures*. Oxford University Press.

Bursztyn, L., Gonzalez, A., & Yanagizawa-Drott, D. (2018). *Misperceived social norms: Female labor force participation in Saudi Arabia* [Working paper]. University of Zurich. https://www.aeaweb.org/articles?id=10.1257/aer.20180975

Butler, J. V., Giuliano, P., & Guiso, L. (2016). The right amount of trust. *Journal of the European Economic Association, 14*(5), 1155–1180.

Cameron, L. A. (1999). Raising the stakes in the ultimatum game: Experimental evidence from Indonesia. *Economic Inquiry, 37*(1), 47–59.

Campa, P., & Serafinelli, M. (2019). Politico-economic regimes and attitudes: Female workers under state-socialism. *Review of Economics and Statistics, 101*(2), 233–248.

Campante, F., & Yanagizawa-Drott, D. (2015). Does religion affect economic growth and happiness? Evidence from Ramadan. *Quarterly Journal of Economics, 130*(2), 615–658.

Campante, F., & Yanagizawa-Drott, D. (2016). *The intergenerational transmission of war* [Working paper]. Harvard Kennedy School.

Cantoni, D., Chen, Y., Yang, D. Y., Yuchtman, N., & Zhang, Y. J. (2017). Curriculum and ideology. *Journal of Political Economy, 125*(2), 338–392.

Cassar, A., Grosjean, P., & Whitt, S. (2013). Legacies of violence: Trust and market development. *Journal of Economic Growth, 18*, 285–318.

Cervellati, M., Chiovelli, G., & Esposito, E. (2019). *Bite and divide: Malaria and ethnolinguistic diversity* [Working paper]. University of Bologna.

Chuang, Y., & Schechter, L. (2015). Stability of experimental and survey measures of risk, time, and social preferences: A review and some new results. *Journal of Development Economics, 117*, 151–170.

Clingingsmith, D., Khwaja, A. I., & Kremer, M. (2009). Estimating the impact of the Hajj: Religion and tolerance in Islam's global gathering. *Quarterly Journal of Economics, 124*(3), 1133–1170.

Cohn, A., & Marechal, M. A. (2016). *Laboratory measure of cheating predicts school misconduct* [CESifo Working paper 5613]. Center for Economic Studies and ifo Institute.

Cohn, A., Marechal, M. A., & Noll, T. (2015). Bad boys: How criminal identity salience affects rule violation. *Review of Economic Studies, 82*(4), 1289–1308.

Cohn, A., Marechal, M. A., Tannenbaum, D., & Zund, C. L. (2019). Civic honesty around the globe. *Science, 365,* 70–73.

Cornelson, K. (2018). *Media role models and Black educational attainment: Evidence from the* Cosby Show [Working paper]. University of Notre Dame.

Corno, L., Hildebrandt, N., & Voena, A. (2020). Age of marriage, weather shocks, and the direction of marriage payments. *Econometrica, 88*(3), 879–915.

Costa-Font, J., Giuliano, P., & Ozcan, B. (2018). The cultural origin of saving behavior. *PLoS ONE, 13*(9), Article e0202290.

Couttenier, M., Grosjean, P., & Sangnier, M. (2017). The wild west is wild: The homicide resource curse. *Journal of the European Economic Association, 15*(3), 558–585.

Dell, M., Lane, N., & Querubin, P. (2019). The historical state, local collective action, and economic development in Vietnam. *Econometrica, 86*(6), 2083–2121.

Dell, M., & Querubin, P. (2018). The historical state, local collective action, and economic development in Vietnam. *Quarterly Journal of Economics, 133*(2), 701–764.

Della Vigna, S., & Kaplan, E. (2007). The Fox News effect: Media bias and voting. *Quarterly Journal of Economics, 122,* 1187–1234.

Depetris-Chauvin, E., Durante, R., & Campante, F. R. (2020). Building nations through shared experiences: Evidence from African football. *American Economic Review, 110*(5), 1572–1602.

Desmet, K., Ortuno-Ortin, I., & Wacziarg, R. (2017). Culture, ethnicity and diversity. *American Economic Review, 107,* 2479–2513.

Desmet, K., & Wacziarg, R. (2019). *The cultural divide* [NBER Working Paper 24630]. National Bureau of Economic Research.

Dohmen, T., Falk, A., Huffman, D., & Sunde, U. (2018). *Patience and comparative development* [Working paper]., University of Bonn.

Duflo, E. (2001). Schooling and labor market consequences of school construction in Indonesia: Evidence from an unusual policy experiment. *American Economic Review, 91*(4), 795–813.

Enke, B. (2019). Kinship, cooperation, and the evolution of moral systems. *Quarterly Journal of Economics, 134*(2), 953–1019.

Enke, B. (2020). Moral values and voting. *Journal of Political Economy, 128*(10), 3679–3729.

Enke, B., & Rodriguez-Padilla, R. (2019). *Moral universalism and the structure of ideology* [Working paper]. Harvard University.

Evans-Pritchard, E. E. (1940). *The Nuer.* Clarendon.

Falk, A., Becker, A., Dohmen, T., Enke, B., Huffman, D., & Sunde, U. (2018). Global evidence on economic preferences. *Quarterly Journal of Economics, 133*(4), 1645–1692.

Falk, A., Becker, A., Dohmen, T., Huffman, D., & Sunde, U. (2016). *The preference survey module: A validated instrument for measuring risk, time, and social preferences* [IZA Discussion Paper 9504]. Institute for the Study of Labor.

Feldman, M. W., Aoki, K., & Kumm, J. (1996). Individual social learning: Evolutionary analysis in a fluctuating environment. *Anthropological Science, 104*(3), 209–232.

Fernandez, R., & Fogli, A. (2009). Culture: An empirical investigation of beliefs, work, and fertility. *American Economic Journal: Macroeconomics, 1*(1), 146–177.

Fernandez, R., Fogli, A., & Olivetti, C. (2004). Mothers and sons: Preference formation and female labor force dynamics. *Quarterly Journal of Economics, 119,* 1249–1299.

Fernandez, R., Parsa, S., & Viarengo, M. (2019). *Coming out in America: AIDS, politics, and cultural change* [Working paper]. New York University.

Figlio, D., Giuliano, P., Ozek, U., & Sapienza, P. (2019). Long-term orientation and educational performance. *American Economic Journal: Economic Policy, 11*(4), 272–309.

Fouka, V. (2020). Backlash: The unintended effects of language prohibition in U.S. schools after World War I. *Review of Economic Studies, 87*(1), 204–239.

Fouka, V., & Schlapfer, A. (2020). Agricultural returns to labor and the origins of work ethics. *Economic Journal, 130*(628), 1081–1113.

Francois, P., Fujiwara, T., & van Ypersele, T. (2010). *Competition builds trust* [Working paper]. University of British Columbia.

Francois, P., Fujiwara, T., & van Ypersele, T. (2018). The origins of human prosociality: Cultural group selection in the workplace and the laboratory. *Science Advances, 4*(9), Article eaat2201.

Galor, O., & Ozak, O. (2016). The agricultural origins of time preference. *American Economic Review, 106*(10), 3064–3103.

Galor, O., & Savitskiy, V. (2018). *Climatic roots of loss aversion* [Working paper]. Brown University.

Gelfand, M. (2018). *Rule makers, rule breakers.* Simon & Schuster.

Gelfand, M. J., Raver, J. L., Nishii, L., Leslie, L. M., Lun, J., Lim, B. C., Duan, L., Almaliach, A., Ang, S., Arnadottir, J., Aycan, Z., Boehnke, K., Boski, P., Cabecinhas, R., Chan, D., Chhokar, J., D'Amato, A., Ferrer, M., Fischlmayr, I. C., . . . Yamaguchi, S. (2011). Differences between tight and loose cultures: A 33-nation study. *Science, 332*(6033), 1100–1104.

Gershman, B. (2019). *Witchcraft beliefs as a cultural legacy of the Atlantic slave trade: Evidence from two continents* [Working paper]. American University.

Giavazzi, F., Petkov, I., & Schiantarelli, F. (2019). Culture: Persistence and evolution. *Journal of Economic Growth, 24*(2), 117–154.

Gigerenzer, G., & Goldstein, D. G. (1996). Reasoning the fast and frugal way: Models of bounded rationality. *Psychological Review, 103*(4), 650–669.

Gigerenzer, G., Todd, P. M., & ABC Research Group. (1999). *Simple heuristics that make us smart*. Oxford University Press.

Giuliano, P. (2007). Living arrangements in western Europe: Does cultural origin matter? *Journal of the European Economic Association, 5*(5), 927–952.

Giuliano, P., & Nunn, N. (2013). The transmission of democracy: From the village to the nation state. *American Economic Review Papers and Proceedings, 103*(3), 86–92.

Giuliano, P., & Nunn, N. (2021). Understanding cultural persistence and change. *Review of Economic Studies, 88*(4), 1541–1581.

Giuliano, P., & Spilimbergo, A. (2014). Growing up in a recession. *Review of Economic Studies, 81*(3), 787–817.

Gorodnichenko, Y., Kukharskyy, B., & Roland, G. (2018). *Cultural distance, firm boundaries, and global sourcing* [Working paper]. University of California Berkeley.

Gorodnichenko, Y., & Roland, G. (2011). Individualism, innovation, and long-run growth. *Proceedings of the National Academy of Sciences of the United States of America, 108*(4), 21316–21319.

Gorodnichenko, Y., & Roland, G. (2015). *Culture, institutions, and democratization* [Working paper]. University of California Berkeley.

Gorodnichenko, Y., & Roland, G. (2017). Culture, institutions, and the wealth of nations. *Review of Economics and Statistics, 99*(3), 402–416.

Grosjean, P. (2014). A history of violence: The culture of honor as a determinant of homicide in the U.S. South. *Journal of the European Economic Association, 12*(5), 1285–1316.

Grosjean, P., & Khattar, R. (2018). It's raining men! Hallelujah? The long-run consequences of male-biased sex ratios. *Review of Economic Studies, 86*(2), 723–754.

Guiso, L., Sapienza, P., & Zingales, L. (2006). Does culture affect economic outcomes? *Journal of Economic Perspectives, 20*(2), 23–48.

Guiso, L., Sapienza, P., & Zingales, L. (2008). Long-term persistence. *Journal of the European Economic Association, 14*, 1401–1436.

Guiso, L., Sapienza, P., & Zingales, L. (2009). Cultural biases in economic exchange. *Quarterly Journal of Economics, 124*(3), 1095–1131.

Hanna, R., & Wang, S.-Y. (2017). Dishonesty and selection into public service: Evidence from India. *American Economic Journal: Economic Policy, 9*(3), 262–290.

Harrington, J. R., & Gelfand, M. J. (2014). Differences between tight and loose cultures: A 33-nation study. *Proceedings of the National Academy of Sciences of the United States of America, 111*(22), 7990–7995.

Heldring, L. (2021). The origins of violence in Rwanda. *Review of Economic Studies, 88*(2), 730–763.

Heller, S. B., Shah, A. K., Guryan, J., Ludwig, J., Mullainathan, S., & Pollack, H. A. (2017). Thinking, fast and slow? Some field experiments to reduce crime and dropout in Chicago. *Quarterly Journal of Economics*, *132*(1), 1–54.

Henrich, J. (2000). Does culture matter in economic behavior? Ultimatum game bargaining among the Machiguenga of the Peruvian Amazon. *American Economic Review*, *90*(4), 973–979.

Henrich, J. (2015). *The secret of our success: How culture is driving human evolution*. Princeton University Press.

Henrich, J., Bauer, M., Cassar, A., Chytilova, J., & Purzycki, B. G. (2019). War increases religiosity. *Nature Human Behavior*, *3*, 129–135.

Henrich, J., Boyd, R., Bowles, S., Camerer, C., Fehr, E., Gintis, H., McElreath, R., Alvard, M., Barr, A., Ensminger, J., Henrich, N. S., Hill, K., Gil-White, F., Gurven, M., Marlowe, F. W., Patton, J. Q., & Tracer, D. (2005). "Economic man" in cross-cultural perspective: Ethnography and experiments from 15 small-scale societies. *Behavioral and Brain Sciences*, *28*, 795–855.

Henrich, J., Boyd, R., Bowles, S., Camerer, C., Gintis, H., McElreath, R., & Fehr, E. (2001). In search of *Homo economicus*: Experiments in 15 small-scale societies. *American Economic Review Papers and Proceedings*, *91*(2), 73–79.

Henrich, J., Ensminger, J., McElreath, R., Barr, A., Barrett, C., Bolyanatz, A., Cardenas, J. C., Gurven, M., Gwako, E., Henrich, N., Marlowe, F., Tracer, D., & Ziker, J. (2010a). Markets, religion, community size, and the evolution of fairness and punishment. *Science*, *327*, 1480–1484.

Henrich, J., Heine, S. J., & Norenzayan, A. (2010b). The weirdest people in the world. *Behavioral and Brain Sciences*, *33*(2/3), 1–75.

Heywood, L. (2009). Slavery and its transformation in the Kingdom of Kongo: 1491–1800. *Journal of African History*, *21*, 1–22.

Hoffman, E., McCabe, K. A., Shachat, K., & Smith, V. L. (1994). Preferences, property rights, and anonymity in bargaining games. *Games and Economic Behavior*, *7*(3), 346–380.

Hofstede, G. (2001). *Culture's consequences: Comparing values, behaviors, institutions, organizations across nations*. Sage Publications.

House, R. J., Hanges, P. J., Javidan, M., Dorfman, P. W., & Gupta, V. (2004). *Culture, leadership and organizations*. Sage Publications.

Jakiela, P., & Ozier, O. (2019). The impact of violence on individual risk preferences: Evidence from a natural experiment. *Review of Economics and Statistics*, *101*(3), 547–559.

Jayachandran, S., & Pande, R. (2017). Why are Indian children so short? The role of birth order and son preference. *American Economic Review*, *107*(9), 2600–2629.

Jensen, R., & Oster, E. (2009). The power of TV: Cable television and women's status in India. *Quarterly Journal of Economics*, *124*(3), 1057–1094.

Johnson, N. D., & Mislin, A. A. (2011). Trust games: A meta-analysis. *Journal of Economic Psychology*, *32*, 865–889.

Kahneman, D. (2011). *Thinking, fast and slow*. Macmillan.

Karaja, E., & Rubin, J. (2017). *The cultural transmission of trust norms: Evidence from a lab in the field on a natural experiment* [Working paper]. Chapman University.

Katz, S., Hediger, M., & Valleroy, L. (1974). Traditional maize processing techniques in the New World. *Science*, *184*(4138), 765–773.

Koelle, S. W. (1854). *Polyglotta Africana; or a comparative vocabulary of nearly three hundred words and phrases, in more than one hundred distinct African languages*. Church Missionary House.

Kosse, F., Deckers, T., Schildberg-Horisch, H., & Falk, A. (2020). The formation of prosociality: Causal evidence on the role of the social environment. *Journal of Political Economy*, *128*(2), 434–467.

Kroell, M., & Rustagi, D. (2019). *Measuring honesty and explaining adulteration in naturally occurring markets* [Working paper]. Brown University.

La Ferrara, E., Chong, A., & Duryea, S. (2012). Soap operas and fertility: Evidence from Brazil. *American Economic Journal: Applied Economics*, *4*(4), 1–31.

Lowes, S. (2018). *Matrilineal kinship and spousal cooperation: Evidence from the matrilineal belt* [Working paper]. Stanford University.

Lowes, S., & Montero, E. (2017). *Mistrust in medicine: The legacy of colonial medicine campaigns in central Africa* [Working paper]. Bocconi University.

Lowes, S., & Montero, E. (2019). *Concessions, violence and indirect rule: Evidence from the Congo Free State* [Working paper]. Stanford University.

Lowes, S., Nunn, N., Robinson, J. A., & Weigel, J. (2017). The evolution of culture and institutions: Evidence from the Kuba Kingdom. *Econometrica*, *85*(4), 1065–1091.

Madestam, A., Shoag, D., Veuger, S., & Yanagizawa-Drott, D. (2013). Do political protests matter? Evidence from the Tea Party movement. *Quarterly Journal of Economics*, *128*(4), 1633–1685.

Madestam, A., & Yanagizawa-Drott, D. (2011). *Shaping the nation: The effect of the Fourth of July on political preferences and behavior in the United States* [Working paper]. Bocconi University.

Michalopoulos, S. (2012). The origins of ethnolinguistic diversity. *American Economic Review*, *102*(4), 1508–1539.

Michalopoulos, S., Naghavi, A., & Prarolo, G. (2018). Trade and geography in the spread of Islam. *Economic Journal*, *128*(616), 3210–3241.

Miguel, E., & Fisman, R. (2007). Corruption, norms and legal enforcement: Evidence from diplomatic parking tickets. *Journal of Political Economy*, *115*(6), 1020–1048.

Miguel, E., Saiegh, S., & Satyanath, S. (2011). Civil war exposure and violence. *Economic and Politics*, *23*(1), 59–73.

Mitrunen, M. (2019). *Can you make an American? Compulsory patriotism and assimilation of immigrants* [Working paper]. University of Chicago.

Mokyr, J. (2018). *A culture of growth: The origins of the modern economy*. Princeton University Press.

Moscona, J., Nunn, N., & Robinson, J. A. (2017). Keeping it in the family: Lineage organization and the scope of trust in sub-Saharan Africa. *American Economic Review Papers and Proceedings, 107*(5), 565–571.

Moscona, J., Nunn, N., & Robinson, J. A. (2019). Kinship and conflict: Evidence from segmentary lineage societies in sub-Saharan Africa. *Econometrica*, forthcoming.

Nguyen, K.-T. (2018). *Trust and innovation within the firm: Evidence from matched CEO-firm data* [Working paper]. London School of Economics.

Nisbett, R. E. (2003). *The geography of thought*. Free Press.

Nunn, N. (2008). The long-term effects of Africa's slave trades. *Quarterly Journal of Economics, 123*(1), 139–176.

Nunn, N. (2009). The importance of history for economic development. *Annual Review of Economics, 1*(1), 65–92.

Nunn, N. (2010). Religious conversion in colonial Africa. *American Economic Review Papers and Proceedings, 100*(2), 147–152.

Nunn, N. (2014). Historical development. In P. Aghion & S. Durlauf (Eds.), *Historical development* (pp. 347–402). North-Holland.

Nunn, N. (2020). The historical roots of economic development. *Science, 367*(6485), Article eaaz9986.

Nunn, N., Qian, N., and Wen, J. (2019). *Distrust and political turnover* [Working paper]. Harvard University.

Nunn, N., & Wantchekon, L. (2011). The slave trade and the origins of mistrust in Africa. *American Economic Review, 101*(7), 3221–3252.

Okoye, D. (2017). *Things fall apart? Missions, institutions, and interpersonal trust* [Working paper]. Dalhousie University.

Olken, B. (2009). Do television and radio destroy social capital? *American Economic Journal: Applied Economics, 1*(4), 1–33.

Qian, N. (2008). Missing women and the price of tea in China: The effects of sex-specific income on sex imbalance. *Quarterly Journal of Economics, 123*(3), 1251–1285.

Ramos-Toro, D. (2019). *Social exclusion and social preferences: Evidence from Colombia's leper colony* [Working paper]. Brown University.

Rao, G. (2019). Familiarity does not breed contempt: Diversity, discrimination, and generosity in Delhi schools. *American Economic Review, 109*(3), 774–809.

Riley, E. (2017). *Increasing students' aspirations: The impact of* Queen of Katwe *on students' educational attainment* [CSAE Working paper WPS/207-13]. Center for the Study of African Economies.

Rogers, A. R. (1988). Does biology constrain culture? *American Anthropologist, 90*(4), 819–831.

Roth, A. E., Prasnikar, V., Okuno-Fujiwara, M., and Zamir, S. (1991). Bargaining and market behavior in Jerusalem, Ljubljana, Pittsburgh, and Tokyo: An experimental study. *American Economic Review, 81*(5), 1068–1095.

Rubin, J. (2014). Printing and protestants: An empirical test of the role of printing in the Reformation. *Review of Economics and Statistics, 96*(2), 270–286.

Rustagi, D. (2019). *Historical self-governance and norms of cooperation* [Working paper]. Brown University.

Sahlins, M. D. (1961). The segmentary lineage: An organization of predatory expansion. *American Anthropologist, 63*(2), 322–345.

Schulz, J. (2017). *The churches' bans on consanguineous marriages, kin networks and democracy* [Working paper]. Yale University.

Schulz, J., Bahrami-Rad, D., Beauchamp, J., & Henrich, J. (2019). The church, intensive kinship, and global psychological variation. *Science, 366*(6466), Article eaau5141.

Schwartz, S. H., & Sagiv, L. (1995). Identifying culture-specifics in the content and structure of values. *Journal of Cross-Cultural Psychology, 26*(1), 92–116.

Spolaore, E., & Wacziarg, R. (2013). How deep are the roots of economic development? *Journal of Economic Literature, 51*(2), 325–369.

Tabellini, G. (2008a). Presidential address. Institutions and culture. *Journal of the European Economic Association, 6*, 255–294.

Tabellini, G. (2008b). The scope of cooperation: Values and incentives. *Quarterly Journal of Economics, 123*(3), 905–950.

Tabellini, G. (2010). Culture and institutions: Economic development in the regions of Europe. *Journal of the European Economic Association, 8*(4), 677–716.

Teso, E. (2019). The long-term effects of demographic shocks on the evolution of gender roles: Evidence from the trans-Atlantic slave trade. *Journal of the European Economic Association, 17*(2), 497–534.

Xue, M. M. (2018). *High-value work and the rise of women: The cotton revolution and gender equality in China* [Working paper]. Northwestern University.

CHAPTER 4

The Pursuit of Honor

Novel Contexts, Varied Approaches, and New Developments

SUSAN E. CROSS AND AYŞE K. ÜSKÜL

Abstract

Why are people around the world willing to sacrifice for honor? This chapter addresses that question with a focus on the little-researched cultural context of Turkey. When compared to European Americans from northern US states, Turkish people have richer conceptions of the concept of *honor*, and they perceive that a greater variety of situations are imbued with honor-related implications. They respond to honor-relevant situations with more intense emotions and are more sensitive to sharing content in social media that could lead to shame or disrepute. This research replicates previous findings of the link between honor and aggression, and it showed that honor threats impair goal pursuit more among Turkish participants. Turkish participants react more strongly to a charge that they behaved dishonestly (i.e., an honor threat) than to a charge that they were incompetent, compared to European American participants in northern US states. This research provides an important extension to previous research focused on the southern states in the United States.

Key Words: culture of honor, Turkey, goal pursuit, honor threat, dignity culture

---

I. INTRODUCTION

A. Overview of the Chapter

Why do people fight and die for honor? That question is part of a larger question: What is honor, and how does concern for honor influence behavior? In

Susan E. Cross and Ayşe K. Üskül, *The Pursuit of Honor* In: *Handbook of Advances in Culture and Psychology.*
Edited by: Michele J. Gelfand, Chi-yue Chiu, and Ying-yi Hong, Oxford University Press. © Oxford University Press 2022.
DOI: 10.1093/oso/9780197631669.003.0004

this chapter, we outline our research on a culture of honor that the field of cultural psychology has largely overlooked: Turkey. Until recently, cultural psychologists have paid relatively little attention to this part of the world and to the values, beliefs, and ideals that shape patterns of behavior in this region.

We begin the chapter by situating our work in the context of the bigger picture of cultural psychology as a field and in the particular domain of earlier research on cultures of honor. We will first walk the reader through the initial work by anthropologists. Then we will provide a quick survey of theory and research on the origins of cultures of honor and their distinctions relative to the other cultural logics of dignity and face, which sets a foundation for our foray into understanding honor in the Turkish context.

Next, we will introduce the reader to our work through five key themes. The first theme describes bottom-up, or *emic*, approaches that we have used to understand the indigenous conceptions of honor in Turkey compared to European-heritage people in the northern United States (encompassing states in the Northeast and upper Midwest, primarily). These studies employ prototype approaches and situation sampling to discover lay beliefs about honor and to begin investigating the cultural similarities and differences in perceptions of the ways that honor-related situations impact individuals and their families. Our next theme acknowledges the existing theories of cultures of honor and examines their generalizability to the Turkish context (an *etic* approach). We apply theories of the distinctive emotions (i.e., shame and anger) that underlie responses to honor threats and investigate the honor–aggression link among Turkish samples. Next, we seek to extend theories of honor's influence on behavior by differentiating types of threats and by examining a new outcome—goal pursuit. Throughout these studies, we have paid attention not only to negative consequences of a concern for honor (as has been the focus of much of the honor-focused research) but also to the positive roles that honor plays in morality and social behavior. This review also highlights the diversity of methodological approaches and paradigms that are part of a cultural psychologist's toolkit. We conclude with suggestions of additional useful techniques and measures, and important questions for researchers to consider.

B. Cultural Psychology at the Turn of the Century

In the early 2000s, the field of cultural psychology was based primarily on comparisons of East or South Asians with Westerners,[1] with a focus on differences in self-construal, cognition, emotion, and motivation. At that time, the research literature had documented that East Asians tended to define the self in terms of close others and group memberships, in contrast to the focus on individual traits, attitudes, beliefs, and goals that defined the self-views of members of Western-heritage societies (Markus & Kitayama, 1991; for a review, see Cross & Lam, 2017). Building on this foundation, researchers demonstrated that East Asians and European Americans make different assumptions about the world, leading to important differences in attention, memory, attribution, and judgment (see Spencer-Rodgers & Peng, 2018, for a review of this literature). These differing patterns of self-conception and cognition are associated with differences in emotional experiences and motivations (e.g., Mesquita & Leu, 2007; Morling & Lee, 2017; Tsai, 2007). This East versus West theory and research laid a key foundation for cultural psychology to build on, and it framed the experiences that we, Susan Cross and Ayşe Üskül, brought to bear in our work.

This foundation based on East–West comparisons excluded much of the world. Africa, Latin America, and the Middle East were largely overlooked in these developments although they were assumed to be similar to the "East" (for exceptions at the time, see, e.g., Adams, 2005; Greenfield, 1997). By the middle of the first decade of the 2000s, however, researchers had begun to examine a particular cultural category that held promise for helping us understand the psychology of members of some of the cultural groups outside the East–West vector: cultures of honor. As described in this chapter, cultures of honor are thought to shape psychological processes in Mediterranean and North African countries, Latin America, parts of South Asia, and the southern and mountain states of the United States. As social psychologists who believed that our field should be a global science, we saw the developing social-psychological research on cultures of honor as a path into the study of often overlooked regions of the world. We were also motivated by our own backgrounds as members of cultures of honor: Uskul was raised in Turkey and lived and worked in different countries, which provided her with a comparative perspective, and Cross was raised in the southern US state of Texas and had some connections to the Middle East. We were both concerned that although the eastern Mediterranean and Middle Eastern countries of the world played important roles in world events, they did not have commensurate representation in social-cultural psychology. Yes, Turkish psychologists had established themselves as a leading voice in the region, but the interpretation of findings obtained in that context did not always take cultural characteristics into consideration (although exceptions, of course, exist, e.g., Kagitcibasi [1994] and Wasti & Erdaş [2019], to give just two examples). Given the fundamental, explicit, yet sometimes contested importance of honor in Turkey, we seized upon this theoretical formulation as a means of making progress in unfolding the social psychology of Turkish and other honor culture populations.

C. What Characterizes Cultures of Honor?

Anthropologists working in the Mediterranean societies of Greece and Spain were the first to identify honor as a key cultural concern. Observing the relations among residents of a small Spanish village, Julian Pitt-Rivers (1965) described honor as "the value of a person in his own eyes, but also in the eyes of his society" (p. 21). In the language of contemporary psychology, this definition marries concern for self-esteem with a concern for one's reputation or social image—how one is viewed by others. Pitt-Rivers does not articulate in this statement the dimensions upon which individuals base their self-esteem and social image, but others have identified culturally specific moral codes, gender-related roles, and economic and social status as the primary sources of these evaluations in traditional cultures of honor (Campbell, 1964; Gilmore, 1987; Peristiany, 1965). A person's honor is maintained by adherence to these codes and roles; by achievement of educational, economic, and social gains; and by swift and firm responses to threats to one's honor. Importantly, honor—especially the respect of others—is easily lost in these contexts, and once lost, it is difficult to regain (Stewart, 1994). Consequently, members of honor cultures have been described as especially attuned to potential insults or threats that challenge their reputation and as prepared to vigorously defend themselves in the face of such threats. The importance of reputation and social respect as a key concern or attribute to be prized, protected, and defended is expressed in the traditional Arabic saying "Honor before bread."

How do cultures of honor arise? The socioecological origins of cultures of honor can be found in subsistence patterns in local environments. Historians (Fischer, 1989; Gastil, 1971; McWhiney, 1988) and anthropologists (Edgerton, 1971; Goldschmidt, 1965) argue that cultures of honor arise in ecological contexts with two primary characteristics: (a) subsistence based primarily on herding animals (or other forms of portable wealth) and (b) weak or absent law enforcement. Picture the rugged terrain of the Scottish Highlands (or the Mongolian steppes where nomadic Turkic peoples originate) prior to the Industrial Revolution: The ecology is mountainous and rocky and therefore not conducive to farming, so people raised cattle, sheep, and pigs to feed their families. These animals could easily be stolen by "rustlers." The herder whose livestock was stolen often had little recourse to legal systems for protection; getting a message to the nearest law enforcement agency could take a day or more. By that time, one's livestock was rebranded, butchered, or hidden away in a remote location. Consequently, the owner of livestock (typically men) had to protect his and his family's livelihood by cultivating a reputation for being a person who was quick to respond to any threat to his property and was unstinting in his retaliation against a threat. He had to cultivate a "tough" persona, so that thieves would choose not to tempt fate by absconding with his herd.

This conception of cultures of honor first proved useful when American sociologists and historians attempted to explain how the US South differed from other parts of the country, particularly the North and Midwest. In particular, scholars noted that the US South was more violent than the northern and midwestern regions of the country (Gastil, 1971, 1989; Hackney, 1969). The initial explanations of this difference focused on differences in climate, poverty rates, and the history of slavery in the region (Anderson, 1989; Loftin & Hill, 1974; de Tocqueville, 1835/1969). Others, however, noted that the European origins of the settlers of the southern region of the United States differed from the origins of the settlers of the northern regions. Whereas the North and Midwest were settled by Anglo-Saxons and northern Europeans, the South was initially settled by large numbers of Scots who originated from the southern border with Britain. As Brown (2016) describes, these settlers came from a region where generations of warfare between British and Scottish forces left the environment decimated and social institutions in shambles. The chief means of subsistence was open-range herding of animals for meat (Fischer, 1989; McWhiney, 1988; Wyatt-Brown, 1982, 1986; see Brown & Osterman, 2012, for a review), which created an environment conducive to the development of a culture of honor.

Consequently, Scottish settlers in the US South brought with them an honor code that included the social principle of *lex talionis*, or the rule of retribution. As a historian of the US South put it, "lex talionis . . . held that a good man must seek to do right in the world, but when wrong was done to him, he must punish the wrongdoer himself by an act of retribution that restored order and justice in the world" (Fischer, 1989, p. 765). In an environment in which state-run enforcement of rules and laws is weak, individuals (especially men) must cultivate a reputation for quick and strong responses to threats to their honor to ensure that others do not consider insulting or aggressing against them, their families, or their possessions. The person who fails in this effort may be easily taken advantage of, disregarded in community decisions, or written out of opportunities for advancement or profit because others do not believe that the person is a trustworthy ally or a responsible caretaker of resources (Cohen et al., 2018; Nowak et al., 2016). Thus, honor cultures are marked by strong norms of reciprocity or payback: The honorable person reciprocates both good things (help and hospitality) and bad things (insults, affronts, and injustices) (Cohen & Vandello, 2004; Leung & Cohen, 2011). Some consequences of this cultural heritage in the US South are high rates of violence among the White population over relatively minor affronts, high levels of gun ownership, high levels of endorsement of violence for self-protection, and other phenomena that fit together into the logic of honor (Brown, 2016; Gul et al., 2021; Nisbett, 1993; Nisbett & Cohen, 1996).

1. The Cultural Logic of Dignity and Face

The theoretical differentiation of honor cultures from other cultural logics has been articulated by Leung and Cohen (2011), who compare three cultural syndromes: honor, dignity, and face. They describe these cultural syndromes as "constellations of shared beliefs, values, behaviors, practices and so on that are organized around a central theme" (p. 508). This organization takes on a sort of internal logic, in which the various components (values, beliefs, practices, institutions, and so on) fit together in a coherent whole, at least from the perspective of insiders in each cultural group.

Societies that share a western European heritage represent what Leung and Cohen (2011) describe as *dignity* cultures. This cultural logic is premised on the belief that a person's worth is inherent and unalterable; it is based on Enlightenment notions of equality and human rights that are accorded to all people, independent of their status in society (at least ideally). In dignity cultures, at least theoretically, a person's worth does not depend on other people's opinions or respect. Good behavior is not driven by worries about what other people think but by one's own values, moral stances, goals, and beliefs. Individuals do not have to rely on a reputation for toughness or payback because an accessible legal system guards individuals' rights and possessions. Payback is a responsibility of the state, not the individual, and so norms of reciprocity or retaliation are relatively weaker in these societies (Miller, 1993; for comparisons with face cultures, see Boiger et al., 2014; Leung & Cohen, 2011).

Dignity and honor cultures both differ from so-called face cultures, largely found in East Asian societies that are based on Confucian, Buddhist, or Daoist philosophical traditions. Leung and Cohen (2011) describe face cultures in terms of three *Hs*: hierarchy, harmony, and humility. In face cultures, one's social worth or respectability is maintained by diligently enacting one's proper role in one's in-groups or social hierarchy and by safeguarding harmony in one's relationships and in-groups. Face cultures are marked by strong social norms and attitudes that focus on avoiding conflict. When an individual is the target of an insult or derogation, they are not obligated to respond immediately or retaliate, as in an honor culture. Instead, the offender is punished by other group members or higher-status individuals. The respectable person does not brag about their achievements or status in an attempt to gain others' admiration; instead, the humble, modest person gains face when a higher-status person calls out their achievements or admirable behavior. So, although both honor and face cultures may be characterized by a collectivist social orientation, they differ in the means by which one gains or maintains reputation and social respect (through retaliation in an honor culture versus humility and harmony in a face culture [see Kim & Cohen, 2010; Kim et al., 2010]). Although the honor, face, and dignity conceptualization provides a valuable framework for investigating cultural patterns of behavior, our focus in this chapter is comparison of honor and dignity cultures (for a comparison of honor, face, and dignity cultures, see e.g., Boiger et al., 2014; Smith et al., 2021).

Much of the research testing theoretical differences between honor and dignity cultures has focused on European-heritage people in the United States who have been socialized into the honor culture of the southern and mountain states or the dignity culture of the upper midwestern and northern states (e.g., Brown, 2016; Cohen et al., 1996; Nisbett & Cohen, 1996; Vandello et al., 2009). Yet vast geographic regions of the world are likely marked by the cultural logic of honor, but they have largely gone unexamined.[2] We have sought to extend culture of honor theory to a relatively less investigated part of the world: Turkey.

2. Turkey as a Culture of Honor

There were several reasons we chose to focus on Turkey in this line of research in comparison with other cultural groups. First, one of us (Ayşe K. Üskül) grew up experiencing the norms, values, and cultural contexts of Turkey; she is aware of the ways in which concerns for honor permeate everyday experiences in people's lives. Second, in the light of existing research in the social-psychological literature on cultures of honor conducted primarily in the southern United States, Spain, and Latin America (e.g., Brown, 2016; Nisbett & Cohen, 1996; Ramirez-Marin & Shafa, 2017; Rodriguez Mosquera et al.,

2002a, 2002b; Vandello & Cohen, 2003; Vandello et al., 2009), the Turkish context presents stark differences in terms of its religious and cultural background, geographic location, and the prevalence of honor in individuals' daily social affairs. Turkey hosts individuals of different religious backgrounds, with the majority of individuals identifying themselves as Muslim. Due to its geographic positioning, Turkey has been at the crossroads of Europe and Asia, which resulted in its shaping by traditions and customs originating from different religious and cultural practices. Its position in the region also made Turkey home for many of the displaced, contributing to its ethnic and cultural diversity. Finally, it is more collectivistic and tight (e.g., having relatively strict enforcement of social norms) compared with other regions studied within the cultures of honor framework (e.g., US South and Spain).

It is in this broad context (which is to some extent similar to neighboring southeast European and Middle Eastern cultural groups) that researchers have pointed to the importance of honor in shaping interpersonal and other social processes (Bagli & Sev'er, 2003; Kardam, 2005; Ozgur & Sunar, 1982). The variety of Turkish terms used to refer to different aspects of honor (e.g., *onur, namus, seref, haysiyet, nam, san, izzet*) (Sev'er & Yurdakul, 2001) and practices that help protect and maintain honor (e.g., the incidence of honor crimes; laws that protect national honor) all attest to honor's influential position in this society. This is in strong contrast to, for example, how honor is backgrounded in the southern US context, where honor is not as explicitly cognized and articulated.

Third, despite similarities in the importance of honor to other cultural groups in the region, we argue that the Turkish context is also different from other Middle Eastern and North African contexts that researchers have recently started investigating (e.g., Alvaro et al., 2018; Aslani et al., 2016; Gelfand et al., 2015) in terms of its imperial past (i.e., the Turkish republic emerged following the abolition of the Ottoman monarchy), its relationship with the "West" (e.g., it is a member of the Council of Europe and the North Atlantic Treaty Organization; it has a customs union with the European Union), and its position as a country of emigration and immigration (e.g., hosting large number of immigrants from the Balkans and, most recently, large number of refugees from countries such as Syria, Iraq, and Afghanistan; having a large diaspora settled in western European countries such as Germany, Belgium, and the Netherlands). These characteristics position Turkey as a gatekeeper country with strong links to Europe.

Finally, we were cognizant of the fact that little systematic and experimental research on honor had taken place outside of the US South, and we aimed to advance this literature by focusing on an understudied cultural context with a starkly different background. Focusing on Turkey would also open the gateway to understanding other understudied cultural groups in southeastern Europe, the Middle East, and North Africa that share certain characteristics with Turkey. This would also contribute more generally to the literature in cultural psychology, where the vast majority of comparative evidence is based on the investigation of psychological processes of individuals in Western contexts, on the one hand (e.g., North America, western Europe), and East Asian contexts, on the other (e.g., Japan, Korea) (De Almeida & Uchida, 2019). Although Turkey has not been systematically studied in comparison with East Asian contexts before, we know from other research that both individualistic and collectivistic orientations exist in the Turkish context (especially in urban settings [see Kagitcibasi & Ataca, 2005, 2015; Uskul et al., 2004]) and that Turkish individuals do not always handle conflict harmoniously, as one would expect in East Asian groups (e.g., Cingöz-Ulu & Lalonde, 2007). Thus, by focusing on Turkey, we also aimed to shed light on a different configuration of the self and pattern of relationships through the study of honor.

II. MAJOR THEMES IN OUR RESEARCH

Our research to date can be characterized by several themes. Some of these themes organize our findings into particular categories, whereas other themes cut across categories. We briefly describe these themes in this section and then spell out our research with respect to them.

A. Bottom-Up Approaches

What characterizes the cultural logic of honor in Turkey? We were reluctant to assume that the lay understanding of honor and the situations, practices, and norms in which honor is embedded were the same across all cultural contexts. Thus, we began our adventure studying honor cultures with a bottom-up assessment of the everyday experience and conception of honor in Turkey. This emic approach investigated the everyday lay understandings of the meaning of honor among individuals from Turkey and northern US. In this work, we sought to identify both cognitive representations of honor (through the identification of prototypes and dimensions that underlie the prototypes) and situations that carry honor-related expectations for behavior.

B. Top-Down Approaches

At the time that we initiated this research, most social-psychological theories of honor cultures were developed with a focus on the US South or Spain. These societies differ from Turkey and other Middle Eastern honor cultures in many ways. Thus, we used an etic approach that tested existing theories in the novel cultural context of Turkey to examine their generalizability.

C. Extending the Reach of the Theory of Honor Cultures

If the pursuit of and maintenance of one's reputation or honor are core motivations in places such as Turkey, then a wide range of activities, relationships, and decisions may be influenced by these motivations. Thus, we have sought to extend the theory to new outcomes and situations, with a goal to expand the literature beyond its common focus on the honor–aggression link. In particular, we have examined how concern for honor can have consequences for individuals' attention to and pursuit of other goals. Furthermore, we have sought to distinguish honor-related motives and behaviors from other types of motives. For example, we have examined how responses to honor threats differ from responses to other kinds of threats (e.g., threats to competence) among members of honor and dignity cultures.

D. Positive and Negative Consequences of Concern for Honor

When we started this line of research, the literature had accumulated considerable evidence on the negative role of honor (e.g., how it can lead to aggressive behavior), while very few studies had examined positive aspects of honor. Yet the concept of honor in contexts such as Turkey is very far-reaching; it includes the value of hospitality, reciprocity, being trustworthy and honest, and adherence to other culturally endorsed codes for positive behavior (Cohen et al., 2018; Leung & Cohen, 2011; Uskul et al., 2019). With a goal to address this limitation, in our research, we recognized both the negative and positive consequences of honor and designed studies to understand both sides of the medallion.

E. Using Multiple Approaches, Methods, and Paradigms

Our final cross-cutting theme is that we aimed to examine cultural conceptualizations of honor and its consequences for a variety of social-psychological processes using a diverse set of approaches, methods, and paradigms. Cultural beliefs, values, motives, and ways of thinking are transmitted and embodied in many different ways: through individuals' attitudes, self-views, and actions as well as through norms and expectations for how one should behave. When we initiated this program of research, the existing literature focused heavily on group comparisons, using national or regional background as a proxy for culture of honor. We focused not only on group differences but also on social norms around honor and situations in which honor is experienced, as well as individual differences in honor endorsement. Thus, one cross-cutting theme in our work is a focus on complementary levels of explanation.

We have also used a variety of methods, paradigms, and outcome variables to examine the cultural logic of honor. These include qualitative methods, survey methods, and experimental methods in both the laboratory and online. We have used self-report outcomes tapping into different cognitive and emotional responses as well as behavioral outcomes to test our hypotheses. Some of our work has combined culture-level analysis with individual differences, in recognition that individuals do not uniformly endorse the values, beliefs, and expectations of their societies (Kitayama et al., 2009). These individual difference measures of the endorsement of honor-related values are used in some cases to explain cultural differences in behavior (as in a mediation model). In other cases, we adopt the Culture × Personality × Situation [CuPS] approach, articulated by Leung and Cohen (2011). This approach does not assume that cultural differences in behavior lie entirely in the individual; instead, it recognizes that a particular individual attribute (e.g., concern for one's reputation) may predict different outcomes in honor, dignity, or face cultural contexts in interaction with different situational characteristics.

In the remainder of the chapter, we articulate how these major themes framed our past and ongoing program of research in cultures of honor and the contributions of this research to our understanding of culturally shaped patterns of behavior.

III. BOTTOM-UP APPROACHES

A. Prototypes of Honor

When you think of the concept of *honor*, what comes to mind? Do you consider how much other people respect you, your perceived morality, or the degree to which you live up to your assigned roles and norms? Or do you think of an award, some sort of recognition, or a person in an esteemed position (as in "Your honor, the judge")?

Our early work on bottom-up approaches investigated lay prototypes of honor, in part as a response to differing theoretical definitions of the construct. As mentioned previously, the initial description of cultures of honor by the anthropologist Pitt-Rivers (1965) articulated a dual theory of honor, which included individuals' feelings of self-worth along with their worth as judged by others. Some scholars have focused primarily on the latter component of Pitt-Rivers' definition—others' judgment and opinion of the individual (Bowman, 2006; Salzman, 2008). In some research, honor is presented as primarily a function of the individual's place in the social dominance hierarchy (Henry, 2009), whereas others have focused on reciprocity as the key feature of an honor culture (Cohen et al., 2018; Miller, 1993; Nisbett & Cohen, 1996). Lay beliefs and prototypes of a construct such as honor may differ in important ways from expert or theoretical perspectives, yet both approaches are important for a thorough understanding of the phenomenon. Examination of lay prototypes of honor can help researchers and theorists articulate the critical components of the construct and capture what people mean when they invoke the construct to explain their own or other people's behavior. This examination can also uncover unexamined assumptions or biases in the existing theories or research, and it can be used to test competing theories (Fehr, 2005). Furthermore, the features and dimensions of the construct identified through a prototype approach can be used to develop new measures. Finally, identification of the prototypical features of a construct in differing cultural contexts can help researchers articulate the foundations of cultural differences in behavior (see Lam et al., 2016).

1. Feature Frequency

The goal of the first step in this process of identifying lay prototypes of a construct is to delineate the range of attributes ascribed to the concept of *honor* in each group. If participants within a cultural group seldom generate the same attributes in describing a concept, one would conclude that there is little agreement or consensus on the meaning of the concept in that group; if many people generate the same attribute(s), then we could conclude that there is considerable consensus about the meaning of the attribute. Given the theoretical and ethnographic research that suggests that honor is a more important motivator in Turkey than in the northern United States, we expected the Turkish participants both to generate more features of the construct and to have more consensus about the features of the construct.

In the first step of this process, 84 Turkish participants (56 women) and 106 European American participants in northern US states (52 women) enrolled in public universities were asked to think about the ways that the word *honor* is used. They then responded to two questions: (a) What comes to your mind when you think of an individual's personal honor? and (b) What does it mean to be a person with honor? In this and other research we have conducted in Turkey, we use the Turkish term *onur* as the translation of the English term *honor*. Other scholars have argued that it is the most similar in meaning to the northern US understanding of honor (Sev'er & Yurdakul, 2001), and it is gender-neutral in its usage.

Coders identified the unique features listed by two or more participants in each context (see Cross et al., 2014, for a description of this process). As expected, Turkish participants generated more individual features of honor than did northern US participants (M_{Turkey} = 7.42, SD = 3.2; M_{US} = 4.97, SD = 2.49; d = 0.85). There was also more agreement among Turkish participants in the features of honor: 40% of the sample generated a feature related to honesty, and 20% mentioned the term *namus* (which can refer either to women's sexual behavior or to reliability). In contrast, the most frequently generated terms among the northern US participants, *doing the right thing* and *being respected*, were generated by only 15% of the sample. Thus, as we hypothesized, Turkish participants not only had a richer conception of honor (i.e., it was characterized by more attributes) but were more likely than US Northerners to share a relatively consensual understanding of the concept of *honor*.

We also examined the overlap between the features generated by the two groups. After translation and backtranslation, the degree to which the two groups' prototypes shared common features was assessed using the *index of inter-prototype similarity* (Cantor et al., 1982). This is simply a ratio of shared to unique attributes in pairs of feature lists; in the Cantor et al. (1982) study of prototypes of situations, the similarities ranged from 0.00 to 1.30. In our study, only 16 of the total set of features (N = 145) were found in both lists, for an index of 0.14. This relatively low score indicates considerable differences in the features of honor generated by these two groups. Furthermore, there was a qualitative difference in the two sets of features: Turkish participants generated more negations such as *not cheating* (30% of the unique features) than did northern US participants (4%). This finding supports the argument that members of honor cultures are highly attuned to actions and behaviors that can lead one to lose honor, with the goal of avoiding these behaviors.

2. Centrality of the Features

In Step 2 of this process, a new sample of participants was invited to rate the combined Turkish and American features for their centrality to their conception of honor. Features that were high in frequency (i.e., generated by a large proportion of the Step 1 sample) and highly central are considered prototypical. For both groups, *honesty*, *trustworthiness*, and *self-respect* were highly prototypical features of honor. The two groups differed, however, in the extent to which specific moral behaviors were rated as highly central. Turkish participants, as mentioned previously, were more likely to view specific moral behaviors that one should not do (*not telling lies, not to steal anything*) as very prototypical, whereas the northern US list of prototypical features included relatively vague statements about morality (*doing the right thing, having morals*).

We then examined whether there were similar underlying dimensions in the centrality ratings of the combined set of features. Exploratory factor analyses revealed three dimensions that were similar for both Turkish and northern US participants: Moral Behavior (with items such as *to be helpful to others, to be honest, not to cheat*), Social Status and Respect (e.g., *to be respectable in society, to be highly regarded by others, to reach a certain status in society*), and Self-Respect (e.g., *to feel proud of myself, to have self-esteem, to be confident*). In short, these results support the dual perspective on honor articulated by Pitt-Rivers (1965) that included a person's value in their own eyes and in the eyes of others in society, but they also go beyond this definition to highlight the importance of moral behavior in conceptualizations of honor in these two cultural groups.

In summary, a lay prototypes approach can help researchers flesh out the ways that a construct is understood in differing cultural contexts. In the process of providing an important "bottom-up" perspective on the components of honor, this work has also contributed to another theme of this chapter: the need to address positive aspects of honor in addition to negative aspects of honor. Honor concerns motivate individuals to keep their word, to be helpful to others, and to be willing to sacrifice for others. Most definitions and theoretical conceptions of *culture of honor* have focused on social status and respect or the role of payback in maintaining others' respect (Leung & Cohen, 2011; Peristiany, 1965); researchers and theorists often understate (or simply assume) the role of moral behavior (with the exception of women's sexual behavior; see Gilmore, 1987; Rodriquez Mosquera, 2016; Saucier et al., 2015; Vandello & Cohen, 2003).

These findings bolster other observations that suggest that members of honor cultures are more likely to have a prevention motivational focus (Gelfand et al., 2015; Higgins, 1996). The generation of negatively phrased features, such as *not to tell lies* and *not to cheat*, supports the contention that honor is easy to lose and difficult to regain when lost (Stewart, 1994). Thus, individuals focus on those behaviors that are most likely to cause one to lose honor (e.g., *not to lie*, *not to steal*). One might expect a US Southerner to list *Don't be a wuss*. In contrast, in a dignity culture, where the occasional lie or moral misstep is not an indicator of one's inherent worth (Leung & Cohen, 2011), individuals may be more likely to focus on the self- and socially enhancing aspects of moral behavior, such as *doing something good for others* and *doing the right thing*. In our follow-up research, we are currently investigating how the dimensions of honor uncovered in this work are related to other attitudes, beliefs, and behaviors.

B. Situations in Everyday Life

A different way of thinking of the concept *honor* would be to visualize it in more concrete terms as experienced within specific situations. What kinds of experiences are thought of as impacting one's honor, either positively or negatively? Or how do individuals envisage honor being threatened or enhanced in different situations? To complement the studies designed to identify lay prototypes of honor and their underlying dimensions described in the previous section, we employed a situation sampling approach to examine the types of honor-relevant situations afforded by the Turkish and northern American cultural worlds. This approach was inspired by previous research (e.g., Kitayama et al., 1997; Morling et al., 2002) that was based on the premise that cultures leave their traces both inside and outside of our heads, not only shaping what we think, feel, and do but also guiding the everyday practices and scripts, norms, and customs that we follow (Kitayama, 2002; Morling & Lamoreaux, 2008). And it is through experiencing different types of situations that we come to adopt certain ways of thinking of ourselves and the world around us (Markus & Hamedani, 2019). Thus, examining social situations in different cultural contexts can give us important insights into the kinds of experiences individuals regularly encounter in different cultural groups and how frequent these experiences are. Once these situations have been identified, they can then be utilized to examine affective or behavioral responses to these situations by individuals from the same cultural group or other cultural groups. To some extent, this methodology allows researchers to circumvent one difficulty experienced in cultural-psychological research, which is the ethically impossible alternative of randomly assigning individuals to experience situations that are encountered in other cultural contexts.

In this research, we followed the situation sampling methodology in a two-step process. In Step 1, we asked Turkish and European American participants from northern US states to list honor-relevant situations (Uskul et al., 2012). In Step 2, we asked new participants to evaluate a subsection of these situations for their impact on their own and close others' feelings, and acquaintances' feelings about their family. We will cover findings from Step 2 later in the section on emotions (see Section IV.A.1). In this section, we limit our focus to the analysis of situations generated by Turkish and northern European American participants, as part of our attempt to understand cultural conceptions of honor in a bottom-up process.

We asked 84 Turkish participants and 97 European-heritage participants from northern US states to list situations that they considered as most effective if someone wanted to (a) attack or insult somebody else's honor or (b) enhance or increase somebody else's honor. We then coded the situations generated by participants in both samples for the kinds of incidents to which they referred (e.g., false accusations, praise) and for who the situations involved (e.g., themselves, close others, groups, audience). We purposefully asked participants to generate situations that focused on somebody else's honor-related experiences, rather than their own, as we aimed to get an insight into culturally common (vs. idiosyncratic) situations that were viewed as effective in either threatening or enhancing honor. Our first observation in this study pointed to group differences in the frequency with which participants generated honor-relevant situations. Independent of the honor-attacking or honor-enhancing nature of the situations, Turkish participants (M = 2.81, SD = 1.82) generated significantly more meaningful units (i.e., independent units of analysis consisting of unique meaning statements such as *saying that he is a liar*) than did northern European American participants (M = 2.03, SD = 1.37, d = 0.48).

1. Honor-Attacking Situations

When we coded honor-attacking situations for content, we found that, overall, honor-attacking situations generated by members of both groups mainly referred to incidents that involved humiliation, false accusation, sexual or physical attack, challenge or criticism, a person being attributed negative character or behavior, or lack of achievement. There were both similarities and differences between the two cultural groups in the frequency with which these situations were generated. On the one hand, Turkish (28.5%) and northern US (31.4%) participants generated comparable numbers of honor-attacking situations that involved an insult or explicit humiliation of another person. On the other hand, Turkish participants generated 8 times more situations that involved false accusation or unfair treatment and 3 times more situations that referred to physical or sexual attacks than did northern US participants. In contrast, northern US participants were 5 times more likely than Turkish participants to generate situations that involved a criticism of a person's ideas or character or situations that focused on a person's lack of integrity.

Coding honor-attacking situations for the target that they involved revealed that, on the one hand, Turkish participants (11.6%) generated significantly more honor-threatening situations than did northern US participants (3.5%) that involved a relational target (e.g., calling someone's sister a liar). On the other hand, the northern US participants (95%) generated a greater number of situations than did Turkish participants (88.4%) that involved an individual target (e.g., accusing someone of being dishonest). Percentage of units involving a collective target (e.g., national group) did not differ across the two groups. In addition, Turkish participants generated a greater number of honor-attacking situations that involved an audience (25.3%), referring to a close other (e.g., mother or sister, 7.8%), or referring to a social group (classroom or sports team, 17.5%) than did European-American participants (4.8%, 0.7%, 4.1%, respectively). These differences highlight the more relational nature of honor as experienced in the Turkish context and point to the need for an integrative understanding of honor which takes into account different cultural dimensions (e.g., individualism–collectivism).

2. Honor-Enhancing Situations

The conception of honor reflected in the types of honor-enhancing situations generated by Turkish and European-American participants from northern states also showed similarities and differences. On the one hand, both groups generated to a similar extent situations that showed integrity or consistency in one's behaviors and situations that revealed positive characteristics and behaviors of a person (Turkish [TR] = 13.2%, US = 8.7%). On the other hand, the largest proportion of situations generated by Turkish participants involved being praised, admired, or appreciated by others (39.6%), as well as a person achieving positive outcomes (20.8%), whereas the largest proportion of situations generated by US participants involved helping or serving others (33.7%). Coding honor-enhancing situations generated by the two groups for the target[3] and audience that they involved did not reveal significant differences across the two cultural groups. The vast majority of honor-enhancing situations generated by both groups focused on the individual, and a very small percentage of them involved an audience.

These findings point to some agreement between the two cultural groups in the honor relevance of different situations (e.g., that a person's honor can be attacked through situations that involve insults and other forms of humiliation and that a person's honor can be enhanced through integrity and consistency in one's behavior). There was, however, considerable disagreement as well. For example, US Northerners seemed to view one's honor being attacked or enhanced primarily through one's own character and behavior (e.g., immoral behavior or having bad character), whereas Turkish individuals seemed to view honor as being impacted to a greater extent by others' negative or positive actions and appraisals (e.g., being attacked by another person, being praised by someone). Turkish participants were also more likely to generate situations that were stronger in terms of the likely consequences they would evoke for the participant and individuals associated with them (e.g., sexual and physical attack, false accusation; see Table 4.1). These findings also highlight, in line with previous findings documenting culturally shaped forms of honor, that European-heritage individuals from northern US states are more likely to experience honor as a person-bound construct, whereas individuals of Turkish background are more likely to experience honor as a more relational (and collective) construct. Finally, the types of situations described as honor-attacking or honor-enhancing varied between the two groups, suggesting that the cognitive representations of honor are likely to show differences.

This initial set of studies that focused on prototypes and situations as units of analysis using a bottom-up approach provides a glimpse into how the concept of honor is understood and lived in the Turkish and northern United States cultural groups. These studies also constituted an important base for our research that followed, in which we relied on the initial studies for selection of situations that would be meaningful to study in both cultural groups.

IV. TOP-DOWN APPROACHES

A. Application of Theories of Honor Culture to Turkish Participants

1. Emotional Consequences of Honor Threats

Both ethnographic and social-psychological evidence so far has shown that honor-relevant events evoke strong emotional responses, especially among

TABLE 4.1: **Categories of Most Commonly Generated Honor-Attacking and Honor-Enhancing Situations by Turkish and Northern US Participants**

	Description (Example)	TR (%)	US (%)
Honor-attacking situations			
Humiliation	Calling someone names, insulting, explicitly humiliating (*Disgrace the name of someone's parents or family*)	28.5	31.4
False accusations	Being falsely accused for acts one has not committed and being subjected to unfair treatments one does not deserve (*Accuse someone of cheating*)	34.3	4.4
Sexual/physical attack	Physically attacking someone (e.g., slapping, hitting), sexually attacking someone (molestation, sexual harassment) (*Sexually harass someone*)	9.5	3.6
Challenge/criticism	Challenging someone, criticizing or attacking their ideas or character features (*Attack their views and morals*)	6.6	29.2
Negative character	Lacking integrity, consistency, and stability in ones' actions (*Prove that the person has the wrong motives*)	0.7	7.3
Achievement/negative	Not being able to achieve/accomplish as expected or where the person is outperformed by others (*Outperform the person in an area that is important to them*)	0	5.1
Revealing negative behaviors of a person	Pointing out someone's negative behaviors (*Catch them in a lie about a serious matter*)	10.2	17.5
Honor-enhancing situations			
Praise	Praising someone's qualities, showing admiration and appreciation (*Praise someone in words or with actions*)	39.6	26.9
Achievement/positive	Achieving/accomplishing positive outcomes/being rewarded for them (*Make the honor roll at school for high grades*)	20.8	3.8
Positive character	Showing integrity, consistency, and stability in ones' actions (*Be an honest person*)	13.2	8.7

(*continued*)

208 Handbook of Advances in Culture and Psychology

TABLE 4.1: **Continued**

	Description (Example)	TR (%)	US (%)
Helping	Helping other people, serving in the community (*Encourage them to do voluntary community service*)	8.5	33.7
Revealing positive characteristics and behaviors of a person	Pointing out someone's positive behaviors, attributes, and characteristics (*Make them look like a great person in how they fight for what they believe in*)	13.2	18.3

Adapted from Uskul, A. K., Cross, S., Gercek-Swing, B., Sunbay, Z., & Ataca, B. (2012). Honor bound: The cultural construction of honor in Turkey and the northern US. *Journal of Cross-Cultural Psychology, 43*, 1131–1151. https://doi.org/10.1177/0022022111422258

members of honor cultures. Until recently, comparative studies have focused primarily on the negative emotional consequences (e.g., shame, anger) triggered by honor-attacking situations. This was perhaps the most logical starting point as negative emotions such as anger have the capacity to mobilize the individual subjected to an honor attack to retaliate against the perpetrator with a goal to restore their honor in their own eyes and in the eyes of others. Similarly, shame attracted considerable attention in this literature as it plays an important functional role in cultures of honor by signaling that one is attached to the honor code and underscores concern for others' appraisal of oneself. Moreover, research so far has primarily used honor-relevant situations that were either set up in the laboratory by researchers, generated by researchers based on examples of participants' real-life experiences, or recalled by participants themselves (e.g., Cohen et al., 1996; Rodriguez Mosquera et al., 2000, 2008). We built on this existing work and extended it by investigating both negative and positive emotional responses to honor-attacking and honor-enhancing events that we collected in a systematic manner in the early phases of our research program and focusing on the role of the cultural origin of the situations in individuals' emotional responses to these situations (Uskul et al., 2012). This approach allowed us to examine how honor is implicated in daily life, as observed in situations typically encountered by members of honor and dignity cultures.

In one set of studies, we capitalized on the honor-attacking and honor-enhancing situations generated by Turkish and northern US participants in Uskul et al. (2012, Study 1) and presented a random subset of these situations to a new sample of Turkish (n = 81) and European-heritage participants from northern US states (n = 76) who evaluated these situations in terms of their likely impact on their own feelings ("How would this situation make you feel about yourself?") and the feelings of their close others ("How would your family and friends feel about themselves?").[4] Participants were presented 160 situations, selected considering the type of situation (honor-attacking vs. -enhancing) as well as the cultural origin (Turkish vs. northern US) and gender (female vs. male) of the participant who generated the situations.

We found that when evaluating honor-attacking situations, Turkish participants, compared with their northern US counterparts, rated their own feelings and close others' feelings about themselves more strongly, especially when they imagined themselves in situations generated by their Turkish peers. When evaluating honor-enhancing situations, this difference held only for close others' feelings about themselves. Furthermore, Turkish participants rated the implications of honor-relevant situations similarly for themselves and their close others, whereas US participants rated the implications of these situations more negatively for themselves than for their close others. Importantly, we also found a significant effect of cultural origin of situations such that both honor-attacking and honor-enhancing situations generated by Turkish participants were evaluated as producing more emotional impact on both themselves and their close others. This finding underlines the more "extreme" nature of the situations generated by Turkish (vs. northern US) participants.

In a different set of studies, we followed up these findings with a goal to extend the study of emotional responses to honor-relevant situations to a large set of meaningful negative and positive emotions (rather than simply asking participants to evaluate the impact of situations on unspecified "feelings" [see Uskul et al., 2014]). We did this also to further investigate the reasons underlying the more potent evaluations that we observed among both Turkish and northern US participants of the situations generated by Turkish participants compared with situations generated by northern US participants. Specifically, we asked whether the potency of Turkish situations was due to their association with stronger positive or negative emotions. To test this possibility, we recruited Turkish (n = 168) and European-American participants from northern US states (n = 228) and asked them to indicate the degree to which honor-threatening or honor-enhancing situations would trigger a large set of emotions. Again, we selected these situations from a list of situations generated by participants in Uskul et al.'s study (2012, Study 1). Before conducting this study, we asked a separate sample of Turkish (n = 200) and northern US (n = 167) participants to rate these situations for how prototypical or central they are to their conceptions of situations that would enhance (or attack) a person's sense of honor. We did this with a goal to examine the role of situation centrality in the emotional responses triggered by honor-relevant situations.

We found that centrality of situations as well as cultural origin of situations played an important role in individuals' emotional responses to honor-attacking situations: Highly central honor-attacking situations (M = 4.39, SD = 1.04) elicited stronger negative emotions than did less central situations (M = 3.73, SD = 1.00; d = 0.65), and situations generated by Turkish participants (M = 4.17, SD = 0.93) elicited stronger negative emotions than did those generated by northern US participants (M = 3.95, SD = 1.02). In addition, the effect of situation centrality depended on situation origin, such that the difference in the intensity of emotions elicited by highly versus less central Turkish situations (d = 1.15) was greater than highly versus less central US situations (d = 0.23). Also, Turkish participants responded similarly to the highly and less central situations generated by US Northerners, suggesting that they did not distinguish between these situations in terms of their emotional consequences.

This pattern held for honor-enhancing situations. Highly central situations elicited stronger positive emotions (M = 4.74, SD = 0.81) than did less central situations (M = 4.58, SD = 0.79; d = 0.20), and situations generated by Turkish participants elicited stronger positive emotions (M = 4.80, SD = 0.79) than did those generated by northern US participants (M = 4.53, SD = 0.83; d = 0.33). Overall, these findings show that Turkish situations were viewed as being associated with stronger emotional consequences than US situations by both Turkish and northern US participants. Perhaps not surprisingly so, given that Turkish situations contained more "extreme" relational characteristics such as accusing someone falsely or sexually or physically attacking them (Uskul et al., 2012).

Findings from these sets of studies designed to focus on the emotional consequences of honor-relevant situations highlight a few important distinctions between the Turkish and northern American cultural worlds in terms of the strength and the nature of the emotional responses evoked by honor-relevant situations. First, in line with previous literature, we found that, in comparisons with members of a dignity culture, members of an honor culture responded more strongly to honor-attacking situations. Second, providing further evidence for the relational nature of honor-related experiences in the context of an honor culture, the findings demonstrated a spillover effect such that the consequences of honor-relevant situations for oneself and close others were evaluated similarly by Turkish participants. Third, both Turkish and US participants evaluated situations generated by Turkish participants as producing more impact on both themselves and their close others than situations generated by US participants, showing that honor is implicated by more potent situations in this cultural group. Fourth, this seemed to be due to the fact that Turkish situations were seen to be associated with stronger negative and positive emotions. Fifth, the prototypicality or centrality of honor situations moderated emotional responses. Overall, the situation sampling approach and the prototype approach that we took to examine honor-relevant situations provided us with an opportunity to examine the construct of honor from the perspective of both participants and the cultural origin of situations and highlighted that individuals' responses (regardless of their cultural background) can be strongly grounded in the characteristics of the situations they encounter.

2. Aggressive Responses to Honor Threats

At the time we started our research in Turkey and the northern United States, there was considerable evidence demonstrating differences between members of honor versus non-honor cultures in their responses to honor-threatening events. In a nutshell, this literature had shown that, when facing an honor threat (e.g., in the form of an insult or another type of offense), members of honor cultures tended to react in retaliatory ways, expressed mostly in violence, aggression, and negative emotions such as anger, and at times, perhaps counterintuitively so, politeness (for a review, see Uskul et al., 2019). Studies that provided this evidence based their predictions on a core theme in honor cultures which revolves around the need to create and maintain reputations for strength and toughness and a preparedness to engage in actions necessary to protect honor when it is under threat.

In our work, we examined whether this prediction would receive support in a different cultural context by asking how members of Turkish cultural contexts (in comparison with European American US Northerners) would respond emotionally and behaviorally to threats to their honor. In our attempts to examine the generalizability of previously observed findings in this domain, we also incorporated in our designs the observations that we made in the studies in which we took a bottom-up approach. Specifically, taking into consideration the relational features of honor as demonstrated in the bottom-up studies that we have summarized previously, we asked how individuals would respond when honor attacks are relational (i.e., when directed to one's close others). We examined retaliation using behavioral measures to overcome limitations associated with using imaginary situations or recalled honor threats that tend to be idiosyncratic. Finally, we also capitalized on the finding that different situations were perceived as honor-attacking by members of honor and dignity cultural groups and examined whether type of honor threat might result in different responses. This allowed us to expand existing research on honor threats beyond the commonly employed threats to masculine honor.

In two studies, we investigated retaliatory responses to an honor threat which took the form of accusing the person of being dishonest (vs. neutral feedback) in a task that involved producing an essay where participants explained the role of honesty in their lives. We chose this particular form of an offense based on our initial studies where we observed that individuals of Turkish and northern US backgrounds reported viewing honesty as central to their lay conception of honor (Cross et al., 2014). In both studies, we found that Turkish participants retaliated more aggressively than did northern US participants against the person who challenged their honesty. Two behavioral measures provided evidence for this. In one study (Uskul et al., 2015, Study 1), they assigned this person significantly more difficult tangrams to solve than easy ones and made it less likely for the participant to be eligible for a prize linked to the number of successfully solved tangrams (see Figure 4.1). In another study (Uskul et al., 2015, Study 2), Turkish participants assigned significantly more intense and potentially painful stimuli (in both studies participants were asked to choose these tasks for the [bogus] participant to complete in an unrelated study that was about to follow). When feedback was neutral (i.e., not honor-threatening), the two groups did not differ from each other, indicating that Turkish participants did not show a generalized tendency to be retaliatory in the absence of threatening feedback. These results, in line with previous research, show one more time that honor threats are more likely to be responded to in a retaliatory manner by members of other honor cultures compared with members of non-honor cultures.

When we examined responses to honor threats that were directed to close others (specifically to honesty of one's parents in the form of accusing them of behaving dishonestly; for procedural details, see Uskul et al., 2015, Study 2), we found that endorsement of honor values (measured by Rodriguez Mosquera et al.'s [2008] Honor Values scale) predicted retaliation in the relational honor threat condition among Turkish participants but not among northern US participants. Thus, Turkish participants who were concerned about their social

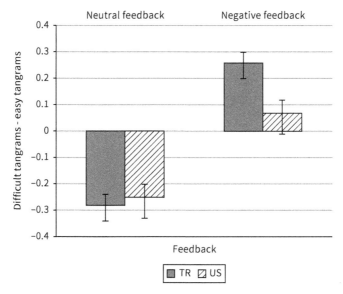

FIGURE 4.1: Difference in the number of difficult tangrams (relative to the number of easy tangrams) assigned to the imaginary participant as a function of type of feedback (neutral vs. negative) and cultural background (Turkish [TR] vs. US).
Adopted from Uskul, A. K., Cross, S., Günsoy, C., Gercek-Swing, B., Alozkan, C., & Ataca, B. (2015). A price to pay: Turkish and American retaliation for threats to personal and family honor. *Aggressive Behavior, 41,* 594–607. https://doi.org/10.1002/ab.21598

image retaliated more when their parents' honesty was attacked than did those who were less concerned about their social image. This finding points to the importance of differentiating between individuals who strongly versus weakly endorse a cultural value within a given cultural context and to the value of considering the three-way interaction between cultural context × person characteristics × situation (see CuPS approach by Leung & Cohen, 2011).

3. Responses to Differing Types of Honor Attacks

In a different line of studies, we examined evaluations of responses to hypothetical situations, once again informed by our initial bottom-up research on honor-relevant situations (Uskul et al., 2012). This time, our predictions were informed by past findings that demonstrated both retaliatory and polite or non-confrontational responses to honor threats. Despite sounding paradoxical, members of honor cultures have been shown to cultivate politeness and hospitality to avoid offending others, with a goal of preventing the start of a cycle of retaliation and retribution. For example, Cohen et al. (1999) found that US Southerners were slower to respond to a series of annoyances compared with US Northerners, but when Southerners responded, their reactions were much more extreme and aggressive than reactions by Northerners (which they termed the "paradox of politeness" in southern states). Based on this, we examined the approval of different types of responses, specifically retaliation versus withdrawal, to honor threats that varied in potency (Cross et al., 2013). We compared participants' evaluations of different honor threat situations, in which the target was subjected to either a rude affront (less potent) or a false accusation (more potent) and the target chose to respond by either withdrawing from the situation or confronting the attacker. We found that Turkish participants were more likely than northern US participants to favor the person who withdrew from the rude affront and the person who confronted the false accusation. This pattern is in line with the notion that members of honor cultures may respond differently to different types of honor threats (e.g., weak in potency or minor annoyances vs. strong in potency or viewed as humiliating); they either avoid starting a cycle of violence (like the US Southerners in Cohen et al.'s [1999] study) or deal with it strongly to signal that the accusation is not correct. Furthermore, we found that endorsement of honor values was associated more strongly with justification and encouragement of confrontational responses among Turkish versus northern US respondents. These findings once again provide insight into the role of cultural norms and individual differences in the ways honor shapes behavior.

In this study, we also examined the normative context by asking participants to report how they thought others in their society would evaluate the target who attacked or withdrew in situations that involved a rude affront or a false accusation and how others in their society would behave in those situations. Furthermore, we assessed the extent to which individuals would encourage others to withdraw or confront in those situations. This approach allowed us to investigate (a) how participants' personal evaluations and behavioral tendencies might be shaped by their social perceptions of societal norms in honor-related situations and (b) how personal evaluations shape societal norms and expectations.

We found that, unlike the pattern observed with personal approval, Turkish participants perceived that other people in their society would be more likely to confront than to withdraw. They also perceived that other people would approve of the person who engaged in confrontational responses in the face of both rude affronts and false accusations. Northern US participants responded similarly; however, this difference in perceptions that others would approve of confrontation more than withdrawal was larger for Turkish than northern US participants. Finally, consistent with the paradox of politeness, Turkish participants were more likely to encourage others to withdraw rather than to confront in the face of rude affronts and more likely to encourage confrontation rather than withdrawal in the face of false accusation (see Figure 4.2). Northern US participants encouraged withdrawal and confrontation at similar levels for rude affronts and were more likely to encourage confrontation than withdrawal in the face of false accusation situations.

This study builds a bridge between culture as represented in individuals' heads and their expectations of their society (for similar approaches, see Chiu et al., 2010; Zou et al., 2009). Based on our bottom-up work, we also recognized that honor-relevant situations can come in different shapes and forms and that responses to those (both personal and, as expected, from other people) can differ. These findings highlight the importance of not treating all honor-related situations similarly, both in research and in applied contexts. By focusing on different types of honor threats, perceived societal norms, and individual values, we tried to capture the complex dynamics that shape how honor operates in our social lives.

4. Honor Concerns in the Context of Social Media

In a fourth set of studies, we examined the consequences of culture of honor norms and values for a relatively new social phenomenon: interaction over social media. One's posts, pictures, and comments on social media have the potential to enhance or to ruin one's reputation, as evidenced by the frequent take-downs of celebrities and politicians based on their cruel, prejudiced, or simply insensitive posts on Facebook, Twitter, or other social media outlets. One critical key to the power of social media is the public shaming that can occur when an individual posts potentially inappropriate or scandalous content (or someone else posts about their inappropriate or scandalous behavior [Scheff & Schorr, 2017]). For the average person, this shaming may be limited to the individual's family, friends, and in-groups; but it can nevertheless result in gossip, ostracism, and a loss of reputation that can have far-reaching effects. In cultures of honor, individuals must be careful to guard not only their own honorable reputation but also that of their family. So, what are the implications of culture of honor concerns for everyday social media behavior?

That was the question addressed in studies that compared Facebook postings by Turkish and northern Euro-American students (Günsoy et al., 2015). The studies focused on students' attitudes toward posting content that was potentially scandalous or that might result in disapproval by family members

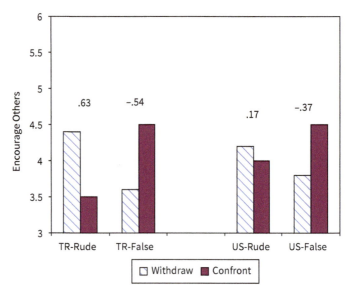

FIGURE 4.2: Responses to the question "Would you encourage your friend/son to behave similarly?" in withdrawal or confrontation and in rude or false accusation scenarios.
Note: Values above the bars represent the effect size (d) for the difference in the two conditions.
Adopted from Cross, S. E., Uskul, A. K., Gercek Swing, B., Alozkan, C., & Ataca, B. (2013). Confrontation vs. withdrawal: Cultural differences in responses to threats to honor. *Group Processes and Intergroup Relations, 16,* 345–362. https://doi.org/10.1177/1368430212461962

or close others. In Turkish contexts, this could include posts related to parties and alcohol or pictures with romantic partners or with opposite-sex friends. As expected, the Turkish participants reported that they were less willing to post such pictures; if they did post such a picture, they reported that they would be less likely than their northern US counterparts to let their relatives see the pictures (see Figure 4.3). In contrast, there were no group differences in the willingness of Turkish and northern US participants to post content that could enhance their honor and reputation, such as pictures of winning an award.

Günsoy and her colleagues also requested permission to download 6 months worth of postings from these participants' Facebook pages. Coders blind to the study's hypotheses coded them into theory-relevant categories, such as achievement-related posts and posts about potentially dishonorable or improper situations (being at a party or holding a drink at a bar). When participants' scores on a commonly used honor values measure were correlated

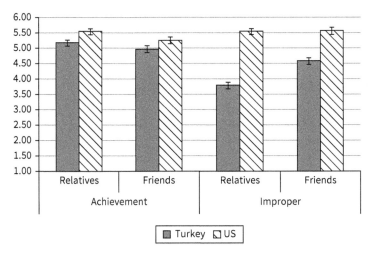

FIGURE 4.3: Willingness to let relatives and friends view one's achievement and potentially improper pictures. Error bars represent standard errors.
Adapted from Günsoy, C., Cross, S. E., Saribay, A., Olcaysoy-Okten, I., & Kurutas, M. (2015). Would you post that picture and let your dad see it? Culture, honor and Facebook. *European Journal of Social Psychology, 45*, 323–335. https://doi.org/10.1002/ejsp.2041

with their posting behavior, an interesting pattern emerged: For the Turkish participants, high scores on the honor values measure were associated with low levels of posting content that could be seen as improper, but they were not associated with rates of posting achievement-related material. For the US Northerners, however, scores on the honor values measure were positively associated with posting achievement-related material among women (but not men) but not to rates of posting potentially improper material. These findings show that endorsement of honor values has different consequences in different cultural contexts (as Leung & Cohen's [2011] CuPS model theorizes): In a context in which avoiding disrepute or scandal is highly valued (e.g., Turkey), individuals who are very concerned about their own and their family's honor will avoid social media behavior that could cause reputation loss. In contrast, in a cultural context in which self-promotion and self-enhancement are common and expected (e.g., northern United States), individuals who strongly endorse the importance of their own and their family's reputation will be more likely to post content that highlights their achievement and competence. Like a hydrangea flower that blooms blue or pink based on whether it is planted in acidic or alkaline soil, concern for one's reputation can result in different behaviors, depending on one's cultural environment.

V. EXPANDING THE THEORY OF HONOR CULTURES

One goal of our work has been to elaborate how concerns for one's honor shape behavior. In recent work, we have pursued that question in two domains. First, we have differentiated among types of threat, to show that for members of an honor culture, particularly Turkish participants, honor threats are construed differently than other kinds of threats. The second domain is in the area of goal pursuit. We have investigated how honor threats can derail goal pursuit among members of an honor culture.

A. Differentiating Honor Threats From Other Types of Threat

Most of the early work on responses to threats to one's honor focused on comparing responses to insults or affronts versus neutral or non-insulting situations. Typically, members of honor cultures respond more aggressively to the insult than to the neutral or non-insulting condition (Cohen et al., 1996). These findings raise the following question: Do members of honor cultures respond aggressively to any threat or criticism, or are they selective in their responses, responding to threats that implicate the components of honor (especially social respect) more strongly than other sorts of criticism?

Theoretically, members of an honor culture should differentiate between challenges that only affect their self-esteem or pride (such as not winning an award or performing poorly on an exam) and those that are related to the other components of honor: morality and social respect. It is these components—morality and social respect—that we expect to most strongly differentiate conceptions of worth in Turkey and other traditional honor cultures from those of dignity cultures. As our other studies have shown, honesty is a core component of the honor code among Turkish participants, and Turkish people respond strongly when their honesty is impugned (Cross et al., 2014; Uskul et al., 2015). A charge that one is dishonest should theoretically implicate a Turkish person's sense of honor or worth more extensively than a charge that one is incompetent, due to the centrality of morality in the honor code of the relatively tight Turkish context and the possibility that dishonorable behavior can be known by others and stain one's social respect. In contrast, for US Northerners socialized in a loose cultural context, a charge of dishonesty is less likely to threaten the internal and inherent sense of worth thought to characterize members of dignity cultures (Leung & Cohen, 2011). Given that one's own self-evaluation is the primary basis of self-worth in dignity cultures, challenges to one's honesty or to one's competence may have similar consequences. We tested these hypotheses in several studies that differentiated threats to one's honesty from threats to one's competence.

1. Responses to True Accusations of Dishonesty Versus Accusations of Incompetence

Most of the existing research on how people respond to insults and accusations in honor and dignity cultures has relied on undeserved insults, false accusations, or accusations that can be discounted (e.g., "I don't think this essay is truthful" [Uskul et al., 2015; see also Beersma et al., 2003; Cohen et al., 1996; Rodriguez Mosquera et al., 2008; van Osch et al., 2013]). Sometimes, however, an accusation of misconduct or dishonesty is accurate or deserved. For members of cultures of honor, a rightful accusation of dishonesty may be especially harmful to social position because the "stain" of the dishonorable behavior is not easily removed or discounted. Compared to insults or false accusations, an accurate or true accusation of misconduct against a person is likely to lead to more distrust, less collaboration, and more ostracism of the immoral actor (Skowronski, 2002; Wojciszke, 2005). Given that honor must be given by others and not just claimed by the individual, a verifiable act of lying, cheating, stealing, or other immorality stains the person's reputation permanently.

In two studies, Günsoy, Cross, and colleagues focused on how members of honor and dignity cultures responded to true accusations of misconduct compared to negative competence feedback on performance. They hypothesized that among Turkish (honor culture) participants, a true accusation of dishonesty would be very honor-threatening, leading to strong, aggressive responses. For members of a dignity culture, however, one's own self-views are theoretically more important than others' opinions of the self, and dishonesty is perhaps more easily dismissed or minimized (Günsoy et al., 2018).

In the first study, participants read scenarios, where they were asked to imagine themselves as a member of a workgroup who is either rightfully accused of misconduct or given negative competence feedback on their performance by the leader of the group. For example, one scenario asks the participant to put themselves in the place of a member of a workgroup who either (a) plagiarizes a project and is called out by their boss (true accusation), (b) forgets to include an important element of a project and is confronted by their boss (competence threat), or (c) is given neutral or slightly positive feedback on their performance on the project (no threat condition). Turkish and White northern US college students read two such situations in their native language and evaluated how negatively they perceived each situation, how they would respond emotionally, and how they would react in each situation. Specifically, participants indicated the extent to which they would want to retaliate against the accuser.

As we expected, the Turkish participants responded more intensely to the true accusation situations than to the negative competence feedback situations; they rated them as more negative ($d = 0.65$) and reported they would feel more anger ($d = 0.69$) and more shame ($d = 0.69$) in the true accusations compared to the negative feedback situations. In contrast, the US Northerners did not distinguish between the two types of situations as much as did the Turkish participants: They rated the two types of situations as equally negative ($d = 0.18$) and equally anger-inducing ($d = 0.03$). They only distinguished between the situations in their ratings of how ashamed they would feel: True accusations engendered greater reports of shame than did negative feedback ($d = 0.61$). Consistent with these reactions, the Turkish participants also said they would be more likely to retaliate against the accuser in the verifiable misconduct situations than in the negative feedback situation ($d = 0.55$). US Northerners, however, did not vary as greatly in their responses to the two types of situations ($d = 0.27$).

These findings provided initial support that true accusations of dishonorable behavior were especially potent for Turkish participants, but they bear the limitations endemic to self-report studies in hypothetical situations. So we followed up with an experimental study that manipulated the morality threat and the negative performance feedback and that allowed the participants to actually retaliate against the source of the threat. To set up the study, we ask you to put yourself in the position of a participant in the morality threat condition in the study.

> You come to the lab, where the experimenter describes the study as an investigation of teamwork, cognition, and decision-making. After signing the consent form and completing some brief questionnaires, you are placed in a room with another participant, given a worksheet with four difficult problems, and told to work individually on two problems and work together on two problems. The experimenter stresses the importance of not helping each other on the individual problems and the value of working together on the team problems. When the experimenter leaves, you and your partner begin working on the problems,

following the instructions to work together on two problems and individually on the others. The final problem is the most difficult, but you have been told to work on it individually. Your partner in this task, however, asks for help, and he pesters you until you give in and give him your answer.

Next, you and your partner individually complete a questionnaire about teamwork, while the experimenter scores your performance on the logic problems. After a few minutes, the experimenter returns, appearing flustered. "There seems to be a problem here," he says, and he asks your partner to go with him to another room. "What problem?" you think, and then the experimenter returns and says "I scored your logic problems, and you appear to have shared answers on one of the problems you were supposed to finish individually. You both had the same wrong answer to the last problem. I wasn't sure what to do, so I called the professor in charge of the study. She said this sounds like a case of cheating, and she would like to talk to you. She has something she has to complete first, but she said to go ahead to the next task while we wait for her."

The experimenter then describes the next task as designed to investigate the relations between emotions and decision-making. You complete a few short measures on the computer about your emotional state, then, after a coin flip, you (not your partner) are selected for the decision-making task with the experimenter. The experimenter explains that part of his payment for being a research assistant is based on this task and that you both could make money depending on the outcomes of the task.

The experimenter goes on to explain the task, which is based on the ultimatum game (Guth et al., 1982). He tells you that there are several rounds in this task, and on each round, he has been given a particular amount of money to divide between himself and you, the participant. For example, he may have $10, and he can give you any fraction of that $10 he chooses (let's say 25% or $2.50). If you accept the offer, you keep $2.50, and he keeps $7.50. If you reject the offer, you both receive nothing. The experimenter tells you that you two will communicate via computer, and that he will be in another room making the offers. He won't see your responses until the end of the task—so his offers are not responses to your decisions to accept or reject his previous offers. Finally, he describes how the computer-based program will randomly select the outcome of two rounds in the task to determine his payment and your payment. So if the computer selects two rounds in which you rejected the offer, you would both leave empty-handed. In contrast, if the computer selects two rounds in which you accept the experimenter's offer of $4 from a total of $10, then you would go home with $8, and the experimenter would leave with $12.

After making sure that you understand the decision-making task, the experimenter goes to another room and begins the proposal–response sequence. You are still seething at the experimenter tattling on you to the professor and worried that the professor could tell others. Do you use this task as an opportunity to get back at the experimenter by rejecting his offers, even though it means you won't make any extra money? Or do you swallow your anger, accept his offers, and hope to go home with a few extra dollars in your pocket?

This was the predicament that one group of Turkish and White northern US participants faced in Günsoy et al.'s (2018) study (adapted from Russano et al., 2005; Scherr & Madon, 2012). Another group of participants was given negative competence feedback: They were told they had performed very badly on the logic problems and that the professor had been consulted and was coming to speak to the participant. Finally, a third group of participants was not given any feedback—neither that they cheated nor that they performed poorly.[5]

How did the participants respond, and did cultural background make a difference? Both condition and cultural background made a difference in the participants' decisions to accept or reject the high-stakes offers (i.e., those high in value). Compared to Turkish participants in both the negative competence feedback and the neutral feedback conditions, the Turkish participants in the true accusation condition rejected more high-value offers. Evidently, being called a cheater is worse than being called incompetent for members of a culture of honor. In contrast, among the northern US participants, there was no difference in the number of rejections of high-value offers by people in the true accusation condition and the negative feedback condition. Participants in both of these conditions rejected the offers more frequently than did participants in the neutral condition. In short, being told one is a cheater has the same effect as being told one is incompetent for northern US participants.

Furthermore, Günsoy and her colleagues (2018) found that the likelihood of rejecting offers in the morality threat condition was stronger among Turkish participants who highly endorsed an honor values measure (Rodriquez Mosquera et al., 2008). This was not the case for the northern US participants, however. In other words, members of an honor culture who strongly endorse the importance of maintaining one's social image were more likely to retaliate against their accuser than were those who did not.

Taken together, these studies show that Turkish participants differentiate between threats to their honesty/morality and threats to their competence more than do US Northerners. In a dignity culture, the "stain" of being called out for cheating or lying is only superficial; the basic dignity or inherent worth of the individual is not contaminated by the behavior. In an honor culture, in contrast, an apology may make the stain of an immoral behavior more permanent because it indicates responsibility for the behavior.

If we map these conditions onto the components of honor identified by our earlier prototype study (Cross et al., 2014), a challenge to one's honesty addresses the morality component of honor. Furthermore, a charge of dishonesty may be more likely to impact others' respect for the individual. Individuals told they are incompetent at a task may experience decreased self-esteem, but this is not as likely to influence others' respect for them as a charge of dishonesty. Given that social respect is a key feature that distinguishes honor cultures from dignity cultures, a potential threat to one's social reputation should have more impact than a threat to one's self-esteem for members of this group. In the study we describe in the next section, we examined the emotional consequences of these two types of threat among members of honor and dignity cultural groups.

2. Emotional Responses to Social Respect and Self-Respect Threats

In one exploration of this question, we examined participants' emotional responses to hypothetical situations that could threaten their reputation compared to situations that primarily threatened their self-respect (Günsoy et al., 2021). Anger and shame are among the common responses examined in the face of reputation threats among members of cultures of honor (Cohen et al., 1996; IJzerman et al., 2007; Maitner et al., 2017; Rodriguez Mosquera et al., 2002b). Anger activates the individual to respond to the source of the threat, whereas shame serves to alert the individual to potential dishonorable behavior and to motivate appropriate behavior in the future (Boiger et al., 2014; Leung & Cohen, 2011).

We hypothesized that Turkish participants would differentiate between the two types of situations more than would northern US participants. In particular, we expected that Turkish participants would view the reputation threat situations as more rude and humiliating than would the northern US participants. In addition, we expected that the Turkish participants would anticipate that they would experience more anger and shame in response to the situations than would the northern US participants.

In this study, Turkish (n = 52) and White northern US (n = 38) undergraduate research participants read brief descriptions of situations (derived from the situations generated in Uskul et al. [2012]). Three situations depicted a reputation threat (e.g., being insulted in front of other people) and three situations depicted a self-respect threat (e.g., being criticized privately). Manipulation checks demonstrated that these two types of situations differed in the extent to which they could harm a person's reputation, but they were rated similarly in importance. Participants were asked to imagine each situation and to appraise how rude and humiliating they would find them and the degree to which they would experience anger and shame-related emotions if they were in the situation.

There were no cultural differences or culture by threat-type interactions in the evaluations of how rude or humiliating the scenarios were. We often find no differences between these groups in appraisals of the situation, indicating that differences in their responses are not due to different perceptions of aspects of the situation (e.g., rudeness or humiliation or, in other studies, negativity, commonality, or importance). Instead, our primary interest was in how these situations prompt differing responses by members of the two groups. Indeed, as expected, there was a significant interaction of cultural group and threat type for ratings of anger and shame (see Figure 4.4). As expected, Turkish participants were more likely to anticipate feeling anger in social respect situations than in self-respect situations, whereas US Northerners anticipated the same level of anger in both types of situations. Of note, there was also a simple effect of cultural group in the anger ratings for the social respect situations, with Turkish participants rating these situations as more anger-provoking than US Northerners (d = 0.52). There was no cultural difference for anger ratings of the self-respect situations.

Ratings of shame revealed marked differences for the two types of situations. Both Turkish and US participants were more likely to anticipate feeling shame in social respect situations than in self-respect situations, but the difference was much greater among Turkish participants than among northern US participants. Curiously, there was no cultural difference in anticipated shame in the social respect situations, but US Northerners anticipated feeling more shame than did Turkish participants for the self-respect situations.

These findings support the argument that members of an honor culture discriminate more between threats to their social standing and reputation versus threats to their self-esteem compared to members of a dignity culture. In a cultural context in which one's reputation is easily damaged by others, resulting in significant losses of other types, an angry response to a public insult communicates to others that the insult is off-base and untrue. The findings for shame reports were more extreme—the social respect situations were

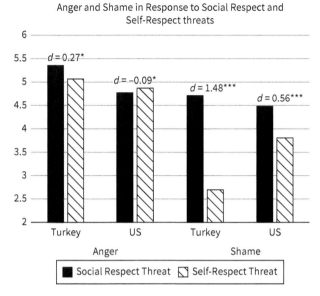

FIGURE 4.4: Turkish and northern US participants' emotional responses to scenarios depicting threats to social respect or self-respect ($*p < 0.05$, $***p < 0.001$).

much more likely to elicit high shame ratings for the Turkish participants than were the self-respect situations. Shame is one of the primary emotional consequences of disrespect and dishonor; consequently, this pattern indicates that, for Turkish participants, a challenge to one's self-esteem is fundamentally different from a challenge to one's reputation. Whereas a challenge to one's beliefs about oneself or one's abilities may have negative consequences for performance, emotion, and other behavioral outcomes, the negative consequences of a threat to one's reputation are potentially far greater in an honor culture. An individual's dishonor can also stain their family members, resulting in social exclusion from important groups, in gossip and rumors, and in ongoing discrimination against the family (Uskul et al., 2012). These differences were much smaller for the US Northerners, suggesting that they view self-respect and social respect situations relatively similarly; the price of threats to one's competence for the US Northerners is a higher level of shame (compared to the Turkish participants).

B. Extending Theories of Honor to Goal Pursuit

In a more recent direction of our research, we were inspired by the literature on goal conflict and aimed to extend some of the predictions emerging from this literature to the study of the role of maintenance and protection of honor acting in competition with other goals in cultures of honor. *Goal conflict* can be defined as a situation in which seemingly incompatible goals exert force in opposing or divergent directions (Kehr, 2003). Leung and Cohen (2011) asserted that the importance put on maintaining or asserting one's honor by members of honor cultures may override other goals, even when the honor-restoring actions are costly, thus leading to a goal conflict. They claimed that this is due to a salient characteristic of members of honor cultures as "dedicated to short-term irrationality in that [they] abhor cost–benefit calculations" (p. 510). For example, it is likely that Zidane experienced goal conflict when he headbutted Materazzi in the World Cup final in 2006 for mentioning his sister in a heated moment. Was he going to respond to Materazzi as would be expected of him (i.e., not leaving an insult to his sister unanswered) or end his football career in a celebratory way? He chose the first and almost 15 years on, he is still remembered for the headbutt.

Following this theorizing and utilizing a goal conflict framework, we suggested that when members of honor cultures face an honor threat in the form of false accusations or insults, the goal of restoring honor may take precedence, and any other goal that they were working toward may become secondary to the honor-relevant goal (Brunstein & Gollwitzer, 1996). In addition, we continued to examine the hypothesis that for members of honor cultures, threats to one's honor (in the form of an accusation of being dishonest) elicited different responses than a non-honor threat (in the form of an accusation of incompetence). Thus, this line of research helped us extend the reach of culture of honor theories by intersecting it with goal conflict literature as well as by differentiating how responses to honor threats differ from responses to other kinds of threats among members of honor and dignity cultures. Finally, we also expanded research on honor cultures by using two different honor groups: Turkish participants and US European-heritage Southerners.

1. Consequences of Honor Threat for Goal Delay

We first tested this prediction in a study where we examined goal delay in the presence of a threat to one's honesty, in the presence of a competence threat, and in a no threat condition. We hypothesized that members of an honor culture cannot let a threat to their honesty or honor pass; they must find a way to respond. Consequently, other goals may take a back seat to the goal of restoring honor, leading the individual to delay initiating action toward them (termed the *predecisional* phase of goal pursuit by Gollwitzer [1996]).

Using a modified version of a laboratory paradigm designed to deliver honor-threatening feedback to participants (see Uskul et al., 2015), we first asked participants to report when (i.e., how soon) they would start working toward several goals (adapted from Guinote, 2007) after an accusation of dishonesty, an accusation of incompetence, or no threat. As predicted, we found that members of cultures of honor (Turkish and US European-heritage Southerners) were more likely to delay pursuit of a goal following an honor threat compared with a competence threat or no threat. They were also more likely to report goal delay in the honor threat condition compared with members of a dignity culture (US European-heritage Northerners [Günsoy et al., 2020, Study 1]).

2. Consequences of Honor Threat for Goal Derailment

To picture the situation participants encountered in this study, imagine yourself in a new workgroup, and one of your group members, Pat, has just insinuated that you are a liar. You are not able to respond immediately to this accusation, but later, you are in a situation in which you must choose a partner from the group to work on a problem-solving task. The best-performing groups will win a monetary prize. The task involves mathematical and statistical skills, and Pat, your accuser, is the only member of your group who has the background and training to perform well on this task. Your dilemma is this: Do you select Pat as a partner in order to increase your odds of performing well and so winning a prize, or do you snub Pat and choose someone else, therefore potentially derailing your own goal of a monetary gain?

This was the decision that faced participants in our second study related to goal pursuit. We set up an analogue of this situation in an online interaction platform (based loosely on the Ostracism Online Manipulation paradigm created by Wolf et al., 2015). Participants created an avatar in the online space, introduced themselves to the other group members with a short statement of their interests and achievements (others' behavior was pre-scripted), and commented on other group members' statements (these were pre-scripted by a computer program to appear to be other research participants). As part of the scripted interaction, other group members commented on the participant's statement. In the honor threat condition, a participant named Pat (or the Turkish equivalent) insinuated that the participant was lying about their achievements. In the competence threat condition, Pat commented that the participant did not write well. In the no threat condition, Pat made very neutral comments on the real participant's introductory statement. Other group members also made scripted neutral comments. In all cases, Pat was presented as the best partner for the upcoming mathematical problem-solving task. The members of the pair who correctly solved the most problems could each win a $30 (50TL) gift card. The "real" participants were faced with the dilemma just described: Do they choose Pat to be their partner for the problem-solving task, and thereby increase their odds of winning a prize, or do they reject Pat due to the insult and choose someone else?

First, to determine that the situation was perceived similarly across all three groups, we examined the degree to which participants from Turkey, the southern United States, and the northern United States (US participants were all from White, European-heritage backgrounds) selected Pat in the no threat condition. This condition is an important manipulation check, to be confident that Pat was largely perceived as the best partner for the problem-solving task. As shown in Figure 4.5, 82%–93% of the participants in these conditions selected Pat as their partner.

As expected, the Turkish participants differentiated between the honor/honesty threat and the competence threat conditions; they were much less likely to select Pat as a partner in the honesty threat condition (32%) than in the competence threat condition (53%). The US Northerners, in contrast, did not differ at all in their rates of selecting Pat in the honesty threat (51%) versus the competence threat (54%) conditions. Finally, the US Southerners in the honesty threat condition selected Pat at about the same rates as the US Northerners (50%) but were somewhat less likely to select Pat as a partner in the competence threat condition (38%). The Southerners' rates of choosing Pat in these two threat conditions did not, however, significantly differ from each other. In short, a significantly higher number of Turkish participants chose to let go of their chance of winning a prize (the goal in the study) by distancing themselves from the person who threatened their honor.

These studies point to three important discoveries. First, Turkish participants let the goal of maintenance of honor take precedence by (1) pushing off other goals to a later time and (2) sacrificing the possibility of winning a prize by not choosing a person who threatened their honor but who could also help them win the prize. Second, members of cultures of honor, especially Turkish participants, differentiated between honor threats and other non-honor threats to a greater extent than did members of the dignity culture group.

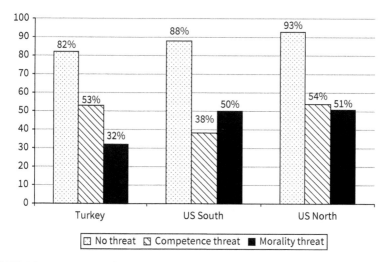

FIGURE 4.5: Percentages of Turkish, US southern, and US northern participants who chose Pat (the accuser in the threat conditions) in the no threat, competence threat, and morality threat conditions.
Adapted from Günsoy, C., Joo, M., Cross, S. E., Uskul, A. K., Gul, P., Wasti, S. A., Salter, P., Haugen, A., Erdaş, K. D., & Yegin, A. (2020). The influence of honor threats on goal delay and goal derailment: A comparison of Turkey, southern US, and northern US. *Journal of Experimental Social Psychology, 88*, Article 103974. http://dx.doi.org/10.1016/j.jesp.2020.103974

Thus, we see that members of honor cultures are not affected comparably by different types of threat; specific threats to one's sense of being a moral person who is respected by others are the ones that are most potent and lead to goal conflict. Third, to our knowledge, these studies provide the first systematic comparison between two different groups of honor cultures: the US South and Turkey. In the goal pursuit studies summarized in this section, we observed both similarities and differences between these two groups, and we can only speculate at this point where these might originate. Reasons such as technical aspects of our studies (e.g., differences in the paradigms or dependent measures employed) as well as differences in the meaning and function of honor among members of different cultures of honor might be underlying these non-uniform patterns of responses obtained in our studies with southern US and Turkish samples. Although previous studies have firmly established differences between the southern and northern regions of the United States, these studies focused almost exclusively on aggressive responses to threats directed to masculine honor. In our studies, we shifted the focus to threats to honesty, and it may be the case that this aspect of honor does not play as important a role in the US South as it does in Turkish society in regulating social behavior.

To assess the accuracy of these speculative interpretations of our results will require further comparisons between different cultures of honor, and we are currently conducting more research to tease apart and understand the ways in which these two groups are similar or different.

VI. THEMES, IMPLICATIONS, AND FUTURE DIRECTIONS

A. Summary of Major Themes of Our Work

In describing the progression of our research on cultures of honor, we have attempted to identify five major themes, either directly or indirectly. Our work began with bottom-up approaches that identified lay prototypes of honor in Turkish and northern US contexts (Cross et al., 2014) as well as situations that implicate honor in each context (Uskul et al., 2012). This approach acknowledges that honor ideologies coexist with and interact with other aspects of a particular cultural niche such as levels of individualism–collectivism, power distance, economic development, and gender equality. In this work we also addressed positive and negative aspects of honor, such as situations that enhanced or threatened one's honor and the positive and negative emotions elicited by these situations. At the time that we initiated this program of research, the focus of most of the existing scholarship was on negative consequences of the honor syndrome, such as retaliation for insults or affronts, honor killings, or domestic violence. Yet the honor complex sustains a variety of positive virtues and practices, and a complete research program should continue to examine both sides of the coin.

In another series of studies, taking a top-down approach, we have examined the generalizability of existing theories of honor cultures for Turkish participants. Following early studies with US Southerners, we conducted experimental studies of the effects of honor threats on the likelihood of behaving aggressively toward the source of a threat (Uskul et al., 2015). Framing honor in terms of concern for one's reputation, we found that members of honor cultures are more sensitive to sharing content in social media that can lead to shame or disrepute (Günsoy et al., 2015). Examination of social media posts also allows us to address cultural differences in both positive, honor-enhancing posts and negative, potentially dishonorable posts. Several of these studies examined the consequences of threats to one's honor for the individual as well as for their families, consistent with our focus on the relatively collective Turkish context. Other studies explicitly addressed the role of social norms in perceptions of people who confront or withdraw from an honor-related conflict (Cross et al., 2013).

We also sought to extend the reach of theories of honor cultures, first by distinguishing between different kinds of threats. For members of honor cultures, for whom one's worth lies not only in their own eyes but also in the eyes of others, a threat to others' opinion of them should have more impact than a threat to their self-esteem that does not impact others' opinions. We found that in several different types of studies—lab experiments, online experiments, and responses to scenarios—Turkish participants reacted more strongly to a charge that they behaved dishonestly (i.e., an honor threat) than to a charge that they were incompetent. Some may claim that an accusation of incompetence is also a type of honor threat; but it does not implicate the morality component of honor that an honesty threat implicates, and it is less likely to damage one's social respect or reputation than an accusation of dishonesty. The US Northerners in our studies did not differentiate between these two types of threats as much as did the Turkish participants, indicating perhaps that the key component of these two types of threat for members of a dignity culture is the threat to self-esteem.

We also extended the reach of theories of honor cultures by examining the consequences of honor threat for goal pursuit. Most theories suggest that members of honor cultures should prioritize the maintenance of their honor over most other goals and that when their honor is challenged, they should delay or abandon other goals in order to address the challenge. In these initial examinations of this hypothesis, we found that Turkish participants were more likely to delay initiation of other goals and to abandon other goals when their honor (honesty) was called into question (Günsoy et al., 2018, 2020). We are continuing to investigate the mechanisms through which concerns for honor can impede the pursuit and achievement of other goals.

Finally, woven through this overview of our work thus far are descriptions of a multiple approaches, methods, and paradigms. We have employed a prototype approach (Fehr, 1994, 2005), situational sampling (Kitayama et al., 1997; Morling et al., 2002), laboratory experiments, online social interactions, social media behaviors, and scenario studies to capture a diverse array of concepts, environments, attitudes, and perceptions that create a culture of honor and a culture of dignity. In several cases, we have identified CuPS interactions, in which individual differences in endorsement of honor lead to differing responses, depending on the situation and the individuals' cultural context. These approaches have allowed us to draw conclusions about how honor

232 Handbook of Advances in Culture and Psychology

threats cause aggression or goal delay and about the role of individual differences in honor-related situations. They show how honor and dignity cultures are represented not only in the heads of individuals but also in the everyday situations they encounter.

B. Implications and Future Directions

There are other approaches, methods, and paradigms that could provide valuable insight into the dynamics of honor and dignity cultures. For example, unfolding how honor is embedded in cultural artifacts and reflected in different linguistic practices would further enrich our understanding of the mutual constitution of mind and cultural context. Recent work by Gelfand and her colleagues (2015) is an important step in this direction, which provides researchers with an Honor Dictionary based on interviews conducted with members of different honor cultures to examine how honor is talked about in terms of gains, loses, or prevention of loss.[6] Other scholars have fruitfully used a variety of archival data sets to test how honor influences behavior in the US South (e.g., Altheimer, 2012; Brown, 2016); international data sets may also provide valuable tests of the theories across a variety of cultural settings. There is also growing interest in manipulating honor to test causal mechanisms (e.g., Leung & Cohen, 2011; Shafa et al., 2015). Given that honor is a multifaceted construct, these attempts would have to choose in a theoretically driven way which aspect(s) of honor should be primed, according to the specific research question. Another growing area of research has focused on the development of different explicit and implicit individual difference measures designed to assess individual endorsement of honor, face, and dignity values, as well as different aspects of honor (e.g., Barnes et al., 2012; Guerra et al., 2013; IJzerman et al., 2007; Imura et al., 2014; Rodriguez Mosquera et al., 2002a; Saucier & McManus, 2014; Saucier et al., 2016; Smith et al., 2017; Vandello et al., 2009). We are currently studying how some of these different measures predict theoretically meaningful variables associated with honor at the intrapersonal and interpersonal levels.

We have begun to examine similarities and differences in two different honor cultures, and this work needs considerable expansion. Two streams of research have contributed to the visibility of honor as a key cultural syndrome: One stream focused on Mediterranean societies such as Spain and Greece, and the other stream focused on southern regions of the United States (for a review, see Uskul et al., 2019). Other regions of the world, especially those based on pastoral subsistence norms and having unstable or inaccessible legal systems, may also be characterized by the beliefs, attitudes, and norms that characterize cultures of honor. For example, research in Pakistan (e.g., Rodriguez Mosquera et al., 2014), Poland (Krys et al., 2017), the Middle East and North Africa (e.g., Abu-Lughod, 1999; Abu-Odeh, 1996; Aslani et al., 2016; Eisner & Ghuneim, 2013; Maitner et al., 2017), and Latin America (e.g., Vandello & Cohen, 2003; Vandello et al., 2009) has uncovered elements of honor in people's behavior, attitudes, and emotions as well as in social norms and cultural products. Most of these regions have received little attention from cultural psychologists, and insight into the diversity of honor cultures can contribute to the advancement of theories and methods in multiple ways. For example, diverse honor contexts may enable researchers to identify which aspects of honor play a bigger or smaller role in shaping responses to honor-threatening and honor-enhancing situations in different cultures of honor, may facilitate the pinpointing of how honor is associated differently with other cultural dimensions across these groups (e.g., looseness/tightness, individualism/collectivism), and may expedite the determination of how honor is construed differently across different groups along the lines of socially constructed categories such as gender, social class, religion, and ethnicity.

This work, while focused primarily on honor cultures, also sheds light on dignity cultural processes, especially those of northern European-Americans. Cultural psychology turns a lens on little-studied cultural groups and societies and their norms, beliefs, values, and behaviors. But it also turns the lens back onto the more frequently studied WEIRD (Western, educated, industrialized, rich, and democratic) societies and provides insights into the sources of behavior that are taken for granted or assumed to be universal. For many people in the world, the responses of members of dignity cultures to accusations of misconduct or to insults are perceived as exceptionally weird: It may seem unimaginable that a person would not respond quickly and aggressively to being called a liar or being the target of a crude epitaph. They may see dignity contexts as an odd social world in which an individual can simply shrug off, discount, minimize, or ignore such treatment and still be considered a good person. In fact, the ability to do that is considered by some in dignity cultures to be the mark of the "bigger" person, the more self-assured person, or the person with a confident sense of their own integrity. In a society influenced by ethical and religious traditions that implore individuals to "turn the other cheek" or "forgive your enemies," individuals who retaliate against insults or false accusations may be viewed as "hot-heads" or "thin-skinned" and disparaged by others. To members of honor cultures, however, failure to respond in these cases is assumed to imply acquiescence to the threat or weakness.

In our work, we have started taking the investigation of honor beyond its original foci (e.g., aggressive responses to masculine honor threats) by extending research into relational aspects of honor (e.g., threats being directed to the self vs. close others), different types of honor threats (e.g., threats targeting one's morality vs. competence), negative and positive aspects and consequences of honor, and different types of social interactions (e.g., cooperating with someone [or not] who has just offended you). Moreover, in more recent studies, we have been working on connecting the literature on cultures of honor with the mainstream social psychology literature by, for example, integrating honor into the goal conflict literature. Our attempts contribute to the increasing cross-fertilization taking place across different subfields of psychology in relation to honor (e.g., honor in the context of negotiations [Aslani et al., 2016; Gelfand et al., 2015], honor in the context of intergroup relations [Levin et al., 2015], and honor in relation to social identities [Maitner et al., 2017]).

While our research has so far shed light on various unknown cultural aspects of honor and its consequences for emotions and actions, it has also highlighted how much more basic and applied research is needed to better grasp this complex construct in its cultural context and to integrate the accumulating evidence into other subfields of psychology. Continuing to research honor in relation to different outcome variables in intrapersonal, interpersonal, and intergroup levels of analysis and the underlying mechanisms will advance our understanding of the role played by honor in different domains of life. Further investigation into who pursues honor in varying situations, why honor is important, and how honor and other motivations and social norms interact to shape behavior can increase the integration of this work in mainstream psychological knowledge and increase its application in real-world settings such as education, health, violence, social work, and legal studies.

NOTES

1. *Westerners* are defined here as western Europeans or people with western European heritage living in North America, New Zealand, or Australia.
2. Exceptions to this include Rodriquez Mosquera's work in Spain and Pakistan (described in Rodriguez Mosquera, 2016), Travaglino's research on the Italian mafiosa (Travaglino et al., 2014), and Gelfand's work in the Middle East (Gelfand et al., 2015). Notably, work in African societies, some of which are likely to have cultures of honor, is missing from the social-psychological research on honor.

3. One exception was that we observed a trend toward northern US participants (5.3%) generating a slightly higher percentage of units focusing on close others than Turkish participants (1.2%), $\chi^2(1) = 3.55$, $p = .06$, Cramér's $\varphi = .14$.
4. We also asked participants to rate the situations for "How would others feel about your family?" Results pertaining to this question can be found in Uskul et al. (2012, Study 2).
5. The other "participant" in this study was actually a confederate of the experimenter. At the end of the study, all participants were carefully debriefed. They were also paid the maximum amount possible assuming acceptance of the two highest offers (15 Turkish lira in Turkey and $8 in the United States).
6. The dictionary is available at https://www.michelegelfand.com/honor-dictionary

REFERENCES

Abu-Lughod, L. (1999). *Veiled sentiments: Honor and poetry in a Bedouin society*. University of California Press.

Abu-Odeh, L. (1996). Crimes of honour and the construction of gender in Arab societies. In M. Yamani (Ed.), *Feminism and Islam: Legal and literary perspectives* (pp. 141–194). Ithaca Press.

Adams, G. (2005). The cultural grounding of personal relationship: Enemyship in North American and West African worlds. *Journal of Personality and Social Psychology*, *88*, 948–968.

Altheimer, I. (2012). Cultural processes and homicide across nations. *International Journal of Offender Therapy and Comparative Criminology*, *57*, 842–886.

Alvaro, S., Sinaceur, M., Madi, A., Tompson, S., Maddux, W. W., & Kitayama, S. (2018). Self-assertive interdependence in Arab culture. *Nature Human Behaviour*, *2*, 830–837.

Anderson, C. A. (1989). Temperature and aggression: Ubiquitous effects of heat on the occurrence of human violence. *Psychological Bulletin*, *106*, 74–96.

Aslani, S., Ramirez-Marin, J., Brett, J., Yao, J., Semnani-Azad, Z., Zhang, Z.-X., Tinsley, C., Weingart, L., & Adair, W. (2016). Dignity, face, and honor cultures: A study of negotiation strategy and outcomes in three cultures. *Journal of Organizational Behavior*, *37*, 1178–1201.

Bagli, M., & Sev'er, S. A. (2003). Female and male suicides in Batman, Turkey: Poverty, social change, patriarchal oppression and gender links. *Women's Health & Urban Life*, *2*, 60–84.

Barnes, C. D., Brown, R. P., & Osterman, L. L. (2012). Don't tread on me: Masculine honor ideology in the US and militant responses to terrorism. *Personality and Social Psychology Bulletin*, *38*, 1018–1029.

Beersma, B., Harinck, F., & Gerts, M. (2003). Bound in honor: How honor values and insults affect the experience and management of conflicts. *International Journal for Conflict Management, 14*, 75–94.

Boiger, M., Güngör, D., Karasawa, M., & Mesquita, B. (2014). Defending honor, keeping face: Interpersonal affordances of anger and shame in Turkey and Japan. *Cognition and Emotion, 28*, 1255–1269.

Bowman, J. (2006). *Honor: A history*. Encounter Books.

Brown, R. P. (2016). *Honor bound: How a cultural ideal has shaped the American psyche*. Oxford University Press.

Brown, R. P., & Osterman, L. L. (2012). Culture of honor, violence, and homicide. In T. K. Shackelford & V. A. Weekes-Shackelford (Eds.), *The Oxford handbook of evolutionary perspectives on violence, homicide, and war* (pp. 218–232). Oxford University Press.

Brunstein, J. C., & Gollwitzer, P. M. (1996). Effects of failure on subsequent performance: The importance of self-defining goals. *Journal of Personality and Social Psychology, 70*, 395–407.

Campbell, J. K. (1964). *Honor, family, and patronage*. Clarendon Press.

Cantor, N., Mischel, W., & Schwartz, J. (1982). A prototype analysis of psychological situations. *Cognitive Psychology, 14*, 45–77.

Chiu, C., Gelfand, M. J., Yamagishi, T., Shteynberg, G., & Wan, C. (2010). Intersubjective culture: The role of intersubjective perceptions in cross-cultural research. *Perspectives on Psychological Science, 5*, 482–493.

Cingöz-Ulu, B., & Lalonde, R. N. (2007). The role of culture and relational context in interpersonal conflict: Do Turks and Canadians use different conflict management strategies? *International Journal of Intercultural Relations, 31*, 443–458.

Cohen, D., Hernandez, I., Gruschow, K., Nowak, A., Gelfand, M. J., & Borkowski, W. (2018). Rationally irrational? The ecologies and economics of honor. In A. K. Uskul & S. Oishi (Eds.), *Socio-economic environment and human psychology* (pp. 77–102). Oxford University Press.

Cohen, D., Nisbett, R. E., Bowdle, B. F., & Schwarz, N. (1996). Insult, aggression, and the southern culture of honor: An "experimental ethnography." *Journal of Personality and Social Psychology, 70*, 945–960.

Cohen, D., & Vandello, J. A. (2004). The paradox of politeness. In M. Anderson (Ed.), *Cultural shaping of violence: Victimization, escalation, response* (pp. 119–132). Purdue University Press.

Cohen, D., Vandello, J., Puente, S., & Rantilla, A. (1999). "When you call me that, smile!" How norms for politeness, interaction styles, and aggression work together in southern culture. *Social Psychology Quarterly, 62*, 257–275.

Cross, S. E., & Lam, B. C.-P. (2017). Cultural models of self: East–West differences and beyond. In T. Church (Ed.), *The Praeger handbook of personality across cultures* (Vol. 2, pp. 1–33). Praeger.

Cross, S. E., Uskul, A. K., Gerçek-Swing, B., Alözkan, C., & Ataca, B. (2013). Confrontation versus withdrawal: Cultural differences in responses to threats to honor. *Group Processes & Intergroup Relations*, *16*, 345–362.

Cross, S. E., Uskul, A. K., Gerçek-Swing, B., Sunbay, Z., Alözkan, C., Günsoy, C., Ataca, B., & Karakitapoğlu-Aygün, Z. (2014). Cultural prototypes and dimensions of honor. *Personality and Social Psychology Bulletin*, *40*, 232–249.

De Almeida, I., & Uchida, Y. (2019). *Is international social psychology diverse enough?* [Manuscript in preparation]. Kyoto University.

de Tocqueville, A. (1969). *Democracy in America* (J. P. Mayer, Ed., G. Lawrence, Trans.). University of Chicago Press. (Original work published 1835)

Edgerton, R. B. (1971). *The individual in cultural adaptation*. University of California Press.

Eisner, M., & Ghuneim, L. (2013). Honor killing attitudes amongst adolescents in Amman, Jordan. *Aggressive Behavior*, *39*, 405–417.

Fehr, B. (1994). Prototype-based assessment of laypeople's views of love. *Personal Relationships*, *1*, 309–331.

Fehr, B. (2005). The role of prototypes in interpersonal cognition. In M. W. Baldwin (Ed.), *Interpersonal cognition* (pp. 180–205). Guilford Press.

Fischer, D. H. (1989). *Albion's seed: Four British folkways in America*. Oxford University Press.

Gastil, R. D. (1971). Homicide and a regional culture of violence. *American Sociological Review*, *36*, 412–427.

Gastil, R. D. (1989). Violence, crime and punishment. In C. R. Wilson & W. Ferris (Eds.), *Encyclopedia of southern culture* (pp. 1473–1476). University of North Carolina Press.

Gelfand, M. J., Severance, L., Lee, T., Bruss, C. B., Lun, J., Abdel-Latif, A.-H., Al-Moghazy, A. A., & Ahmed, S. M. (2015). Getting to yes: The linguistic signature of the deal in the U.S. and Egypt. *Journal of Organizational Behavior*, *36*, 967–989.

Gilmore, D. D. (1987). *Honor and shame and the unity of the Mediterranean*. American Anthropological Association.

Goldschmidt, W. (1965). Theory and strategy in the study of cultural adaptability. *American Anthropologist*, *67*, 402–407.

Gollwitzer, P. M. (1996). The volitional benefits of planning. In P. M. Gollwitzer & J. A. Bargh (Eds.), *The psychology of action: Linking cognition and motivation to behavior* (pp. 287–312). Guilford Press.

Greenfield, P. M. (1997). You can't take it with you: Why ability assessments don't cross cultures. *American Psychologist*, *52*, 1115–1124.

Guerra, V. M., Gouveia, V. V., Araújo, R. C. R., Andrade, J. M., & Gaudêncio, C. A. (2013). Honor scale: Evidence on construct validity. *Journal of Applied Social Psychology*, *43*, 1273–1280.

Guinote, A. (2007). Power and goal pursuit. *Personality and Social Psychology Bulletin, 33*, 1076–1087.

Gul, P., Cross, S. E., & Uskul, A. K. (2021). Implications of culture of honor theory and research for practitioners and prevention researchers. *American Psychologist, 76*, 502–515.

Günsoy, C., Cross, S. E., Sarıbay, A., Olcaysoy-Ökten, I., & Kurutaş, M. (2015). Would you post that picture and let your dad see it? Culture, honor, and Facebook. *European Journal of Social Psychology, 45*, 323–335.

Günsoy, C., Cross, S. E., Saribay, S. A., Wasti, S. A., Altinoz, E., & Yildiz, D. (2018). *Better to be a cheater or a failure? Cultural background and honor values predict aggressive responses to negative evaluation* [Unpublished manuscript]. Clemson University.

Günsoy, C., Cross, S. E., Uskul, A. K., & Gercek-Swing, B. (2021). The role of culture in appraisals, emotions, and helplessness in response to threats. *International Journal of Psychology, 55*, 472–477.

Günsoy, C., Joo, M., Cross, S. E., Uskul, A. K., Gul, P., Wasti, S. A., Salter, P., Haugen, A., Erdaş, K. D., & Yegin, A. (2020). The influence of honor threats on goal delay and goal derailment: A comparison of Turkey, southern US, and northern US. *Journal of Experimental Social Psychology, 88*, Article 103974.

Güth, W., Schmittberger, R., & Schwarze, B. (1982). An experimental analysis of ultimatum bargaining. *Journal of Economic Behavior & Organization, 3*, 367–388.

Hackney, S. (1969). Southern violence. *The American Historical Review, 74*, 906–925.

Henry, P. J. (2009). Low status compensation: A theory for understanding the role of status in cultures of honor. *Journal of Personality and Social Psychology, 97*, 451–466.

Higgins, E. T. (1996). The "self-digest": Self-knowledge serving self-regulatory functions. *Journal of Personality and Social Psychology, 71*, 1062–1084.

IJzerman, H., van Dijk, W. W., & Gallucci, M. (2007). A bumpy train ride: A field experiment on insult, honor, and emotional reactions. *Emotion, 7*, 860–875.

Imura, M., Burkely, M., & Brown, R. P. (2014). Honor to the core: Measuring implicit honor ideology endorsement. *Personality and Individual Differences, 59*, 27–31.

Kagitçibaşi, C. (1994). Psychology in Turkey. *International Journal of Psychology, 29*, 729–738.

Kagitcibasi, C., & Ataca, B. (2005). Value of children and family change: A three-decade portrait from Turkey. *Applied Psychology: An International Review, 54*, 317–337.

Kagitcibasi, C., & Ataca, B. (2015). Value of children, family change, and implications for the care of the elderly. *Cross-Cultural Research, 49*, 374–392.

Kardam, F. (2005). *The dynamics of honor killings in Turkey: Prospects for action*. United Nations Development Programme & Population Association.

Kehr, H. M. (2003). Goal conflicts, attainment of new goals, and well-being among managers. *Journal of Occupational Health Psychology, 8,* 195–208.

Kim, Y.-H., & Cohen, D. (2010). Information, perspective, and judgments about the self in face and dignity cultures. *Personality and Social Psychology Bulletin, 36,* 537–550.

Kim, Y.-H., Cohen, D., & Au, W.-T. (2010). The jury and abjury of my peers: The self in face and dignity cultures. *Journal of Personality and Social Psychology, 98,* 904–916.

Kitayama, S. (2002). Cultural and basic psychological processes—Toward a system view of culture: Comment on Oyserman et al. (2002). *Psychological Bulletin, 128,* 189–196.

Kitayama, S., Markus, H. R., Matsumoto, H., & Norasakkunkit, V. (1997). Individual and collective processes in the construction of the self: Self-enhancement in the US and self-criticism in Japan. *Journal of Personality and Social Psychology, 72,* 1245–1267.

Kitayama, S., Park, H., Sevincer, A. T., Karasawa, M., & Uskul, A. K. (2009). A cultural task analysis of implicit independence: Comparing North America, western Europe, and East Asia. *Journal of Personality and Social Psychology, 97,* 236–255.

Krys, K., Xing, C., Zelenski, J. M., Capaldi, C. A., Lin, Z., & Wojciszke, B. (2017). Punches or punchlines? Honor, face, and dignity cultures encourage different reactions to provocation. *Humor, 30,* 303–322.

Lam, B. C. P., Cross, S. E., Wu, T., Yeh, K., Wang, Y., & Su, J. C. (2016). What do you want in a marriage? Examining marriage ideals in Taiwan and the United States. *Personality and Social Psychology Bulletin, 42,* 703–722.

Leung, A. K., & Cohen, D. (2011). Within- and between-culture variation: Individual differences and the cultural logics of honor, face, and dignity cultures. *Journal of Personality and Social Psychology, 100,* 507–526.

Levin, S., Roccas, S., Sidanius, J., & Pratto, F. (2015). Personal values and intergroup outcomes of concern for group honor. *Personality and Individual Differences, 86,* 374–384.

Loftin, C., & Hill, R. H. (1974). Regional subculture and homicide: An examination of the Gastil-Hackney thesis. *American Sociological Review, 39,* 714–724.

Maitner, A. T., Mackie, D. M., Pauketat, J. V. T., & Smith, E. R. (2017). The impact of culture and identity on emotional reactions to insults. *Journal of Cross-Cultural Psychology, 48,* 892–913.

Markus, H. R., & Hamedani, M. G. (2019). People are culturally-shaped shapers: The psychological science of culture and culture change. In D. Cohen & S. Kitayama (Eds.), *Handbook of cultural psychology* (2nd ed., pp. 11–52). Guilford Press.

Markus, H., & Kitayama, S. (1991). Culture and the self: Implications for cognition, emotion and motivation. *Psychological Review, 98*, 224–253.

McWhiney, G. (1988). *Cracker culture: Celtic ways in the old South*. University of Alabama Press.

Mesquita, B., & Leu, J. (2007). The cultural psychology of emotions. In S. Kitayama & D. Cohen (Eds.), *Handbook for cultural psychology* (pp. 734–759). Guilford Press.

Miller, W. I. (1993). *Humiliation*. Cornell University Press.

Morling, B., Kitayama, S., & Miyamoto, Y. (2002). Cultural practices emphasize influence in the U.S. and adjustment in Japan. *Personality and Social Psychology Bulletin, 28*, 311–323.

Morling, B., & Lamoreaux, M. (2008). Measuring culture outside the head: A meta-analysis of cultural products. *Personality and Social Psychology Review, 12*, 199–221.

Morling, B., & Lee, J. M. (2017). Culture and motivation. In A. T. Church (Ed.), *The Praeger handbook of personality across cultures: Culture and characteristic adaptations* (Vol. 2, pp. 61–89). Praeger/ABC-CLIO.

Nisbett, R. E. (1993). Violence and U.S. regional culture. *American Psychologist, 48*, 441–449.

Nisbett, R. E., & Cohen, D. (1996). *Culture of honour: The psychology of violence in the South*. Westview Press.

Nowak, A., Gelfand, M., Borkowski, W., Cohen, D., & Hernandez, I. (2016). The evolutionary basis of honor cultures. *Psychological Science, 27*, 12–24.

Ozgur, S., & Sunar, D. (1982). Social psychological patterns of homicide in Turkey: A comparison of male and female convicted murders. In C. Kagitcibasi (Ed.), *Sex roles, family and community in Turkey* (pp. 349–382). Indiana University Press.

Peristiany, J. G. (1965). *Honor and shame: The values of Mediterranean society*. Weidenfeld and Nicolson.

Pitt-Rivers, J. (1965). Honour and social status. In J. G. Peristiany (Ed.), *Honour and shame: The values of Mediterranean society* (pp. 19–78). Weidenfeld and Nicolson.

Ramirez Marin, J., & Shafa, S. (2017). Social rewards: The basis for collaboration in honor cultures. *Cross Cultural Management: An International Journal, 25*, 53–69.

Rodriguez Mosquera, P. M. (2016). On the importance of family, morality, masculine and feminine honor for theory and research. *Social and Personality Psychology Compass, 10*, 431–443.

Rodriguez Mosquera, P. M., Fischer, A. H., Manstead, A. S. R., & Zaalberg, R. (2008). Attack, disapproval, or withdrawal? The role of honor in anger and shame responses to being insulted. *Cognition and Emotion, 22*, 1471–1498.

Rodriguez Mosquera, P. M., Manstead, A. S. R., & Fischer, A. H. (2000). The role of honor- related values in the elicitation, experience, and communication of pride, shame, and anger: Spain and the Netherlands compared. *Personality and Social Psychology Bulletin, 26*, 833–844.

Rodriguez Mosquera, P. M., Manstead, A. S. R., & Fischer, A. H. (2002a). Honor in the Mediterranean and northern Europe. *Journal of Cross-Cultural Psychology, 33*, 16–36.

Rodriguez Mosquera, P. M., Manstead, A. S. R., & Fischer, A. H. (2002b). The role of honor concerns in emotional reactions to offenses. *Cognition & Emotion, 16*, 143–163.

Rodriguez Mosquera, P. M., Tan, L., & Saleem, F. (2014). Shared burdens, personal costs: On the emotional and social consequences of family honor. *Journal of Cross-Cultural Psychology, 45*, 400–416.

Russano, M. B., Meissner, C. A., Narchet, F. M., & Kassin, S. M. (2005). Investigating true and false confessions within a novel experimental paradigm. *Psychological Science, 16*, 481–486.

Salzman, P. C. (2008). *Culture and conflict in the Middle East*. Humanity Books.Saucier, D. A., & McManus, J. L. (2014). Men of honor: Examining individual differences in masculine honor beliefs. In J. Gelfer (Ed.), *Masculinities in a global era* (pp. 85–100). Springer.

Saucier, D. A., Stanford, A. J., Miller, S. S., Martens, A. L., Miller, A. K., Jones, T. L., McManus, J. L., & Burns, M. D. (2016). Masculine honor beliefs: Measurement and correlates. *Personality and Individual Differences, 94*, 7–15.

Saucier, D. A., Strain, M. L., Hockett, J. M., & McManus, J. L. (2015). Stereotypic beliefs about masculine honor are associated with perceptions of rape and women who have been raped. *Social Psychology, 46*, 228–241.

Scheff, S., & Schorr, M. (2017). *Shame nation: The global epidemic of online hate*. Sourcebooks.

Scherr, K. C., & Madon, S. (2012). You have the right to understand: The deleterious effect of stress on suspects' ability to comprehend Miranda. *Law and Human Behavior, 36*, 275–282.

Sev'er, A., & Yurdakul, G. (2001). Culture of honor, culture of change: A feminist analysis of honor killings in rural Turkey. *Violence Against Women, 7*, 964–998.

Shafa, S., Harinck, S., Ellemers, N., & Beersma, B. (2015). Regulating honor in the face of insults. *International Journal of Intercultural Relations, 47*, 158–174.

Skowronski, J. J. (2002). Honesty and intelligence judgements of individuals and groups: The effects of entity-related behavior diagnosticity and implicit theories. *Social Cognition, 20*, 136–169.

Smith, P. B., Easterbrook, M. J., Blount, J., Koc, Y., Harb, C., Torres, C., Ahmad, A. H., Ping, H., Celikkol, G. C., Loving, R. D., & Rizwan, M. (2017). Culture as perceived context: An exploration of the distinction between dignity, face and honor cultures. *Acta de Investigación Psicológica, 7*, 2568–2576.

Smith, P. B., Easterbrook, M. J., Koc, Y., et al. (2021). Is emphasis on dignity, honor and face more an attribute of individuals or of cultural groups? *Cross-Cultural Research, 55*, 95–126.

Spencer-Rodgers, J., & Peng, K. (Eds.). (2018). *The psychological and cultural foundations of East Asian cognition.* Oxford University Press.

Stewart, F. H. (1994). *Honor.* University of Chicago Press.

Travaglino, G. A., Abrams, D., de Moura, G. R., & Russo, G. (2014). Organized crime and group-based ideology: The association between masculine honor and collective opposition against criminal organizations. *Group Processes & Intergroup Relations, 17*, 799–812.

Tsai, J. L. (2007). Ideal affect: Cultural causes and behavioral consequences. *Perspectives on Psychological Science, 2*, 242–259.

Uskul, A. K., Cross, S., Alozkan, C., Gercek-Swing, B., Ataca, B., Günsoy, C., & Sunbay, Z. (2014). Emotional responses to honor situations in Turkey and the U.S. *Cognition and Emotion, 28*, 1057–1075.

Uskul, A. K., Cross, S. E., Günsoy, C., Gercek-Swing, B., Alozkan, C., & Ataca, B. (2015). A price to pay: Turkish and American retaliation for threats to personal and family honor. *Aggressive Behavior, 41*, 594–607.

Uskul, A. K., Cross, S. E., Günsoy, C., & Gul, P. (2019). Cultures of honor. In D. Cohen & S. Kitayama (Eds.), *Handbook of cultural psychology* (2nd ed., pp. 793–821). Guilford Press.

Uskul, A. K., Cross, S. E., Sunbay, A., Gerçek-Swing, B., & Ataca, B. (2012). Honor bound: The cultural construction of honor in Turkey and the northern US. *Journal of Cross-Cultural Psychology, 43*, 1131–1151.

Uskul, A. K., Hynie, M., & Lalonde, R. (2004). Interdependence as a mediator between culture and interpersonal closeness for Euro-Canadians and Turks. *Journal of Cross-Cultural Psychology, 35*, 174–191.

Vandello, J. A., & Cohen, D. (2003). Male honor and female fidelity: Implicit cultural scripts that perpetuate domestic violence. *Journal of Personality and Social Psychology, 84*, 997–1010.

Vandello, J. A., Cohen, D., Grandon, R., & Franiuk, R. (2009). Stand by your man: Indirect cultural prescriptions for honorable violence and feminine loyalty. *Journal of Cross-Cultural Psychology, 40*, 81–104.

van Osch, Y., Breugelmans, S. M., Zeelenberg, M., & Boluk, P. (2013). A different kind of honor culture: Family honor and aggression in Turks. *Group Processes and Intergroup Relations, 16*, 334–344.

Wasti, S. A., & Erdaş, K. D. (2019). The construal of workplace incivility in honor cultures: Evidence from Turkey. *Journal of Cross-Cultural Psychology, 50*(1), 130–148.

Wojciszke, B. (2005). Morality and competence in person- and self-perception. *European Review of Social Psychology, 16*, 155–188.

Wolf, W., Levordashka, A., Ruff, J. R., Kraaijeveld, S., Lueckmann, J. M., & Williams, K. D. (2015). Ostracism online: A social media ostracism paradigm. *Behavior Research Methods, 47*, 361–373.

Wyatt-Brown, B. (1982). *Southern honor: Ethics and behavior in the old South.* Oxford University Press.

Wyatt-Brown, B. (1986). *Honor and violence in the old South.* Oxford University Press.

Zou, X., Tam, K., Morris, W. M., Lee, L., Lau, I., & Chiu, C. Y. (2009). Culture as common sense: Perceived consensus vs. personal beliefs as mechanisms of cultural influence. *Journal of Personality and Social Psychology, 97*, 579–597.

CHAPTER 5

Culture and Negotiation Strategy

JEANNE M. BRETT

Abstract

This chapter reviews the theory and research linking culture, negotiation strategy, and joint gains. It distinguishes between motivational and behavioral theories of negotiation strategy but concludes that two theories of strategy are functionally equivalent with respect to predicting joint gains as both measure value-claiming and value-creating strategy. It explains how the intersection of cultural levels of trust and tightness–looseness account for cultural differences in the use of negotiation strategy. It concludes, based on a meta-analysis, that value-creating negotiation strategy as conceptualized and measured by motivational or behavioral theory predicts joint gains in Western, but not in non-Western, culture negotiations.

Key Words: negotiation strategy, joint gains, creating value, claiming value, motivational theory, behavioral theory, trust, tightness–looseness

---

I. INTRODUCTION

There is a problem with the theory of negotiation strategy: It does not hold across cultures! A recent meta-analysis concluded that both behavioral and motivational theoretical perspectives on negotiation strategy, as negotiation strategy relates to joint gains, is Western culture–bound (Brett et al., 2021). This chapter surveys the research, taking the theory of negotiation strategy beyond Western culture to that meta-analysis finding and beyond.

Jeanne M. Brett, *Culture and Negotiation Strategy* In: *Handbook of Advances in Culture and Psychology*. Edited by: Michele J. Gelfand, Chi-yue Chiu, and Ying-yi Hong, Oxford University Press. © Oxford University Press 2022.
DOI: 10.1093/oso/9780197631669.003.0005

The chapter begins by introducing key concepts in negotiation strategy research, defining negotiation strategy, and introducing the negotiation outcome of joint gains. The chapter then introduces two major theories of negotiations, the motivational theory and the behavioral theory. This section describes the origins of these two theories in psychology and game theory. It explains these theories' development of two negotiation strategy concepts: (1) cooperative versus competitive and problem-solving versus contending from motivational theory and (2) integrative versus distributive from behavioral theory. It discusses the method of measurement characteristically used by motivational theorists—self-report and behavioral theorists—coding of negotiators' speech. It reviews empirical evidence of the relationship between negotiation strategy conceptualized motivationally and behaviorally and joint gains. The section ends by reporting the new meta-analysis, which has three major findings. First, the two theories are functionally equivalent with respect to predicting joint gains. Second, the two methods are functionally equivalent with respect to predicting joint gains. Third, both theories are culture-bound to Western culture. Negotiation strategy as conceptualized and measured by motivational or behavioral theory does not predict joint gains in non-Western cultures.

The second section of the chapter focuses on culture, negotiation strategy, and joint gains. It begins with a model explaining how culture affects negotiations. It then turns to evidence of cultural differences in the use of negotiation strategy. It describes a model based on cultural levels of trust and tightness–looseness to explain cultural differences in the use of strategy and reviews theory and evidence supporting that model. This section then turns to cultural differences in joint gains. It reviews evidence for the effectiveness of multi-issue offers (MIOs) as an alternative to value-creating strategy for negotiating joint gains. It concludes by reviewing new empirical evidence of an alternative use of negotiation strategy—MIOs—that a recent meta-analysis (Yao et al., 2021) shows is an effective strategy, independent of value creation, to negotiate joint gains and that is valid in both Western and non-Western cultures. The section concludes with a review of theory and evidence of strategic adaptation in intercultural negotiations.

The chapter concludes by summarizing the implications for future research on culture and negotiation strategy and for classroom teaching. There are many opportunities for future research focused on understanding the use of negotiation strategy across intra- and intercultural contexts.

II. KEY CONCEPTS

Negotiation is the process by which two or more parties with conflicting goals, interests, or priorities try to reach an agreement. In some negotiations, parties are interdependent with respect only to their negotiated agreement; in other negotiations, they also are interdependent with respect to what happens if they do not reach agreement (Brett, 2014). For example, if two parties who are engaged in deal-making, that is, buying and selling, cannot reach agreement, the parties are independent in the aftermath. The buyer seeks an alternative seller, and the seller seeks an alternative buyer. In contrast, if two neighbors who are in conflict over who is responsible for the dead trees on their joint property line cannot reach agreement, they are interdependent in the aftermath. The conflict does not go away. One, the other, or both parties may escalate the conflict. The focus of this chapter is research on negotiations in which parties are interdependent with respect only to their negotiated agreement.

A key criterion for evaluating a negotiated outcome is whether negotiators' agreements maximize their joint gains. The term *joint gains* refers to the total value created in a negotiation (Raiffa, 1982). Joint gains are the sum of the individual negotiators' gains. Joint gains have certain structural characteristics depending on the number and types of issues in the negotiation. When there is only a single issue and it cannot subdivided, joint gains are fixed. Game theory labels such negotiations *zero-sum*. When negotiators can subdivide a single issue, for example, the classic story of the two sisters and the orange (attributed to Mary Parker Follett), or there are multiple issues, joint gains are variable. Game theory labels these negotiations *variable-sum*. Whether negotiators take full advantage of the potential variable value embedded in variable-sum negotiations depends on their generating insight, that is identifying trade-offs between low- and high-priority issues and/or issues for which they have compatible interests—for example, the two sisters learning that their interests are compatible because one sister wants the orange rind and the other wants the orange juice. Joint gains are a particularly important outcome of negotiation (Pruitt & Rubin, 1986) because they imply that negotiators received more of their high-priority interests, which in turn implies that negotiators should be satisfied and therefore more likely to implement their agreements (Raiffa, 1982). The focus of this chapter is research on variable-sum negotiations with joint gains potential.

Negotiation strategy refers to the goal-directed behaviors, sometimes called *tactics*, that negotiators use in trying to reach agreement (Weingart et al., 1990). Strategy is an important construct in negotiation research because it serves both as an immediate cause of negotiation outcomes and as a mechanism that explains contextual and individual difference effects on negotiation outcomes.

III. ORIGINS OF NEGOTIATION STRATEGY THEORY

The conceptualization of negotiation strategy theory seemingly emerged in parallel in psychology (Deutsch, 1949) and game theory (Luce & Raiffa, 1957), resulting in two theoretical models, motivational and behavioral, that are different in focus but ultimately highly related in practice. The psychological approach focuses on negotiators' motivations—their concerns about their own and the other party's outcomes (Pruitt & Rubin, 1986) and how those two different motivations manifest in cooperation versus competition (Deutsch, 1949, 1973), problem-solving (collaborating) versus contending (competing) versus yielding (accommodating) versus inaction (avoiding) (Pruitt & Rubin, 1986; Thomas, 1976). The behavioral approach focuses on negotiators' behaviors—how they seek and use information about trade-offs to generate joint gains (i.e., *integrative strategy*) or about the other's vulnerabilities to influence the counterpart to make concessions (i.e., *distributive strategy*) (Walton & McKersie, 1965).

These two different theoretical perspectives have stimulated extensive empirical research on negotiation strategy and joint gains. Researchers typically follow one or the other theoretical perspective, and they also typically take different approaches to measurement; for example, motivational researchers ask negotiators to self-report on their motives and use of strategy (e.g., DeDreu et al., 2001), while behavioral researchers mostly, but not exclusively, code use of strategy from negotiators' verbal behavior (e.g., Weingart et al., 1990).

IV. MOTIVATIONAL THEORY

The motivational theoretical perspective grew from social psychologist Morton Deutsch's (1949) cooperative–competitive theory into the two-dimensional dual-concern theory (Pruitt & Rubin, 1986; Rahim, 1983). Deutsch wrote about two different types of social situations in which people are interdependent. In cooperative situations, Deutsch proposed that one party's goal achievement depends to some degree on the other party's goal achievement. That is, if I facilitate your goal achievement, I am also facilitating my own goal achievement. In competitive situations, Deutsch proposed that one party's goal achievement diminishes the other party's goal achievement. That is, I achieve my goal at your expense. Deutsch (1949) clearly understood the interrelationships between these two different types of goals because he illustrated the concepts of cooperation and competition with the example of a basketball team. For the team to win, he pointed out, the members had to cooperate, that is, share the ball; for one team member to be a star, that team member had to compete, that is hog the ball.

Although perhaps unfair to Deutsch's distinct conceptualization of cooperation and competition, psychologists criticized cooperative–competitive theory for being one-dimensional (e.g., Pruitt & Rubin, 1986; Rahim, 1983, 1986; Thomas, 1976; Van de Vliert & Kabanoff, 1990), ultimately leading researchers into two-dimensional motivational territory with what eventually came to be known as dual-concern theory. Dual-concern theory leans heavily on Blake and Mouton's (1964) managerial grid that proposes that the strength of concern for people versus concern for production can account for different conflict management behavioral styles (e.g., avoiding, accommodating, collaborating, competing, and compromising). Different researchers have given somewhat different names for the conflict management behavioral styles; for example, collaborating is sometimes called *problem-solving* (Ben Yoav & Pruitt, 1984), but the only real conceptual changes in the meaning of the constructs from the managerial grid to dual-concern theory were not in the conflict management behaviors but in the two dimensions underlying them. Concern for production became *assertiveness*, and concern for people became *cooperativeness* in Ruble and Thomas' (1976) conceptualization. Ultimately, assertiveness turned into the social motive *concern for self* (proself [Messick & McClintock, 1968]) and cooperativeness into the social motive *concern for others* (prosocial [Pruitt & Rubin, 1986]). Figure 5.1 reproduces the dual-concern model.

Messick and McClintock (1968) conceptualized social motives[1] as a way to understand the psychology underlying choice behavior in games simulating situations of social interdependence. Game theory predicts that a single motive, rational self-interest, predicts behavior. Messick and McClintock (1968), however, observed decision makers in their lab studies making not only self-interested but also cooperative decisions. They labeled the motives underlying these decisions as *cooperative concern* for the joint outcome and *competitive concern* for the relative outcome (e.g., not doing worse than the other party), choices originally identified by Deutsch (1960).

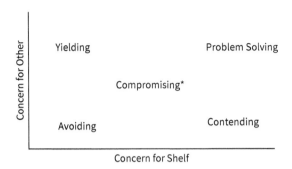

FIGURE 5.1: The Dual-Concern Model
*Note *Compromising* is in some, but not all, conceptualizations of the dual-concern model.

To classify negotiators' social motives, many dual-concern theory researchers use the triple-dominance measure of social values (TDMSV) (Van Lange et al., 1997). The TDMSV presents participants with nine decomposed games (Messick & McClintock, 1968) in the form of choices among three alternative allocations of points to themselves and another unknown person: The individualistic or proself alternative maximizes own outcome, the cooperative or prosocial alternative maximizes joint outcome, and the competitive alternative maximizes own outcome relative to the other's outcome. Researchers classify participants who make six consistent choices as having the social motive associated with their six choices. A meta-analysis of studies since 1973 using the TDMSV method reported that 57% of classifiable participants were prosocial, 27% were proself, and 15% were competitive (Eek & Garling, 2008 [citing Au & Kwong, 2004, which was unavailable to me]).

The TDMSV data I collected in a pre-class survey of 930 managers from around the world—U.S. (163), China (146), Brazil (56) Hong Kong (44), Germany (200), Israel (144), India (135), and Jordan, Palestine, Syria (22) — show a similar pattern. Across cultures, 50% were cooperatively motivated, 38% individualistically motivated, 4% were competitively motivated, and 8% had no dominant social motive (Brett, 2007).[2] There were some cultural differences: the Israelis (37%) and the Middle Easterners from Jordan, Palestine, and Syria (23%) were the least likely, while the Germans were the most likely (71%) to be prosocial. The Israelis (54%) and the Middle Easterners (54%), followed by the Brazilians (45%) were the most likely to be proself, with the Germans (22%) the least likely to be proself. These cultural data using the TDMSV suggest that, although there may be some cultural component to social motives, for the most part, social motives are traits and so more likely to explain within- than between-culture differences.

DeDrue and Van Lange (1995) summarize the research using the TDMSV in experimental games research as follows: People with prosocial motives initiate cooperation with others but will retreat to competition if the counterpart does not reciprocate. People with proself motives initiate competitive strategy but will switch to cooperation if it is in their self-interest to do so, for example, because their counterpart is playing tit-for-tat (Rappaport, 1960). Competitive people initiate and maintain competitive strategy.

The question for negotiation strategy researchers is whether the cooperative–competitive and dual-concern motivational models predict behavior in negotiations, as they seem to in experimental games. Experimental games differ from multi-issue negotiations in several ways (Weingart et al., 2007). In games, parties' choices (options), typically only two, determine their outcomes. In negotiations, parties usually have multiple options for an agreement that determines their outcomes. In games, parties have complete information about each other's outcome depending on the choices made. In negotiations, parties do not know the value of settlement options to the other party, often even after they reach agreement. In games, parties can only express a cooperative intention by making a cooperative choice. In negotiations, there are a myriad of ways to signal cooperative and competitive intentions, for example, via information-sharing and concession patterns.

Researchers have developed three different instruments to operationalize the conflict management behaviors predicted by the dual-concern model. Practitioners use the Thomas-Kilmann Conflict Mode Instrument (TKI) (https://psycho-tests.com/test/conflict-mode) to give people feedback on their conflict management style. Descriptive studies of the preferred style of, for example, doctors versus nurses abound. One of the more interesting of the descriptive studies (Kass et al., 2010) analyzed the conflict-handling styles of three crews of four people each before and after a 264-day space flight simulation that was conducted in Russia in 1999–2000. Researchers defined conflict for participants as a situation in which the concerns of two or more individuals appear to be incompatible. The results showed no significant differences between crews (I believe these were mixed-culture crews) or between pre- and post-isolation. The TKI appears to be a reliable measure of style. However, the TKI is difficult to use in hypothesis-testing research because, like the TDMSV, it forces choices and categorizes styles. The negotiator cannot be a strong proponent of collaborating and contending. The largest proportion of space crews opted for the TKI compromise style.

Instead, negotiation researchers testing hypotheses derived from the dual-concern model use the Rahim (1983) or the Dutch Test for Conflict Handling (DUTCH), originally developed by van de Vliert (1997) and updated by DeDreu and colleagues (2001). Both are survey measures that negotiators complete by responding to a set of Likert-style questions. The widest use of the Rahim measure is as an alternative to the TKI to measure styles, although with a bit of editing it could be used to describe the use of strategy after the negotiation. The DUTCH asks negotiators to describe their own and the counterpart's behaviors on dual-concern behavioral styles after the negotiation. For example, Beersma and DeDreu (1999) manipulated negotiators' social motives and found that prosocially motivated negotiators reported more problem-solving, less contending, and higher joint gains than proself motivated negotiators. A meta-analysis by DeDreu et al. (2000) confirmed these relationships between social motives and conflict management behavior and joint gains. Prosocial negotiating dyads[3] engaged in more problem-solving and less contending[4] and reached higher joint gains than proself dyads under two conditions when resistance to yielding was high. These results support dual-concern theory, although it takes a bit of explaining to get there.

What takes some disentangling is (1) why the second dimension of the dual-concern model in this research is resistance to yielding, not concern for self (proself), and (2) what the meaning of resistance to yielding is. Research using the TDMSV cannot use both prosocial and proself motives to characterize a negotiator or dyad because the measure is categorical. Individuals who split their choices among the three motives measured by the TDMSV have no dominant social motive, and the experimental game research treats them as unpredictable.[5] Resistance to yielding is a concept from negotiation research. It refers to the negotiator's reluctance to make concessions (Kelley, 1967). High concern for self (proself) according to Kelley (1967) is likely to produce high resistance to yielding.[6] Thus, dual-concern theory researchers (e.g., Ben Yoav & Pruitt, 1984; DeDreu et al., 2000) have used resistance to yielding as a proxy for the proself motive when they use the TDMSV to measure social values.

Overall, DeDreu and colleagues' (2000) meta-analysis provides evidence of the relevance of both cooperative–competitive and dual-concern motivational theories predicting use of conflict management behavior and joint gains, at least when both members of the dyad have the same social motive.[7] Although this meta-analysis suggests that engaging in problem-solving and not engaging in contending leads to joint gains, it does not formally test conflict management behaviors as the mechanism explaining the relationship between social motives and joint gains.

V. BEHAVIORAL THEORY

The behavioral theory of negotiation strategy grew out of game theory made accessible to social and behavioral scientists by Luce and Raiffa (1957) and applied to labor management negotiations by Walton and McKersie (1965). Behavioral theory takes a distinctly rational, thus cognitive, as opposed to motivational perspective. The economist and arms control theorist Thomas Schelling (1960/1980) soundly rejected the motivational perspective, defining *strategy* as "rational, conscious, artful kind of behavior" (p. 3). Walton and McKersie (1965) took the rational perspective on strategy one step further, defining strategy in terms of negotiators' goal-directed behaviors and identifying two different types of strategy, with the unfortunate consequence of naming the strategies for the outcomes that they theoretically promoted: *Distributive strategy*, in theory, facilitates distributive, zero-sum, win–lose, individual-gains outcomes; *integrative strategy*, in theory, facilitates integrative, variable sum, win–win, joint-gains outcomes.

Distributive and integrative strategies focus on how negotiators seek and share information with each other. Distributive strategy consists of tactics and behaviors that focus on acquiring information to understand the counterpart's utilities for outcomes and using that information, for example, via threats or emotional tactics (putdowns, demands, appeals to logic, persuasive arguments), to modify the counterpart's utilities and induce the counterpart to make concessions (Walton & McKersie, 1965). In contrast, integrative strategy consists of tactics that focus on mutually defining the problem and identifying and searching for alternative solutions which benefit both parties or that, at a minimum, do not represent "equal sacrifices" (Walton & McKersie, 1965, p. 9) and selecting the best solution. Integrative negotiation strategy consists of behaviors that focus on acquiring information about negotiators' interests (motives, concerns) and priorities and using trade-offs to integrate those interests (Follett, 1940). These behaviors include information-sharing and -seeking as well as asking and answering questions about negotiators' interests and priorities (Gunia et al., 2011; Hüffmeier et al., 2014; Pruitt, 1981; Weingart et al., 1990).

Pruitt (1981) presented a slightly different conceptualization of behavioral negotiation strategy, distinguishing three types of strategy and suggesting that all three, at least in principle, can generate joint gains. Pruitt understood from his own empirical research (1981, summarized in Chapter 6) that to negotiate joint gains negotiators needed to use information to generate insight into their counterpart's interests and priorities.[8] Pruitt suggested that they could do so by engaging in explicit information exchange, implicit information exchange, and/or heuristic trial and error (1981, p. 82).

Explicit information-sharing rests on reciprocal exchange of information about parties' priorities and, I would add, interests. In study after study from Weingart et al. (1990) to Kong et al.'s (2014) meta-analysis, explicit information-sharing about priorities and interests is a direct route to joint gains because it generates insight (Pruitt, 1981; Thompson & Hastie, 1990). Conceptually and operationally, explicit information-sharing, as defined by Pruitt (1981), and integrative negotiation strategy, as defined by Walton and McKersie (1965), are essentially the same set of behaviors.

Implicit information-sharing, as defined by Pruitt (1981), and distributive negotiation strategy, as defined by Walton and McKersie (1965), also are conceptually and operationally the same set of behaviors. However, Pruitt suggests that negotiators should be able to generate insight about other negotiators' priorities and interests from implicit information embedded in a distributive information exchange. He observed negotiators in his lab asking their counterparts to make extremely large concessions on issues that were particularly high-priority to the negotiators and fiercely defending their own positions on high-priority issues. Pruitt theorized that negotiators' positions as well as the arguments that negotiators use to defend their positions inevitably reveal information about the negotiators' underlying motives. Aside from some studies in his lab (Kimmel et al., 1980; Pruitt et al., 1978), there do not seem to be other studies documenting negotiators doing so (although see Adair et al., 2001).

Pruitt also explained why negotiators were unlikely to use this strategy to generate joint gains. First, negotiators in his lab who were using this strategy did not regard themselves as acting cooperatively, and they did not see themselves as searching for a mutually acceptable agreement. Instead, they thought they were engaged in a win–lose competition and were using self-interested offers and persuasion to try to win that competition. Second, inferring priorities and interests successfully requires rather high-level information-processing that may be hard to come by in negotiations that parties view as competitions as opposed to opportunities to identify a mutually beneficial agreement.

Heuristic trial and error is "an ambitious search model," consisting of "a variety of [multi-issue] proposals . . . to generate a series of alternatives and a simple heuristic—concede on low priority issues and hold firm positions on high priority issues—until you find an alternative proposal that the counterpart can endorse" (Pruitt, 1981). Pruitt also thought that this strategy could lead to joint gains, but he suggested that the mechanism linking heuristic trial and error to joint gains was the heuristic, not insight. Pruitt observed that although some negotiators in his studies used this heuristic strategy to reach high joint gains, they did not comprehend why their counterparts found their offers acceptable; that is, they lacked insight.

Four very important contributions of Pruitt's behavioral research on negotiation strategy and joint gains go beyond Walton and McKersie's (1965) initial conceptualization. First, Pruitt recognized that insight was the mechanism by which direct information about negotiators' priorities and interests translated into joint gains. Second, he recognized that direct information-sharing about interests and priorities required trust. Negotiators were not about to share information directly if they expected their counterparts to exploit it. (I return to insight and the importance of trust for integrative negotiation strategy to generate joint gains in Section VI.) Third, Pruitt understood that there was information about priorities and interests embedded in the negotiators' use of offers and influence tactics. Fourth, Pruitt saw that joint gains agreements were more likely if negotiators considered issues simultaneously rather than sequentially. (I also return to this insight about MIOs and joint gains in Section VI.)

A. Measuring Behavioral Strategy

Behavioral theorists' usual choice to operationalize negotiation strategy is coding of the negotiators' verbal exchanges, from audio or video recordings, email, or chat. There are several published behavioral coding schemes for negotiation strategy. For example, Weingart and colleagues (1990) measured nine tactics (behaviors) which they reduced to three dimensions: distributive tactics (D), integrative tactics (I), and social support (SS). The nine tactics were: single-issue offer (SIO; D), MIO (D), suggest trade-offs (I), ask for information (I), concern for other (I/SS), provide information (D/I), negative reaction (D), positive reaction (SS), and threat (D), In another study, Weingart and colleagues (2007) coded 33 categories of behavior, which they reduced to six strategy clusters: integrative information (e.g., asking questions about information and priorities), integrative action (e.g., behaviors revealing insight), distributive information (e.g., asks about other's bottom line [walkaway]), distributive action (e.g., make a threat), and two clusters of process-management behaviors (time management, asking for reciprocity). Brett, Yao, and Zhang's

(2018) OFFER coding scheme uses just five codes: information about interests or priorities (Q&A); substantiation about positions (S), that is, justifying and arguing for positions; making an offer on a single issue; making a multi-issue offer; and miscellaneous (M), greatly simplifying behavioral coding. There are also unique behavioral coding schemes, for example, Gelfand et al.'s (2015) use of linguistic inquiry and word count (LIWC) (Pennebaker & Graybeal, 2001) to code cognitive mechanisms, moral integrity, image, and strength.

B. Factors Affecting Use of Behavioral Strategy

There has been a great deal of research grounded in behavioral theory on factors affecting negotiators' use of strategy and individual and joint gains. Meta-analyses show that the frequency of use of distributive strategy increases negotiators' individual gains (Hüffmaier et al., 2014), whereas frequency of use of integrative strategy increases and use of distributive strategy decreases their joint gains (Brett et al., 2021; Kong et al., 2014).

Individual studies (e.g., Elahee & Brooks, 2004; Gunia et al., 2011) and a meta-analysis (Kong et al., 2014) confirm Pruitt's (1981) prediction that trust facilitates use of integrative strategy and joint gains. Trust is the willingness to make oneself vulnerable to another person (Rousseau et al., 1998). Sharing information in negotiation invites vulnerability. Trust mitigates this risk because trusting negotiators believe that their counterparts will use shared information to identify mutually beneficial opportunities (Kimmel et al., 1980). Negotiators who trust their counterparts are more likely to share information (Butler, 1999; Kimmel et al., 1980; Kong et al., 2014; Pruitt & Lewis, 1975), acquire insight, and maximize joint gains (Gunia et al., 2011; Olekalns & Smith, 2003a, 2003b, 2005).

Negotiators' goals affect their own and their counterparts' use of strategy and individual and joint gains (Liu & Wilson, 2011). Negotiators for whom competitive goals are more important than cooperative goals use more distributive and less integrative strategy, which reduces their counterparts' profit. Counterparts of negotiators for whom competitive goals are important use fewer integrative tactics, which in turn hurts the negotiators' own profit. Negotiating dyads with competitive goals in this study had lower joint gains than those with cooperative goals.

The research on negotiators' emotions and use of strategy focuses mainly on anger. Early research showed that negotiators' anger that reinforced old slights or prior reputations generated lower joint gains than anger that provided new information (Allred et al., 1997). Following up, Van Kleef and colleagues' (2004a, 2004b) documented the effectiveness of anger on concession-making and proposed the EASI (emotion as social information) model (Van Kleef, 2009). EASI predicts that when anger provides new information (e.g., about the negotiator's own higher limits), conveys a threat (Sinaceur et al., 2011), or signals dominance (Belkin et al., 2013), it motivates the counterpart to make concessions. Subsequent research, however, has detailed a myriad of social and structural characteristics of the negotiation that negate the generality of this finding (see Brett & Thompson, 2016, for a review). Expressions of anger risk negative outcomes for both negotiators, such as low joint gains (Allred et al., 1997), impasses (Friedman et al., 2004), and covert retaliation (Wang et al., 2012).

Power in negotiation may be associated with the quality of the negotiators' alternatives, or BATNA, an acronym for best alternative to a negotiated agreement (Fisher et al., 2011), or with personal qualities of the negotiator, such as status "the extent to which an individual or group is respected or admired by others" (Magee & Galinsky, 2008, p. 359). BATNA power affects use of strategy and individual, but not apparently joint, gains. Negotiators with better BATNAs set higher goals (Pinkley, 1995; Wong, 2014), use threats (Lawler, 1992), and take more for themselves (Komorita & Leung, 1985; Pinkley et al., 1994).

Power based on status may have a different effect on negotiation than power based on BATNA. In interpersonal interactions, status leads to respect, deference, and obedience from others. At the same time, people may expect high-status others to take responsibility for caring for low-status others' welfare (Magee & Galinsky, 2008). Despite this prediction, there is little empirical evidence of this phenomenon in negotiation research. Suggestive evidence from Blader and Chen (2012) shows that relative to low-status parties, high-status parties treated others in more procedurally just ways, listening to their counterparts' concerns and considering their counterparts' wishes, opinions, and needs; but this effect was limited to those high-status parties who were also in the low–BATNA power condition. Most of the research on status in negotiation is confounded with gender and negotiation studies where gender stereotypes confer status on men relative to women. This literature suggests that social category status (e.g., male) implies competency in negotiations, and so the "right" to propose agreements (Miles & Clenney, 2010), presumably favorable to themselves.

The perceived reputation of the counterpart influences negotiators' use of strategy. Glick and Croson (2001) report that over time in a negotiation class students develop reputations for being a liar or being tough. Students negotiated more competitively with a classmate who had a reputation of being a liar but more cooperatively with a classmate regarded as "tough." They negotiated competitively with classmates regarded as soft apparently because these classmates were viewed as easy to exploit. In another study (Tinsley et al., 2002) novices negotiating with experts with "distributive" (competitive) reputations used more distributive and less integrative strategy, which ultimately reduced their joint gains. The relative experts had a bargaining advantage but only if their distributive reputation was known. In a different study, compared to the control condition, novices negotiating with experts with "integrative" (cooperative) reputations shared information about their interests, needs, priorities, and achieved joint gains (Tinsley et al., 2006).

C. Dynamics of Use of Negotiation Strategy—Behavioral Theory

A key question in behavioral strategy negotiation research is the process by which negotiators, whose different social motives, trust, goals, emotions, power, and reputations generate different strategic orientations, interact to reach joint gains. This is also a fundamental question for intercultural negotiation research. For example, prosocial negotiators adjust their use of integrative and distributive strategies in response to the social-motive composition of the other parties with whom they are negotiating, but proself negotiators do not (Weingart et al., 2007).

Linda Putnam (1983) spearheaded this line of research on the dynamics of the negotiation process, describing negotiation as a series of reoccurring actions and reactions. Multiple studies show that the pattern of sequential use of behaviors (tactics) embedded in integrative or distributive strategy fits a second-order Markov chain (Kern et al., 2020; Olekalns & Smith, 2003b; Weingart et al., 1999, 2007). To predict the negotiator's behavior at time t requires knowing the counterpart's behavior at time $t - 1$ and the negotiator's behavior at time $t - 2$. In addition, these negotiation sequences follow three different patterns (Weingart et al., 2007). One pattern, *reciprocity*, refers to responding using the same strategic tactic. For example, the negotiator shares information, the counterpart reciprocates, and the negotiator shares more information. A second pattern, *complementarity*, refers to responding in a strategically similar but not identical way. For example, the negotiator shares information, the counterpart suggests a trade-off, and the negotiator expresses insight—all value-creating behaviors. The third pattern, *structural*, reveals a strategic change. For example, the negotiator makes a threat, the counterpart asks a question about interests, and the negotiator answers the question about interests. Reciprocity and complementarity of integrative behaviors lead to joint gains, but reciprocity and complementarity of distributive behaviors lead to impasses or unclaimed value (Druckman, 1986; Olekalns & Smith, 2000; Putnam & Jones, 1982; Weingart et al., 1990, 2007).

The research suggests that four different types of structural sequences are effective in breaking reciprocal sequences of distributive behavior: (1) refusing to reciprocate and responding with an integrative behavior; (2) reciprocating the distributive behavior but also responding with an integrative behavior; (3) responding with a comment about the process (Brett et al., 1998; see also Olekalns & Smith, 2000); and (4) recognizing that if no progress is being made, there is nothing to lose by sharing information more candidly (Druckman, 1986). (See Druckman & Olekalns [2011] for a review of the turning points in literature and theory.)

A different approach to the dynamics of the negotiation process addresses the trajectory of the use of strategy over the duration of the negotiation. Adair and Brett (2005) divided 70-minute negotiations into quarters depending on speaking turns. They identified two different trajectories. One trajectory began with a strong emphasis on direct information-sharing behavior. This focus on information-sharing continued throughout the negotiation. However, as the negotiation progressed beyond the midpoint, negotiators also substantially increased their use of offers. The other trajectory began with an emphasis on offers with very little direct information-sharing. In this trajectory, the use of offers increased dramatically over time. (See also Adair et al. [2007] for a similar observation.)

VI. MOTIVATIONAL AND BEHAVIORAL THEORIES: A COMPARISON

Behavioral and motivational theories of negotiation strategy have important conceptual similarities and differences. Both view strategy as goal-related behavior and ultimately conceptualize two different types of strategy: integrative versus distributive, competitive (contending) versus cooperative (problem-solving). Behavioral and motivational theories differ in their underlying conceptualization of strategy. Behavioral theory conceptualizes strategy in terms of the information negotiators seek from and share with each other. It focuses on what negotiators do. The motivational theories, competitive–cooperative and dual-concern, view strategy in terms of negotiators' motives and so focus on what negotiators are trying to do. In addition, although some studies use self-reports to measure behavioral strategy (e.g., Aslani et al., 2016; Gunia et al., 2011), most researchers use self-reports to operationalize motivational theory and behavioral coding to operationalize behavioral theory.

A recently completed meta-analysis addresses the similarities and differences of motivational and behavioral theories and self-report and behavioral coding operationalizations as these two strategic perspectives relate to joint gains (Brett et al., 2021). It reveals two surprising findings regarding the theory and measurement of negotiation strategy and one shocking finding regarding culture.

The data for the meta-analysis consisted of 3899 unique negotiations from 76 independent, same-culture samples reported in 46 different papers. Inclusion criteria were as follows. (1) At least two parties from an undergraduate, MBA, executive, or mixed population completed a simulated multi-issue negotiation either in person or virtually. (2) Researchers measured distributive, competitive, or contending strategy and/or integrative, cooperative, or problem-solving strategy using behavioral coding or self-report.[9] Pre-negotiation surveys indicating negotiators' intent to use strategies did not meet inclusion criteria. (3) Data was available to compute a correlation between strategy and joint gains. When evaluating papers published or presented within 5 years, the authors sought and received unpublished correlational data from 14 authors. (4) The negotiation context was deal-making, not dispute resolution. (5) The negotiation was intracultural not intercultural. The reason to exclude intercultural negotiations is that if there are cultural differences in use of negotiation strategy, then, as the model introduced in the next section suggests, intercultural negotiators may experience strategic conflict, which would negate the effectiveness of either intercultural negotiator's strategy.

The surprising results from the meta-analysis are that motivational and behavioral theories and self-report and behavioral coding methods of conceptualizing and measuring negotiation strategy are essentially functionally equivalent, significant predictors of joint gains. One theory does not outperform the other in predicting joint gains nor does one method of measurement. To avoid confusion in the rest of this chapter, I use the terms from Lax and Sebenius (1986): *value-creating* to refer to integrative, cooperative, or problem-solving strategy and *value-claiming* to refer to distributive, competitive, and contending strategy. The meta-analysis revealed a positive relationship of value-creating with joint gains and a negative relationship of value-claiming with joint gains.

The implications for researchers of the functional equivalency of theories and methods of measurement of negotiation strategy are that choosing a theoretical perspective should depend on the nature of the research question and choosing a measurement method should depend on the research question and expediency. For example, a question about how a manipulation or context variable affects negotiators' motivations would imply a motivational theoretical perspective, whereas a question about how a manipulation or context variable affects information exchange would imply a behavioral theoretical perspective. However, without very clear theoretical guidance, the choice of self-report or behavioral coding comes down strongly in favor of self-report because of the costs and challenges of behavioral coding. Future research may show that negotiators do not self-report some specific elements of strategy reliably, for example, the frequency of use of different types of offers. However, negotiators appear to be able to self-report the variation in their cooperative, problem-solving, information-sharing motives and behaviors and their competitive, contending, and influence-seeking motives and behaviors as reliably as coders blind to the hypotheses of the study can code those behaviors.

The meta-analysis also revealed one shocking finding. The relationships of value-creating (positive) and value-claiming (negative) with joint gains were culture-bound to Western culture samples. The relationships between value-creating and value-claiming strategy and joint gains were non-significant in study populations from East Asia, South Asia, and the Middle East. This result does not appear to be a small sample problem. There were adequate numbers of independent observations (same culture samples) in Western (45 for value-creating and 40 for value-claiming) and non-Western (20 for value-creating and 18 for value-claiming) cultures.

In retrospect, perhaps we should not have been so shocked. We knew from our research at the interface of culture and negotiation strategy that culture affects how negotiators use strategy, but it took the meta-analysis to understand just how much! The meta-analytic evidence that Western motivational and behavioral theories of negotiation strategy are culture-bound, at least with respect to joint gains, justifies culture and negotiation researchers' systematic program of documenting and interpreting cultural effects on negotiation strategy—the theme of the rest of this chapter.

VII. CULTURE AND NEGOTIATION STRATEGY AND JOINT GAINS

This section begins with a model explaining how culture affects negotiations. It then turns to evidence of cultural differences in the use of negotiation strategy. It describes a model based on cultural levels of trust and tightness–looseness

262   Handbook of Advances in Culture and Psychology

to explain cultural differences in the use of strategy and reviews theory and evidence supporting that model. The section next addresses cultural differences in joint gains. It reviews evidence for the effectiveness of MIOs as an alternative to value-creating strategy for negotiating joint gains. It continues by reviewing new empirical evidence of an alternative use of negotiation strategy—MIOs—that a recent meta-analysis shows is an effective strategy, independent of value creation, to negotiate joint gains and that is valid in both Western and non-Western cultures. The section concludes with a review of theory and evidence of strategic adaptation in intercultural negotiations.

A. Model

Brett (2000) identifies factors influencing negotiators from two different cultures.[10] The key concepts in her model are (1) factors in the negotiators' environments, (2) negotiators' interests and priorities, (3) their use of negotiation strategy, (4) the integrative outcome potential, (5) social interaction, and (6) outcome. Her model proposes that factors in the negotiators' environments, including elements of their cultures, affect negotiators' interests, priorities, and use of strategy. Negotiators' interests and priorities affect their potential for joint gains. The social interaction resulting from the fit or misfit of negotiators' strategies influences the degree to which negotiators' outcomes realize their potential for joint gains.

There are several cultural entry points identified by Brett's (2000) model. Negotiation occurs in a rich cultural environment, which consists of the culturally prototypical values, norms, and beliefs about negotiations that individuals bring to the negotiation, as well as systems of law, government, religion, economy, and society that structure and limit social interaction, including negotiations, within a culture. Culture and negotiation researchers assume that negotiators bring their cultural orientations toward negotiations with them. Thus, the cultural effects that researchers have identified in controlled simulations of negotiations may be pale shadows of cultural effects on real-world negotiation.

The cultural environment can affect negotiators' alternatives to agreement with each other. For example, in a culture in which there is widespread government control of assets, negotiators' alternatives to reaching an agreement to buy and sell an asset may be to forgo the sale or the acquisition. Other things, such as the negotiator's skill or motivation, being equal, the negotiator with the better alternatives, whether those alternatives come in the form of access to resources, social status, or information, is the more powerful negotiator.

Culture can affect negotiators' interests—their reasons for the positions they take on the issues they must negotiate. Positions are what negotiators' want; interests answer the why question. For example, a negotiator may take a demanding position because her interest is that others view her as someone who cannot be taken advantage of. Understanding interests in negotiation is important because, although there only may be one way to satisfy a position, there may be multiple ways to satisfy an interest.

Culture can affect negotiators' priorities—the relative importance of the issues. What we see in the culture and negotiation literature, for example, is that negotiators in some cultures may prioritize establishing a status-based relationship with their counterparts over realizing an outcome that maximizes economic potential (Gelfand et al., 2015). Their prioritization of relationship over economic outcome may be a product of a cultural environment in which the rule of law is lax, such that if the relationship is not solid, the negotiated economic gains are unlikely to materialize.

Culture can affect negotiators' strategic behaviors. As I have reviewed, factors such as social motives, goals, trust, power, reputation, and their counterparts' use of strategy all can affect how much negotiators engage in value-claiming versus value-creating negotiation strategy. However, research shows that the use of strategy varies systematically with negotiators' culture, as does the effectiveness of strategy for generating joint gains (Brett, Gunia & Teucher, 2017).

The model introduces the concept of *outcome potential*—the value that the negotiators can jointly achieve by trading off low-priority interests for high-priority interests. It proposes that whether negotiators achieve joint gains is a function of their outcome potential and the patterns of social interaction at the negotiating table—that is, how the two negotiators use strategy.

In the next section, I summarize Brett, Gunia, and Teucher's (2017) review of the research documenting cultural differences in the use of negotiation strategy and in the subsequent outcomes.

B. Evidence of Cultural Differences in Use of Negotiation Strategy

The research on cultural differences in use of negotiation strategy and in negotiation outcomes takes a comparative cultural perspective, testing between-versus within-group differences, where groups typically are national cultures. Using national and even regional boundaries to delineate different cultures is appropriate because these boundaries define the political, legal, economic, and social contexts within which people negotiate and which may affect not only their strategic approach to negotiation but also their interests and priorities—both cultural entry points in the Brett (2000) model. Significant between-culture differences reflect distinct central tendencies or cultural norms but certainly do not mean that all negotiators in a culture use the same negotiation strategy or that negotiators use the same strategy all the time. All negotiators use a mix of value-creating and value-claiming strategies, but in some cultures, negotiators emphasize value-claiming over value-creating strategies and in others just the opposite.

Brett, Gunia, and Teucher (2017) identified 19 studies providing comparative culture, strategy, and outcome data from negotiators in 18 different cultures. These studies shared several characteristics: (1) They reported data from two or more independent intracultural samples negotiating the same quantified simulation, (2) the negotiation setting allowed for joint gains, and (3) the researchers used either self-reports or behavioral coding to measure strategy.

To classify a national culture as value-creating or value-claiming prototypical, Brett and colleagues collected all the studies comparing the use of negotiation strategy in a focal culture with the use of negotiation strategy in other cultures. For example, three studies reported data comparing Chinese and US negotiators' use of strategy (Aslani et al., 2016; Dong, 2006; Liu, 2009). In all three studies, the Chinese negotiators used value-claiming statistically more frequently than the US negotiators, and the US negotiators used value-creating statistically more frequently than the Chinese negotiators. A fourth study (Lügger et al., 2015) compared German and Chinese negotiators. The Chinese used value-claiming statistically more often than the Germans, and the Germans used value-creating statistically more often than the Chinese. Brett, Gunia, and Teucher (2017) interpreted patterns of significant statistical results like these, which they report were remarkably consistent across studies, samples, and simulations, to classify a culture as value-creating or value-claiming prototypical. They cautioned that in classifying a national culture as value-creating or value-claiming prototypical, they did not mean to imply that negotiators in that culture exclusively used value-creating or value-claiming negotiation strategy. Rather, the extant research implies that negotiators from some cultures use value-claiming relatively more and value-creating relatively less than negotiators from other cultures.

These authors' classification of national cultures as value-creating versus value-claiming prototypical illustrated in their Figure 1 (Brett, Gunia, & Teucher, 2017) revealed similarities within and differences between four regions of the world that global organizations, such as the World Bank (2016), commonly use to organize and report economic activity. These regions are the West, East Asia, "Latin cultures" (including Latin America, Spain, and Portugal), and the Middle East/South Asia. Recognizing that the number of comparative culture studies available was extremely limited, the regional classification reveals Western culture nations (Germany, Israel, Norway, Sweden, United States) as value-creating prototypical and East Asian (China, Hong Kong, Japan, Thailand) and Middle Eastern/South Asian nations (India, Qatar) as value-claiming prototypical. The studies reporting on the use of negotiation strategy within the Latin cultures show a mix of value-creating (prototypical in Brazil) and value-claiming (prototypical in Mexico and Spain). Figure 1 in their article (Brett, Gunia, & Teucher, 2017) displays the frequency of comparative studies classifying a culture as prototypically value-claiming or value-creating aggregated to the regional level.

Brett, Gunia, and Teucher (2017) drew two conclusions from their review of the comparative negotiation strategy data. First, they observed that there are systematic national cultural differences in the use of negotiation strategy and that these cultural differences cluster regionally. Second, they concluded that although use of value-creating strategy involves a high level of information-sharing about interests and priorities and trust in negotiation promotes use of value-creating strategy, cultural levels of trust do not fully explain the pattern of cultural differences in the use of value-claiming and especially value-creating negotiation strategy. Third, they propose that the intersection of cultural levels of trust by cultural tightness–looseness may provide a better explanation of cultural differences in use of negotiation strategy than cultural levels of trust alone.

C. Trust, Tightness–Looseness, Negotiation Strategy, and Culture

At the cultural level, *trust* refers to the general belief that others are trustworthy. Brett, Gunia, and Teucher (2017) analyzed World Bank regional differences in trust using national-level data from the World Values Survey trust question: Can other people be trusted? Yes or no. They illustrate in Figure 2 of their article that trust is higher in cultures in the Western and East Asian regions than in cultures in the Latin American and Middle Eastern/South Asian regions. Comparing Figures 1 and 2 from Brett, Gunia, and Teucher (2017), it is clear that regional cultural patterns of trust do not fully correspond to the regional cultural patterns of use of the value-creating negotiation strategy. For example, their Figure 2 shows that trust is high in East Asian and Western cultures, but their Figure 1 shows that value-claiming, not value-creating, strategy is prototypical of East Asian negotiators. Counter to the meta-analytic research linking trust to value-creating strategy (Kong et al., 2014), cultural levels of trust in East Asian cultures manifest in prototypical use of value-claiming strategy. Further, if trust is so low in Latin American cultures, negotiators from cultures in these regions should be relying heavily on value-claiming negotiation strategy; but Brett, Gunia, and Teucher (2017) report studies that show Brazilians use a mix of value-creating and value-claiming strategy (see Figure 1 in Brett, Gunia, & Teucher, 2017).

To explain these anomalies, Brett, Gunia, and Teucher (2017) proposed that trust alone was not sufficient to account for cultural differences in prototypical use of negotiation strategy but that the intersection of cultural levels of trust and cultural tightness–looseness might be. *Tightness–looseness* is the degree to which cultural institutions support conformity to cultural norms and monitor and sanction violations (Gelfand et al., 2006). In tight cultures, cultural institutions, such as family, community, and religion, convey behavioral expectations for interpersonal interaction and enforce conformity via monitoring and sanctioning, leaving individuals little leeway for improvisation or interpretation (Boldt, 1978a, 1978b; Boldt & Roberts, 1979). In contrast, in loose cultures social norms are relatively flexible and informal (Gelfand, 2018; Gelfand et al., 2006). Norms in loose cultures signal behavioral expectations but permit individuals to engage in a "range of tolerable behavior within which [they] may exercise their own preferences" (Gelfand et al., 2011; see also Boldt, 1978a, 1978b; Boldt & Roberts, 1979; Ford et al., 1967). Enactment and enforcement of social norms in loose cultures are largely under individuals' control, providing opportunities for improvisation.

Just as there are regional differences in cultural levels of trust, there are regional differences in cultural tightness–looseness. Figure 3 in Brett, Gunia, and Teucher (2017) illustrates these regional differences using data reported by Gelfand and colleagues (2011). East Asian, South Asian, and Middle Eastern cultures are tight relative to Latin American and most Western cultures.

Brett, Gunia, and Teucher (2017) integrate the patterns of data represented in their Figures 1–3 in their Figure 4, which places cultural differences in the prototypical use of negotiation strategy within the intersection of cultural levels of trust and tightness–looseness. (At the cultural level, trust and tightness–looseness are not correlated [Brett, Gunia, & Teucher, 2017].) Their Figure 4 shows relatively high trust, tight East Asian cultures prototypically using value-claiming strategy; relatively high trust, loose Western cultures prototypically using value-creating strategy; relatively low trust, tight Middle Eastern and South Asian cultures prototypically using value-claiming strategies; and relatively low trust, loose Latin American cultures using value-creating (Brazil) and value-claiming (Mexico) strategies.

Brett, Gunia, and Teucher (2017) theorize that the cultural patterns of use of negotiation strategy illustrated by their Figure 6 occur because (1) cultural tightness generates institutional trust, whereas cultural looseness generates the capacity for interpersonal trust and (2) institutional trust does not generalize into trust in negotiation as well as interpersonal trust. Their theorizing was heavily influenced by Yamagishi and colleagues' research and theorizing.

The Yamagishi trust, faith, and social dilemma studies with Japanese and American participants experimented turning sanctioning for defection on and off (e.g., Takahashi et al., 2008; Yamagishi et al., 1998; Yamagishi & Yamagishi, 1994). When the sanctioning for defection system was on, there were no cultural differences between Japanese and American participants in trust and cooperation. When the sanctioning system was off, American participants trusted and cooperated more than Japanese participants.

To interpret these data, Yamagishi (2009) concluded that there are two different trust mechanisms: institutional trust and interpersonal trust. *Institutional trust* generates trustworthy behavior—willingness to make oneself vulnerable to another in social interaction—because of the presence of social institutions that impose norms and engage in monitoring and sanctioning of deviant behavior (tight culture). *Interpersonal trust* generates trustworthy behavior because, lacking institutional assurances (loose cultures), individuals engage in social intelligence to identify who is and is not trustworthy (Yamagishi & Yamagishi, 1994). Indeed, Yamagishi (2009) goes so far as to propose that so long as strong institutions remain a force in controlling social interaction, individuals living in cultures with strong social norms (tight cultures) "do not need social intelligence to find out who is trustworthy—trust is not needed" (p. 3). Yamagishi is implying that individuals in tight cultures can assume others are trustworthy because they wish to avoid sanctioning. He is also implying that individuals in tight cultures may have much less experience developing interpersonal trust than individuals in loose cultures where social norms are flexible and sanctioning systems are weak (Gunia et al., 2011).

These underlying tight–loose cultural differences between institutional and interpersonal trust provide an explanation for the anomalies in use of negotiation strategy in East Asian and Latin American cultures. East Asian cultures are high-trust but tight. And East Asian negotiators rely heavily on value-claiming strategy (Brett, Gunia, & Teucher, 2017). This theorizing and the pattern of empirical results suggest that they do so because the institutional trust that leads to trustworthy behavior in everyday social interaction does not extend to negotiation. In contrast, Latin American cultures are low-trust but, relative to East Asian cultures, much looser. Latin American negotiators, according to the limited data available to Brett, Gunia, and Teucher (2017), engage in both value-claiming and value-creating strategies. Low trust certainly inclines these negotiators to defensive value-claiming strategy; but cultural looseness implies that Latin American negotiators have plenty of experience in everyday social interaction in gathering social intelligence to determine trustworthiness, which their use of value-creating strategy suggests they are willing to use in negotiations.

The use of negotiation strategy in the Middle East/South Asia and the West suggests a more straightforward theoretical interpretation of the intersection of cultural trust and tightness–looseness. In everyday social interaction in high-trust, loose Western cultures, trust is interpersonal. Trust is not only grounded in an underlying cultural assumption that others are trustworthy but also due to extensive social experience in testing whether that assumption is valid. This Western culture combination of the cultural assumption that others are trustworthy and cultural practice of testing that assumption manifests in Western culture negotiators' reliance on value-creating strategy. In contrast, in tight, low-trust Middle Eastern/South Asian cultures, negotiators' reliance on value-claiming strategy is a rational defense against being taken advantage of.

D. Evidence of Cultural Differences in Joint Gains

Many intracultural comparison studies using different negotiation simulations report cultural differences in joint gains—for example, Lügger and colleagues (2015), where Chinese negotiators' joint gains were lower than those of German negotiators; Gelfand and colleagues (2015), where Egyptian negotiators' joint gains were lower than those of US negotiators; Natlandsmyr and Rognes (1995), where Mexican negotiators' joint gains were lower than those of Norwegian negotiators; and Aslani and colleagues (2016), where Qatari negotiators' joint gains were lower than those of US negotiators. The results of all these studies are consistent with the theory of negotiation strategy: Joint gains are a function of use of value-creating strategy; negotiators who use value-claiming strategy generate lower joint gains. Cultural differences in joint gains are associated with the value-creating versus value-claiming strategic prototype of the culture.

Brett (2007), however, provides a somewhat different perspective. She reports joint gains data from intracultural negotiations from 11 different national cultures—all using the same simulation. Joint gains were higher in some cultures (e.g., Brazil, France, Germany, Israel, Japan, and the United States) than in other cultures (e.g., China, Hong Kong, India, Russia, and Thailand). However, these differences were due more to negotiators leaving the optional compatible issue out of the agreement and less to negotiators failing to realize the trade-off. Adair and Brett's (2005) analysis of these negotiators' use of strategy shows that in the first and second quarters of the negotiation, Western culture negotiators were exchanging information about interests and priorities (value-creating strategy) significantly more frequently than non-Western negotiators, and non-Western culture negotiators were exchanging offers and influence attempts more frequently than Western culture negotiators. Western culture negotiators continued to exchange information (integrative strategy) throughout the negotiation and caught up to the non-Western negotiators' exchange of offers and influence attempts in the third and fourth quarters of their negotiations. There were no significant differences in joint gains between Western and non-Western negotiators.

These 2005 Adair and Brett results presage the 2021 meta-analytical results (Brett et al., 2021) reported previously, which found no significant effects of strategy on joint gains in non-Western culture samples. They indicate that Western culture negotiators prototypically engage in value-creating, direct information-sharing and then consolidate their knowledge using offers, whereas non-Western culture negotiators who prototypically use the value-claiming strategy of offers nevertheless do not necessarily negotiate lower joint gains than Western culture negotiators. The question is, how do they do it? Recall that Pruitt (1981) theorized that there was indirect information embedded in influence attempts and offers (value-claiming strategy). Pruitt (1981) also proposed that a MIO strategy, which he called *heuristic trial and error*, provides a heuristic structure for reaching joint gains but not insight. The heuristic is to make only MIOs, concede over time on low-priority issues, and hold firm positions on high-priority issues. Yao et al. (2021) set out to

270 Handbook of Advances in Culture and Psychology

see whether non-Western culture negotiators were generating insight and negotiating joint gains using value-creating or -claiming negotiation strategy or MIOs.

E. Theory and Evidence Accounting for Cultural Differences in Joint Gains

Yao and colleagues (2021) report several studies testing whether negotiators can use MIOs to achieve high joint gains as an alternative to value-creating, information-sharing, and value-claiming influence attempts and SIOs. Their theorizing builts on Pruitt's (1981) identification of negotiation strategy that might provide indirect information to use to generate insight as to what trade-offs might lead to joint gains and Brett's (2014) theorizing that negotiators processing information holistically would be better at generating insight than their linearly analytic reasoning counterparts. The idea is that if negotiators assume their counterparts follow Pruitt's heuristic trial and error rule of only making MIOs and only conceding on low-priority issues, the pattern of a counterpart's concessions across a series of MIOs should reveal the counter-part's interests and priorities. Putting this priority information together with the negotiator's own priorities should generate insight into what trade-offs both parties can accept. Such trade-offs are the foundation of joint gains.

Pruitt (1981), Brett (2014), and Yao et al. (2021) all concede that infer-ring insight from the patterns of change in a series of MIOs requires second-order information-processing. Brett, Gunia, & Teucher (2017) proposed that negotiators with a holistic mindset should be more adapt at second-order information-processing and therefore better at inferring insight from MIOs than negotiators with an analytic mindset. They explained, "A mindset is a system of thought that directs attention and reasoning" (Nisbett et al., 2001). People with holistic versus analytic mindsets use fundamentally different cognitive processes. Those with holistic mindsets tend to consider an object's context, using associative reasoning to understand the situation as a whole. For example, they may rely on metaphors and stories to cue associations and, when confronted with contradictory perspectives, try to transcend the con-tradictions (Nisbett et al., 2001). Conversely, people with an analytic mindset focus on content, assigning objects to categories based on their attributes. They tend to use linear reasoning to understand each aspect of a situation in turn, and they may experience discomfort with contradictions. Faced with contradictions, analytic thinkers often prefer to choose one perspective over another (Nisbett et al., 2001). Nisbett and colleagues also summarized the evidence that mindset varies systematically between Eastern and Western cultures, with Easterners often categorized as holistic and Westerners as analytic (Chua et al., 2005; Ji et al., 2000; Kitayama et al., 2003; Masuda et al., 2008; Masuda & Nisbett, 2006; Nisbett & Masuda, 2003; Nisbett & Miyamoto, 2005; Norenzayan et al., 2002).

Yao and colleagues' Study 1 (2021) used meta-analysis to test the hypothesis that negotiators can use MIOs as an alternative to value-creating information-sharing to generate joint gains. They noted that prior research sometimes treats MIOs as a value-claiming strategy (Weingart et al., 1990), sometimes as a value-creating strategy (Weingart et al., 2007), and sometimes as a strategy separate from value-creating or value-claiming (Liu & Wilson, 2011). Sorting these confounds out and focusing on MIOs versus information-sharing versus influence attempts, Yao and colleagues (2021) found that use of the MIO strategy positively predicted joint gains in Western and non-Western intracultural samples. Results for intercultural negotiations were not significant. Use of the SIO strategy negatively predicted joint gains in Western, but not non-Western, cultures. When offers reported in the study were a mix of single and multiple issues, there was no relationship with joint gains in either Western or non-Western culture samples. The effect of the MIO strategy on joint gains remained significant even after controlling for negotiators' use of information-sharing (value-creating) and influence (value-claiming) strategy. Thus, MIO is a strategy that negotiators can use effectively to negotiate joint gains and that negotiators do use in addition to their well-documented use of information-sharing embedded in value-creating strategy.

Yao and colleagues' Study 2 unpacked the MIO joint gains relationship. They proposed that the MIO strategy should be particularly beneficial to low-trust negotiators, that insight is the mechanism accounting for the MIO–joint gains relationship,[11] and that mindset moderates the MIO–insight relationship. Their results with a non-Western culture managerial sample supported all three hypotheses.

VIII. INTERCULTURAL NEGOTIATION STRATEGIC ADJUSTMENT AND OUTCOMES

The model I proposed of factors influencing negotiators from different cultures (Brett, 2000) implies that negotiators from different cultural backgrounds may have very different interests and priorities. These differences may generate good potential for creating value via trade-offs. However, I also proposed that if the normative use of negotiation strategy is different for these negotiators, they may have difficulty identifying the value potential when they meet at the negotiation table. In short, their lack of strategic fit may impede their success in negotiating joint gains. An alternative perspective, based on social identity theory (Tajfel et al., 1979), is that intercultural negotiators' joint gains will be lower than intracultural negotiators' joint gains simply because intercultural negotiations are by definition between members of out-groups and people are less cooperative when interacting with out-group than in-group members (Halevy et al., 2008). A third perspective, based on Kelley and Thibaut's (1978) triangle hypothesis to explain behavioral choice in games, is that the least common denominator to avoid exploitation in negotiation is value-claiming. If value-claiming is the culturally normative strategy of one of the intercultural negotiators, the other will also engage in value-claiming strategy. The triangle theory proposes that a prosocial decision maker will change away from cooperation when faced with a proself decision maker but that a proself decision maker will not change away from competition when faced with a prosocial decision maker.

The standard design for intercultural negotiation research picks two different cultures and runs the same study within each culture and between cultures (e.g., Brett & Okumura, 1998). Most of these studies use Western culture negotiators (e.g. US, German, Norwegian), where value-creating strategy dominates, and non-Western culture negotiators (e.g., Japanese, Chinese, Mexican), where value-claiming strategy dominates.

Ramirez-Marin and colleagues (2019) concluded after identifying and reviewing papers with this design[12] that intercultural joint gains usually are lower than one of the two intracultural comparison samples but not lower than both. A comparison of the intracultural and the intercultural data presented in Brett (2007) illustrate this point. Other studies for which samples are not sojourners (e.g., Adler & Graham [1989], United States–Japan; Lügger et al. [2015], Germany–China; Natlandsmyr & Rognes [1995], Norway–Mexico; Ramirez-Marin et al. [2019], United States–Mexico) report similar results. Although there are not many intercultural negotiation strategy studies, reviewing these studies reveals that negotiators from primarily value-creating cultures do not always abandon that strategy when negotiating with counterparts from value-claiming cultures (e.g., Lügger et al., 2015) and vice versa. Negotiators from cultures where value-claiming is the prototype do not always maintain their normative approach when negotiating with a value-creating intercultural counterpart (e.g., Adair et al., 2001).

To explain these data, Ramirez-Marin and colleagues (2019) propose that there are two types of strategic adaptation. In one type of adaptation, negotiators move strategically toward their counterparts' culturally normative strategy. For example, negotiators from cultures where value-claiming is normative may increase use of value-creating strategy that is prototypical in their intercultural counterparts' cultures. Alternatively, negotiators may move strategically away from their own culture's prototypical negotiation strategy. For example, negotiators from value-claiming cultures may decrease use of value-claiming. Furthermore, negotiators are not limited to one or the other type of strategic adaptation. Intercultural negotiators may engage in both types simultaneously by moving toward their counterparts' culturally dominant strategy and moving away from their own culturally dominant strategy.

Ramirez-Marin and colleagues (2019) propose that *reciprocity*, the general tendency to return what one receives (Gouldner, 1960), explains both types of adaptation. The assumption is that negotiators carry their culture's prototypical strategic behavior with them from intracultural to intercultural situations. This implies that intercultural negotiators will start negotiating using the strategy that is prototypical in their culture and that because reciprocity is reinforcing and socially validating (Brett et al., 2004), reciprocity will govern strategic adaptation. For example, if the focal negotiator's culturally normative strategy is value-creating and the counterpart reciprocates, the strategic adaptation hypothesis predicts that the focal negotiator will continue to rely primarily on that culturally normative strategy and that the counterpart will engage in the focal negotiator's strategy more than would be normative in an intracultural negotiation. This is the pattern that Adair et al. (2001) report in a study comparing intra- and intercultural Japanese and US negotiators. The intercultural negotiations occurred in English in the United States, and the Japanese reciprocated to the US negotiators' use of value-creating strategy by reducing their use of value-claiming strategy relative to Japanese intracultural negotiators. However, this prediction ignores the fact that cultural norms may also be sticky. In Lügger and colleagues' (2015) study of Chinese and Germans negotiating via email, the Chinese negotiators did not adapt to the value-creating Germans. The German negotiators increased their level of value-claiming behavior but did not decrease their use of value-creating behavior relative to the German intracultural negotiators.

Ramirez-Marin and colleagues (2019) concluded that strategic adaptation in intercultural negotiation is much more complicated than social identity theory or the triangle hypothesis predicts. Strategic adaptation with mechanisms of culturally prototypical negotiation strategy and reciprocity provides a better account of the evidence of strategic adaptation in intercultural negotiations. What is missing from the intercultural literature, besides studies contrasting many different cultures, is a theory that identifies what factors beyond reciprocity affect whether a negotiator engages fully or partially in strategic adaptation.

IX. DISCUSSION AND FUTURE DIRECTIONS

Some scholars may believe that negotiation strategy is a mature research area with few opportunities for new insights. To be sure, negotiation strategy research has a long history relative to some of the currently hot topics in behavioral science research. However, the research reviewed in the second half of this chapter challenges the notion that there is nothing more to learn about negotiation strategy.

First, although motivational and behavioral theories of negotiation strategy are conceptually different, they apparently are functionally, at least with respect to predicting joint gains, equivalent.[13] The implication of this is not that the motivational versus behavioral theoretical distinction is invalid but that motivation and behavior work together to facilitate goal achievement in negotiation. This deeper understanding of the similarities of the two different theoretical perspectives also does not mean that researchers should abandon identifying their theoretical perspectives but it does imply that researchers should use their theoretical perspective as a driving force underlying their hypotheses, such that they coordinate their theory with their choices of independent variables and of mediators and moderators.

Second, the evidence that self-report and behavioral coding measurement of negotiation strategy are functionally equivalent in predicting joint gains should facilitate research on negotiation strategy. Behavioral coding is expensive, tedious, difficult, and, based on the available evidence, unnecessary when it comes to measuring value-claiming and value-creating negotiation strategies as a mediating mechanism to explain the effects of strategy on negotiation outcomes. Negotiators can tell the researcher whether they were cooperative, sharing information, or competitive, trying to influence the counterpart to make concessions. Thus, self-report should be sufficient for most research that is using negotiation strategy as an explanation for why an independent variable affects a negotiation outcome. The evidence that self-reports of strategy, which are made at the end of the negotiation, and behavioral coding of strategy from data collected during the negotiation are functionally equivalent also has implications for addressing causation. Functional equivalency implies that post-negotiation self-reports are valid indicators of process and not overly biased by the negotiation outcome.

There are some instances when behavioral coding will be necessary. Negotiators may not be able to self-report their use of SIOs and MIOs accurately. Following up and developing insight regarding the new research showing the importance of MIOs as a low-trust strategy for negotiating joint gains will probably require behavioral coding of offers. It also seems unlikely that negotiators can self-report the trajectory of their use of negotiation strategy. For example, Adair and Brett (2005) reported how strategy evolved over the four quarters of a negotiation simulation that required 60–75 minutes to complete. It would not be possible to study how context, for example, the social motive composition of a negotiating group, affected the reciprocal, complementary, or structural Markov sequences used by negotiators (e.g., Weingart et al., 2007) without behavioral coding that documents who said what when. That said, given the strength of behavioral theory, it seems difficult to justify the detailed level of coding that has been done in the past; for example, Weingart et al. (2007) used 33 codes. Brett, Yao, and Zhang's (2017) five-code approach—value-claiming (information-sharing, cooperation), value-claiming (influence, competitive and self-interested behavior), SIOs, MIOs and miscellaneous—perhaps supplemented by special codes related to the study's research question should be sufficient. Researchers could even justify having negotiators self-report their value-creating and value-claiming behaviors and just code offers and whatever behaviors are specific to the study's research question.

Third, evidence that negotiation strategy theory of value-creating and value-claiming does not predict joint gains in non-Western cultural samples should stimulate much new research. The low-hanging research fruit is to identify under what conditions in non-Western cultures negotiation strategy, as it is conceived motivationally or behaviorally, does predict joint gains. Two other research questions are more challenging and more interesting. The first is what is happening in non-Western cultures to mitigate the negative relationship between value claiming strategy and joint gains. So far, the research suggests that a plausible explanation needs to integrate understanding of cultural levels of trust, the cultural nature of trust (interpersonal vs. institutional), and the implications of cultural tightness. The second is what does predict joint gains across cultures? The meta-analytic research on MIOs is extremely promising, but already in their Study 2 Yao and colleagues (2021) identified a boundary condition. As predicted by Pruitt (1981), negotiators need to engage in higher-order processing to use MIOs to generate the insight that leads to joint gains. Yao and colleagues identified an individual difference, holistic mindset, that facilitated doing so. An interesting question is whether it is possible to motivate negotiators who normally and naturally process information analytically to engage in holistic analysis. What other conditions can motivate the higher-level processing that is necessary to turn MIOs into the insight that generates joint gains?

Finally, in intercultural negotiation, who adapts to whom and why, is a field wide open for new research. The review by Ramirez-Marin et al. (2019) of the admittedly sparse empirical literature reveals that social identity theory and the triangle hypothesis of adaptation are not sufficiently complex to model the empirical data. The data show that adaptation patterns are multifaceted, with negotiators increasing their use of their own culturally prototypical strategy, reducing it, or holding firm, while increasing their use of the counterpart's strategy, reducing it, or holding firm. If researchers could manipulate which of these adaptation patterns emerges, they are likely to begin to identify mechanisms beyond reciprocity that control strategic adaptation.

Although there has been much research on negotiation strategy and there are even a reasonable number of comparative cultural studies of negotiation strategy, at this stage the theorizing about how culture affects negotiation strategy theory is ahead of the data. There is not enough comparative culture research testing these new theoretical ideas about culture and negotiation strategy. There are opportunities for research testing theory about cultural differences in use of MIOs and other strategies, on strategic adaptation in intercultural negotiations, and on cultural differences in trust development. That said, there is also an opportunity for more theorizing. There may be other strategies uniquely in use at the table in specific non-Western cultures that so far research based on current negotiation strategy theory has ignored because the strategy does not fit with the current theory or because current measurement does not cover the concept. Relationship-building comes to mind. It seems to underlie the way negotiators in low-trust tight and loose cultures went about the process of determining trust in Brett and Mitchell's (2022) interview study and may underlie the moral integrity constructs that Gelfand and colleagues (2015) identified as operating in their study.

Culture matters in negotiation strategy research. Culture matters because comparative culture research reveals differences systematically associated with culture. More importantly, culture also matters because comparative culture research on negotiation strategy has revealed the limitations of negotiation strategy theory, which has been accepted as gospel for many years.

Alongside the view that negotiation strategy is a mature research area is the complementary view that comparative culture research is nothing more than stereotyping, which ignores the rich variability within cultures. To be sure, comparative culture research reveals central tendencies, but central tendencies emerge thanks to the discipline of statistics partitioning within- versus between-group variation. Comparative cultural research does not ignore within-culture variation; it would not be possible without it. It may be useful to think about cultures as a set of nesting dolls in which there are dolls within dolls within dolls. Although each doll has its own structure, the structure of the larger doll influences the structure within which the smaller and smaller dolls fit. The challenge for culture and negotiation researchers is to understand what that structure is and how it affects negotiation strategy.

As a negotiation researcher, I have a different way of approaching the cultural level of analysis problem. I work from boundaries that are national or regional and then try to use cultural theory to explain, culturally and psychologically, the differences in the phenomena I study. This is a distinctly non-psychological approach, but there are reasons for taking this approach, certainly not always appreciated by reviewers. First, national boundaries constrain negotiators because they delineate political, social, and economic systems within which negotiations take place. They also reflect cultural norms, beliefs, and values in a symbiotic relationship between psychology and structure. Political and economic systems may vary within regional boundaries, but history and geography, as well as simply distance, unite the social outlook within regions—the larger doll in the example of nesting dolls. Second, there is a plethora of cultural constructs available to researchers interested in explaining cultural differences. Which one to use? There is little guidance. Moreover, starting with a cultural construct poses two research risks. One risk is that it reorients the research to the level of individual differences in cultural values rather than cultural group differences. Another risk is that the construct of choice may not account for the cultural differences.

Finally, there is the view that, because people are becoming global citizens, the research question should not be about how citizens of one country or region negotiate but how global citizens negotiate. What about their global experience influences their use of negotiation strategy and outcomes? How globalization of identity affects negotiations poses an interesting set of research questions (Janssens et al., 2019). There may be differences depending on types of global experience. For example, people with deep as opposed to broad global experience seem to be more creative (Godart et al., 2015). However, global versus local would seem to be a comparison that is not going to disappear given the drive to preserve local culture in the face of an actual or illusory challenge from an influx of people from other cultures.

A. Practical Implications

Negotiation research has had the remarkable status of being a field in which its scholarship moved rapidly into the classroom. Business schools around the world and many US law schools offer courses in negotiation that address the implications of the theory and research. These classes teach the benefits of joint gains and the mechanisms for achieving joint gains via value-creating and value-claiming strategies. A business school student will get the same curriculum in business school whether taking the course in India, China, Spain, Great Britain, the United States, or Canada. If the conclusions of the research reviewed in the second half of this chapter continue to hold, the global negotiation curriculum needs to be restructured.

Step 1 is to add use of MIOs to a negotiation curriculum that already teaches students to share information about interests and priorities in order to negotiate joint gains. Students, even those who are initially skeptical, learn very quickly to ask for and share information about interests and priorities. It is what the instructor is asking them to do; it means they reach high-quality outcomes in the classroom exercises and do so efficiently. Trust is a two-edged sword. It facilitates information-sharing and so joint gains, but negotiators may take advantage of trusting counterparts (Olekalns & Smith, 2007). If the only way a student knows to reach a joint gains agreement is by trusting the counterpart, the current negotiation curriculum is breeding lambs and releasing them blithely into meadows of wolves. Use of MIOs appears to be an effective alternative strategy for negotiating joint gains when trust is low. Using MIOs to generate insight does take practice with higher-level processing, but practice is why students take negotiation classes.

Step 2 is teaching students about trust and tightness–looseness around the world. Many negotiation students want to know not only what to do to improve their negotiation outcomes but why. When negotiators understand why, they can make their own adjustments in strategy as their negotiations unfold. What to teach? First, in many parts of the world people, much less negotiators, do not assume that others are trustworthy. Deciding whether a potential business partner is trustworthy is a process, and the process is not the same around the world (Brett & Mitchell, 2022). What deciding to trust has in common in regions of the world where trust in negotiation is low is that it takes much more time and personal engagement than Western culture negotiators are used to. Second, what looks like interpersonal trust may be institutional trust, and institutional trust does not extend to the negotiation table. Institutional trust may take some explaining. One way into this concept is to introduce cultural tightness–looseness and explain how in tight cultures strong monitoring and sanctioning systems enforce norms so that social interaction that looks like trust only occurs within social bounds.

Step 3 is addressing whether joint gains should be the primary criterion for evaluating negotiation outcomes. Joint gains are a short-term outcome with supposedly long-term benefits (Raiffa, 1982): Joint gains should facilitate implementation, because joint gains should mean that the negotiators agreement integrated their interests and priorities. However, an agreement that maximizes negotiators' short term interests may not maximize long term interests, if the agreement fails to take account of relationship issues. There is certainly acknowledgment in the literature (Gelfand et al., 2015) that in some cultures the relationship is equally or even a more important outcome of negotiations than joint gains. Relationship seems to mean more than satisfaction or subjective value (Curhan et al., 2006), or trust, defined as the willingness to be vulnerable to actions of the other (Gunia et al., 2011). Relationship pushes the boundaries of benevolence. Relationship in some cultures seems to imply confidence that the other party will not just cut and run in the face of adversity but actively help to combat it. Is such a relationship a likely outcome of negotiation in Western culture? Probably not, for all kinds of reasons, ranging from rule of law to the separation of professional and personal relationships as described by Sanchez-Burkes (2005). In non-Western cultures? Perhaps yes, if the process of deciding whether a potential new business partner is the prolonged social vetting that Brett and Mitchell (2022) describe as characterizing trust development in Latin American and Middle Eastern/South Asian cultures.

X. CONCLUSION

Negotiation strategy theory and research only seems like a mature research area if you do not consider culture. With the new meta-analyses showing that negotiation strategy theory does not predict joint gains in non-Western cultures and that MIO does predict joint gains independently of information-sharing in Western and non-Western cultures and is particularly helpful to low-trust negotiators, whole new vistas of culture and negotiation strategy research open.

NOTES

1. *Social motive* is the term for when the researcher is treating the concept as a state, potentially variable associated with context or manipulation. *Social value orientation* is the term used for when the researcher is treating the concept as a trait, a stable individual difference. This chapter, while recognizing the differences, treats social values and social motives as a single construct.
2. Data reanalyzed from Brett (2007, p. 22).
3. Note that both members of the dyad had the same social motive.
4. Although the dual-concern theory identifies four distinct strategies, empirical studies frequently collapse the four strategies into two: problem-solving and contending (e.g., Beersma & De Dreu, 2005).
5. In my data (Brett, 2007) 8% (range 4%–13%) of managers had no dominant social motive.
6. Factors that reduce resistance to yielding, for example, time pressure, are not likely to similarly affect the negotiator's proself social motive, especially if a social motive is considered to be a trait.
7. I found no significant differences between prosocial and proself negotiators' joint gains. Across cultures, regardless of the social motive or culture of the counterpart, competitive negotiators reported lower joint gains (M = \$3.64m, SD = \$1.23m, n = 50) than either prosocial (M = \$4.034m, SD = \$1.01m, n = 776) or proself (M = \$4.03m, SD = \$1.02m, n = 526) ($F_{(2,1339)}$ = 3.398, p < .05) negotiators. My data were not available at the time of the DeDreu et al. meta-analysis. I did not collect data on problem-solving or contending, the conflict management strategies associated with dual-concern theory. It seems entirely possible that prosocial negotiators without the motivational boost of resistance to yielding satisfice and proself negotiators, while motivated to do well for themselves, overlook the possibility of negotiating more for self by negotiating more for the other party, generating similar levels of joint gains (Brett, 2007).
8. Thompson & Hastie (1990) is heavily cited for the finding that it is not just information about priorities but insight into negotiators' priorities (what issue is more and what issue less important) that leads to joint gains. However, Pruitt's own research (e.g., Carnevale et al., 1981; Kimmel et al., 1980; Pruitt et al., 1978) showed that when giving instructions to engage in problem-solving, negotiators' information-sharing about priorities increased along with their joint gains. Pruitt used the concept insight to explain logrolling from information acquired during negotiation in his 1981 book.
9. The meta-analysis also included studies using the LIWC to code strategy. Linguistic Inquiry and Word Count (LIWC) (Pennebaker & Graybeal, 2001) is a general framework for coding social interaction. I do not discuss this aspect

of the meta-analysis, as it showed no significant relationships between LIWC coding of strategy and joint gains, perhaps because of few observations.

10. Although I proposed this model to conceptualize intercultural negotiations, it also can be used to organize and examine the research on negotiation more broadly. It organizes the factors that negotiators bring to negotiation and that affect their interests and priorities and or use of negotiation strategy, thereby affecting the nature of the interaction at the negotiation table (Brett & Thompson, 2016).

11. Too few studies identified for the meta-analysis measured insight for this mediation hypothesis to be tested.

12. They did not include papers in which participants in one of the intercultural samples were sojourners because of the expectation that cultural adjustments would have already been made in everyday living that would transfer to the intercultural negotiation.

13. Brett et al. (2021) did not report their results with satisfaction as the dependent variable; however, they found that motivational and behavioral theories were also functionally equivalent in predicting negotiators' satisfaction.

REFERENCES

Adair, W., & Brett, J. M. (2005). The negotiation dance: Time, culture, and behavioral sequences in negotiation. *Organizational Science*, *16*(1), 33–51.

Adair, W. L., Okumura, T., & Brett, J. M. (2001). Negotiation behavior when cultures collide: The United States and Japan. *Journal of Applied Psychology*, *86*(3), 371–385.

Adair, W. L., Weingart, L. R., & Brett, J. M. (2007). The timing and function of offers in US and Japanese negotiations. *Journal of Applied Psychology*, *92*(4), 1056–1068.

Adler, N. J., & Graham, J. L. (1989). Cross-cultural interaction: The international comparison fallacy? *Journal of International Business Studies*, *20*(3), 515–537.

Allred, K. G., Mallozzi, J. S., Matsui, F., & Raia, C. P. (1997). The influence of anger and compassion on negotiation performance. *Organizational Behavior and Human Decision Processes*, *70*(3), 175–187.

Aslani, S., Ramirez-Marin, J., Brett, J., Yao, J., Semnani-Azad, Z., Zhang, Z. X., Tinsley, C., Weingart, L., & Adair, W. (2016). Dignity, face, and honor cultures: A study of negotiation strategy and outcomes in three cultures. *Journal of Organizational Behavior*, *37*(8), 1178–1201.

Beersma, B., & De Dreu, C. K. (1999). Negotiation processes and outcomes in prosocially and egoistically motivated groups. *International Journal of Conflict Management*, *10*(4), 385–402.

Beersma, B., & De Dreu, C. K. (2005). Conflict's consequences: Effects of social motives on post negotiation creative and convergent group functioning and performance. *Journal of Personality and Social Psychology*, *89*(3), 358–374.

Belkin, L. Y., Kurtzberg, T. R., & Naquin, C. E. (2013). Signaling dominance in online negotiations: The role of affective tone. *Negotiation and Conflict Management Review, 6*(4), 285–304.

Ben-Yoav, O., & Pruitt, D. G. (1984). Resistance to yielding and the expectation of cooperative future interaction in negotiation. *Journal of Experimental Social Psychology, 20*(4), 323–335.

Blader, S. L., & Chen, Y. R. (2012). Differentiating the effects of status and power: A justice perspective. *Journal of Personality and Social Psychology, 102*(5), 994–1014.

Blake, R., & Mouton, J. (1964). *The managerial grid: The key to leadership excellence.* Gulf Publishing.

Boldt, E. D. (1978a). Structural tightness and cross-cultural research. *Journal of Cross-Cultural Psychology, 9*(2), 151–165.

Boldt, E. D. (1978b). Structural tightness, autonomy, and observability: An analysis of Hutterite conformity and orderliness. *Canadian Journal of Sociology, 3*(3), 349–363.

Boldt, E. D., & Roberts, L. W. (1979). Structural tightness and social conformity: A methodological note with theoretical implications. *Journal of Cross-Cultural Psychology, 10*(2), 221–230.

Brett, J. M. (2000). Culture and negotiation. *International Journal of Psychology, 35*(2), 97–104.

Brett, J. M. (2007). *Negotiating globally: How to negotiate deals, resolve disputes, and make decisions across cultural boundaries* (2nd ed.). Jossey-Bass.

Brett, J. M. (2014). *Negotiating globally: How to negotiate deals, resolve disputes, and make decisions across cultural boundaries* (3rd ed.). Jossey-Bass.

Brett, J. M., Gunia, B. C., & Teucher, B. M. (2017). Culture and negotiation strategy: A framework for future research. *Academy of Management Perspectives, 31*(4), 288–308.

Brett, J. M., & Mitchell, T. (2022). *Searching for trust in the global economy.* University of Toronto Press

Brett, J. M., & Okumura, T. (1998). Inter and intra-cultural negotiation: U.S. and Japanese negotiators. *Academy of Management Journal, 41*(5), 495–510.

Brett, J. M., Ramirez-Marin, J., & Galoni, C. (2021). Negotiation strategy: a cross-cultural meta-analytic evaluation of theory and measurement. *Negotiation and Conflict Management Research, 14*(4).

Brett, J. M., Shapiro, D. L., & Lytle, A. L. (1998). Breaking the bonds of reciprocity in negotiations. *Academy of Management Journal, 41*(4), 410–424.

Brett, J. M., & Thompson, L. (2016). Negotiation. *Organizational Behavior and Human Decision Processes, 136*, 68–79.

Brett, J., Weingart, L., & Olekalns, M. (2004). Baubles, bangles, and beads: Modeling the evolution of negotiating groups over time. In *Time in groups* (pp. 39–64). Emerald Group Publishing.

Brett, J. M., Yao, J. J., & Zhang, Z-X. (2017). OFFER: Behaviorally coding indirect and direct information exchange in negotiations. In E. Brauner, M. Boos, & M. Kolbe (Eds.), *Handbook of group interaction analysis* (pp. 483–490). Cambridge University Press.

Butler, J. K. (1999). Trust expectations information sharing climate of trust and negotiation effectiveness and efficiency. *Group and Organization Management, 24*(2), 217–238.

Carnevale, P. J. D., Pruitt, D. G., & Seilheimer, S. D. (1981). Looking and competing: Accountability and ad visual access in integrative bargaining. *Journal of Personality and Social Psychology, 40*(1), 111–120.

Chua, H. F., Boland, J. E., & Nisbett, R. E. (2005). Cultural variation in eye movements during scene perception. *Proceedings of the National Academy of Sciences of the United States of America, 102,* 12629–12633.

Curhan, J. R., Elfenbein, H. A., & Xu, H. (2006). What do people value when they negotiate? Mapping the domain of subjective value in negotiation. *Journal of Personality and Social Psychology, 91*(3), 493–512.

De Dreu, C. K., Evers, A., Beersma, B., Kluwer, E. S., & Nauta, A. (2001). A theory-based measure of conflict management strategies in the workplace. *Journal of Organizational Behavior, 22*(6), 645–668.

De Dreu, C. K., & Van Lange, P. A. (1995). The impact of social value orientations on negotiator cognition and behavior. *Personality and Social Psychology Bulletin, 21*(11), 1178–1188.

De Dreu, C. K. W., Weingart, L. R., & Kwon, S. (2000). Influence of social motives on integrative negotiations: A meta-analytic review and test of two theories. *Journal of Personality and Social Psychology, 78,* 889–905.

Deutsch, M. (1949). A theory of co-operation and competition. *Human Relations, 2*(2), 129–152.

Deutsch, M. (1960). The effect of motivational orientation upon trust and suspicion. *Human Relations, 13*(2), 123–139.

Deutsch, M. (1973). *The resolution of conflict: Constructive and destructive processes.* Yale University Press.

Dong, R. (2006). *How does culture influence the joint gains of a negotiation? A close study on the U.S. and Chinese intracultural negotiations* [Unpublished undergraduate thesis]. Northwestern University.

Druckman, D. (1986). Stages, turning points, and crises: Negotiating military base rights, Spain and the United States. *Journal of Conflict Resolution, 30*(2), 327–360.

Druckman, D., & Olekalns, M. (2011). Turning points in negotiation. *Negotiation and Conflict Management Research, 4*(10), 1–7.

Eek, D., & Gärling, T. (2008). A new look at the theory of social value orientations: Prosocials neither maximize joint outcome nor minimize outcome differences but prefer equal outcomes. In *New issues and paradigms in research on social dilemmas* (pp. 10–26). Springer.

Elahee, M., & Brooks, C. M. (2004). Trust and negotiation tactics: Perceptions about business-to-business negotiations in Mexico. *Journal of Business & Industrial Marketing, 19*(6), 397–404.

Fisher, R., Ury, W., & Patton, B. (2011). *Getting to yes*. Penguin.

Follett, M. P. (1940). Constructive conflict. In H. C. Metcalf & L. Urwick (Eds.), *Dynamic administration: The collected papers of Mary Follett* (pp. 30–49). Harper and Brothers.

Ford, J., Young, D., & Box, S. (1967). Functional autonomy, role distance and social class. *British Journal of Sociology, 18*(4), 370–381.

Friedman, R., Anderson, C., Brett, J., Olekalns, M., Goates, N., & Lisco, C. C. (2004). The positive and negative effects of anger on dispute resolution: Evidence from electronically mediated disputes. *Journal of Applied Psychology, 89*(2), 369–376.

Gelfand, M. J. (2018). *Rule makers: Rule breakers*. Scribner.

Gelfand, M. J., Nishii, L. H., & Raver, J. L. (2006). On the nature and importance of cultural tightness-looseness. *Journal of Applied Psychology, 91*(6), 1225–1244.

Gelfand, M. J., Raver, J. L., Nishii, L., Leslie, L. M., Lun, J., Lim, B. C., Duan, L., Almaliach, A., Ang, S., Arnadottir, J., Aycan, Z., Boehnke, K., Boski, P., Cabecinhas, R., Chan, D., Chhokar, J., D'Amato, A., Ferrer, M., Fischlmayr, I. C., . . . Yamaguchi, S. (2011). Differences between tight and loose cultures: A 33-nation study. *Science, 332*, 1100–1104.

Gelfand, M. J., Severance, L., Lee, T., Bruss, C. B., Lun, J., Abdel-Latif, A. H., Al-Moghazy, A. A., & Moustafa Ahmed, S. (2015). Culture and getting to yes: The linguistic signature of creative agreements in the United States and Egypt. *Journal of Organizational Behavior, 36*(7), 967–989.

Glick, S., & Croson, R. (2001). Reputations in negotiation. In S. Hoch & H. Kunreuther (Eds.), *Wharton on making decisions* (pp. 177–186). John Wiley & Sons.

Godart, F. C., Maddux, W. W., Shipilov, A. V., & Galinsky, A. D. (2015). Fashion with a foreign flair: Professional experiences abroad facilitate the creative innovations of organizations. *Academy of Management Journal, 58*(1), 195–220.

Gouldner, A. W. (1960). The norm of reciprocity: A preliminary statement. *American Sociological Review, 25*(2), 161–178.

Gunia, B. C., Brett, J. M., Nandkeolyar, A., & Kamdar, D. (2011). Paying a price: Culture, trust, and negotiation consequences. *Journal of Applied Psychology, 96*(4), 774–789.

Halevy, N., Bornstein, G., & Sagiv, L. (2008). "In-group love" and "out-group hate" as motives for individual participation in intergroup conflict: A new game paradigm. *Psychological Science, 19*(4), 405–411.

Hüffmeier, J., Freund, P. A., Zerres, A., Backhaus, K., & Hertel, G. (2014). Being tough or being nice? A meta-analysis on the impact of hard- and soft-line strategies in distributive negotiations. *Journal of Management, 40*(3), 866–892.

Janssens, M., Maddux, W., & Nguayen, T. (2019). Globalization: Current issues and future research directions [Special issue]. *Negotiation and Conflict Management Research, 12*(2), 174–185.

Ji, L., Peng, K., & Nisbett, R. E. (2000). Culture, control and perception of relationship in the environment. *Journal of Personality and Social Psychology, 78,* 943–955.

Kass, R., Kass, J., Binder, H., & Kraft, N. (2010). Conflict-handling mode scores of three crews before and after a 264-day spaceflight simulation. *Aviation, Space, and Environmental Medicine, 81(5),* 502–505. https://www.ncbi.nlm.nih.gov/pubmed/20464818

Kelley, H. H. (1967). Attribution theory in social psychology. In *Nebraska symposium on motivation* (Vol. 15, pp. 192–238). University of Nebraska Press.

Kelley, H. H., & Thibaut, J. W. (1978). *Interpersonal relations: A theory of interdependence.* John Wiley & Sons.

Kern, M. C., Brett, J. M., Weingart, L. R., & Eck, C. S. (2020). The "fixed" pie perception and strategy in dyadic versus multiparty negotiations. *Organizational Behavior and Human Decision Processes, 157,* 143–158.

Kimmel, M. J., Pruitt, D. G., Magenau, J. M., Konar-Goldband, E., & Carnevale, P. J. D. (1980). Effects of trust, aspiration, and gender on negotiation tactics. *Journal of Personality and Social Psychology, 38*(1), 9–22.

Kitayama, S., Duffy, S., Kawamura, T., & Larsen, J. T. (2003). Perceiving an object and its context in different cultures: A cultural look at the new look. *Psychological Science, 14,* 201–206.Komorita, S. S., & Leung, K. (1985). The effects of alternatives on the salience of reward allocation norms. *Journal of Experimental Social Psychology, 21*(3), 229–246.

Kong, D. T., Dirks, K. T., & Ferrin, D. L. (2014). Interpersonal trust within negotiations: Meta-analytic evidence, critical contingencies, and directions for future research. *Academy of Management Journal, 57*(5), 1235–1255.

Lawler, E. J. (1992). Power processes in bargaining. *Sociological Quarterly, 33*(1), 17–34.

Lax, D. A., & Sebenius, J. K. (1986). *The manager as negotiator.* Free Press.

Liu, M. (2009). The intrapersonal and interpersonal effects of anger on negotiation strategies: A cross-cultural investigation. *Human Communication Research, 35*(1), 148–169.

Liu, M., & Wilson, S. R. (2011). The effects of interaction goals on negotiation tactics and outcomes: A dyad-level analysis across two cultures. *Communication Research, 38*(2), 248–277.

Luce, R. D., & Raiffa, H. (1957). *Games and decisions: Introduction and critical survey.* John Wiley & Sons. https://books.google.fr/books?hl=en&lr=

&id=zT-KAAAAQBAJ&oi=fnd&pg=PA1&dq=luce+and+raiffa+1957&ots=
Uec3I0Z9EH&sig=v6WKIH9E5pGuwyLH7eJU9Sf_5RM&redir_esc=y#v=
onepage&q=luce%20and%20raiffa%201957&f=false

Lügger, K., Geiger, I., Neun, H., & Backhaus, K. (2015). When East meets West at the bargaining table: Adaptation, behavior and outcomes in intra- and intercultural German–Chinese business negotiations. *Journal of Business Economics*, *85*(1), 15–43.

Magee, J. C., & Galinsky, A. D. (2008). Social hierarchy: The self-reinforcing nature of power and status. *Academy of Management Annals*, *2*(1), 351–398.

Masuda, T., Gonzalez, R., Kwan, L., & Nisbett, R. E. (2008). Culture and aesthetic preference: Comparing the attention to context of East Asians and Americans. *Personality and Social Psychology Bulletin*, *34*, 1260–1275.

Masuda, T., & Nisbett, R. E. (2006). Culture and change blindness. *Cognitive Science*, *30*, 381–399.Messick, D. M., & McClintock, C. G. (1968). Motivational bases of choice in experimental games. *Journal of Experimental Social Psychology*, *4*(1), 1–25.

Miles, E. W., & Clenney, E. F. (2010). Gender differences in negotiation: A status characteristics theory view. *Negotiation and Conflict Management Research*, *3*(2), 130–144.

Natlandsmyr, J., & Rognes, J. (1995). Culture, behavior, and negotiation outcomes: A comparative and cross-cultural study of Mexican and Norwegian negotiators. *International Journal of Conflict Management*, *6*(1), 5–29.

Nisbett, R. E., & Masuda, T. (2003). Culture and point of view. *Proceedings of the National Academy of Sciences of the United States of America*, *100*, 11163–11170.

Nisbett, R. E., & Miyamoto, Y. (2005). The influence of culture: Holistic versus analytic perception. *Trends in Cognitive Sciences*, *9*, 467–473.

Nisbett, R. E., Peng, K., Choi, I., & Norenzayan, A. (2001). Culture and systems of thought: Holistic vs. analytic cognition. *Psychological Review*, *108*, 291–310.

Norenzayan, A., Smith, E. E., Kim, B. J., & Nisbett, R. E. (2002). Cultural preferences for formal versus intuitive reasoning. *Cognitive Science*, *26*, 653–684.

Olekalns, M., & Smith, P. L. (2000). Understanding optimal outcomes. The role of strategy sequences in competitive negotiations. *Human Communication Research*, *26*(4), 527–557.

Olekalns, M., & Smith, P. L. (2003a). Social motives in negotiation: The negotiators' motivational orientations, strategy choices, and outcomes. *International Journal of Conflict Management*, *14*, 233–254.

Olekalns, M., & Smith, P. L. (2003b). Testing the relationship among negotiator's motivational orientations, strategy choices, and outcomes. *Journal of Experimental Psychology*, *39*, 101–117.

Olekalns, M., & Smith, P. L. (2005). Moments in time: Metacognition, trust, and outcomes in dyadic negotiation. *Personality and Social Psychology Bulletin*, *31*, 1696–1707.

Olekalns, M., & Smith, P. L. (2007). Loose with the truth: Predicting deception in negotiation. *Journal of Business Ethics, 76*(2), 225–238.

Pennebaker, J. W., & Graybeal, A. (2001). Patterns of natural language use: Disclosure, personality, and social integration. *Current Directions in Psychological Science, 10*(3), 90–93.

Pinkley, R. L. (1995). Impact of knowledge regarding alternatives to settlement in dyadic negotiations: Whose knowledge counts? *Journal of Applied Psychology, 80*(3), 403–417.

Pinkley, R. L., Neale, M. A., & Bennett, R. J. (1994). The impact of alternatives to settlement in dyadic negotiation. *Organizational Behavior and Human Decision Processes, 57*(1), 97–116.

Pruitt, D. G. (1981). *Negotiation behavior*. Academic Press.

Pruitt, D. G., Kimmel, M. J., Britton, S., Carnevale, P. J., Magenau, J. M., Peragallo, J., & Engram, P. (1978). The effect of accountability and surveillance on integrative bargaining. *Contributions to Experimental Economics, 7*, 310–343.

Pruitt, D. G., & Lewis, S. A. (1975). Development of integrative solutions in bilateral negotiations. *Journal of Personality and Social Psychology, 31*(4), 621–633.

Pruitt, D. G., & Rubin, J. Z. (1986). *Social conflict: Escalation, impasse, and resolution*. Addison-Wesley.

Putnam, L. L. (1983). The interpretive perspective: An alternative to functionalism. In L. L. Putnam & M. E. Pacanowsky (Eds.), *Communication and organizations: An interpretive approach* (pp. 31–54). SAGE Publications.

Putnam, L. L., & Jones, T. S. (1982). Reciprocity in negotiations: An analysis of bargaining interaction. *Communication Monographs, 49*(3), 171–191.Rahim, M. A. (1983). A measure of styles of handling interpersonal conflict. *Academy of Management Journal, 26*(2), 368–376.

Rahim, M. A. (1986). Referent role and styles of handling interpersonal conflict. *The Journal of Social Psychology, 126*(1), 79–86.

Raiffa, H. (1982). *The art and science of negotiation*. Harvard University Press.

Ramirez-Marin, J., Brett, J. M., & Munduate, L. (2019). *Strategic adaptation in intercultural negotiation: Spanish honor and U.S. dignity negotiations* [Working paper].

Rappaport, A. (1960). *Fights, games, and debates*. University of Michigan Press.

Rousseau, D. M., Sitkin, S. B., Burt, R. S., & Camerer, C. (1998). Not so different after all: A cross-discipline view of trust. *Academy of Management Review, 23*, 393–404.

Ruble, T. L., & Thomas, K. W. (1976). Support for a two-dimensional model of conflict behavior. *Organizational Behavior and Human Performance, 16*(1), 143–155.

Sanchez-Burks, J. (2005). Protestant relational ideology: The cognitive underpinnings and organizational implications of an American anomaly. *Research in Organizational Behavior, 26*, 265–305.

Schelling, T. (1980). *The strategy of conflict*. Harvard University Press. (Original work published 1960)

Sinaceur, M., Van Kleef, G. A., Neale, M. A., Adam, H., & Haag, C. (2011). Hot or cold: Is communicating anger or threats more effective in negotiation? *Journal of Applied Psychology, 96*(5), 1018–1032.

Tajfel, H., Turner, J. C., Austin, W. G., & Worchel, S. (1979). An integrative theory of intergroup conflict. *Organizational identity: A reader, 56*(65), 9780203505984-16.

Takahashi, C., Yamagishi, T., Liu, J. H., Wang, F. X., Lin, Y. C., & Yu, S. (2008). The intercultural trust paradigm: Studying joint cultural interaction and social exchange in real time over the internet. *International Journal of Intercultural Relations, 32*(3), 215–228.

Thomas, K. W. (1976). Conflict and conflict management. In M. D. Dunnette (Ed.), *Handbook of industrial and organizational psychology* (pp. 889–935). Rand-McNally.

Thompson, L., & Hastie, R. (1990). Social perception in negotiation. *Organizational Behavior and Human Decision Processes, 47*, 98–123.

Tinsley, C. H., O'Connor, K. M., & Sullivan, B. A. (2002). Tough guys finish last: The perils of a distributive reputation. *Organizational Behavior and Human Decision Processes, 88*(2), 621–642.

Tinsley, C. H., Cambria, J. J., & Schneider, A. K. (2006). Reputations in negotiation. In A. K. Schneider & C. Honeyman (Eds.), *The negotiator's fieldbook: The desk reference for the experienced negotiator, 203–214.

Van de Vliert, E. (1997). *Complex interpersonal conflict behaviors*. Psychology Press.

Van de Vliert, E., & Kabanoff, B. (1990). Toward theory-based measures of conflict management. *Academy of Management Journal, 33*(1), 199–209.

Van Kleef, G. A. (2009). How emotions regulate social life the emotions as social information (EASI) model. *Current Directions in Psychological Science, 18*, 184–188.

Van Kleef, G. A., De Dreu, C. K., & Manstead, A. S. (2004a). The interpersonal effects of anger and happiness in negotiations. *Journal of Personality and Social Psychology, 86*(1), 57–76.

Van Kleef, G. A., De Dreu, C. K. W., & Manstead, A. S. R. (2004b). The interpersonal effects of emotions in negotiations: A motivated information processing approach. *Journal of Personality and Social Psychology, 87*, 510–528.

Van Lange, P. A., De Bruin, E., Otten, W., & Joireman, J. A. (1997). Development of prosocial, individualistic, and competitive orientations: Theory and preliminary evidence. *Journal of Personality and Social Psychology, 73*(4), 733–746.

Walton, R. E., & McKersie, R. B. (1965). *A behavioral theory of labor negotiations.* McGraw-Hill.

Wang, L., Northcraft, G. B., & Van Kleef, G. A. (2012). Beyond negotiated outcomes: The hidden costs of anger expression in dyadic negotiation. *Organizational Behavior and Human Decision Processes, 119*(1), 54–63.

Weingart, L. R., Brett, J. M., Olekalns, M., & Smith, P. L. (2007). Conflicting social motives in negotiating groups. *Journal of Personality and Social Psychology, 93*(6), 994–1010.

Weingart, L. R., Prietula, M. J., Hyder, E. B., & Genovese, C. R. (1999). Knowledge and the sequential processes of negotiation: A Markov chain analysis of response-in-kind. *Journal of Experimental Social Psychology, 35*(4), 366–393.

Weingart, L. R., Thompson, L. L., Bazerman, M. H., & Carroll, J. S. (1990). Tactical behavior and negotiation outcomes. *International Journal of Conflict Management, 1*(1), 7–31.

Wong, R. (2014). Same power but different goals: How does knowledge of opponents' power affect negotiators' aspiration in power-asymmetric negotiations? *Global Journal of Business Research, 8*(3), 77–89.

World Bank. (2016). *The World Bank annual report 2016.* https://thedocs.worldbank.org/en/doc/596391540568499043-0340022018/original/worldbank-annualreport2016.pdf

Yamagishi, T. (2009, June 16). *Trust in China and Japan: Findings from "joint-cultural" experiments* [Paper presentation]. IACM Conference, Kyoto, Japan.

Yamagishi, T., Cook, K. S., & Watabe, M. (1998). Uncertainty, trust, and commitment formation in the United States and Japan. *American Journal of Sociology, 104*(1), 165–194.

Yamagishi, T., & Yamagishi, M. (1994). Trust and commitment in the United States and Japan. *Motivation and Emotion, 18*(2), 129–166.

Yao, J., Brett, J. M., Zhang, Z. X., & Ramirez-Marin, J. (2021). Multi-issue offers strategy and joint gains in negotiations: How low-trust negotiators get things done. *Organizational Behavior and Human Decision Processes, 162*, 9–23.

CHAPTER 6

Foresight, Punishment, and Cooperation

SERGEY GAVRILETS

Abstract

Understanding the evolution of social behaviors, norms, and institutions, which are at the core of all human cultures, requires understanding human decision-making processes. Two important characteristics of humans are that people care about future payoffs and that they have the "theory of mind" which allows them to predict to a certain extent the reaction of their social partners to their own actions. In evolutionary game theory, these characteristics can be modeled by a recently introduced strategy update method called foresight. This chapter discusses applications of foresight to several evolutionary games describing the effects of punishment on cooperation in repeated dyadic or group interactions. It is argued that foresight is able to solve both the first and second order free-rider problems, simplifying cooperation and the evolution of social institutions. Moreover, it can maintain social norms. Foresight can also undermine cooperation by allowing for manipulation and tactical deception.

Key Words: cooperation, conflict, punishment, evolutionary game theory, social norm, manipulation, strategy revision

---

I. INTRODUCTION

In my research, I use mathematical models to study complex evolutionary processes.[*] The earlier part of my career was spent attempting to shed theoretical light on various puzzles in the field of evolutionary biology. Although most of my models were not specifically designed for understanding humans or their psychology but rather focused on general evolutionary processes, some of my

---

[*] The editors asked me to start by outlining the development of my research program.

Sergey Gavrilets, *Foresight, Punishment, and Cooperation* In: *Handbook of Advances in Culture and Psychology.*
Edited by: Michele J. Gelfand, Chi-yue Chiu, and Ying-yi Hong, Oxford University Press. © Oxford University Press 2022.
DOI: 10.1093/oso/9780197631669.003.0006

results would also apply to humans. I have worked on models of phenotypic plasticity and genotype–environment interaction, the dynamics and maintenance of genetic variation in multiple loci, fitness landscapes, coevolution and adaptation, sexual selection and sexual conflict, homosexuality, multicellularity, and some other related topics. A significant proportion of these efforts has focused on developing a mathematical theory of the origins and evolution of biodiversity via the process of speciation which Darwin (2003/1859) called a "mystery of mysteries." That work led to a monograph entitled *Fitness Landscapes and the Origin of Species* (Gavrilets, 2004), which represented an attempt to, first, formalize the arguments of evolutionary biologists of the 20th century on how new species arise and, second, provide additional theoretical insights into these processes. (The term *theoretical work* may mean different things in different disciplines. Here, by *theoretical work*, I will mostly mean mathematical modeling.)

A. Why Models?

Complex evolutionary processes such as speciation are affected by many different forces (genetic, ecological, developmental, environmental, etc.) interacting in nonlinear ways. Both this complexity and the difficulties of experimental approaches, coming in particular from the very long timescales that are typically involved, imply that mathematical models have to play a very important role in evolutionary research. The abilities of models to offer insights into the complex processes, to develop or strengthen our intuition, to provide a general framework for synthesizing accumulated knowledge and generating hypotheses to test, and to identify key components as well as relevant spatial scales and timescales in their dynamics are invaluable. Therefore, it is not a surprise that developing mathematical models and testing their predictions empirically have played a central role in evolutionary biology research for 100 years now, starting with the work of Fisher, Haldane, and Wright (Provine, 1971, 1986).

The common wisdom is that a picture is worth a thousand words. In the exact sciences, an equation can be worth a thousand pictures. Equations, their predictions, and interpretations are the most concrete results a theoretician can come up with. Some say that the maturity of a science correlates with the degree of its mathematical sophistication. From this point of view, evolutionary biology as well as population ecology (where mathematical modeling was pioneered by Lotka and Volterra in the 1920s) and epidemiology (where modeling started with Roos and Kermack and McKendrick in the 1910s–1920s) are indeed mature sciences. The application of mathematical modeling in social sciences in general and for studies of cultural evolution in particular has a shorter history, but it is growing steadily. It goes without saying that mathematical models must be based on solid empirical foundations and that close collaboration of empiricists and theoreticians is crucial for scientific progress in any area.

B. Human Origins

Turning back to the development of my research program, after completion of my book, I came to realize that the time was ripe for attacking the ultimate speciation event—the origin of our own species (Darwin, 1871). Human origins and our subsequent cultural and social evolution should be explainable using the logic of general evolutionary processes, and many of the tools, methods, ideas and models developed by empirical and theoretical evolutionary biologists should be useful for understanding human behavior and psychology. Nevertheless, it was apparent to me that the puzzle of human origins and distinctiveness needed much more empirical and theoretical work. It also became clear to me that research on human origins and our subsequent cultural and social evolution was vital for understanding, mitigating, and solving some of the most pressing challenges faced by our society (Gavrilets et al., 2021). For example, humans strongly react to inequality and injustice, a behavior that we share with other primates (Brosnan & de Waal, 2014). Understanding the evolution of our sense of fairness may help us build a more just society. Similarly, studies of sexual selection as well as genetic and cultural diversity can shed light on gender-, race-, and ethnicity-related prejudices; their consequences for human behavior; and ways to mitigate undesirable effects. Insights into the factors shaping human (pro)sociality can be leveraged to improve the efficiency and benevolence of collective actions in businesses and communities. They can foster more efficient economic, political, social, and educational policies. Such insights can also be applied to better understanding of motivations leading to the onset and maintenance of both violent and non-violent conflicts, which can increase societal resilience to external and internal shocks. Our long-term persistence requires addressing existential risks from climate change, biodiversity loss, depletion of non-renewable resources, and security threats posed by unstable political systems. Humans have evolved various psychological mechanisms and biases for making collective decisions which need to be considered when developing policies for sustainability (Brooks et al., 2018).

C. Human Distinctiveness

One factor that influenced and motivated me greatly initially was the discussion of human uniqueness (and its origins) in the writings of Richard Alexander (1987, 1989, 1990) and others (Flinn et al., 2005). There were a number of evolutionary puzzles related to this yet to be solved. For example, how can we use evolutionary theory to explain and model the evolution of human cognition, of pair-bonding, of our sense of fairness, of coalition formation? I began working on these topics (Bissonette et al., 2015; Gavrilets, 2008, 2012a, 2012b; Gavrilets & Vose 2006; Mesterton-Gibbons et al., 2011). I also started collaborations with primatologists and anthropologists whose domains of research interest are positioned, in a sense, on the opposite side of the major evolutionary transition I was interested in. Later I came to understand, mostly through my interactions with Frans de Waal, that it probably makes much more sense to talk about "human distinctiveness" rather than "human uniqueness" as most differences between humans and "the higher animals, great as [they are], certainly [are ones] of degree and not of kind," as clearly stated by Darwin (1871, p. 85) himself. I note that the 150th anniversary of Darwin's *The Descent of Man* offered scientists a unique opportunity to advance the appreciation of science in general, of life and the social sciences in particular, and of a diversity of topics related to human origins and evolution (Gavrilets et al., 2020).

D. Cooperation and Conflict

As often happens in one's scientific career, my interests expanded into "adjacent" research areas, and I became interested in the processes happening in historical and contemporary humans and their societies. I started discussions and collaborations with psychologists, sociologists, economists, political scientists, and cultural evolutionists. In particular, through my collaboration with Peter Turchin and Peter Richerson, I got deeply involved in the issues of the evolution of human social complexity, cultural evolution, as well as cooperation and conflict in human groups and societies.

Cooperation can potentially be very profitable for all parties involved because cooperating groups can acquire material benefits that would be completely out of reach (or too costly) for single individuals (Smith, 1776/2008). To realize this potential, however, group members have to be able to overcome certain hurdles: They have to effectively coordinate their actions, resolve potential conflicts, and eliminate or minimize free-riding. The collective action problem (i.e., free-riding of group members) is generic for both human and non-human animal groups and can easily undermine within-group cooperation (Hardin, 1982; Olson, 1965; Pecorino, 2015; Sandler, 1992). Collective action problems can be (partially) resolved by several mechanisms including kin cooperating with each other, direct reciprocity (when individuals directly exchange favors), indirect reciprocity (when individuals cooperate with others who have reputation of being cooperative), punishment, group selection (when certain individually costly behaviors increase group survival), selective incentives (when cooperators are rewarded by the group), within-group heterogeneity (when certain individuals benefit from a collective action more than others), leadership, as well as social norms and social institutions regulating individual and group behavior (Bowles & Gintis, 2011; Gavrilets, 2015; McElreath & Boyd, 2007; Nowak, 2006; Olson, 1965; Richerson & Boyd 2005).

A significant effort has been devoted to theoretical and experimental studies of the effects of punishment of free-riders on cooperation (Boyd & Richerson, 1992; Boyd et al., 2003; Fehr & Fischbacher 2004; Fehr & Gächter, 2002; Heckathorn, 1989; Panchanathan & Boyd, 2004). Initially it appeared that punishment was a very powerful way to enforce cooperation and solve the collective action problem (Boyd & Richerson, 1992). However, it was quickly realized that if punishing others is costly, the act of punishment itself becomes a collective good which leads to a second-order free-rider problem as one would prefer others to administer costly punishment. Subsequently, theoreticians devoted a lot of their efforts to solving this second-order free-rider problem. The proposed solutions include meta-punishment (when there is a social norm requiring punishment of individuals who violate social norms), conformism, signaling (when individuals punish others to increase their own reputation), and group selection (Andreoni, 1988; Boyd et al., 2003; Gilby et al., 2015; McElreath & Boyd, 2007; McGinty & Milam, 2013; Olson, 1965; Ostrom, 2000; Panchanathan & Boyd, 2004).

But, from my own real-life experience, it was obvious that something important was missing in these theories. Indeed, when a child does something bad, most parents would discipline them. Naturally, it is never a pleasant experience, but parents would do it with a specific, bigger goal in mind—to modify the child's future behavior. So a parent would expect that the immediate cost of disciplining a child would, in a sense, be compensated by future benefits to both the parents and the child. Naturally, similar reasoning applies to many other situations and social interactions.

E. Foresight

These intuitions led me to propose a particular mechanism (and a corresponding mathematical model) for decision-making regarding punishment that can solve collective action problems. I called it *foresight*. Foresight is based on two postulates: First, individuals care about future payoffs and, second, they are able to predict to a certain extent the reaction of their social partners to their own actions. These "postulates" are not just based on common knowledge but are also well established in the scientific literature, and strong empirical evidence supporting them is in plain sight.

Indeed, humans have the ability to represent mentally what might happen in the future (captured in the notion of prospection [Szpunar et al., 2014]) and are routinely engaged in making intertemporal choices when they have to trade off costs and benefits at different points in time (Berns et al., 2007; Frederick et al., 2002). Intertemporal choices imply self-control (Hayden, 2019), which is also found in other animals (MacLean et al., 2014; Miller et al., 2019). Consideration of future payoffs is also explicit in many game-theoretic models, where it often comes under the rubric of the "shadow of the future" (Axelrod, 1984). The latter essentially is the idea that people behave differently when they expect to interact with someone repeatedly over time. For example, consider a classical repeated prisoner's dilemma game where an individual can provide benefit b to the partner at the cost c to themselves. Let w be the probability of another encounter between the same two individuals so that they will play on average $1/(1 - w)$ rounds. Then consideration of expected payoffs over $1/(1 - w)$ rounds shows that the tit-for-tat strategy is an evolutionarily stable strategy if probability w exceeds the cost-to-benefit ratio c/b of the altruistic act (Nowak, 2006). Another example of consideration of future payoffs in game theory is the backward induction principle (von Neumann & Morgenstern, 1944), which is an iterative process of reasoning backward in time used to study sequential games in which players make moves in a particular order.

In a similar way, the ability to mentally construct possible events in the future, travel mentally in time, and build mentally various scenarios plays an important role in discussions of human distinctiveness, consciousness, intelligence, and shared intentionality in the psychological literature (Alexander, 1987; Call, 2009; Suddendorf & Corballis, 1997; Tomasello et al., 2005). In particular, it is well accepted that this ability has evolved because it contributes to the future survival of individuals and groups through processes of social competition and/or cooperation (Alexander, 1989; Suddendorf & Corballis, 1997; Tomasello et al., 2005). More recent work draws attention to these abilities as a factor in the evolution of cumulative culture (Vale et al., 2012) and the evolution of effective learning strategies (Fogarty et al., 2012). The understanding that others will change their actions in response to one's own actions is a consequence of humans' *theory of mind*—the ability to reason about the knowledge and thought processes of others. The theory of mind is a well-established trait in humans (Premack & Woodruff, 1978; Tomasello et al., 2005), and it is thought to be key in promoting cooperation within groups (Tomasello et al., 2005). Humans can use the theory of mind recursively (Hedden & Zhang, 2002; Perner & Wimmer, 1985), which implies thinking about how others think about you.

It should also be obvious that similar considerations and forces also work in many non-human animals. For example, a subordinate male in a group of chimpanzees will rarely attempt to take food or a mating opportunity from a dominant individual because punishment will likely be immediate and severe. The existence of the theory of mind has been demonstrated experimentally in apes (Call & Tomasello, 2008; Kano et al., 2019; Krupenye et al., 2016). A more general set of examples are common cases of manipulation and tactical deception in animals, which are thought to have evolved as an evolutionary response to mind-reading (Hall & Brosnan, 2016; Krebs & Dawkins, 1984).

Theoretical and experimental studies of cooperation and punishment provide further evidence for foresight. For example, in his highly cited paper "An Evolutionary Approach to Norms," Axelrod (1986) gives an extensive discussion of eight different mechanisms that can support cooperative behavior. His Mechanism 4 was called *deterrence*. Its logic was straightforward: "players may have a great enough understanding of the situation to do some forward-looking calculations. . . . In particular, a person may realize that even if punishing a defection is costly now, it might have long-term gains by discouraging other defections later" (p. 1104). Fehr and Gächter (2002), in their classical experimental study of the effect of punishment on cooperation in a public goods game, observed that "the punishment threat was immediately effective" (p. 138), as was evident by the big increase in investments (see Figure 6.1) when the punishment opportunity was introduced, that is, even before any actual punishment took place. Krasnow et al. (2012) studied a two-round trust game with punishment. They observed that "subjects direct[ed] their cooperative efforts preferentially towards defectors they have punished and away from those they haven't punished" and "subjects were just as likely to

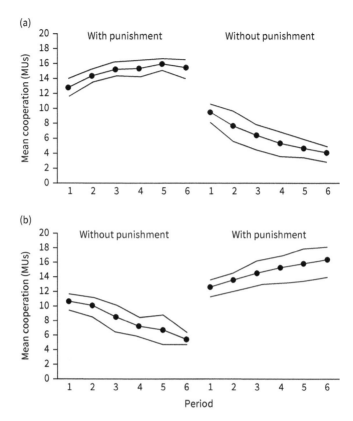

FIGURE 6.1: Time trend of mean group contributions in a public goods game together with the 95% confidence interval. (a) During the first six periods, subjects have the opportunity to punish the other group members. Afterward, the punishment opportunity is removed. (b) During the first six periods, punishment of other group members is ruled out. Afterward, punishment is possible. MU are money units used.
Source: Fehr & Gächter (2002, Figure 2) (reproduced with permission).

cooperate in round two with a defector whom they had punished in round 1 as with a partner who had cooperated in round 1." That is, individuals expected that the punishment they administered earlier was effective in modifying the target's behavior. (I note that punishment can, of course, have other purposes besides deterrence [Carlsmith, 2008; Carlsmith et al., 2002; Cushman, 2015], which I do not consider here.)

My final example is rather broad and general. It concerns social norms which are central to human behavior. (As Tomasello [2011, p. 20] puts it, "Humans live in a sea of social norms that govern pretty much all aspects of their lives.") There are different types of social norms (Bicchieri, 2006; Ensminger & Henrich, 2014; Grusec & Kuczynski; 1997; Lapinski & Rimal,

2005). For example, descriptive norms involve perceptions of which behaviors are typically performed and what people actually do. In contrast, injunctive social norms are behaviors that one is expected to follow and expects others to follow in a given social situation. That is, they refer to what people ought to do. One of the reasons people follow injunctive social norms (and as a consequence often behave in a way that reduces their immediate material well-being) is because they are afraid of being punished and/or disapproved of as a result of norm violation. That is, people know that if they go after an immediate material benefit by violating a social norm, their action may trigger punishment or disapproval by others. Often, such foresight is sufficient to prevent a norm-violating behavior.

To reiterate, the fact that people care about the future and are able to foresee to a certain extent the reaction of their social partners to their action is well established. However, these facts and ideas have so far not been incorporated in theoretical models. In the following section, I first outline how I define foresight mathematically. Then I discuss applications of foresight to several evolutionary games, describing the effects of punishment on cooperation in repeated dyadic or group interactions. I argue that foresight is able to solve both the first- and second-order free-rider problems, simplifying cooperation and the evolution of social institutions. Moreover, it can maintain social norms. Foresight can also undermine cooperation by allowing for manipulation and tactical deception.

II. THEORETICAL FRAMEWORK AND MAJOR CONCEPTS

Game theory is the most appropriate theoretical tool for studying strategic interactions between multiple individuals (Binmore, 1990; Fudenberg & Tirole, 1992; von Neumann & Morgenstern, 1944). In classical game theory, a game-theoretic model has three main components: players, their possible actions ("strategies"), and the "payoffs" that each player gets after each possible social interaction. In classical game theory, players have complete information about the game, are fully rational, and can identify most beneficial strategies. Then one can, at least in principle, find certain states (Nash equilibria) that no player would want to deviate from once this state is reached, the expectation being that these states will somehow be realized.

Three relatively recent extensions of classical game theory have played an important role in my work on foresight: strategy update methods, utility

300 Handbook of Advances in Culture and Psychology

functions combining material and normative costs and benefits, and methods for modeling errors in the decision-making process.

A. Strategy Revision Method

The assumptions of classical game theory about unbounded knowledge and rationality are very strong and clearly unrealistic. Evolutionary game theory is an extension of the classical theory, which does not rely on these assumptions. Instead, evolutionary game theory brings an additional component to each model—a strategy update method which specifies how players change their strategies from one interaction to another. Then, as players go through multiple rounds of interactions and strategy updates, the distribution of strategies in the population evolves through time, potentially converging to a certain attractor (e.g., a Nash equilibrium).

In the original formulation (Maynard Smith, 1982; Maynard Smith & Price, 1973), which was inspired by population genetic models in evolutionary biology, the players are genetically hardwired to always play a particular strategy. At the individual level, their strategy changes only as a result of a random mutation (usually at birth). At the population level, the changes in the distribution of strategies happen as a result of differential birth and death rates, with players with high-payoff strategies leaving more surviving offspring than players utilizing low-payoff strategies. Under this approach, the details of the strategy update method (i.e., mutation rate) play a secondary role in evolutionary dynamics, with mutation merely supplying the necessary variation while the population evolution is mostly driven by differences in payoff (which is interpreted as biological fitness).

Later research has, however, brought in a number of additional and more realistic strategy update methods to the forefront of evolutionary game theory. These include individual learning, selective imitation (e.g., payoff-biased), myopic best response, and level-k modeling (Hofbauer & Sigmund, 1998; Sandholm, 2010). Rather than assuming that individuals are hardwired to behave in a particular way, these methods grant some free will and bound rationality to the players. For example, individuals using best response attempt to answer the question, What is my best option given the current strategies of all of my social partners? Individuals using level-1 modeling (which is a special case of level-k modeling) attempt to answer the question, What is my best option given my social partners choose strategies randomly? Likewise, individuals using selective payoff–biased imitations try to identify a player with the highest payoff among their social partners and copy the corresponding strategy. From a formal modeling point of view, foresight is a new strategy update method allowing for bounded rationality of players.

In evolutionary biology, mutation is viewed as random and consequently does not play a creative or large role in evolutionary processes (although mutation biases do exist and can be important under some conditions). In contrast, in modern developments of evolutionary game theory, selection can happen at the level of new strategy generation (Sandholm, 2010), for example, when agents evaluate different possible strategies mentally with respect to expected payoffs. As a result, changing a strategy update method, while keeping all other components of a game-theoretic model the same, can strikingly change the resulting evolutionary dynamics.

Consider, for example, a classical model in evolutionary game theory in which individuals are randomly paired to play the standard rock–scissors–paper game (e.g., Hofbauer & Sigmund, 1998). There are three strategies such that rock beats scissors, scissors beats paper, and paper beats rock. Players are motivated to increase their payoffs. They change their strategies according to a particular strategy revision protocol, for example, by choosing a best response to the previous game of the opponent (best response protocol) or by choosing a strategy that had overall the highest payoff in the previous round (replicator dynamics protocol). The state of the population can be characterized by the frequencies of the three strategies which can be visualized as a point on an equilateral triangle, while evolutionary dynamics can be described by a curve (trajectory) on this triangle (as in Figure 6.2). In this game, there is an equilibrium at which all three strategies are present at equal frequencies. This equilibrium exists under all standard strategy revision protocols. However, whether this equilibrium is approached asymptotically and the pattern and speed of convergence vary dramatically between different strategy revision protocols (see Figure 6.2).

One consequence of this is that, while the first- and second-order free-rider problems exist independently of the strategy update method, people's decision-making process can greatly affect the ability of groups to overcome these problems. For example, selective payoff–biased imitation is not able to solve the first- or second-order free-rider problem without invoking additional mechanisms (e.g., group selection or reduced migration and inbreeding). In contrast, a group of individuals capable of foresight can overcome these problems.

B. Utility Function

Cultural evolutionists often express unhappiness with what they perceive as economists' focus on material payoffs and disregard of normative values in

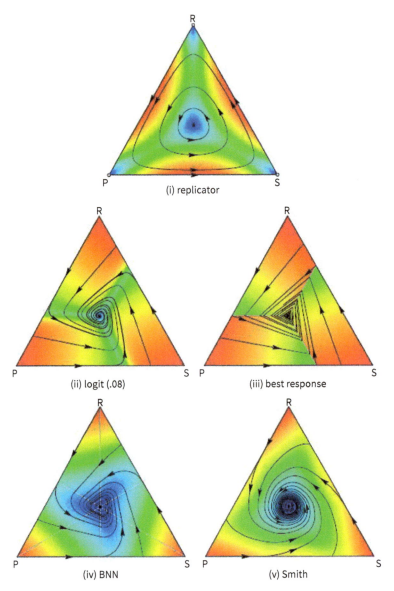

FIGURE 6.2: Strikingly different deterministic dynamics in standard rock–paper–scissors game under five different strategy update methods (labeled replicator, login, best response, Brown-von Neumann-Nash (BNN), and Smith). Colors represent speeds: Red is fastest; blue is slowest.
Source. Sandholm (2009, Figure 1).

the economists' models. I do not think this view is justified. Economists have developed a very powerful notion of utility function which can capture both material and immaterial/normative costs and benefits (e.g., Akerlof, 1980; Azar, 2004, 2008; Berhheim, 1994; Nyborg, 2018). For example, to mathematically capture the idea that changing an action/strategy x can have material consequences, for example, changing payoffs $\pi(x)$, as well as affect some normative values $v(x)$ for individuals, one can postulate that in making a decision on a possible action x, individuals attempt to maximize a utility function

$$u(x) = (1 - \eta)\pi(x) + \eta v(x)$$

where $0 \leq \eta \leq 1$ is a parameter measuring the importance of normative values relative to material payoffs (Gavrilets & Richerson, 2017). Note that if $\eta = 0$, individuals care only about material benefits: $u(x) = \pi(x)$. In contrast, if $\eta = 1$, individuals care only about normative values: $u(x) = v(x)$. (In the terminology of Wrong [1961], individuals with $\eta = 0$ are undersocialized, while individuals with $\eta = 1$ are oversocialized.)

C. Errors

It is natural to expect that when individuals attempt to find an action or strategy that maximizes their payoff (or utility), some errors are inevitable. It is also reasonable to assume that the error becomes more likely as the differences in payoffs/utilities between different options become small. A simple and powerful way to capture these intuitions is to assume that individuals chose a particular strategy x with probability proportional to its utility. For example, assuming logit errors, we can set this probability to $\exp(\lambda u[x])$, where $0 \leq \lambda \leq \infty$ is a non-negative precision parameter. If λ is very small, different actions will be chosen with similar probabilities; if λ is very large, the action with the highest utility u will be most definitely chosen. Using this stochastic approach leads to a powerful generalization of Nash equilibrium known as quantal response equilibrium (Goeree et al., 2016).

D. Modeling Foresight

Now we are in a position to introduce the strategy update method foresight formally. Assume that agents are engaged in repeated interactions happening at discrete moments in time. For example, the agents could be playing a two-stage game: a collective goods game, followed by peer punishment. After each such round, the agents are given an opportunity to update their strategy with probability v. The agents may expect that if they chose a particular behavior for the next round, their social partners will likely react to this behavior by adjusting their own strategy accordingly in the subsequent round. We then postulate that the focal agent attempts to maximize a generalized utility function

$$U(x) = (1 - \omega)u(x) + \omega u'(x) \tag{1}$$

which is a weighted sum of the expected utility at the next game $u(x)$ and the expected utility at the subsequent game $u'(x)$ (Perry et al., 2018). Parameter $0 \leq \omega \leq 1$ measures the importance of future payoffs. The case of $\omega = 0$ corresponds to myopic best response (i.e., no foresight). To evaluate utilities u and u', the focal agent needs to be able to predict how their social partner(s) will behave in the next and the subsequent rounds. This can be done, for example, by asking the question, What would I do in their place, or alternatively by assuming that social partners use a simple strategy update protocol, such as myopic best response. In the numerical implementations of foresight to be illustrated, the players mentally generate a number of "candidate strategies" x and then pick one of them with a probability proportional to $\exp(\lambda U[x])$, where λ represents the precision with which an agent estimates utilities.

Before I illustrate the applications of this method, several clarifications are in order. First, this approach is an example of bounded rationality (Gigerenzer & Selten, 2001). It can be viewed as a generalization of standard myopic best response for the case of individuals with a bounded ability to anticipate the actions of their group-mates and care about future payoffs. At the same time, foresight is related to level-k modeling (Nagel, 1995; Stahl & Wilson, 1995) but with a different definition of level-0 play. In the standard approach, level-0 players choose their strategies randomly. In contrast, in our approach level-0 players do not change their strategy from the previous round. That makes best responders equivalent to level-1 players. This apparently small difference in the assumption about level-0 play actually turns out to be important (Perry & Gavrilets, 2020). The term *foresight* was used earlier in game-theoretic models considering expected future benefits but with a different meaning. In Jehiel (1995, 1998, 2001) and Heller (2015), players differed in their *foresight*, which was defined as the ability to predict after how many rounds from the current one a repeated prisoner's dilemma game will end. In their models, having longer foresight would result in a payoff advantage. In Mengel (2014), players formed beliefs about the behavior of their social partners by relying on past experience in the same situation and then using the best response to these beliefs over t periods ahead. Note also that earlier Blume (1995) showed that myopic best response arises whenever future payoff is discounted heavily or opportunities to revise a strategy arise sufficiently rarely. However, in all these models the players do not attempt to predict how their peers will adjust behavior in response to their actions. In contrast, the level-k models do attempt to capture the theory of mind. However, in level-k models players do not consider future payoffs or change their strategies/action depending on the behavior of their group-mates. The foresight in our implementation brings the ideas from these two approaches into the same modeling framework.

III. MAJOR PREDICTIONS AND EVIDENCE

The ideas and approaches outlined in this section were developed with my students and collaborators. I will start by introducing a model without foresight, which will serve as a reference point for illustrating the effects of foresight in other models to be considered subsequently.

A. Collective Action Problems in Heterogeneous Groups

Assume there is a population of individuals subdivided into a number of groups each of size n individuals. We consider two types of collective action (Gavrilets, 2015a). The first type focuses on group activities such as hunting and gathering, defense from predators, and building/maintaining shelter. The success of an individual group in these activities is largely unaffected by actions of neighboring groups. We refer to these actions as "us versus nature" games. In contrast, limited space, resources, and mating opportunities can result in direct competition between groups of individuals of the same species. This means that as the success of one group increases, the resources available to other groups decrease. We refer to such games as "us versus them."

1. *Efforts*. Assume that individual i in a focal group makes an effort x_i toward the group's success in a collective action. Effort x_i can be

treated as a binary variable (i.e., taking only two values: 0 and 1) or a non-negative continuous variable. Individual efforts of group members are aggregated into a group effort X. In the simplest case, the group effort is just the sum of individual efforts:

$$X = \sum_i x_i$$

2. *Probability of success in a collective action.* In the case of "us versus nature" games, I define the probability the focal group is successful as

$$P = X/(X + X_0)$$

where X_0 is a half-effort parameter (which specifies the group effort at which $P = 50\%$). The larger X_0, the more group effort X is needed to secure the collective good. In the case of "us versus them" games, I define

$$P = X/\overline{X}$$

where $\overline{X}$ is the average effort over all competing groups (including the focal one). Mathematically, in "us versus nature" actions, group members participate in a generalized public goods game which can also be viewed as a generalized volunteer's dilemma (Archetti, 2009; Diekmann, 1985). In "us versus them" actions, the groups compete in a contest (Konrad, 2009; Rusch & Gavrilets, 2020). The key distinction between these two types of collective action is that in the former the absolute group effort is critical for obtaining resources, while in the latter it is the group effort relative to that of the other competing group that matters.

3. *Payoffs.* Assume further that groups survive to the next generation with a probability proportional to their success in a collective action P. For individuals from surviving groups, the payoff (which is treated as biological fitness) is defined as

$$\pi_i = \pi_{0,i} + b v_i P - c x_i,$$

where $\pi_{0,i}$ is the baseline payoff, v_i is the share of the group reward going to individual i, and b and c are parameters measuring the benefit and cost of contributing to the collective action.

4. *Predictions.* Gavrilets and Fortunato (2014) and Gavrilets (2015a) studied this model assuming that individuals within each group were different with respect to their strength (which was assigned randomly according to a certain distribution). Individual strengths in turn controlled their shares/valuation v_i of the reward so that stronger individuals were getting a large share of the reward. The focus of modeling was on individual x_i and group X efforts and on relative individual shares of reproduction $f_i = \pi_i / \Sigma \, \pi_j$ observed at evolutionarily stable states. Note that variable f_i can be interpreted as relative fertility of individual i. Some of their results are illustrated in Figure 6.3. In general, individuals defect (i.e., choose $x = 0$) if they are "weak" so that their shares v_i of the rewards are small but cooperate (i.e., choose $x > 0$) if they are "strong" so that their shares v_i are large. This is what Olson (1965) called "the exploitation of the great by the small." In many cases, individual share of reproduction f_i grows with rank/valuation v_i.

However, under conditions of strong between-group competitions, the highest valuators (who are simultaneously the biggest contributors) end up with lower relative fertility f_i than other individuals because of the costs paid. This is the *altruistic bully effect* when strong and dominant individuals who grab the biggest share of the reward from their group-mate effectively become altruists in between-group conflicts, making the biggest effort and paying the largest costs. The reason for this apparent altruism is that the high-ranked individuals are effectively competing with their peers in other groups, and the most efficient way to do so is to increase their own efforts. Modeling results also show that increasing the reward size b causes an increase in the efforts of high valuators, but it can also decrease the efforts of low valuators who would increasingly free-ride. Allowing for group extinction results in two main effects. First, there are no free-riders anymore, and all group members contribute proportionally to their valuations. Second, individual and group efforts significantly increase. The effects of the group size n and the degree of inequality (characterized by the distribution of v_i values in the group) on the overall group effort X depend on the degree of non-linearity of various functions. That is, under some conditions, smaller groups can outperform larger

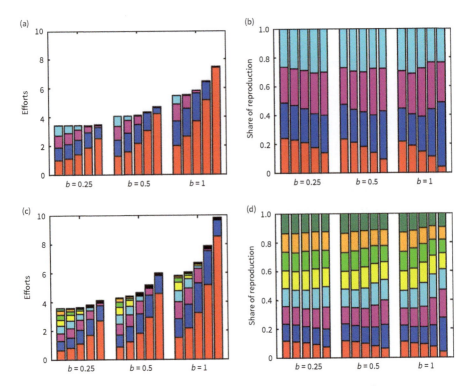

FIGURE 6.3: Collective action in the basic model. Summary results over with group size $n = 4$ (a, b) and $n = 8$ (c, d) individuals per group and cost $c = 0.5$. The values are averages over individuals of the same rank in all groups in the population. Colors show the relevant amounts for individuals of different ranks, from the highest-rank individual at the bottom (red) to the lowest-rank individual at the top. Each set of bars corresponds to a specific value of benefit b. Each bar within a set corresponds to a specific value of within-group inequality, from the smallest on the left to the largest on the right.
(a) Individual efforts with group size $n = 4$; the height of the bar is the total group effort X. (b) Shares of reproduction for individuals of different rank with group size $n = 4$.
(c) Individual efforts with group size $n = 8$; the height of the bar is the total group effort X. (d) Shares of reproduction for individuals of different rank with group size $n = 8$. Reproduced from Gavrilets & Fortunato (2014, Figure 4).

groups, while within-group inequality can have positive or negative effect on group effort.

B. Collective Action Problems in Heterogeneous Groups With Peer Punishment

In Perry et al. (2018), this model was generalized in several directions. First, we allowed for peer punishment. Specifically, besides deciding on the contribution

x_i to a collective action, each individual would choose a punishment threshold y_i and would consider punishing any group-mate whose contribution falls below y_i. We assumed that the cost inflicted by punishment was proportional to the difference between y_i and the contribution x_j of the group-mate. That is, we used a graduated punishment method (Gao et al., 2012; Helbing et al., 2010; Iwasa & Lee, 2013; Shimao & Nakamaru, 2013). The actual punishment happened only if the punisher was sufficiently strong relative to the target. Second, using agent-based simulations, we contrasted two strategy update methods: random mutation and best response. We allowed for three different types of group events happening with fixed probabilities: an "us versus nature" collective action, an "us versus them" contest against another randomly chosen group, and a "cultural group selection" event when members of one group would copy strategies of members of a higher-payoff group. In line with earlier work, we observed no cooperation or punishment in these models which was a result of the second-order free-rider problem. Consequently, our third step then was to introduce foresight.

Using the logic outlined before, we postulated that in making their decisions on the cooperative efforts x_i and punishment threshold y_i individuals attempt to maximize the weighted sum of the material payoffs of this and the next rounds (see Equation 1). The factors included in the model accounted for the benefits and costs of collective action as well as the costs of inflicted and received punishment. In making their decision, each actor would generate K pairs of candidate strategies (x', y') and would choose one of the them with probabilities proportional to the corresponding expected generalized utilities. To predict the actions of social partners, our agents assumed that their peers would best respond to their previous action.

Allowing for foresight immediately resulted in striking differences in behavior (see Figure 6.4). First, foresight allowed for the establishment of punishment, thus solving the second-degree free-rider problem. As a consequence, group efforts X in collective actions increased. Second, foresight resulted in the emergence of a division of labor in which more powerful individuals specialized in punishment, while less powerful individuals mostly contributed to the production of collective goods. Recall that without foresight we observed higher efforts and low payoffs of the strongest individuals (i.e., the *exploitation of the great by the small* effect and *altruistic bully* effects). With foresight, the situation has changed, and we observed the exploitation of the small by the great, where powerful individuals enjoyed higher payoffs than their group-mates. Interestingly, while foresight increases cooperation,

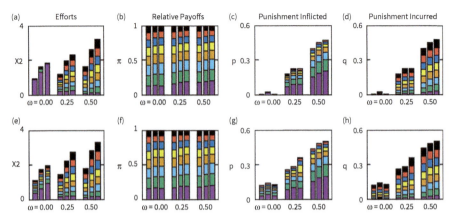

FIGURE 6.4: Effects of the foresight parameter ω on the group efforts X and relative payoffs π, the punishment inflicted p, and the punishment incurred q for individuals of different ranks in the full model with perfect (λ = ∞, first row) and imperfect (λ = 40, second row) precision. For each value of ω, the three bars correspond to groups mostly engaged in the "us versus nature" game (left bars), mostly "us versus them" games (right bars), and an equal frequencies of the two games (middle bars). The segments of each bar correspond to particular individuals, with the dominant at the bottom (purple) and the weakest at the top. Results are the averages of 20 simulations using: n = 8, b = 1.0, c = 0.5, β = 1, K = 2.
Reproduced from Perry et al. (2018, Figure 4).

it does not necessarily result in higher payoffs because much effort becomes wasted on punishment. We also observed that while between-group conflicts promoted within-group cooperation, as shown before, the effects of cultural group selection on cooperation were relatively small.

C. Evolution of Institutions

Our results on peer punishment can be interpreted as demonstrating evolutionary emergence on informal leadership, where strong individuals become leaders and weak individuals become followers. Our next step was to assume that such a division of labor is already established and collectively endorsed by group members, that is, that the punishment has become institutionalized. We wanted to look at its subsequent evolution in more detail.

The models that I will describe next belong to a class of models for the evolution of social institutions. Institutions that regulate social life are ubiquitous and are viewed as a key feature enabling the success of our species (Alesina & Giuliano, 2015; North, 1990; Powers et al., 2016; Richerson & Boyd, 2005; Singh et al., 2017). A question of particular theoretical and practical importance is how social institutions for collective action become effective and stable.

One powerful method of optimizing individual behavior is random innovation coupled with payoff-biased social learning when individuals observe and evaluate actions and payoffs of others and adapt strategies resulting in a higher payoff. Selective imitation can also drive cultural group selection, resulting in the spread of beneficial institutions across different groups (Richerson et al., 2016; Richerson & Boyd, 2005; Turchin, 2016). It has been argued recently that cultural group selection is the most important (or even the only) mechanism that can account for institutionalized cooperation in human societies (Chudek at al., 2013; Richerson et al., 2016; Turchin, 2016). However, there are questions about the power and usefulness of selective imitation within the context of collective action. At the level of individuals, because free-riders have higher payoffs than cooperators, their strategies are more likely to be imitated, which would undermine cooperation (Burton-Chellew et al., 2017; Molleman et al., 2014; van den Berg et al., 2015). Additionally, because of between-individual variation, a strategy that is good for one will not necessarily be beneficial or even feasible for another. At the level of groups, copying of institutions requires information flow between (potentially competing) groups and the deep knowledge of relevant details. Even if all this is readily available, institutions might not be transferable "off the shelf" because of social, cultural, or environmental differences among groups (Aoki, 2001; Powers et al., 2016; Singh et al., 2017).

An alternative view is that evolution of institutions is a result of within-group design processes driven by the motivation of the whole group or some of its subgroups to increase their material well-being or some more general utility. For example, Ostrom (1990) outlines a number of "design principles" for stable and successful management of common resources by local communities. Early 18th-century pirates created democratic institutions (with separation of power, checks and balances, and written constitutions) which helped to make pirate predatory groups very efficient (Defoe, 1972/1724; Leeson, 2009). Similar examples exist among contemporary prison gangs (Skarbek, 2012). Singh et al. (2017) forcefully argue for the importance of self-interested design in the creation of institutions. They also put forward a *self-interested enforcement* hypothesis, according to which many group-level traits and institutions can be explained by the differences in relative enforcement capabilities of different group segments. We note that the idea of self-interested design also captures key aspects of human social life—that we can in fact make guesses about the future and the future behavior of our peers. One can view the strategy update method foresight as an example of self-interested design.

One goal of the work outlined next was to extend our approach to the case of collective actions under institutionalized punishment in small-scale societies. Specifically, our assumption was that the division of labor between leaders who punish cheaters and the rest of the group who produce collective goods is already established and collectively endorsed (Garfield et al., 2019, Wiessner, 2019). We wanted to see how it would evolve in small-scale societies. (Note that Isakov and Rand [2012] and Roithmayr et al. [2015] studied institutionalized punishment in more modern states.) Our second goal was to compare selective imitation and foresight with respect to their ability to identify and converge to cooperative social institutions.

We studied the evolution of institutionalized punishment using two models. In the first model (Perry & Gavrilets, 2020), each group consists of just two players: a subordinate who is charged with producing a collective good and a leader whose responsibility is to monitor the effort of the subordinate and punish them if they shirk. The simplicity of this model allowed for substantial analytical progress in understanding its behavior. In the second, more general model (Gavrilets & Duval Shrestha, 2020), each group has n subordinates producing a collective good and a single leader monitoring their effort. In spite of the complexity of this model, some analytical progress was also possible. We also used agent-based simulation to advance our understanding of both models.

1. *Two-player leader-subordinate game.* In Perry and Gavrilets (2020), we consider a simple 2 x 2 game between a leader and a subordinate, which is based on the inspection game (Fudenberg & Tirole, 1992). The subordinate is tasked with producing a benefit at a personal cost to themselves, while the leader has a vested interest in seeing that the good is produced.

The subordinate can either produce the good ($x = 1$) or shirk on the production of the good ($x = 0$). If the subordinate produces the good, they pay a cost of c to produce a good of value b. The leader receives share $0 \leq \theta \leq 1$ of the good produced as tax, while the subordinate keeps the remaining share $1 - \theta$. The leader can either enforce production via inspection ($y = 1$) or not ($y = 0$). Inspection costs the leader h, but in the event that a leader inspects a non-producing subordinate, they inflict a punishment of d at a cost of h. We assume that all parameters are positive. Table 6.1 describes the corresponding payoff matrix.

Since we are interested in drawing parallels with the first- and second-order free-rider problems in collective action, we make assumptions in such

Foresight, Punishment, and Cooperation   313

TABLE 6.1: **Payoff matrix for the leader–subordinate game**

	Leader		
Subordinate		Inspect	Don't Inspect
	Produce	$(1 - \theta)b - c, \theta b - h$	$(1 - \theta)b - c, \theta b$
	Shirk	$-d, -h - k$	$0, 0$

a way that the subordinate has no incentive to see the good be produced unless they are facing punishment. First, given that the subordinate contributes (i.e., $x = 1$), the benefit to the leader exceeds its cost of inspection (i.e., $\theta b > h$). Second, we assume that without punishment (i.e., if $y = 0$) the subordinate is not motivated to contribute, but facing the threat of punishment (i.e., if $y = 1$), the subordinate, however, is motivated to contribute: $- d \le (1 - \theta)b - c \le 0$.

In this game, the only Nash equilibrium is the one where the subordinate does not produce and the leader does not inspect. We then extended this model by considering mixed Nash equilibria, level-k cognition (which captures some aspects of the theory of mind), and two methods of learning: reinforcement learning (Borgers & Sarin, 1997) and payoff-biased selective imitation (Hofbauer & Sigmund, 1998). In the former case, after each round, the probability of playing a particular strategy is increased by a value proportional to the payoff received. In the latter case, individuals compare their payoff with that of a peer and choose to either copy the selected individual (if their payoff is higher than the focal individual's) or keep their own strategy. In all these extensions, the state of nothing being done remains the only equilibrium.

We then introduced foresight into the model. While allowing that foresight for the subordinate did not result in any differences, the introduction of foresight for the leader allows for the emergence of a new Nash equilibrium ($x = 1$, $y = 1$) where the leader always inspects and the subordinate always produces. This equilibrium appears if the weight of the future payoff is sufficiently large:

$$\omega > h / (\theta b + h)$$

Under this condition, the cost of inspection for the leader $(1 - \omega) h$ is overcompensated by the future benefit $\omega \theta b$ coming from the subordinate's production effort in the next round.

We also showed the same Nash equilibrium (1, 1) appears if, instead of relying on foresight, leaders copy the action of other leaders who have higher payoffs. That is, both foresight and selective payoff–biased imitation result in leaders enforcing commoners' production.

2. *Collective action problems with institutionalized punishment.* In a follow-up paper (Gavrilets & Duval Shretha, 2021) each group has not just one but an arbitrary number of subordinates. However, our main results were similar: Foresight increases leaders' willingness to punish free-riders, which in turn leads to a boost in cooperation. Overall this leads to the emergence of an effective institution for collective action as measured by increased production and monitoring. We also observed that largely similar outcomes can be achieved by selective imitation when leaders copy other, more successful leaders. Foresight and selective imitation can interact synergistically, leading to a faster convergence to an equilibrium. What seems to happen is that foresight design leads to a faster establishment of a social innovation in a single group, while selective imitation speeds up its spread across other groups. One difference with the earlier two-player model was that while in the simpler model the equilibria under foresight and selective imitation were exactly the same, this was not the case anymore in the model with multiple subordinates.

I want to stress that although both selective imitation and foresight can result in similar outcomes, their prerequisites differ. Selective imitation is a cognitively simple optimization method based on learning from others with whom the focal agent (i.e., an individual or a group) shares important characteristics (so that the strategy used by the "model" remains feasible and successful for the "mimic"). The agent using selective imitation aims to be as successful as its model. Foresight and, more generally, self-interested design also use social information and learning about the behavior of others. However, they are not restricted to interactions with similar agents, and agents using them can become more successful than their social partners. Cognitive skills needed for foresight, as modeled here, are not too demanding. Predicting others' behavior requires some theory of mind, which can be formed on the basis of previous observations or just by asking a question: What would I do if I were in their place? With respect to group traits (such as social institutions), foresight could work within a single group. In contrast, selective imitation requires multiple groups, the transfer of relevant information between them, and (cultural) group selection.

In our simulations, we assumed the same rates of strategy revision for both mechanisms. However, imitation of institutions from other groups is likely to be a rarer event than attempts to improve poorly functioning institutions by local "means." This implies that the relative rate of social evolution by cultural group selection will likely be slower than that by self-interested design. If, however, selective imitation is unconstrained, the timing of adoption of a new effective institution by different groups will be more similar than that under self-interested design because it will spread in an infection-like fashion.

Overall, these results support the power of foresight in promoting cooperation. We have shown that foresight makes monitoring and punishment a utility-increasing option (Perry et al., 2018). This, in turn, leads to increased production and cooperation and the emergence of an effective institution for collective action by self-interested design (Singh et al., 2017). Richerson et al. (2016) questioned the existence of "the alternatives to [cultural group selection that] can easily account for the institutionalized cooperation that characterizes human societies" (p. 16). These results offer one such alternative.

3. *Dynamics of injunctive social norms in heterogeneous groups.* Here, following Gavrilets (2020), I illustrate how the idea of foresight can be applied to model the decision-making of individuals influenced by injunctive social norms.

Consider a very common situation: You need to cross the street, there are no cars or police around, but the crosswalk sign says "don't walk", and there are several people waiting for it to change. You know that you are supposed to wait. You also expect that if you break the norm and cross the street, the other people will likely disapprove of you. But you are in a rush. What do you do?

To approach this question theoretically, consider a focal individual who can either follow the (injunctive) norm and wait for the traffic light to turn green ($x = 1$) or jaywalk ($x = 0$). Let b be the expected net material benefit of crossing the street rather than waiting. (Parameter b can also account for the cost of being observed by the police or being hit by a car when jaywalking.) Let v be an intrinsic value of following the norm (which can be viewed as the strength of norm internalization). We posit that an individual violating the norm assumes that others who do follow it disapprove of their behavior if they observe it (Fehr & Schurtenberger, 2018).

Let p be the focal individual's estimate of the frequency of such people (e.g., based on previous observations). Let κp be the expected normative cost of their disapproval, where κ is the maximum normative cost of passive disapproval by others for the focal individual. Then the utility of action x, where x can equal 0 or 1, can be written as

$$u = vx + b(1 - x)$$

Acting according to the norm will result in approval by other followers, the value of which is $v_a p$, while violating it will cause disapproval, the value of which is $-\kappa p$, where v_a is the maximum normative value of approval. Therefore, an individual equipped with foresight can infer that their current action x will also have a future consequence captured by the utility function

$$u' = v_a px - \kappa p(1 - x)$$

Following our approach, we can combine the two utility functions into one:

$$U = (1 - \omega)u + \omega u' = [(1 - \omega)v + \omega v_a p] x + [(1 - \omega)b - \omega \kappa p](1 - x)$$

We thus predict that the individual will comply with the norm (i.e., choose $x = 1$) if the expression in the first pairs of parentheses is larger than that in the second pair of parentheses, that is, if

$$(1 - \omega)v + \omega(v_a + \kappa)p > (1 - \omega)b$$

If $\omega = 1/2$, the above equation simplifies to $v + (v_a + \kappa)p > b$. That is, the sum of the intrinsic value of following the norm and normative benefits of approval and costs of disapproval by others has to be larger than the material benefit of violating the norm.

Note that an individual with a low normative value v relative to the potential material benefit b will still comply with the norm if the expected normative cost of disapproval κp and/or approval $v_a p$ by others is high enough. Both these terms increase with the estimated frequency p of people following the norm.

In the first three models, foresight motivates individuals to engage in costly punishment. In the last model, it provides a motivation to follow a social norm to avoid punishment. I will now, in the final example, show that individuals with foresight can also engage in costly acts of manipulation or deception to obtain future benefits from their group-mates.

4. *Tactical deception.* McNally and Jackson (2013) introduced the following model (see also Szolnokii & Perc, 2014). There is a population of individuals engaged in dyadic games of the prisoner's dilemma type. In any given interaction, individuals can choose to cooperate by providing a fixed benefit b to their partner at a fixed cost c to themselves ($b > c$) or to defect and pay no costs. There are three possible strategies: conditional cooperator (CC), tactical deceiver (TD), and honest defector (HD). CCs intend to cooperate only with other cooperative individuals and to not cooperate with defectors. HDs always defect. TDs always defect as well but attempt to deceive the partner by pretending they will cooperate. The act of deceiving has cost d but can fool CCs with probability q, who may then provide a benefit b. It is assumed that the cost of deception is smaller than the cost of cooperation ($d < c$).

In this model, if q decreases with the frequency of TDs (which can happen if CC individuals learn to recognize TDs better as they become more common), there is a polymorphic equilibrium where CCs and TDs coexist at equilibrium, while HDs are absent. McNally and Jackson (2013) did not discuss foresight, but their model essentially postulates it. Indeed, in their model, tactical deceivers effectively trade the immediate cost d of a deceiving act for the future benefit bq to be received from a deceived conditional cooperator. McNally and Jackson (2013) argue that the benefit of eliciting cooperation at lower cost may help select for tactical deception in species with more frequent and diverse forms of cooperation. Obviously, deception can have other benefits in humans and animals besides in the context of cooperation, for example, in mating behavior and aggressive interactions (Hall & Brosnan, 2016; McNally & Jackson 2013; Mokkonen & Lindstedt, 2016).

IV. IMPLICATIONS

The basic idea of foresight is simple: Pay certain costs (or forfeit getting certain benefits) now to get more benefits (or avoid paying larger costs) in the future.

Empirical facts on which the strategy update method foresight is based are well established in psychology. As argued, foresight can be important in punishment, cooperation, learning, cumulative culture, social norms, and social institutions. Having these ideas captured in mathematical models allows one to use a diverse set of theoretical tools from game theory and evolutionary biology to further advance studies of human decision-making and the processes of social and cultural evolution. One can also bring mathematical modeling into the studies of prospection, mental time traveling, and intertemporal choices, which are becoming increasingly important in psychology (Berns et al., 2007; Frederick et al., 2002; Szpunar et al., 2014). Next, I highlight three additional general implications of our results.

A. Game Theory and Human Rationality

Classical game theory assumes, usually implicitly but often explicitly, that players have complete and common knowledge of the structure of the game and that they have the ability to go through all necessary calculations to identify the corresponding Nash equilibria in pure or mixed strategies. On the other hand, evolutionary game theory typically assumes, by analogy with population genetic processes in evolutionary biology, a complete absence of rationality and free will or awards rather limited cognitive abilities to players (who use myopic best response or selective payoff–biased imitation). There have been only limited attempts to bridge the huge theoretical gap between these two extremes. These earlier attempts include various level-k models (Nagel, 1995; Stahl & Wilson, 1995) as well as models where players are able to predict when the dyadic interactions they are engaged in will end (Heller, 2015; Jehiel, 1995, 1998, 2001). This earlier work as well as our results on foresight point to the importance of extending the toolkit of game theory by adding more realism to assumptions about cognition and decision-making.

The earlier work in evolutionary game theory validated the importance of Nash equilibria in many models by demonstrating that individual players or populations of players with rather limited cognitive abilities (implied by myopic best response or selective imitation strategy update protocols) can nevertheless incrementally converge to the corresponding Nash equilibria (Hofbauer & Sigmund 1998; Sandholm, 2010). Foresight as modeled here may provide a way to access a wider or a more profitable array of Nash equilibria, further bridging the classical and evolutionary approaches in game theory.

B. Cooperation

Although potentially very profitable, cooperation is difficult to establish and maintain, especially if multiple players are involved. Intensive research over the last half a century by evolutionary biologists and social scientists has uncovered multiple mechanisms that promote cooperation. These include kin selection, direct and indirect reciprocity, selective incentives (i.e., reward and punishment), group selection, within-group heterogeneity, leadership, social norms, and institutions. Some of these mechanisms emerge naturally as a result of particular biological or social processes (e.g., kin selection, reputation, or group selection), while the appearance of others (e.g., punishment, social norms, and institutions) requires an additional level of explanation to avoid second-order free-rider problems. Most of the theoretical work done in this field has assumed very limited cognitive abilities of players. The models of foresight show that allowing for moderate cognitive abilities can greatly simplify the conditions for the emergence of punishment, leadership, and social institutions, which in turn make cooperation easier. In particular, foresight can motivate individuals to punish free-riders or norm violators, and simultaneously it can motivate cooperation or norm following. Foresight can also motivate leaders to ignore the immediate costs of monitoring, coordination, and norm promotion in order to enjoy future benefits of cooperation.

C. Selective Imitation, Cultural Group Selection, and Designs

Ideas, methods, and models of cultural evolution theory are currently moving to the forefront of many social sciences including anthropology, economics, psychology, and political sciences (Bowles, 2016; Gintis, 2016; Henrich, 2016; Petersen, 2016; Petersen & Aarøe, 2015; Turchin, 2016). A particularly powerful force of cultural evolution is selective payoff–biased imitation, which can work at both the individual and group levels. Human capacity for cultural learning and selective imitation has no doubt greatly contributed both to our uniqueness as a species (Boyd et al., 2011; Henrich, 2016) and to the cooperative social institutions we have built (Richerson et al., 2016). However as with almost any other evolutionary force, selective imitation is most efficient under some conditions but can fail under others. The foresight models discussed draw attention to an alternative mechanism—self-interested design— which can work in tandem with selective imitation or in situations where selective imitation is not effective. These models also show that development of group-level adaptations benefiting some subgroups or the whole group does not require between-group selection or competition. Selection is still crucial though, but it happens at the level of mental processes and scenario-building.

V. EXTENSIONS

There are several important directions this approach can be extended to.

A. Other Game-Theoretic Models

Our results indicate that foresight can affect the basic dynamics of a game by altering the structure of Nash equilibria. So far we have looked at public goods games and the leadership game. It would be a worthwhile exercise to study the effects of one-step foresight in a wider range of classical games such as the prisoner's dilemma and related 2 × 2 games, various coordination games, rock–scissors–paper, and versions of the volunteer's dilemma. It would also be interesting to contrast foresight with other strategy revision protocols as well as with various conditional strategies, such as those that are extortion-like (Press & Dyson, 2012; Stewart & Plotkin, 2013). In simple cases, one can expect to obtain some analytical results.

We have studied only one-step foresight, generalizing myopic optimization. However, individuals may be using higher-order theories of mind and care about longer-term payoffs (de Weerd & Verbrugge, 2011; de Weerd et al., 2013, 2014, 2015). Models capturing these features would be much more complex and require numerical investigation but would be potentially more realistic. It would be important to combine Bayesian inference about peers' strategies into foresight framework (see Khalvati, Mirbagheri, et al., 2019; Khalvati, Park, et al., 2019). Moreover, rather than predicting individual behavior, agents can evaluate common knowledge in their group and then attempt to predict the group's intention and sentiments (Shteynberg, 2015, 2018). A consensus of what a particular person might do in a particular situation would make punishment more acceptable to the other group members.

B. Foresight in Leadership

There are a number of important directions for extending our work, such as explicitly considering the dynamics of population densities (as in Powers & Lehmann, 2013, 2014), allowing for the simultaneous presence of competition of egalitarian and hierarchical groups (as in Hooper et al., 2010; Powers

& Lehmann, 2013, 2014), and allowing for changeable rather than fixed taxes as well as for a market for leaders (as in Hooper et al., 2010). Also, so far we have only modeled leaders as punishers. One can use a similar approach where leaders' effort is directed toward coordination or norm promotion. One can also conceptualize laws as punishers and model their effects on individual and group behaviors.

C. Evolution of Foresight

In our work, we have taken for granted that foresight is already present and sought only to show how it could be an effective route to overcoming the first- and second-order free-rider problem. An important evolutionary question is under what conditions foresight would evolve in a population where it is initially absent. As argued elsewhere (Alexander 1987, 1989, 1990), costly foresight could evolve if it increases biological fitness. Evolution of foresight can be driven by selection for increased individual reproductive success under the action of asocial or social factors. In the latter case, it could be selection arising from competitive interactions (e.g., as implied in Machiavellian intelligence hypothesis [Byrne & Whiten, 1988; Gavrilets & Vose, 2006; Whiten & Byrne, 1997), or selection can be due to potential benefits of cooperation (Dunbar, 1998, 2003, 2009; Gavrilets, 2015b) that can be achieved by individuals having the theory of mind. Potential benefits of cooperation can be augmented by group selection. All these ideas are worth exploring theoretically.

D. Model Validation

As I have argued, the facts that both humans and non-human animals care about the future and are able to predict to a certain extent the behavior of their group-mates are undeniable. The models outlined in this chapter aim to capture these facts in simple mathematical terms in order to predict the dynamics of cooperation and punishment in groups. Whether these simple models are adequate for describing real-world phenomena is an open empirical question. As with other game-theoretical approaches, validating the models can be done at different levels. One is a level of individual decision-making. Another is a level of group behavior. My hope is that existing methods of experimental economic games, surveys, and observational approaches can be appropriately adapted for studying foresight.

VI. CONCLUSION

Classical game theory assumes complete rationality and availability of all relevant information to the players. On the other hand, evolutionary game theory usually makes minimalistic assumptions about human (and animal) decision-making processes. Both these theories have been useful in establishing foundations of a general theory of social behavior. Starting with this foundation, we can now move toward more realism in our models by capturing in them not only the "shadow of the future" but also the theory of mind. Such a step allows us to take a new look at old problems but also to uncover new challenges in understanding social and cultural evolution and their theoretical and practical solutions.

ACKNOWLEDGMENTS

I am grateful to M. Gelfand for the invitation to contribute this chapter; to M. Duval Shretha, L. Perry, and M. D. Vose with whom these ideas have been developed; and to Chiu Cy, L. Gaertner, M. Gelfand, D. Ruck, G. Shteynberg, and D. Tverskoi for comments and suggestions. Supported by the US Army Research Office (grants W911NF-14-1-0637 and W911NF-18-1-0138), the Office of Naval Research (grant W911NF-17-1-0150), the National Institute for Mathematical and Biological Synthesis (through National Science Foundation award EF-0830858), and the University of Tennessee, Knoxville.

REFERENCES

Akerlof, G. (1980). A theory of social custom, of which unemployment may be one consequence. *Quarterly Journal of Economics, 94*(4), 749–775.

Alesina, A., & Giuliano, P. (2015). Culture and institutions. *Journal of Economic Literature, 53*, 898–944.

Alexander, R. D. (1987). *The biology of moral systems*. Aldine de Gruyter.

Alexander, R. D. (1989). Evolution of the human psyche. In P. Mellars & C. Stringer (Eds.), *The human revolution: Behavioural and biological perspectives on the origin of modern humans* (pp. 455–513). Princeton University Press.

Alexander, R. D. (1990). *How did humans evolve? Reflections on the uniquely unique species*. University of Michigan, Museum of Zoology.

Andreoni, J. (1988). Privately provided public goods in a large economy: The limits of altruism. *Journal of Public Economics, 35*(1), 57–73.

Aoki, K. (2001). Theoretical and empirical aspects of gene-culture coevolution. *Theoretical Population Biology, 59*, 253–261.

Archetti, M. (2009). Cooperation as a volunteer's dilemma and the strategy of conflict in public goods games. *Journal of Evolutionary Biology, 22*, 2192–2200.

Axelrod, R. (1984). *The evolution of cooperation*. Basic Books.

Axelrod, R. (1986). An evolutionary approach to norms. *American Political Science Review, 80*(4), 1095–1111.

Azar, O. (2004). What sustains social norms and how they evolve? The case of tipping. *Journal of Economic Behavior & Organization, 54*(1), 49–64.

Azar, O. H. (2008). Evolution of social norms with heterogeneous preferences: A general model and an application to the academic review process. *Journal of Economic Behavior & Organization, 65*(3–4), 420–435.

Bernheim, B. (1994). A theory of conformity. *Journal of Political Economy, 102*(5), 841–877.

Berns, G. S., Laibson, D., & Loewenstein, G. (2007). Intertemporal choice—Toward an integrative framework. *Trends in Cognitive Sciences, 11*(11), 482–488.

Bicchieri, C. (2006). *The grammar of society: The nature and dynamics of social norms*. Cambridge University Press.

Binmore, K. (1990). *Essays on the foundations of game theory*. Basil Blackwell.

Bissonnette, A., Perry, S., Barrett, L., Mitani, J. C., Flinn, M., Gavrilets, S., & de Waal, F. B. M. (2015). Coalitions in theory and reality: A review of pertinent variables and processes. *Behaviour, 152*(1), 1–56.

Blume, L. E. (1995). Evolutionary equilibrium with forward-looking players. *Game Theory and Evolution, 27*, Article 9509001.

Borgers, T., & Sarin, R. (1997). Learning through reinforcement and replicator dynamics. *Journal of Economic Theory, 77*(1), 1–14.

Bowles, S. (2016). *The moral economy: Why good incentives are no substitute for good*. Yale University Press.

Bowles, S., & Gintis, H. (2011). *A cooperative species: Human reciprocity and its evolution*. Princeton University Press.

Boyd, R., Gintis, H., Bowles, S., & Richerson, P. J. (2003). The evolution of altruistic punishment. *Proceedings of the National Academy of Sciences of the United States of America, 100*(6), 3531–3535.

Boyd, R., & Richerson, P. (1992). Punishment allows the evolution of cooperation (or anything else) in sizable groups. *Ethology and Sociobiology, 13*, 171–195.

Boyd, R., Richerson, P. J., & Henrich, J. (2011). Rapid cultural adaptation can facilitate the evolution of large-scale cooperation. *Behavioral Ecology and Sociobiology, 65*(3), 431–444.

Brooks, J. S., Waring, T. M., Borgerhoff Mulder, M., & Richerson, P. J. (2018). Applying cultural evolution to sustainability challenges: an introduction to the special issue. *Sustainability Science, 13*, 1–8.

Brosnan, S. F., & de Waal, F. B. M. (2014). Evolution of responses to (un)fairness. *Science, 346*, 314–322.

Burton-Chellew, M. N., El Mouden, C., & West, S. A. (2017). Social learning and the demise of costly cooperation in humans. *Proceedings of the Royal Society London B, 284*(1853), Article 20170067.

Byrne, R. W., & Whiten, A. (1988). *Machiavellian intelligence: Social expertise and the evolution of intellect in monkeys, apes, and humans.* Clarendon Press.

Call, J. (2009). Contrasting the social cognition of humans and nonhuman apes: The shared intentionality hypothesis. *Topics in Cognitive Science, 1*, 368–379.

Call, J., & Tomasello, M. (2008). Does the chimpanzee have a theory of mind? 30 years later. *Trends in Cognitive Sciences, 12*(5), 187–192.

Carlsmith, K. M. (2008). On justifying punishment: The discrepancy between words and actions. *Social Justice Research, 21*(2), 119–137.

Carlsmith, K., Darley, J., & Robinson, P. (2002). Why do we punish? Deterrence and just deserts as motives for punishment. *Journal of Personality and Social Psychology, 83*(2), 284–299.

Chudek, M., Zhao, W., & Henrich, J. (2013). Culture–gene coevolution, large-scale cooperation and the shaping of human social psychology. In R. Joyce, K. Sterelny, & B. Calcott (Eds.), *Signaling, Commitment, and emotion* (pp. 425–458). MIT Press.

Cushman, F. (2015). Punishment in humans: From intuitions to institutions. *Philosophy Compass, 10*(2), 117–133.

Darwin, C. (2003). *On the origin of species by means of natural selection, or the preservation of favoured races in the struggle for life.* Signet. (original work published in 1859).

Darwin, C. (1871). *The descent of man, and selection in relation to sex.* John Murray.

Defoe, D. (1972). *A general history of the pyrates.* Mineola. (Original work published in 1724.)

De Weerd, H., & Verbrugge, R. (2011). Evolution of altruistic punishment in heterogeneous populations. *Journal of Theoretical Biology, 290*, 88–103.

De Weerd, H., Verbrugge, R., & Verheij, B. (2013). How much does it help to know what she knows you know? An agent-based simulation study. *Artificial Intelligence, 199–200*, 67–92.

de Weerd, H., Verbrugge, R., & Verheij, B. (2014). Theory of mind in the Mod game: an agent-based model of strategic reasoning. In *Proceedings of the European Conference on Social Intelligence (ECSI-2014) CEUR Workshop Proceedings* (Barcelona), 128–136.

De Weerd, H., Verbrugge, R., & Verheij, B. (2015). Higher-order theory of mind in the tacit communication game. *Biologically Inspired Cognitive Architectures, 11*, 10–21.

Diekmann, A. (1985). Volunteer's dilemma. *Journal of Conflict Resolution, 29*, 605–610.

Dunbar, R. I. M. (1998). The social brain hypothesis. *Evolutionary Anthropology, 6,* 178–190.

Dunbar, R. I. M. (2003). The social brain: Mind, language, and society in evolutionary perspective. *Annual Review of Anthropology, 32,* 163–181.

Dunbar, R. I. M. (2009). The social brain hypothesis and its implications for social evolution. *Annals of Human Biology, 36,* 562–572.

Ensminger, J., & Henrich, J. (2014). *Theoretical foundations: The coevolution of social norms, intrinsic motivation, markets, and the institutions of complex societies.* Russel Sage Foundation.

Fehr, E., & Fischbacher, U. (2004). Third-party punishment and social norms. *Evolution and Human Behavior, 25,* 63–87.

Fehr, E., & Gächter, S. (2002). Altruistic punishment in humans. *Nature, 415,* 137–140.

Fehr, E., & Schurtenberger, I. (2018). Normative foundations of human cooperation. *Nature Human Behaviour, 2,* 458–468.

Flinn, M. V., Geary, D. C., & Ward, C. V. (2005). Ecological dominance, social competition, and coalitionary arms races: Why humans evolved extraordinary intelligence? *Evolution and Human Behavior, 26,* 10–46.

Fogarty, L., Rendell, L., & Laland, K. (2012). Mental time travel, memory and the social learning strategies tournament. *Learning and Motivation, 43,* 241–246.

Frederick, S., Loewenstein, G., & O'Donoghue, T. (2002). Time discounting and time preference: A critical review. *Journal of Economic Literature, 40*(2), 351–401.

Fudenberg, D., & Tirole, J. (1992). *Game theory.* MIT Press.

Gao, J., Li, Z., Cong, R., & Wang, L. (2012). Tolerance-based punishment in continuous public goods game. *Physica A: Statistical Mechanics and Its Applications, 391*(16), 4111–4120.

Garfield, Z. H., Hubbard, R. L., & Hagen, E. H. (2019). Evolutionary models of leadership: Tests and synthesis. *Human Nature, 30,* 23–58.

Gavrilets, S. (2004). *Fitness landscapes and the origin of species.* Princeton University Press.

Gavrilets, S. (2012a). Human origins and the transition from promiscuity to pair-bonding. *Proceedings of the National Academy of Sciences of the United States of America, 109,* 9923–9928.

Gavrilets, S. (2012b). On the evolutionary origins of the egalitarian syndrome. *Proceedings of the National Academy of Sciences of the United States of America, 109,* 14069–14074.

Gavrilets, S. (2015a). Collective action problem in heterogeneous groups. *Philosophical Transactions of the Royal Society London B, 370,* Article 20150016.

Gavrilets, S. (2015b). Collective action and the collaborative brain. *Interface, 12,* article 20141067.

Gavrilets, S. (2020). The dynamics of injunctive social norm. *Evolutionary Human Sciences, 2*, e60.

Gavrilets, S., & Fortunato, L. (2014). A solution to the collective action problem in between-group conflict with within-group inequality. *Nature Communications, 5*, Article 3526.

Gavrilets, S., & Richerson, P. J. (2017). Collective action and the evolution of social norm internalization. *Proceedings of the National Academy of Sciences of the United States of America, 114*, 6068–6073.

Gavrilets, S., & Shretha, M. D. (2021). Evolving institutions for collective action by selective imitation and self-interested design. *Evolution and Human Behavior, 42*(1), 1–11.

Gavrilets, S., & Vose, A. (2006). The dynamics of Machiavellian intelligence. *Proceedings of the National Academy of Sciences of the United States of America, 103*, 16823–16828.

Gavrilets, S., Duenez-Guzman, E. A., & Vose, M. D. (2008). Dynamics of coalition formation and the egalitarian revolution. *PLOS One, 3*, Article e3293.

Gavrilets, S., Richerson, P. J., & de Waal, F. (2021). Celebrating the 150th anniversary of the *Descent of Man*. *Evolutionary Human Sciences, 3*, e17.

Gigerenzer, G., & Selten, R. (2001). *Bounded rationality: The adaptive toolbox*. MIT Press.

Gilby, I. C., Machanda, Z. P., Mjungu, D. C., Rosen, J., Muller, M. N., Pusey, A. E., & Wrangham, R. W. (2015). "Impact hunters" catalyse cooperative hunting in two wild chimpanzee communities. *Philosophical Transactions of the Royal Society B, 370*(1983), Article 20150005.

Gintis, H. (2016). *Homo ludens: The moral and material bases of social life*. Princeton University Press.

Goeree, J. K., Holt, C. A., & Palfrey, T. R. (2016). *Quantal response equilibrium*. Princeton University Press.

Grusec, J. E., & Kuczynski, L. (1997). *Parenting and children's internalization of values: A handbook of contemporary theory*. John Wiley & Sons.

Hall, K., & Brosnan, S. F. (2016). Cooperation and deception in primates. *Infant Behavior and Development, 48*(Pt A), 38–44.

Hardin, R. (1982). *Collective action*. John Hopkins University Press.

Hayden, B. Y. (2019). Why has evolution not selected for perfect self-control? *Philosophical Transactions of the Royal Society B, 374*(1766), 20180139.

Heckathorn, D. D. (1989). Collective action and the second-order free-rider problem. *Rationality and Society, 1*(1), 78–100.

Hedden, T., & Zhang, J. (2002). What do you think I think you think? Strategic reasoning in matrix games. *Cognition, 85*(1), 1–36.

Helbing, D., Szolnoki, A., Perc, M., & Szabó, G. (2010). Punish, but not too hard: How costly punishment spreads in the spatial public goods game. *New Journal of Physics, 12*(8), Article 083005.

Heller, Y. (2015). Three steps ahead. *Theoretical Economics, 10*(1), 203–241.

Henrich, J. (2016). *The secret of our success*. Princeton University Press.

Hofbauer, J., & Sigmund, K. (1998). *Evolutionary games and population dynamics*. Cambridge University Press.

Hooper, P. L., Kaplan, H. S., & Boone, J. L. (2010). A theory of leadership in human cooperative groups. *Journal of Theoretical Biology, 265*(4), 633–646.

Isakov, A., & Rand, D. (2012). The evolution of coercive institutional punishment. *Dynamic Games and Applications, 2*, 97–109.

Iwasa, Y., & Lee, J.-H. (2013). Graduated punishment is efficient in resource management if people are heterogeneous. *Journal of Theoretical Biology, 333*, 117–125.

Jehiel, P. (1995). Limited horizon forecast in repeated alternate games. *Journal of Economic Theory, 67*(2), 497–519.

Jehiel, P. (1998). Learning to play limited forecast equilibria. *Games and Economic Behavior, 22*(2), 274–298.

Jehiel, P. (2001). Limited foresight may force cooperation. *Review of Economic Studies, 68*(2), 369–391.

Kano, F., Krupenye, C., Hirata, S., Tomonaga, M., & Call, J. (2019). Great apes use self-experience to anticipate an agent's action in a false-belief test. *Proceedings of the National Academy of Sciences of the United States of America, 116*, 20904–20909.

Khalvati, K., Mirbagheri, S., Park, S. A., Dreher, J.-C., & Rao, R. P. N. (2019, December 8–14). A Bayesian theory of conformity in collective decision making [Paper presentation]. 33rd Conference on Neural Information Processing Systems, Vancouver, Canada.

Khalvati, K., Park, S. A., Mirbagher, S., Philippe, R., Sestito, M., Dreher, J.-C., & Rao, R. P. N. (2019). Modeling other minds: Bayesian inference explains human choices in group decision making. *Science Advances, 5*(11), Article eaax8783.

Konrad, K. (2009). *Strategy and dynamics in contests*. Oxford University Press.

Krasnow, M. M., Cosmides, L., Pedersen, E. J., & Tooby, J. (2012). What are punishment and reputation for? *PLoS ONE, 7*(9), Article e45662.

Krebs, J. R., & Dawkins, R. (1984). Animal signals: Mind-reading and manipulation. In J. R. Krebs & R. Dawkins (Eds.), *Behavioral ecology: An evolutionary approach* (pp. 380–401). Blackwell.

Krupenye, C., Kano, F., Hirata, S., Call, J., & Tomasello, M. (2016). Great apes anticipate that other individuals will act according to false beliefs. *Science, 354*, 110–114.

Lapinski, M. K., & Rimal, R. N. (2005). An explication of social norms. *Communication Theory, 15*, 127–147.

Leeson, P. (2009). *The invisible hook: The hidden economics of pirates*. Princeton University Press.

MacLean, E. L., Hare, B., Nunn, C. L., Addessi, E., Amici, F., Anderson, R. C., Aureli, F., Baker, J. M., Bania, A. E., Barnard, A. M., Boogert, N. J., Brannon, E. M., Bray, E. E., Bray, J., Brent, L. J. N., Burkart, J. M., Call, J., Cantlon, J. F., Cheke, L. G., . . . Zhao, Y. (2014). The evolution of self-control. *Proceedings of the National Academy of Sciences of the United States of America, 111*(20), E2140–E2148.

McNally, L., & Jackson, A. L. (2013). Cooperation creates selection for tactical deception. *Proceedings of the Royal Society London B, 280*, 20130699.

Maynard Smith, J. (1982). *Evolution and the theory of games.* Cambridge University Press.

Maynard Smith, J., & Price, G. R. (1973). The logic of animal conflict. *Nature, 246*, 15–18.

McElreath, R., & Boyd, R. (2007). *Mathematical models of social evolution: A guide for the perplexed.* University of Chicago Press.

McGinty, M., & Milam, G. (2013). Public goods provision by asymmetric agents: Experimental evidence. *Social Choice and Welfare, 40*(4), 1159–1177.

Mengel, F. (2014). Learning by (limited) forward looking players. *Journal of Economic Behavior and Organization, 108*, 59–77.

Mesterton-Gibbons, M., Gavrilets, S., Gravner, J., & Akcay, E. (2011). Models of coalition or alliance formation. *Journal of Theoretical Biology, 274*, 187–204.

Miller, R., Boeckle, M., Jelbert, S. A., Frohnwieser, A., Wascher, C. A. F., & Clayton, N. S. (2019). Self-control in crows, parrots and nonhuman primates. *Wiley Interdisciplinary Reviews. Cognitive Science, 10*(6), Article e1504.

Mokkonen, M., & Lindstedt, C. (2016). The evolutionary ecology of deception. *Biological Reviews of the Cambridge Philosophical Society, 91*, 1020–1035.

Molleman, L., van den Berg, P., & Weissing, F. J. (2014). Consistent individual differences in human social learning strategies. *Nature Communications, 5*, Article 3570.

Nagel, R. (1995). Unraveling in guessing games: An experimental study. *The American Economic Review, 85*(5), 1313–1326.

North, D. C. (1990). *Institution, institutional change and economic performance.* Cambridge University Press.

Nowak, M. (2006). *Evolutionary dynamics.* Harvard University Press.

Nyborg, K. (2018). Social norms and the environment. *Annual Review of Resource Economics, 10*, 405–423.

Olson, M. (1965). *The logic of collective action: Public goods and the theory of groups.* Harvard University Press.

Ostrom, E. (1990). *Governing the commons: The evolution of institutions for collective action.* Cambridge University Press.

Ostrom, E. (2000). Collective action and the evolution of social norms. *Journal of Economic Perspectives, 14*(3), 137–158.

Panchanathan, K., & Boyd, R. (2004). Indirect reciprocity can stabilize cooperation without the second-order free rider problem. *Nature, 432*, 499–502.

Pecorino, P. (2015). Olson's logic of collective action at fifty. *Public Choice, 162*, 243–262.

Perner, J., & Wimmer, H. (1985). "John thinks that Mary thinks that . . ." Attribution of second-order beliefs by 5-to 10-year-old children. *Journal of Experimental Child Psychology, 39*(3), 437–471.

Perry, L., & Gavrilets, S. (2020). Foresight in the game of leadership. *Scientific Reports, 10*, Article 2251.

Perry, L., Shrestha, M. D., Vose, M. D., & Gavrilets, S. (2018) Collective action problem in heterogeneous groups with punishment and foresight. *Journal of Statistical Physics, 172*, 293–312.

Petersen, M. B. (2016). Evolutionary political psychology. In D. M. Buss (Ed.), *Handbook of evolutionary psychology* (pp. 1084–1102). John Wiley & Sons.

Petersen, M. B., & Aaroe, L. (2015). Evolutionary theory and political behavior. In R. A. Scott & S. M. Kosslyn (Eds.), *Emerging trends in the social and behavioral sciences* (pp. 1–15). John Wiley & Sons.

Powers, S., & Lehmann, L. (2013). The co-evolution of social institutions, demography, and large-scale human cooperation. *Ecology Letters, 16*, 1356–1364.

Powers, S., & Lehmann, L. (2014). An evolutionary model explaining the Neolithic transition from egalitarianism to leadership and despotism. *Philosophical Transactions of the Royal Society London B, 281*, Article 20141349.

Powers, S. T., van Schaik, C. P., & Lehmann, L. (2016). How institutions shaped the last major evolutionary transition to large-scale human societies. *Philosophical Transactions of the Royal Society London B, 371*, Article 20150098.

Premack, D., & Woodruff, G. (1978). Does the chimpanzee have a theory of mind? *Behavioral and Brain Sciences, 1*(4), 515–526.

Press, W., & Dyson, F. (2012). Iterated prisoner's dilemma contains strategies that dominate any evolutionary opponent. *Proceedings of the National Academy of Sciences of the United States of America, 109*, 10409–10413.

Provine, W. B. (1971). *The origins of theoretical population genetics*. University of Chicago Press.

Provine, W. B. (1986). *Sewall Wright and evolutionary biology*. University of Chicago Press.

Richerson, P., Baldini, R., Bell, A. V., Demps, K., Frost, K., Hillis, V., Mathew, S., Newton, E. K., Naar, N., Newson, L., Ross, C., Smaldino, P. E., Waring, T. M., & Zefferman, M. (2016). Cultural group selection plays an essential role in explaining human cooperation: A sketch of the evidence. *Behavioral and Brain Sciences, 39*, Article e30.

Richerson, P. J., & Boyd, R. (2005). *Not by genes alone: How culture transformed human evolution*. University of Chicago Press.

Roithmayr, D., Isakov, A., & Rand, D. (2015). Should law keep pace with society? Relative update rates determine the co-evolution of institutional punishment and citizen contributions to public goods. *Games, 6*(2), 124–149.

Rusch, H., & Gavrilets, S. (2020). The logic of animal intergroup conflict: A review. *Journal of Economic Behavior & Organization, 178*, 1014–1030.

Sandholm, W. H. (2009). Evolutionary game theory. In R. A. Meyers (Ed.), *Encyclopedia of complexity and systems science* (pp. 3176–3205). Springer.

Sandholm, W. H. (2010). *Population games and evolutionary dynamics.* MIT Press.

Sandler, T. (1992). *Collective action: Theory and applications.* University of Michigan Press.

Shimao, H., & Nakamaru, M. (2013). Strict or graduated punishment? Effect of punishment strictness on the evolution of cooperation in continuous public goods games. *PLoS ONE, 8*(3), Article e59894.

Shteynberg, G. (2015). Shared attention. *Perspectives on Psychological Science, 5*, 579–590.

Shteynberg, G. (2018). A collective perspective: Shared attention and the mind. *Current Opinion in Psychology, 23*, 93–97.

Singh, M., Wrangham, R., & Glowacki, L. (2017). Self-interest and the design of rules. *Human Nature, 28*, 45–480.

Skarbek, D. (2012). Prison gangs, norms, and organizations. *Journal of Economic Behavior & Organization, 82*, 702–716.

Smith, A. (2008). *An inquiry into the nature and causes of the wealth of nations: A selected edition Adam Smith (author)* (K. Sutherland, Ed.). Oxford University Press. (Original work published 1776)

Stahl, D. O., & Wilson, P. W. (1995). On players' models of other players: Theory and experimental evidence. *Games and Economic Behavior, 10*(1), 218–254.

Stewart, A. J., & Plotkin, J. B. (2013). From extortion to generosity, evolution in the iterated prisoner's dilemma. *Proceedings of the National Academy of Sciences of the United States of America, 110*, 15348–15353.

Suddendorf, T., & Corballis, M. C. (1997). Mental time travel and the evolution of the human mind. *Genetic, Social, and General Psychology Monographs, 123*(2), 133–167.

Szolnoki, A., & Perc, M. (2014). Costly hide and seek pays: Unexpected consequences of deceit in a social dilemma. *New Journal of Physics, 16*, Article 113003.

Szpunar, K. K., Spreng, R. N., & Schacter, D. L. (2014). A taxonomy of prospection: Introducing an organizational framework for future-oriented cognition. Proceedings of the National Academy of Sciences, *111*(52), 18414–18421.

Tomasello, M. (2011). Human culture in evolutionary perspective. In M. J. Gelfand, C. yue Chiu, & Y. yi Hong (Eds.), *Advances in culture and psychology* (Vol. 1, pp.5–51). Oxford University Press.

Tomasello, M., Carpenter, M., Call, J., Behne, T., & Moll, H. (2005). Understanding and sharing intentions: The origins of cultural cognition. *Behavioral and Brain Sciences*, *28*(5), 675–691.

Turchin, P. (2016). *Ultrasociety: How 10,000 years of war made humans the greatest cooperators on earth*. Beresta Books.

Vale, G., Flynn, E., & Kendal, R. (2012). Cumulative culture and future thinking: Is mental time travel a prerequisite to cumulative cultural evolution? *Learning and Motivation*, *43*, 220–230.

van den Berg, P., Molleman, L., & Weissing, F. J. (2015). Focus on the success of others leads to selfish behavior. *Proceedings of the National Academy of Sciences of the United States of America*, *112*(9), 2912–2917.

von Neumann, J., & Morgenstern, O. (1944). *Theory of games and economic behavior*. Princeton University Press.

Whiten, A., & Byrne, R. W. (1997). *Machiavellian intelligence II. Extensions and evaluations*. Cambridge University Press.

Wiessner, P. (2019). Collective action for war and for peace. A case study among the Enga of Papua New Guinea. *Current Anthropology*, *60*(2), 224–244.

Wrong, D. (1961). The oversocialized concept of man in modern sociology. *American Sociological Review*, *26*, 183–193.

INDEX

Tables and figures are indicated by *t* and *f* following the page number.

absolute *vs.* relative judgments, 8
accumulated culture, 127, 157
Adair, W., 259, 269, 273, 275
adherence to Islam, 140*t*, 155–56,
 162*t*. *See also* ideologies/belief
 systems
adolescents. *See also* children/youth
 global trends
 period/menarche, 68*t*, 71, 72
 subcultures, 70*t*, 76
African American educational
 attainment, 137*t*, 156–57
age segregation trends, 68*t*
Aghion, P., 163*t*
aging, 10, 12, 15–16, 17*f*, 23*f*, 31–35,
 35*f*
agriculture
 labor-intensive, 136*t*
 marginal returns/labor of crop
 mix, 138*t*
 plow, 136*t*, 147–49, 148*f*
 suitability/traditional crops, 138*t*
 suitability variation, 140*t*
 wheat, 136*t*
Ahmed, R. A., 95
AIDS epidemic, 152*t*
Alesina, A., 136*t*, 151*t*, 158
Alexander, R., 294
Algan, Y., 158, 163*t*, 166
alloparenting, 63*t*, 64
Alsan, M., 136*t*, 145, 171–72
altruism, 153*t*, 169
altruistic bully effect, 307
Alzheimer's disease (AD), 34, 35*f*

analytic *vs.* holistic processing, 6
ancestors in leper colony, 140*t*, 145
Andersen, T. B., 136*t*
Ang, J. B., 136*t*
anger/shame, 223–25, 225*f*, 256–57
annoyances, 213–14
Ashraf, N., 163*t*, 172
Aslani, S., 268
assertiveness, 249
assimilation, cultural, 152–53*t*, 157,
 176
Atkin, D., 163*t*
atoxyl, 171
attitudes towards United States, 138*t*
authoritative parenting style, 137*t*
autocratic *vs.* democratic national
 government, 164*t*
Axelrod, R., 297

banking deregulation, 152*t*
Bau, N., 151*t*, 173–74
Bauer, M., 151*t*
Bazzi, S., 136*t*
Beaman, L., 151*t*, 175
Becker, A., 136*t*, 150
Becker, S. O., 137*t*, 144–45, 163*t*, 175
Becoming a Man (BAM) program, 173
Beersma, B., 252
behavioral theory, 253–61, 274,
 280nn8–9, 281n13
behaviors
 behavioral theory, 253–61, 274,
 280nn8–9, 281n13
 cheating, 130

333

334 Index

behaviors (*cont.*)
civic honesty, 131, 132*f*, 146
concern for self/others, 249, 252
conflict management, 251–53
honor culture, 207*t*, 208*t*
moral behavior, 194–95, 202, 203, 206
other-regarding, 153*t*
prosociality, 140*t*, 146–47, 151*t*, 158–59, 174–75
revealing negative, 207*t*
revealing positive, 208*t*
self-efficacy/civic mindedness, 139*t*, 146
self-report *vs.* behavioral coding, 260–61, 274–75
trust game behavior, 131
ultimatum game, 129–30, 134
universal/limited morality, 138*t*
work ethic, 136*t*, 138*t*
belief in Christianity, 140*t*. *See also* ideologies/belief systems
Bentzen, J. S., 151*t*
BenYishay, A., 137*t*
Bergh, A., 151*t*
bias
gender norms/bias, 153*t*
in-group/out-group, 151*t*, 153*t*
male-biased sex ratio, 139*t*, 149–50
bicultural individuals, 30
Blader, S. L., 257
Blake, R., 249
Boduroğlu, A., 15
Booth, A., 151*t*
Boserup, E., 147
Boyd, R., 127
brain regions involved in memory, 6–9, 7*f*, 20–21, 28–35, 35*f*
breastfeeding/co-sleeping, 67*t*, 70–71
Brett, J. M., 255–56, 259, 262, 264–68, 269, 270, 272, 275, 279, 281n13
bride price/bride wealth, 163*t*, 172

Brodmann area 18/19, 28
Brown, R. P., 193
Bursztyn, L., 151*t*
Butler, J. V., 163*t*, 167

cable/satellite TV, 153*t*, 156–57
Cahuc, P., 158, 163*t*, 166
Campa, P., 137*t*, 150, 175
Campante, F., 137*t*, 151*t*, 157, 163*t*
Cantoni, D., 152*t*
Cantor, N., 201
capital accumulation, 164*t*
Cassar, A., 152*t*
categorical false memories, 14–16, 16–17*f*
categorization, 7, 8, 33
categorization strategies, 13–14
Catholic Church's medieval policies, 141*t*
Catholic Order of Cistercians, 136*t*
caudate, 35*f*
causality research, 134–35, 142–45, 177, 178n7
Cervellati, M., 137*t*
challenge to competence, 218–23, 231, 235n5
challenge to honesty, 207*t*, 212, 213*f*, 218–23, 231, 235n5
chastity value/girls, 69*t*
cheating behaviors, 130
Chee, M., 10
Chen, Y. R., 257
Chiao, J., 5
childhood stunting, 164*t*
child labor, 67*t*, 102
child mortality rates/life expectancy, 67*t*
child preference, differential, 151*t*
children/youth global trends
adolescent period/menarche, 68*t*, 71, 72
adolescent subcultures, 70*t*, 76
age segregation, 68*t*

Index **335**

alloparenting, 63*t*, 64

breastfeeding/co-sleeping, 67*t*, 70–71

challenges to growing up, 108–10

chastity value/girls, 69*t*

child labor, 67*t*, 102

child mortality rates/life expectancy, 67*t*

China, 66, 73–79, 101, 106, 112

consumerism impacts, 70*t*

digital information societies, 54, 58, 60*t*, 65–66, 67–72*t*, 73–74, 90–92, 98, 101

ecological knowledge impacts, 55–57

economic basis, 59, 61*t*

education fever, 55, 80–81

education/literacy, 62*t*, 66, 68*t*, 72–83, 92–94, 93*f*, 109

family systems, 60–63*t*, 67–70*t*

fertility rates (TFR), 55, 66, 90–92

forcibly displaced/refugee children, 104–5

foreign students/South Korea, 82–83

gender inequality, 59, 62*t*, 72

gender roles, 61–62*t*, 65, 66, 72–73, 93, 97–100

global child mortality rates, 86–88, 86*f*

globalization, 54, 105–6

global perspectives in Western psychology, 110–11

global teenage culture(s) impacts, 70*t*

glocal identities, 54–55

growing up by society type, 67–70*t*

historical background, 51–53

hunter–gatherer societies, 52, 54, 58–64, 60–63*t*, 66–72, 67–72*t*

ideologies/belief systems impacts, 57, 59, 61*t*, 66, 73, 93, 99–100

individualism/collectivism, 70*t*, 73, 101, 106

infanticide, 70, 70*t*

innovations impacts, 53–57, 61–62*t*, 71–72

intelligence rate increases, 94–95

intergenerational knowledge, 69*t*

kinship systems, 65

left-behind children/China, 75–78

malnutrition, 67*t*, 73–74, 87–89

marriage, arranged/semi-arranged, 69*t*, 101

marriage age/boys, 69*t*, 74

marriage age/girls, 69*t*, 74, 109

mass media exposure, 66, 70*t*, 105–6

migration/migrant children, 75–79, 102–4

multicultural students/South Korea, 81–84

obedience/responsibility training, 67*t*, 101

parent-child relationship effects, 95–97, 101

peasant societies, 52, 54, 58, 60*t*, 64–65, 67–72*t*, 72–73, 97–98, 101

peer group influences, 69*t*

population size/density, 59, 61*t*, 84–86, 85*f*

privacy, 68*t*

puberty/adulthood rites, 69*t*, 74

public policy in improvement of lives, 89–90, 106–10

returned students/China, 78–79

siblings number/influence, 68*t*

socialization, 63*t*, 67*t*, 71, 97–100

social relations, kin/strangers, 65, 68*t*

societal change, 61*t*, 100–101

societal complexity, 59, 61*t*

societal evolution, 57–59, 60–63*t*

societal threats to welfare, 70–71, 70*t*

socioecological approach, 54–57, 56*f*

336 Index

children/youth global trends (*cont.*)
  socioeconomic stratification/
    division of labor, 59, 61*t*, 64–65
  South Korea, 55, 66, 73–74, 79–84,
    112
  tradition-innovation balance, 59,
    61*t*, 71
  violence against females, 62*t*, 65,
    70*t*, 72, 78, 109
China
  children/youth global trends, 66,
    73–79, 101, 106, 112
  left-behind children, 75–78
  returned students, 78–79
civic honesty, 131, 132*f*, 146
climatic volatility, 138*t*, 159–61,
    160–61*f*
Clingingsmith, D., 152*t*, 155–56
Cohen, D., 194–95, 199, 213–14, 226
Cohn, A., 131
collective action/free-riders problem,
    294–95, 305–14, 308*f*, 310*f*, 313*t*
colonialism
  medical campaigns, 139*t*, 170–71
  mission stations, 140*t*, 145
  production quotas, 137*t*
  rule (direct *vs.* indirect), 137*t*
communism, 136–37*t*, 150, 151*t*
competence, challenge to, 218–23,
    231, 235n5
competition, competitiveness, 151–52*t*,
    249, 251, 254, 257–58
complementarity, 258–59
concern for self/others, 249, 252
conditional cooperation, 141*t*
conflict
  foresight modeling, 294–95
  goal conflict/goal pursuit, 225–30, 229*f*
  history of, 137*t*, 146–47, 151–53*t*,
    157, 170
  management behaviors, 251–53
  Thomas-Kilmann Conflict Mode
    Instrument (TKI), 251

cooperation
  conditional, 141*t*
  contribution to public good, 137–
    38*t*, 165*t*, 174–75
  foresight modeling, 294–95, 314–
    15, 319
  in negotiation strategy, 249, 251,
    254, 257–58
  problem-solving *vs.* contending
    negotiation strategy, 249
coral reefs presence, 137*t*
Cornelson, K., 137*t*
Corno, L., 163*t*
corruption culture, 130
Cosby Show role models, 137*t*,
    156–57
co-sleeping/breastfeeding, 67*t*, 70–71
cotton weaving, 141*t*, 149
Couttenier, M., 138*t*
crops. *See* agriculture
Croson, R., 257–58
Cross, S. E., 191, 219
cultural assimilation, 152–53*t*, 157,
    176
cultural difference between countries,
    164*t*
culture of honor. *See* honor culture
CuPS approach, 199, 212–13, 231–32

Dai Viet Kingdom, 138*t*
Daly, M., 98
De Dreu, C. K., 251, 252
Dell, M., 138*t*
Della Vigna, S., 152*t*, 156–57
democracy
  autocratic *vs.* democratic national
    government, 164*t*
  medieval, 141*t*, 146
  support for, 138*t*, 146
Depetris-Chauvin, E., 152*t*, 156
Desmet, K., 131–33
deterrence, foresight modeling,
    297–98

Dettwyler, K. A., 86
Deutsch, M., 248–49
de Waal, F., 294
differential child preference, 151*t*
digital information societies, 54, 58, 60*t*, 65–66, 67–72*t*, 73–74, 90–92, 98, 101
dignity culture, honor culture *vs.*, 194–95, 203, 210, 212, 218–23, 233, 234n2
disadvantaged youth outcomes, 173
distributive *vs.* integrative negotiation strategy, 253, 254, 256, 258–59, 269
distrust, 163*t*
Doepke, M., 74
Dohmen, T., 164*t*
dual-concern theory, 249–53, 250*f*, 259–61, 280nn3-9
Dutch Test for Conflict Handling (DUTCH), 252

earthquakes, 151*t*
EASI (emotion as social information) model, 257
economics and culture studies
accumulated culture, 127, 157
adherence to Islam, 140*t*, 155–56, 162*t*
African American educational attainment, 137*t*, 156–57
agricultural suitability/traditional crops, 138*t*
agricultural suitability variation, 140*t*
AIDS epidemic, 152*t*
altruism, 153*t*, 169
ancestors in leper colony, 140*t*, 145
attitudes towards United States, 138*t*
authoritative parenting style, 137*t*
autocratic *vs.* democratic national government, 164*t*

banking deregulation, 152*t*
belief in Christianity, 140*t*
bilateral trade, 164*t*
bride price/bride wealth, 163*t*, 172
cable/satellite TV, 153*t*, 156–57
capital accumulation, 164*t*
Catholic Church's medieval policies, 141*t*
Catholic Order of Cistercians, 136*t*
causality research, 134–35, 142–45, 177, 178n7
cheating behaviors, 130
childhood stunting, 164*t*
civic honesty, 131, 132*f*, 146
climatic volatility, 138*t*, 159–61, 160–61*f*
colonial medical campaigns, 139*t*, 170–71
colonial mission stations, 140*t*, 145
colonial production quotas, 137*t*
colonial rule (direct *vs.* indirect), 137*t*
communism, 136–37*t*, 150, 151*t*
competitiveness, 151*t*
conceptual framework, 126–28
conditional cooperation, 141*t*
cooperation (contribution to public good), 137–38*t*, 165*t*, 174–75
coral reefs presence, 137*t*
corruption culture, 130
Cosby Show role models, 137*t*, 156–57
cotton weaving, 141*t*, 149
cultural assimilation, 152–53*t*, 157, 176
cultural difference between countries, 164*t*
Dai Viet Kingdom, 138*t*
democracy, support for, 138*t*, 146
differences, consequences of, 162–70, 163–65*t*
differential child preference, 151*t*
disadvantaged youth outcomes, 173

338 Index

economics and culture studies (*cont.*)
  distrust, 163*t*
  earthquakes, 151*t*
  economic growth, 163–64*t*, 166
  economic output, 163*t*
  education, 154*t*, 163–64*t*, 172–74
  election violence exposure, 153*t*
  environment similarity across
    generations, 139*t*
  ethnic affiliation, 140*t*
  ethnic affiliation/endogamy, 137*t*,
    157, 158
  experimental games measures,
    129–30
  falsification testing, 144
  female education, 163*t*
  female empowerment, 153*t*
  female genital cutting, 136*t*
  female labor force participation,
    141*t*, 147–50, 175
  female wartime employment/WWII,
    138*t*, 175
  fertility norms, 153*t*, 156, 158
  fertility norms, drought-related,
    163*t*
  firm competition, 152*t*
  food preferences, 163*t*
  forced rubber collection, 139*t*,
    146–47
  foreign direct investment, 162–66,
    164*t*
  foreign outsourcing, 164*t*
  Fourth of July festivities, 153*t*, 155
  Fox News access, 152*t*, 156
  frontier experience, 136*t*
  gay marriage attitudes, 136*t*
  gender norms/bias, 153*t*
  gender quotas, 163*t*, 176
  gender roles/gender attitudes, 136*t*,
    138–39*t*, 141*t*, 147–50, 148*f*,
    151–52*t*, 156–58, 170
  German reunification, 151*t*, 158
  gold rush/ 19th century, 137*t*

government pensions, 151*t*, 173–74
government redistribution
  preferences, 136*t*, 151–52*t*
government regulation, 163*t*
Habsburg Empire, 137*t*
Habsburg *vs.* Ottoman/Russian
  state, 139*t*, 144–45, 175
Hajj pilgrimage, 152*t*, 155–56
happiness, 163*t*
historical determinants, 128, 134–35,
  177n3
history of conflict, 137*t*, 146–47,
  151–53*t*, 157, 170
homicides, 138*t*
homosexuality, attitudes towards,
  137*t*, 152*t*
honor culture, 139*t*
income, 163–64*t*, 167–68
individualism/collectivism, 136*t*,
  164*t*, 169
industrial specialization of
  production, 163*t*
information provision, 151*t*
in-group/out-group bias, 151*t*, 153*t*
in-group/out-group trust, 140*t*, 169
innovation, 165*t*, 168
inspirational movies, 154*t*
instrumental variables, 144
kinship ties, 136*t*, 138*t*, 141*t*, 164*t*,
  165*t*, 168, 170
knowledge transmission, 128,
  155–57
lab-in-the-field experiments, 130–
  31, 132*f*
labor-intensive agriculture, 136*t*
language restrictions, 152*t*
long-run determinants, 134–50,
  136–41*t*
long-term orientation, 164*t*
loss aversion, 138*t*
luck *vs.* effort attitudes, 152*t*
malaria prevalence, 137*t*
male-biased sex ratio, 139*t*, 149–50

male–female sex ratio, 136*t*, 149
malnutrition, 163*t*
marginal returns/labor of crop mix, 138*t*
marriage, 163*t*, 170
mathematical models, 127
matrilineal inheritance, 137*t*
matrilineal kinship, 165*t*, 170
matrilocality/patrilocality, 151*t*, 173–74
medical system trust, 136*t*, 139*t*, 145, 171–72
medieval democracy, 141*t*, 146
medieval independent city-states, 139*t*, 146
mentor program, 153*t*
military bombing, 138*t*
mineral discoveries timing, 138*t*
movement to new country, 151*t*
national soccer team victories, 152*t*, 156
national vs.coethnic identity, 152*t*, 156, 176
norms, 127, 133–34, 158
obedience to state, 139*t*, 165*t*, 175
other-regarding behaviors, 153*t*
pastoralism, 136*t*, 150
patience, 164*t*
patriotism, 153*t*, 176
persistence/chance, 157–62, 160–61*f*
plow agriculture, 136*t*, 147–49, 148*f*
political beliefs/attitudes, 152*t*
political preferences (voting), 152*t*, 153*t*, 155, 164*t*, 168, 169
political turnover, 165*t*, 168
printing press access, 140*t*
prosociality, 140*t*, 146–47, 151*t*, 158–59, 174–75
public policy in, 170–76
Ramadan fasting, 151*t*
recession, 152*t*, 168

regression-discontinuity identification strategy, 144–45
religiosity, 134, 151*t*, 153*t*
religiosity/fasting, 163*t*
religious beliefs (Protestantism), 140*t*, 163*t*
risk aversion, 153*t*
rule following, 139*t*, 165*t*, 175
school curricula, 152*t*
Scotch-Irish immigration, 139*t*
segmentary lineage organization, 140*t*, 165*t*, 170
self-efficacy/civic mindedness, 139*t*, 146
sex ratios, 136*t*
short-run determinants, 150–57, 151–54*t*
slave trades, 135–44, 138*t*, 140–42*t*, 143*f*, 147, 149
social cohesion, 139–40*t*, 147, 152*t*, 156
state bureaucracy trust, 137*t*
state formation, 139*t*
supernatural beliefs, 138*t*
survey measures, 128–29, 131–33
Tea Party protests, 153*t*, 155
television soap operas, 153*t*, 156
trade routes/land suitability, 140*t*
tradition, importance of, 127, 139*t*, 159–62, 160–61*f*, 170
traditional village leadership, 138*t*
traits, global variation in, 128–34, 132*f*
trust, generalized, 163*t*, 165*t*, 167–68
trust, interpersonal, 137*t*, 139*t*, 147, 162–67, 165*t*
trust between countries, 162–66, 164*t*
trust game behavior, 131
trust in CEOs, 165*t*, 167
trust in institutions, 137*t*, 144–45
trust levels studies, 135–46, 140*t*, 151–53*t*, 158

340 Index

economics and culture studies (*cont.*)
  Tuskegee experiment, 136*t*, 145, 171–72
  TV/radio introduction, 140*t*
  ultimatum game, 129–30, 134
  universal/limited morality, 138*t*
  universal *vs.* group-based morality, 164*t*, 169
  voting in US presidential elections, 164*t*, 168
  well-being, 151*t*, 165*t*
  wheat agriculture, 136*t*
  within- *vs.* between-group differences, 131–34, 147
  women in politics attitudes, 151*t*
  work ethic, 136*t*, 138*t*
  workplace obedience, 163*t*
education/literacy
  African American educational attainment, 137*t*, 156–57
  children/youth global trends, 62*t*, 66, 68*t*, 72–83, 92–94, 93*f*, 109
  economics and culture studies, 154*t*, 163–64*t*, 172–74
  education curriculum, 278–79
  education fever, 55, 80–81
  female education, 163*t*
  negotiation strategy, 278–79
  school curricula, 152*t*
emotion-induced trade-off effect, 25–27, 27*f*
End of Childhood Index, 89–90
Enke, B., 138*t*, 164*t*, 168, 169
entorhinal cortex, 35*f*
errors
  in foresight modeling, 303
  heuristic trial and error, 254–55, 269–70
  memory, 11–16, 16–17*f*
  in negotiation strategy, 254–55, 269–70
ethnic affiliation/endogamy, 137*t*, 140*t*, 157, 158

evolutionary game theory. *See* foresight modeling
evolutionary theory (Darwinian), 100
executive function/frontal control processes, 28–31
experimental games measures, 129–30

face culture, 194–95, 234n2
Falk, A., 133
false accusations, 207*t*, 214
false memories, categorical, 14–16, 16–17*f*
falsification testing, 144
family systems, 60–63*t*, 67–70*t*
fasting, 163*t*
Fehr, E., 297
females
  education, 163*t*
  empowerment, 153*t*
  genital cutting, 136*t*
  labor force participation, 141*t*, 147–50, 175
  male–female sex ratio, 136*t*, 149
  matrilineal inheritance, 137*t*
  matrilineal kinship, 165*t*, 170
  matrilocality/patrilocality, 151*t*, 173–74
  sex ratios, 136*t*
  sexual/physical attack, 204–6, 207*t*, 210
  violence against, 62*t*, 65, 70*t*, 72, 78, 109
  wartime employment/WWII, 138*t*, 175
  women in politics attitudes, 151*t*
Fernandez, R., 138*t*, 152*t*, 157
fertility rates (TFR)
  children/youth global trends, 55, 66, 90–92
  fertility norms, 153*t*, 156, 158
  fertility norms, drought-related, 163*t*
Figlio, D., 164*t*

Index **341**

firm competition, 152t
Fisman, R., 130
fMRI studies, of memory, 8–10, 12, 19–21, 28, 31
food preferences, 163t
forcibly displaced/refugee children, 104–5
foreign direct investment, 162–66, 164t
foreign outsourcing, 164t
foreign students/South Korea, 82–83
foresight modeling
  altruistic bully effect, 307
  characterization, 303–5
  conflict, 294–95
  cooperation, 294–95, 314–15, 319
  deterrence, 297–98
  errors, 303
  evolution of, 321
  foresight, 296–99, 298f, 309–10, 310f, 314–18
  free-riders/collective action problem, 294–95, 305–14, 308f, 310f, 313t
  heterogeneous groups, 305–10, 308f, 310f
  human origins/distinctiveness, 293–94
  human rationality, 318
  leadership, 320–21
  leader-subordinate game, 312–14, 313t
  model rationale, 292–93
  model validation, 321
  mutation rates, 300–301, 309
  Nash equilibria, 299, 300, 303, 313–14, 318, 320
  primate models, 297
  public goods game, 297–98, 298f
  punishment, 295, 297–98, 298f, 308–15, 310f
  reciprocity, 295
  rock–paper–scissors game, 301, 302f

selective imitation, 295, 310–11, 314–15, 319–20
self-interested enforcement hypothesis, 311
social institutions evolution, 310–17, 313t
social norms, 298–99, 315–17
strategy revision, 300–301, 302f, 315
tactical deception, 317
theoretical framework/concepts, 299–305
theory of mind, 297
utility function, 301–3, 315
Fortunato, L., 307
Fouka, V., 138t, 152t, 176
Fourth Industrial Revolution, 58
Fourth of July festivities, 153t, 155
Fox News access, 152t, 156
frame-switching, 30
Francois, P., 152t
Fredriksson, P. G., 136t
free-riders/collective action problem, 294–95, 305–14, 308f, 310f, 313t
frontal control/executive function processes, 28–31
frontier experience, 136t
frontoparietal control network, 7–9, 7f, 29–30
frontostriatal network, 34, 35f
Fuchs-Schundeln, N., 136t, 151t, 158

Gächter, S., 297
Gakidou, E., 87–88
Galor, O., 138t
game theory, 247, 299–300
Gavrilets, S., 307, 312, 315
gay marriage attitudes, 136t
Gelfand, M. J., 232, 266, 268, 276
gender
  differences in honor culture, 201, 217, 217f
  inequality, 59, 62t, 72

gender (*cont.*)
    norms/bias, 153*t*
    quotas, 163*t*, 176
    violence against females, 62*t*, 65,
        70*t*, 72, 78, 109
gender roles/attitudes
    children/youth global trends, 61–62*t*,
        65, 66, 72–73, 93, 97–100
    economics and culture studies, 136*t*,
        138–39*t*, 141*t*, 147–50, 148*f*,
        151–52*t*, 156–58, 170
    honor culture, 201, 217, 217*f*
General Social Survey, 131–33
genital cutting, 107–9
German reunification, 151*t*, 158
Gershman, B., 138*t*
Giavazzi, F., 158–59
Gielen, U. P., 71
Giuliano, P., 138–39*t*, 152*t*, 159
Glick, S., 257–58
Global Childhood Report, 54
global child mortality rates, 86–88, 86*f*
globalization
    children/youth global trends, 54,
        105–6
    of identity, 277–78
Global Preferences Survey (GPS), 133
global teenage culture(s) impacts, 70*t*
glocal identities, 54–55
goal conflict/goal pursuit, 225–30, 229*f*
Goh, J., 10, 12, 34
gold rush/ 19th century, 137*t*
Gorodnichenko, Y., 164*t*, 167–68, 169
government
    autocratic *vs.* democratic national
        government, 164*t*
    civic honesty, 131, 132*f*, 146
    medieval independent city-states,
        139*t*, 146
    pensions, 151*t*, 173–74
    redistribution preferences, 136*t*,
        151–52*t*
    regulation, 163*t*

Grosjean, P., 139*t*, 149
Guiso, L., 139*t*, 146, 164*t*, 166
Gunia, B. C., 264–68, 270
Günsoy, C., 216, 219, 222
Gutchess, A. H., 12

Habsburg Empire, 137*t*
Habsburg *vs.* Ottoman/Russian state,
    139*t*, 144–45, 175
Hajj pilgrimage, 152*t*, 155–56
happiness, 163*t*
Hastie, R., 280n8
Hedden, T., 8, 29–30
Heldring, L., 139*t*, 175
Heller, S. B., 173
Henrich, J., 129–30, 134, 153*t*
hierarchical modeling analysis, 20
hippocampus, 5, 21, 35*f*
holistic *vs.* analytic processing, 6
homicides, 138*t*
homosexuality
    attitudes towards, 137*t*, 152*t*
    children/youth global trends,
        99–100
    gay marriage attitudes, 136*t*
honesty, challenge to, 207*t*, 212, 213*f*,
    218–23, 231, 235n5
honor culture
    achievement/negative, 207*t*,
        220–22
    achievement/positive, 207*t*, 216–
        17, 217*f*
    anger/shame, 223–25, 225*f*
    annoyances, 213–14
    bottom-up approaches, 197
    challenge/criticism, 207*t*
    challenge to competence, 218–23,
        231, 235n5
    challenge to honesty, 207*t*, 212,
        213*f*, 218–23, 231, 235n5
    characterization, 192–94, 199–200,
        230, 234n1
    cultural logic of, 195, 199, 234n2

CuPS approach, 199, 212–13, 231–32
dignity culture *vs.*, 194–95, 203, 210, 212, 218–23, 233, 234n2
diversity of, 232–33
everyday situations/contexts, 203–6
face culture, 194–95, 234n2
false accusations, 207t, 214
feature frequency/centrality, 200–203, 210
gender differences, 201, 217, 217f
goal pursuit, 225–31, 229f
helping, 205, 208t, 220
honor-attacking situations, 204–5, 207t, 209
honor-enhancing situations, 205–6, 207–8t, 209, 210, 235n3
honor threats, 205, 206
honor threats, aggressive responses to, 192–95, 211–15, 213f
honor threats, emotional consequences of, 206–11, 235n4
honor threats differentiation, 217–19
humiliation, 204–6, 207t, 214, 215, 220, 223–25, 225f
inter-prototype similarity index, 201
moral behavior, 194–95, 202, 203, 206
negative character, 207t
paradox of politeness, 213–15
positive character, 207t
positive/negative consequences of, 198, 209–11
praise, 204–6, 207t
prototypes of, 199–203
psychological processes in, 190–92
relational impacts, 205–6, 209–13, 216–17, 217f, 223–25, 225f, 235n4
retaliation, 192–95, 211–15, 213f

revealing negative behaviors, 207t
revealing positive behaviors, 208t
sampling methodology, 204
sexual/physical attack, 204–6, 207t, 210
social media impacts, 215–17, 217f, 230–31
social perceptions/societal norms, 201, 214–15, 216f, 231
social status/respect, 193–94, 202, 219, 222–25, 225f
terminology, 196, 201
top-down approaches, 198, 230
transmission/embodiment of, 198–99
Turkey as, 195–97
Honor Dictionary, 232, 235n6
hukou system, 75–79
human origins/distinctiveness, 293–94
human rationality, 318
humiliation, 204–6, 207t, 223–25, 225f
hunter–gatherer societies, 52, 54, 58–64, 60–63t, 66–72, 67–72t

identity
globalization of, 277–78
glocal, 54–55
national vs.coethnic, 152t, 156, 176
self-efficacy/civic mindedness, 139t, 146
ideologies/belief systems
adherence to Islam, 140t, 155–56, 162t
belief in Christianity, 140t
Catholic Church's medieval policies, 141t
Catholic Order of Cistercians, 136t
children/youth global trends, 57, 59, 61t, 66, 73, 93, 99–100
fasting, 163t
Hajj pilgrimage, 152t, 155–56

344 Index

ideologies/belief systems (*cont.*)
  political beliefs/attitudes, 152*t*
  Ramadan fasting, 151*t*
  religiosity, 134, 151*t*, 153*t*, 163*t*
  religious beliefs (Protestantism),
    140*t*, 163*t*
  supernatural beliefs, 138*t*
immigration
  forcibly displaced/refugee children,
    104–5
  migration/migrant children, 75–79,
    102–4
  Scotch-Irish, 139*t*
income studies, 163–64*t*, 167–68
individualism/collectivism
  bicultural individuals, 30
  children/youth global trends, 70*t*,
    73, 101, 106
  economics and culture studies, 136*t*,
    164*t*, 169
  memory, cultural differences, 2–4,
    20
industrial specialization of production,
  163*t*
infanticide, 70, 70*t*
infibulation, 150
information provision, 151*t*
in-group/out-group bias, 151*t*, 153*t*
in-group/out-group trust, 140*t*, 169
innovations
  children/youth global trends, 53–57,
    61–62*t*, 71–72
  economics and culture studies,
    165*t*, 168
  tradition-innovation balance, 59,
    61*t*, 71
inspirational movies, 154*t*
integrative *vs.* distributive negotiation
  strategy, 253, 254, 256, 258–59,
  269
intercultural studies, negotiation
  strategy, 260–61, 264–65, 271–74,
  281n10, 281n12

intracultural studies, negotiation
  strategy, 260, 264, 268–71
Islam, adherence to, 140*t*, 155–56, 162*t*

Jackson, A. L., 317
Jakiela, P., 153*t*
Jayachandran, S., 164*t*
Jenkins, L. J., 12
Jensen, R., 153*t*
Johnson, N. D., 131
joint gains, 247, 253–61, 268–76, 279,
  280nn7–8
judgments, absolute *vs.* relative, 8

Kahneman, D., 173
Kaplan, E., 152*t*, 156–57
Karaja, E., 139*t*, 175
Kelley, H. H., 252, 272
Khattar, R., 139*t*, 149
Kim, S., 71
kinship
  children/youth global trends, 65
  matrilineal, 165*t*, 170
  ties, economic, 136*t*, 138*t*, 141*t*,
    164*t*, 165*t*, 168, 170
knowledge
  ecological knowledge impacts,
    55–57
  intergenerational, 69*t*
  transmission of, 128, 155–57
Koelle, S., 135
Kong, D. T., 254
Korea. *See* South Korea
Kosse, F., 153*t*
Krasnow, M. M., 297
Ksander, J. C., 28

lab-in-the-field experiments, 130–31,
  132*f*
labor
  child labor, 67*t*, 102
  female labor force participation,
    141*t*, 147–50, 175

labor-intensive agriculture, 136*t*
marginal returns/labor of crop mix,
138*t*
socioeconomic stratification/
division of, 59, 61*t*, 64–65
La Ferrara, E., 153*t*, 156
Lax, D. A., 260
leadership
foresight modeling, 320–21
leader-subordinate game, 312–14,
313*t*
village leadership tradition, 138*t*
Lenski, G., 57
Leung, A. K., 194–95, 199, 226
lex talionis (rule of retribution), 193
life expectancy/child mortality rates,
67*t*
Linguistic Inquiry and Word Count
(LIWC), 280n9
literacy. *See* education/literacy
Loftus, E., 5
loss aversion, 138*t*
Lowes, S., 139*t*, 145–47, 165*t*, 170–
71, 175, 176
Luce, R. D., 253
luck *vs.* effort attitudes, 152*t*
Lügger, K., 268, 273

Machiguenga, 129–30
Madestam, A., 153*t*, 155
maize processing, 127
malaria prevalence, 137*t*
male-biased sex ratio, 139*t*, 149–50
male–female sex ratio, 136*t*, 149
malnutrition, 67*t*, 73–74, 87–89,
163*t*
marginal returns/labor of crop mix,
138*t*
marriage
age/boys, 69*t*, 74
age/girls, 69*t*, 74, 109
arranged/semi-arranged, 69*t*, 101
gay marriage attitudes, 136*t*

mass media exposure, 66, 70*t*, 105–6
mathematical models, 127
matrilineal inheritance, 137*t*
matrilineal kinship, 165*t*, 170
matrilocality/patrilocality, 151*t*,
173–74
McKersie, R. B., 253, 254, 255
McNally, L., 317
Mead, M., 112
medicine
colonial medical campaigns, 139*t*,
170–71
medical system trust, 136*t*, 139*t*,
145, 171–72
medieval democracy, 141*t*, 146
medieval independent city-states,
139*t*, 146
memory, cultural differences
absolute *vs.* relative judgments, 8
aging, 10, 12, 15–16, 17*f*, 23*f*, 31–35,
35*f*
analytic *vs.* holistic processing, 6
attentional influences, 23*f*, 25–27,
33–34, 37
automatic *vs.* controlled processes,
33
bicultural individuals, 30
bottom-up influences, 22–24
brain regions involved in, 6–9, 7*f*,
20–21, 28–35, 35*f*
categorical false memories, 14–16,
16–17*f*
categorization, 7, 8, 33
categorization strategies, 13–14
cognitive neuroscience, 5
cognitive persistence, 30–31
collectivism *vs.* individualism, 2–4,
20
content type, 7, 8
context, 4–5, 26
cultural change, 37–38
culture-invariant *vs.* culture-
saturated, 31–32

346 Index

memory, cultural differences (*cont.*)
emotion-induced trade-off effect,
25–27, 27*f*
eye-tracking studies, 10, 21–22
fMRI studies, 8–10, 12, 19–21, 28,
31
frame-switching, 30
framework, 6–9, 21–24, 23*f*
frontal control/executive function
processes, 28–31
hierarchical modeling analysis, 20
malleability of, 5–6
memory errors, 11–16, 16–17*f*
memory specificity, 9–13, 11*f*, 17–21,
18*f*, 28, 34–36
motivational/experiential
influences, 23*f*, 24–25, 33–34, 37
neural activation patterns, 6–9, 7*f*,
20–21, 28–35, 35*f*
object adaptation studies, 10–11,
11*f*
object–background binding, 12
object *vs.* background processing,
9–13, 11*f*, 21
plasticity, 5, 34–35, 35*f*
sampling, 4–5, 37
self-reference effect, 4, 24–25, 26*f*,
33
social factors in, 2–4, 20, 35–36
task difficulty, 7–8, 7*f*
theoretical background, 2–6
top-down influences, 22–24, 33–34
visual influences, lower-level, 23*f*,
27–29
working memory, 7–8
mentor program, 153*t*
Michalopoulos, S., 140*t*
migration/migrant children, 75–79,
102–4
Miguel, E., 130
military bombing, 138*t*
mineral discoveries timing, 138*t*
Mislin, A. A., 131

Mitchell, T., 279
Mitrunen, M., 153*t*, 176
Mokyr, J., 161–62
Montero, E., 139*t*, 145–47, 170–71
morality
moral behavior, 194–95, 202, 203,
206
moral behavior in honor culture,
194–95, 202, 203, 206
moral integrity, 256, 276
negotiation strategy, 256, 276
universal/limited, 138*t*
universal *vs.* group-based, 164*t*, 169
mortality
child mortality rates/life expectancy,
67*t*
global child mortality rates, 86–88,
86*f*
Moscona, J., 140*t*, 165*t*, 170
motivational theory, 248–53, 250*f*,
259–61, 274, 280nn3–9, 281n13
Mouton, J., 249
movies, inspirational, 154*t*
multicultural students/South Korea,
81–84
multi-issue offers (MIOs), 269–71,
275–76, 281n11
mutation rates, 300–301, 309

Nash equilibria, 299, 300, 303, 313–14,
318, 320
national soccer team victories, 152*t*,
156
Natlandsmyr, J., 268
negotiation strategy
anger in, 256–57
assertiveness, 249
BATNA, 257
behavioral theory, 253–61, 274,
280nn8–9, 281n13
comparative cultural research,
276–77
comparison of theories, 259–61

complementarity, 258–59
concepts, definitions, 247–48, 280n1
concern for self/others, 249, 252
conflict management behaviors, 251–53
cooperative *vs.* competitive, 249, 251, 254, 257–58
culture effects on, 261–71, 276–77, 281n10
dynamics of, 258–59
EASI (emotion as social information) model, 257
education curriculum, 278–79
globalization of identity, 277–78
heuristic trial and error, 254–55, 269–70
holistic *vs.* analytic mindsets in, 270–71
information processing in, 270–71, 280n8
institutional/interpersonal trust, 267, 279
integrative *vs.* distributive, 253, 254, 256, 258–59, 269
intercultural studies, 260–61, 264–65, 271–74, 281n10, 281n12
intracultural studies, 260, 264, 268–71
joint gains, 247, 253–61, 268–76, 279, 280nn7–8
moral integrity, 256, 276
motivational theory, 248–53, 250*f*, 259–61, 274, 280nn3–9, 281n13
multi-issue offers (MIOs), 269–71, 275–76, 281n11
OFFER coding scheme, 255–56
outcome potential, 263
problem-solving *vs.* contending, 249
reciprocity in, 258–59, 273
relationship-building in, 276, 279
self-report *vs.* behavioral coding, 260–61, 274–75

single-issue offers (SIOs), 255, 270–71, 275
status effects, 257–58, 263
structural, 258–59
theory origins, 248
tightness–looseness, 265–68, 278–79
triangle theory, 272, 276
trust in, 255, 256, 265–68, 278–79
value claiming, 260–61, 264–65, 268, 269, 272–75
value creating, 247, 258–61, 264–65, 268–71, 275
variable-sum negotiations, 247
zero-sum negotiations, 247
neural activation patterns, in memory, 6–9, 7*f*, 20–21, 28–35, 35*f*
Nguyen, K.- T., 165*t*, 167
niacin absorption, 127
Nisbett, R./Nisbett's theory, 2–4, 270–71
Nolan, P., 57
norms
economics and culture studies, 127, 133–34, 158
fertility norms, 153*t*, 156, 158
fertility norms, drought-related, 163*t*
foresight modeling, 298–99, 315–17
gender norms/bias, 153*t*
honor culture, 201, 214–15, 216*f*, 231
Nunn, N., 138–39*t*, 140*t*, 147, 159, 165*t*

obedience
obedience/responsibility training, 67*t*, 101
rule following, 139*t*, 165*t*, 175
to state, 139*t*, 165*t*, 175
workplace, 163*t*

objects
adaptation studies, 10–11, 11*f*
object–background binding, 12
object *vs.* background processing, 9–13, 11*f*, 21
OFFER coding scheme, 255–56
Ohrvall, R., 151*t*
Okoye, D., 140*t*, 145
Olken, B., 140*t*
Olson, M., 307
Ortiz-Ospina, E., 85, 92
Oster, E., 153*t*
Ostrom, E., 311
other-regarding behaviors, 153*t*
Our World in Data, 54
overweight, 86
Ozak, O., 138*t*
Ozier, O., 153*t*

Paige, L. E., 28
Pande, R., 164*t*
paradox of politeness, 213–15
parenting
alloparenting, 63*t*, 64
authoritative style, 137*t*
parent-child relationship, 95–97, 101
siblings number/influence, 68*t*
Park, D., 5, 31–32
Pashtunwali code, 98
pastoralism, 136*t*, 150
patrilocality/matrilocality, 151*t*, 173–74
peasant societies, 52, 54, 58, 60*t*, 64–65, 67–72*t*, 72–73, 97–98, 101
peer group influences, 69*t*
pellagra, 127
Perry, L., 308, 312
Pitt-Rivers, J., 192, 200, 202
plasticity, 5, 34–35, 35*f*
politeness, paradox of, 213–15
political preferences (voting), 152*t*, 153*t*, 155, 164*t*, 168, 169

political turnover, 165*t*, 168
polygamy, 100
posterior cingulate gyrus, 35*f*
praise, 204–6, 207*t*
precuneus, 35*f*
primate models, 297
primogeniture, 72
printing press access, 140*t*
processes, processing
analytic *vs.* holistic, 6
automatic *vs.* controlled, 33
frontal control/executive function, 28–31
holistic *vs.* analytic, 6
information, 270–71, 280n8
object *vs.* background, 9–13, 11*f*, 21
psychological, in honor culture, 190–92
production, industrial specialization of, 163*t*
prosociality, 140*t*, 146–47, 151*t*, 158–59, 174–75
Pruitt, D. G., 253–55, 270, 276, 280n8
public goods game, 297–98, 298*f*
public policy
in economics and culture studies, 170–76
in improvement of lives, 89–90, 106–10
punishment, 295, 297–98, 298*f*, 308–15, 310*f*
putamen, 35*f*
Putnam, L., 258

Qian, N., 153*t*, 168
Querubin, P., 138*t*

Rahim, M. A., 252
Raiffa, H., 253
Ramadan fasting, 151*t*
Ramirez-Marin, J., 272–74, 276
Ramos-Toro, D., 140*t*, 145
Rao, G., 153*t*, 174

recession, 152*t*, 168
reciprocity
  in foresight modeling, 295
  in negotiation strategy, 258–59, 273
regression-discontinuity identification
    strategy, 144–45
relationships
  building in negotiation strategy,
    276, 279
  parent-child relationship effects,
    95–97, 101
religiosity, 134, 151*t*, 153*t*, 163*t*
respect/social status, 193–94, 202,
    219, 222–25, 225*f*
responsibility. *See* obedience
retaliation, in honor culture, 192–95,
    211–15, 213*f*
retrosplenial cortex, 35*f*
revealing negative behaviors, 207*t*
revealing positive behaviors, 208*t*
Richerson, P. J., 127, 294
Riley, E., 154*t*
risk aversion, 153*t*
Robinson, J. A., 170
rock–paper–scissors game, 301, 302*f*
Rodriguez-Padilla, R., 164*t*, 168, 169
Rogers, A. R., 127
Rognes, J., 268
Rohner, R. P., 95, 96
Roland, G., 164*t*, 167–68, 169
Roser, M., 54, 85, 92
Rubin, J., 139*t*, 140*t*, 175
Ruble, T. L., 249
rule following, 139*t*, 165*t*, 175
Rustagi, D., 141*t*, 146

Sanchez-Burkes, J., 279
Savitskiy, V., 138*t*
Schelling, T., 253
Schlapfer, A., 138*t*
school curricula, 152*t*
Schulz, J., 141*t*
Schwartz, A. J., 16

Schwartz Values Scale, 36–37
Sebenius, J. K., 260
segmentary lineage organization, 140*t*,
    165*t*, 170
selective imitation, 295, 310–11,
    314–15, 319–20
self-efficacy/civic mindedness, 139*t*, 146
self-interested enforcement
    hypothesis, 311
self-reference effect, 4, 24–25, 26*f*, 33
self-report *vs.* behavioral
    coding, 260–61, 274–75
Serafinelli, M., 137*t*, 150, 175
sex ratios, 136*t*
sexual/physical attack, 204–6, 207*t*, 210
shame/anger, 223–25, 225*f*, 256–57
Shen, Y., 77, 78
siblings number/influence, 68*t*
signal detection theory, 23
Singh, M., 311
single-issue offers (SIOs), 255, 270–71,
    275
slave trades, 135–44, 138*t*, 140–42*t*,
    143*f*, 147, 149
sleeping sickness, 171
soccer team victories, 152*t*, 156
social cohesion, 139–40*t*, 147, 152*t*, 156
social institutions evolution, 310–17,
    313*t*
social media influences, 66, 105–6
social status/respect, 193–94, 202,
    219, 222–25, 225*f*
societal change, 61*t*, 100–101
societal complexity, 59, 61*t*
societal evolution, 57–59, 60–63*t*
societal norms. *See* norms
socioeconomic stratification/division
    of labor, 59, 61*t*, 64–65
South Korea
  children/youth global trends, 55,
    66, 73–74, 79–84, 112
  foreign students, 82–83
  multicultural students, 81–84

350 Index

Spilimbergo, A., 152*t*
State of the World's Children, The, 54
strategy revision, 300–301, 302*f*, 315
stunting, 86
superior frontal gyrus, 35*f*
System 1/System 2 cognitions, 173

Tabellini, G., 146, 174
tactical deception, 317
Tea Party protests, 153*t*, 155
television soap operas, 153*t*, 156
temporo-parietal network, 34–35, 35*f*
Teso, E., 141*t*, 149, 150
Teucher, B. M., 264–68, 270
TFR. *See* fertility rates (TFR)
theory of mind, 297
Thibaut, J. W., 272
Third Industrial Revolution, 58
Thomas, K. W., 249
Thomas-Kilmann Conflict Mode
    Instrument (TKI), 251
Thompson, L., 280n8
tightness–looseness in negotiation
    strategy, 265–68, 278–79
trade-off effect, emotion-induced, 25–
    27, 27*f*
trade routes/land suitability, 140*t*
tradition
    importance of, 127, 139*t*, 159–62,
        160–61*f*, 170
    tradition-innovation balance, 59,
        61*t*, 71
    village leadership, 138*t*
triple-dominance measure of social
    values (TDMSV), 250–52
trust
    in CEOs, 165*t*, 167
    between countries, 162–66, 164*t*
    game behavior, 131
    generalized, 163*t*, 165*t*, 167–68
    in-group/out-group, 140*t*, 169
    institutional/interpersonal, 267,
        279

in institutions, 137*t*, 144–45
interpersonal, 137*t*, 139*t*, 147, 162–
    67, 165*t*
medical system trust, 136*t*, 139*t*,
    145, 171–72
in negotiation strategy, 255, 256,
    265–68, 278–79
trust levels studies, 135–46, 140*t*,
    151–53*t*, 158
Turchin, P., 294
Turkey, 195–97. *See also* honor
    culture
Tuskegee experiment, 136*t*, 145, 171–72
TV/radio introduction, 140*t*

Uksul, A. K., 191, 195, 209–10
ultimatum game, 129–30, 134
UN Convention on the Rights of the
    Child (CRC), 53, 106–10
United States, attitudes towards, 138*t*
universal *vs.* group-based morality,
    164*t*, 169
utility function, 301–3, 315

value claiming, 260–61, 264–65, 268,
    269, 272–75
value creating, 247, 258–61, 264–65,
    268–71, 275
van de Vliert, E., 252
Van Kleef, G. A., 257
Van Lange, P. A., 251
variable-sum negotiations, 247
violence against females, 62*t*, 65, 70*t*,
    72, 78, 109
voting
    political preferences in, 152*t*, 153*t*,
        155, 164*t*, 168, 169
    in US presidential elections, 164*t*,
        168

Wacziarg, R., 131–33
Walton, R. E., 253, 254, 255
Wanamaker, M., 136*t*, 145, 171–72

Wantchekon, L., 135, 140*t*, 147
wasting, 86
Weingart, L. R., 254, 255, 275
welfare, societal threats to, 70–71, 70*t*
well-being, 151*t*, 165*t*
Welsh, R. C., 12
Wen, J., 168
wheat agriculture, 136*t*
Wilson, M., 98
within- *vs.* between-group differences, 131–34, 147
Woesmann, L., 163*t*, 175
women in politics attitudes, 151*t*
work ethic, 136*t*, 138*t*
working memory, 7–8

workplace obedience, 163*t*
World Values Surveys, 131, 146

Xue, M. M., 141*t*, 149

Yamagishi, T., 267
Yanagizawa-Drott, D., 137*t*, 151*t*, 153*t*, 155, 157, 163*t*
Yao, J. J., 255–56, 269–71, 275–76
youth global trends. *See* children/youth global trends

zero-sum negotiations, 247
Zhang, W., 24
Zhang, Z- X., 255–56, 275
Zilibotti, F., 74